D1798273

J. MIDDLETON MURRY

Selected Criticism 1916–1957

J. MIDDLETON MURRY

Selected Criticism 1916-1957

Chosen and introduced by
RICHARD REES

London
OXFORD UNIVERSITY PRESS
NEW YORK TORONTO
1960

Oxford University Press, Amen House, London E.C.4
GLASGOW NEW YORK TORONTO MELBOURNE WELLINGTON
BOMBAY CALCUTTA MADRAS KARACHI KUALA LUMPUR
CAPE TOWN IBADAN NAIROBI ACCRA

PRINTED IN GREAT BRITAIN

CONTENTS

INTRODUCTION

Starting in 1916, Middleton Murry wrote an average of more than a book a year for the next forty years. Several million words. It is arguable that the books would have been better, had they been fewer, and no doubt Murry himself would have thought so. But he had to make a living and, as he once said, the only way he could afford to think about a subject was to write a book about it. He was born in 1889 in South London, to parents whose economic status was on the borderline between genteel and sheer poverty; but, thanks to scholarships, he obtained a good classical education at Christ's Hospital and Brasenose. After editing three small but lively magazines he was appointed in 1919 to the editorship of *The Athenaeum*; and in what Mr. Eliot has described as the 'brief and brilliant' life of that journal under Murry's editorship most of the outstanding new writers of the post-war years collaborated. Many of them, indeed, must have owed their first success very largely to his encouragement. But *The Athenaeum* was soon merged with *The Nation* (later to be absorbed by the *New Statesman*), and in 1923, after the death of his first wife, Katherine Mansfield, Murry founded a new monthly review, *The Adelphi*.

This new venture was at first an unexpected success, but in time it alienated many of his former collaborators, including D. H. Lawrence, for whom Murry had intended it to serve as a platform. Murry's association with *The Adelphi* continued for the next twenty-five years, and during this period his editorials expounded, in addition to his literary interests, an unorthodox Christianity and an equally unorthodox politics. But after 1948 literature regained the ascendancy and his later books are mostly concerned with it.

It is sometimes said that he would have done better to confine himself to literary subjects. But he was a mystic, and his mysticism was of a kind which made a life-long specialization in literary criticism impossible. It involved a kind of resignation and, at the same time, a kind of purposiveness which almost amounted to a state of being 'possessed'. His pen was at most times amazingly well controlled by his critical intelligence, but the force that drove it was passionately intense. And as soon as a book was finished, it was done with. He was resigned to its faults and already absorbed in the next phase of his activity. If you objected that certain passages of a book were off the note—the epilogue to *Shakespeare,* for example, or several parts of *God*, that rather brusque 'introduction to the Science of Metabiology'—you might get some such reply as this: There's nothing I can do about it now, and anyway the book's faults are part of the book; it may as well be seen as it really is, warts and all.

This Cromwellian resignation is unexpected in a literary man. It is perhaps partly explained by the fact that Murry was not altogether what is usually meant by a literary man. He possessed extraordinary critical gifts but he undoubtedly thought of those gifts, and of literature itself, as ancillary to some extra-literary purpose. For him, as he wrote in his Journal (quoted by Mrs. Murry in her memoir [1]), criticism 'depended on values—a delineation of what is good for man. And I had to find out'. I think this attitude to literature, which was also Lawrence's, and Dostoevsky's, is clear in the extract I have chosen from the book on Dostoevsky (1916) which was his first critical work.

To write a competent introduction to Murry's criticism one would have to be as well read and as deeply read as he. There is fortunately no need for me to do anything more than refer to Mr. Philip Mairet's British Council pamphlet.[2] Inevitably, the limitations of my own taste will be exposed in the selections I have made for this anthology, but I have tried to find substantial and characteristic examples of Murry's general attitude in each stage of his development from 1916 to 1957. The two essays from *Pencillings* (a title not chosen by Murry himself) are not substantial; but they appeared in a weekly column which he contributed to *The Times* in 1922 and this seems to me to give them a period interest as examples of the best literary journalism at that date. In the same series he wrote an article upon the artistic snobbery which often prevents genuinely original writers from receiving their fair share of critical attention:

> Superficially they do not look like literary artists, as, for example, Mr. W. W. Jacobs does not. But Mr. Jacobs has created a world, a little world, it is true, but a world of his own. He is a much more important figure in literature than a dozen younger writers whose works are always received with respectful attention. But Mr. Jacobs is comic and popular: *snobisme oblige*. How can serious criticism deal with a figure like the Night Watchman?

Most of Murry's writing, however, was devoted to far weightier themes than this, and I do not believe any editor could succeed in giving, within the limits of a moderate-sized volume, a selection that would indicate the full range of his gifts. All the passages have been chosen for their literary and general interest and not in order to em-

[1] *To Keep Faith*, by Mary Middleton Murry (Constable).

[2] *John Middleton Murry*, by Philip Mairet (published for the British Council and National Book League by Longmans Green and Co.).

phasise the didactic and mystical strains in Murry's writing; and the book could have been made many times longer without any sacrifice of quality. An almost equally interesting book could be made from Murry's more autobiographical writings and his essays on social and political subjects, and in this case it would contain a larger proportion of pages dealing with D. H. Lawrence. I do not think such a book would compromise the impression of over-all consistency which the present book makes upon me. Murry was often accused of inconsistency, of switching abruptly from one extreme position to another, and he did sometimes behave in a way which seemed to justify this criticism. But although he was sometimes over-impetuous, he was never fundamentally inconsistent. A man whose thought is continually developing and for whom the development of an idea involves, as it always did for Murry, the testing of it in practice, may appear to make a *volte-face* when he is in fact making a zig-zag progress—which may, of course, look very ridiculous to people who do not take ideas so seriously.

When Murry founded *The Adelphi* in 1923 it was not a literary gesture, it was an *act* of adherence to the doctrine, as he understood it, of Lawrence's *Aaron's Rod* and *Fantasia of the Unconscious*. He was prepared at that time to follow Lawrence as a leader in the simple sense of the word. Soon after he had written, too hastily, *The Necessity of Communism*, he was trying to found a new political party; and after writing *The Necessity of Pacifism*, he actually founded a farm colony for conscientious objectors. He later renounced his pacifism, but not the principles which had led him to embrace it. Mr. Mairet seems to me to put this aspect of Murry in exactly the right perspective when he says:

> In groups of this kind, both his fixed principles and his liability to sudden changes in his estimate of possibilities were apt to inconvenience his associates. . . . Murry's highly idealised version of Marxian doctrine was virtually a refutation of it. . . . His temporary adoption of 'communism' in the *Adelphi* amounted to an innocent, and socially valuable betrayal of a bad cause.

In other words, it often happened that Murry's criticism revealed what was valuable in the subjects he studied, while refuting the 'party spirit', which is always, whether in philosophy, literature or politics, exclusive, monopolistic and dogmatic.

I have mentioned his tendency to spoil some of his best work by the inclusion of discordant and inferior passages (none of which, I trust, will be found in these pages); and here, it might be thought, he is in the best of company. An anthology of the worst prose of the best modern critics would be an extraordinary volume. But Murry usually wrote so very well that his lapses are strangely bathetic. It would make an interesting study, and Mr. Lea has provided some material for it in his biography of Murry,[1] to examine the reason for these lapses of taste in a writer who is usually so remarkable for refinement and delicacy of perception. They certainly do something to account for the neglect and underestimation which his work has sometimes suffered. I would look for an explanation in the fact of his being one of the most conspicuous victims of the bad competitive system in education—what he himself described as the 'immoral and degrading race' for scholarships. Intellectually, he was something of a child prodigy, and his fate was similar to and worse than J. S. Mill's. His father's determination forced him up the educational ladder from a much humbler starting point. I suspect that after the years of unnatural overwork and cramming as a child his mind was in the condition of a musical instrument in which certain strings are overstrained.

But the early forcing of his intellectual growth had no ill effect upon the practical ability for which he was also remarkable. In an appreciation of Murry published in 1934,[2] Mr. Heppenstall presented him as an example of 'excellent normality', suggesting that, unlike many intellectuals, he could easily be imagined as a successful professional man in some such career as the Navy, the Law or Medicine; and this intuition was confirmed by the fact that Murry did, in late middle age, succeed in turning himself into a highly efficient and knowledgeable farmer. But farming did not prevent him from writing, and I doubt if Murry could ever have devoted himself to a career which interfered with his activity as an intellectual crusader. (*Community Farm* (1952) is probably one of his best-known books, but it contains passages on the economics and ethics of farming which should almost suffice, by themselves, to establish him among the profoundest and most timely of contemporary thinkers.)

There is no need, in introducing an anthology of his criticism, to attempt to describe or define the nature of the crusade, but it seems to me that Murry himself summed it up fairly adequately, with the help of Coleridge, in this passage from his remarkable book on education, *The Price of Leadership:*

> It is by no accident that we have been developing, almost unwittingly, the great Coleridgian position, 'that Christianity rightly understood is identical with the highest philosophy, and that, apart from all question of historical evidence, the essential doctrines of Christianity are necessary and eternal truths of reason—truths which man, by the vouchsafed light of nature, may always and everywhere discover for himself'.

* * *

[1] *The Life of John Middleton Murry*, by F. A. Lea (Methuen).
[2] *Middleton Murry: A Study in Excellent Normality*, by Rayner Heppenstall (Cape).

Some of the essays written in the 1920's are now only available in editions printed in the 1950's, but they are here presented in roughly chronological order. The titles are Murry's and the selections consist of complete essays or chapters from books, except where otherwise stated. For permission to use them I am indebted to the following: Mrs. Middleton Murry, the Oxford University Press, the Student Christian Movement Press, and Messrs. Jonathan Cape, William Collins and Sons, Peter Nevill, and Martin Secker. Mr. F. A. Lea has kindly provided bibliographical information. Any surviving bibliographical errors will be my own.

I have not drawn upon Murry's uncollected articles in *The Times Literary Supplement, Criterion, Adelphi, London Magazine, Aryan Path* and elsewhere. They would more suitably provide material for a new volume of essays.

Richard Rees

1

THE FUNCTION OF CRITICISM

From Aspects of Literature *(Cape, 1934). This essay first appeared in 1920.*

It is curious and interesting to find our younger men of letters actively concerned with the present condition of literary criticism. This is a novel preoccupation for them and one which is, we believe, symptomatic of a general hesitancy and expectation. In the world of letters everything is a little up in the air, volatile and uncrystallised. It is a world of aversions and velleities; in spite of outward similarities, a strangely different world from that of half a dozen years ago. Then one had a tolerable certainty that the new star, if the new star was to appear, would burst upon our vision in the shape of a novel. To-day we feel it might be anything. The cloud no bigger than a man's hand might even be, like Trigorin's in 'The Sea-gull', like a piano; it has no predetermined form.

This sense of incalculability, which has been aroused by the prodigious literary efflorescence of late years, reacts upon its cause; and the reaction tends by many different paths to express itself finally in the ventilation of problems that hinge about criticism. There is a general feeling that the growth of the young plant has been too luxuriant; a desire to have it vigorously pruned by a capable gardener, in order that its strength may be gathered together to produce a more perfect fruit. There is also a sense that if the *lusus naturæ*, the writer of genius, were to appear, there ought to be a person or an organisation capable of recognising him, however unexpected the scent or the shape of the leaves. Both these tasks fall upon criticism. The younger generation looks round a little apprehensively to see if there is a gardener whom it can trust, and decides, perhaps a little prematurely, that there is none.

There is reviewing, but no criticism, says one icy voice that we have learned to respect. There are pontiffs and potential pontiffs, but no critics, says another disrespectful young man. Oh, for some more Scotch Reviewers to settle the hash of our English bards, sighs a third. And the *London Mercury*, after whetting our appetite by announcing that it proposed to restore the standards of authoritative criticism, still leaves us a little in the dark as to what these standards are. Mr. T. S. Eliot deals more kindly, if more frigidly, with us in the *Monthly Chapbook*. There are, he says, three kinds of criticism—the historical, the philosophic, and the purely literary.

> Every form of genuine criticism is directed towards creation. The historical or philosophic critic of poetry is criticising poetry in order to create a history or a philosophy; the poetic critic is criticising poetry in order to create poetry.

These separate and distinct kinds, he considers, are but rarely found to-day, even in a fragmentary form; where they do exist, they are almost invariably mingled in an inextricable confusion.

Whether we agree or not with the general condemnation of reviewing implicit in this survey of the situation, or with the division of criticism itself, we have every reason to be grateful to Mr. Eliot for disentangling the problem for us. The question of criticism has become rather like Glaucus the sea-god, encrusted with shells and hung with weed till his lineaments are hardly discernible. We have at least a clear sight of him now, and we are able to decide whether we will accept Mr. Eliot's description of him. Let us see.

We have no difficulty in agreeing that historical criticism of literature is a kind apart. The historical critic approaches literature as the manifestation of an evolutionary process in which all the phases are of equal value. Essentially, he has no concern with the greater or less literary excellence of the objects whose history he traces—their existence is alone sufficient for him; a bad book is as important as a good one, and much more important than a good one if it exercised, as bad books have a way of doing, a real influence on the course of literature. In practice, it is true, the historical critic generally fails of this ideal of unimpassioned objectivity. He either begins by making judgments of value for himself, or accepts those judgments which have been endorsed by tradition. He fastens upon a number of outstanding figures and more or less deliberately represents the process as one from culmination to culmination; but in spite of this arbitrary foreshortening he is primarily concerned, in each one of the phases which he distinguishes, with that which is common to every member of the group of writers which it includes. The individuality, the quintessence, of a writer lies outside his view.

We may accept the isolation of the historical critic then, at least in theory, and conceive of him as a fragment of a social historian, as the author of a chapter in the history of the human spirit. But can we isolate the philosophic critic in the same way? And what exactly *is* a philosophic critic? Is he a critic with a philosophical scheme in which art and literature have their places, a critic who therefore approaches literature with a definite conception of it as one among many parallel manifestations of the human spirit, and with a system of values derived from his metaphysical scheme? Hegel and Croce are philosophical critics in this sense, and Aristotle is not, as far as we can judge from the Poetics, wherein he considers the literary work of Greece as an isolated phenomenon, and examines it in and for itself. But for the moment, and with the uneasy sense that we have not thoroughly laid the ghost of philosophic criticism, we will assume that we have isolated him, and pass to the consideration of the pure literary critic, if indeed we can find him.

What does he do? How shall we recognise him? Mr. Eliot puts before us Coleridge and Aristotle and Dryden as literary critics *par excellence* arranged in an ascending scale of purity. The concatenation is curious, for these were men possessed of very different interests and faculties of mind; and it would occur to few to place Dryden, as a critic, at their head. The living centre of Aristotle's criticism is a conception of art as a means to a good life. As an activity, poetry 'is more philosophic than history', a nearer approach to the universal truth in particular appearances; and as a more active influence, drama refines our spiritual being by a purgation through pity and terror. Indeed, it would not be an exaggeration to say that the pith and marrow of Aristotle's literary criticism is a system of moral values derived from his contemplation of life. It was necessary that this relation should exist, because for Aristotle literature was, essentially, an imitation of life, thought we must remember to understand imitation according to our final sense of the theme which is the golden, persistent thread throughout the Poetics. The imitation of life in literature was for Aristotle, the creative revelation of the ideal actively at work in human life. The tragic hero failed because his composition was less than ideal; but he could only be a tragic hero if the ideal was implicit in him and he visibly approximated to it. It is this constant reference to the ideal which makes of 'imitation' a truly creative principle and the one which, properly understood, is the most permanently valid and pregnant of all; it is also one which has been constantly misunderstood. Its importance is, nevertheless, so central that adequate recognition of it might conceivably be taken as the distinguishing mark of all fruitful criticism.

To his sympathetic understanding of this principle Coleridge owed a great debt. It is true that his efforts to refine upon it were not only unsuccessful, but a trifle ludicrous; his effort to graft the vague transcendentalism of Germany on to the rigour and clarity of Aristotle was, from the outset, unfortunately conceived. But the root of the matter was there, and in Coleridge's fertile mind the Aristotelian theory of imitation flowered into a magnificent conception of the validity and process of the poetic imagination. And partly because the foundation was truly Aristotelian, partly because Coleridge had known what it was to be a great poet, the reference to life pervades the whole of what is permanently valuable in Coleridge's criticism. In him, too, there is a strict and mutually fertilising relation between the moral and the æsthetic values. This is the firm ground beneath his feet when he—too seldom—proceeds to the free exercise of his exquisite æsthetic discrimination.

In Dryden, however, there was no such organic interpenetration. Dryden, too, had a fine sensibility, though less exquisite, by far, than that of Coleridge; but his theoretical system was not merely alien to him—it was in itself false and mistaken. *Corruptio optimi pessima.* He took over from France the sterilised and lifeless Aristotelianism which has been the plague of criticism for centuries; he used it no worse than his French exemplars, but he used it very little better than they. It was in his hands, as in theirs, a dead mechanical framework of rules about the unities. Dryden, we can see in his critical writing, was constantly chafed by it. He behaves like a fine horse with a bearing rein: he is continually tossing his head after a minute or two of 'good manners and action', and saying, 'Shakespeare was the best of them, anyhow'; 'Chaucer beats Ovid to a standstill.' It is a gesture with which all decent people sympathise, and when it is made in language so supple as Dryden's prose it has a lasting charm. Dryden's heart was in the right place, and he was sometimes not afraid to show it; but that does not make him a critic, much less a critic to be set as a superior in the company of Aristotle and Coleridge.

Our search for the pure literary critic is likely to be arduous. We have seen that there is a sense in which Dryden is a purer literary critic than either Coleridge or Aristotle; but we have also seen that it is precisely by reason of the 'pureness' in him that he is to be relegated into a rank inferior to theirs. It looks as though we might have to pronounce that the true literary critic is the philosophic critic. Yet the pronouncement must not be prematurely made; for there is a real and vital difference between those for whom we have accepted the designation of philosophic critics, Hegel or Croce, and Aristotle or Coleridge. Yet three of these (and it might be wise to include Coleridge as a fourth) were professional philosophers. It is evidently not the philosophy as such that makes the difference.

The difference depends, we believe, upon the nature of the philosophy. The secret lies in Aristotle. The true literary critic must have a humanistic philosophy. His inquiries must be modulated, subject to an intimate, organic governance, by an ideal of the good life. He is not the mere investigator of facts; existence is never for him synonymous with value, and it is of the utmost importance that he should never be deluded into believing that it is. He will not accept from Hegel the thesis that all the events of human history, all man's spiritual activities, are equally authentic manifestations of Spirit; he will not even recognise the existence of Spirit. He may accept from Croce the thesis that art is the expression of intuitions, but he will not be extravagantly grateful, because his duty as a critic is to distinguish between intuitions and to decide that one is more significant than another. A philosophy of art that lends him no aid in this and affords no indication why the expression of one intuition should be preferred to the expression of another is of little value to him. He will incline to say that Hegel and Croce are the scientists of art rather than its philosophers.

Here, then, is the opposition: between the philosophy that borrows its values from science and the philosophy which shares its values with art. We may put it with more cogency and truth: the opposition lies between a philosophy without values and a philosophy based upon them. For values are human, anthropocentric. Shut them out once and you shut them out for ever. You do not get them back, as some believe, by declaring that such and such a thing is true. Nothing is precious because it is true save to a mind which has, consciously or unconsciously, decided that it is good to know the truth. And the making of that single decision is a most momentous judgment of value. If the scientist appeals to it, as indeed he invariably does, he too is at bottom, though he may deny it, a humanist. He would do better to confess it, and to confess that he too is in search of the good life. Then he might become aware that to search for the good life is in fact impossible, unless he has an ideal of it before his mind's eye.

An ideal of the good life, if it is to have the internal coherence and the organic force of a true ideal, *must inevitably be æsthetic*. There is no other power than our æsthetic intuition by which we can imagine or conceive it; we can express it only in æsthetic terms. We say, for instance, the good life is that in which man has achieved a harmony of the diverse elements in his soul. For the good life, we know instinctively, is one of our human absolutes. It is not good with reference to any end outside itself. A man does not live the good life because he is a good citizen; but he is a good citizen because he lives the good life. And here we touch the secret of one of the most magnificently human of all books that have ever been written—Plato's *Republic*. In the *Republic* the good life and the life of the good citizen are identified; but the citizenship is not of an earthly but of an ideal city, whose proportions, like the duties of its citizens, are determined by the æsthetic intuition. Plato's philosophy is æsthetic through and through, and because it is æsthetic it is the most human, the most permanently pregnant of all philosophies. Much labour has been spent on the examination of the identity which Plato established between the good and the beautiful. It is labour lost, for that identity is axiomatic, absolute, irreducible. The Greeks knew by instinct that it is so, and in their common speech the word for a gentleman was the *καλὸς κἀγαθὸς*, the beautiful-good.

This is why we have to go back to the Greeks for the principles of art and criticism, and why only those critics who have returned to bathe themselves in the life-giving source have made enduring contributions to criticism. They alone are—let us not say philosophic critics but—critics indeed. Their approach to life and their approach to art are the same; to them, and to them alone, life and art are one. The interpenetration is complete; the standards by which life and art are judged the same. If we may use a metaphor, in the Greek view art is the consciousness of life. Poetry is more philosophic and more highly serious than history, just as the mind of a man is more significant than his outward gestures. To make those gestures significant the art of the actor must be called into play. So to make the outward event of history significant the poet's art is needed. Therefore a criticism which is based on the Greek view is impelled to assign to art a place, the place of sovereignty in its scheme of values. That Plato himself did not do this was due to his having misunderstood the nature of that process of 'imitation' in which art consists; but only the superficial readers of Plato—and a good many readers deserve no better name—will conclude from the fact that he rejected art that his attitude was not fundamentally æsthetic. Not only is the *Republic* itself one of the greatest 'imitations', one of the most subtle and profound works of art ever created, but it would also be true to say that Plato cleared the way for a true conception of art. In reality he rejected not art, but false art; and it only remained for Aristotle to discern the nature of the relation between artistic 'imitation' and the ideal for the Platonic system to be complete and four-square, a perpetual inspiration and an everlasting foundation for art and the criticism of art.

Art, then, is the revelation of the ideal in human life. As the ideal is active and organic so must art itself be. The ideal is never achieved, therefore the process of revealing it is creative in the truest sense of the word. More than that, only by virtue of the artist in him can man appreciate or imagine the ideal at all. To discern it is essentially the work of divination or intuition. The artist divines the end at which human life is aiming; he makes men who are his characters completely expressive of themselves, which no actual man ever has been. If he works on a smaller canvas he aims to make himself completely expressive of himself. That, also, is the aim of the greater artist who expresses himself through the medium of a world of characters of his own creation. He needs that machinery, if a clumsy metaphor may be tolerated, for the explication of his own intuitions of the ideal, which are so various that the attempt to express them through the *persona* of himself would inevitably end in confusion. That is why the great poetic genius is never purely lyrical, and why the greatest lyrics are as often as not the work of poets who are only seldom lyrical.

Moreover, every act of intuition or divination of the ideal in act in the world of men must be set, implicitly or explicitly, in relation to the absolute ideal. In subordinating its particular intuitions to the absolute ideal art is, therefore, merely asserting its own sovereign autonomy. True criticism is itself an organic part of the whole activity of art; it is the exercise of sovereignty by art upon itself, and not the imposition of an alien. To use our previous metaphor, as art is the consciousness of life, criticism is the consciousness of art. The essential activity of true criticism is the harmonious control of art by art. This is at the root of a confusion in the thought of Mr. Eliot, who, in his just anxiety to assert the full autonomy of art, pronounces that the true critic of poetry is the poet and has to smuggle the anomalous Aristotle in on the hardly convincing ground that 'he wrote well about everything', and has, moreover, to elevate Dryden to a purple which he is quite unfitted to wear. No, what distinguishes the true critic of poetry is a truly æsthetic philosophy. In the present state of society it is extremely probable that only the poet or the artist will possess this, for art and poetry were never more profoundly divorced from the ordinary life of society than they are at the present day. But the poet who would be a critic has to make his æsthetic philosophy conscious to himself; to him as a poet it may be unconscious. This necessary change from unconsciousness to consciousness is by no means easy, and we should do well to insist upon its difficulty, for quite as much nonsense is talked about poetry by poets and by artists about art as by the profane about either. Moreover, it is important to remember that in proportion as society approaches the ideal—there is no continual progress towards the ideal; at present society is as far removed from it as it has ever been—the chance of the philosopher, of the scientist even, becoming a true critic of art grows greater. When the æsthetic basis of all humane activity is familiarly recognised, the values of the philosopher, the scientist, and the artist become consciously the same, and therefore interchangeable.

Still, the ideal society is sufficiently remote for us to disregard it, and we shall say that the principle of art for art's sake contains an element of truth when it is opposed to those who would inflict upon art the values of science, of metaphysics, or of a morality of mere convention. We shall also say that the principle of art for art's sake needs to be understood and interpreted very differently. Its implications are tremendous. Art is autonomous, and to be pursued for its own sake, precisely because it comprehends the whole of human life; because it has reference to a more perfectly human morality than any other activity of man; because, in so far as it is truly art, it is indicative of a more comprehensive and unchallengeable harmony in the spirit of man. It does not demand impossibilities, that man should be at one with the universe or in tune with the infinite; but it does envisage the highest of all attainable ideals, that man should be at one with himself, obedient to his own most musical law.

Thus art reveals to us the principle of its own governance. The function of criticism is to apply it. Obviously it can be applied only by him who has achieved, if not the actual æsthetic ideal in life, at least a vision and a sense of it. He alone will know that the principle he has to elucidate and apply is living, organic. It is indeed the very principle of artistic creation itself. Therefore he will approach what claims to be a work of art first as a thing in itself, and seek with it the most intimate and immediate contact in order that he may decide whether it too is organic and living. He will be untiring in his effort to refine his power of discrimination by a return to the finest work of the past, so that he may be sure of himself when he decides, as he must, whether the object before him is the expression of an æsthetic intuition at all. At the best he is likely to find that it is mixed and various; that fragments of æsthetic vision jostle with unsubordinated intellectual judgments.

But, in regarding the work of art as a thing in itself, he will never forget the hierarchy of comprehension, that the active ideal of art is indeed to see life steadily and see it whole, and that only he has a claim to the title of a great artist whose work manifests an incessant growth from a merely personal immediacy to a coherent and all-comprehending attitude to life. The great artist's work is in all its parts a revelation of the ideal as a principle of activity in human life. As the apprehension of the ideal is more or less perfect, the artist's comprehension will be greater or less. The critic has not merely the right, but the duty, to judge between Homer and Shakespeare, between Dante and Milton, between Cézanne and Michelangelo, Beethoven and Mozart. If the foundations of his criticism are truly æsthetic, he is compelled to believe and to show that among would-be artists some are true artists and some are not, and that among true artists some are greater than others. That what has generally passed under the name of æsthetic criticism assumes as an axiom that every true work of art is unique and incomparable is merely the paradox which betrays the unworthiness of such criticism to bear the name it has arrogated to itself. The function of true criticism is to establish a definite hierarchy among the great artists of the past, as well as to test the production of the present; by the combination of these activities it asserts the organic unity of all art. It cannot honestly be said that our present criticism is adequate to either task.

2

POETRY AND PROSE

From The Problem of Style *(Oxford University Press, 1922). A series of lectures delivered at Oxford in 1921.*

In my last lecture I tried to expand a conception which I put forward in my first. I will repeat the original phrase, not because I attach any particular value to the wording, but because it is central to this discussion of style. I said originally that 'the test of a true individuality of style is that we should feel it to be inevitable; in it we should be able to catch the reference back to a whole mode of experience that is consistent with itself. If this reference is perceptible to us, it will be accompanied by a conviction that the peculiarity of style was necessary, and that the originating emotion of which we are sensible demanded this method of expression and this alone'. In my last lecture I did what I could to bring this somewhat abstract conception down to earth.

To-day I propose to examine, more or less in the light of this notion, the familiar distinction between prose and poetry, and to see whether we can gain from this examination any further indications for a more complete and detailed anatomy of style.

It is fairly obvious that this conception of style presupposes that there is no essential difference between prose and poetry. Whether the expression of the comprehensive and self-consistent mode of experience is achieved in the form of prose or verse will depend upon circumstances which are in the main accidental. Indeed, I think that the fashion of the age is perhaps the most important factor. As the Elizabethan age was the age of the drama, the nineteenth century has been the age of the novel. At a certain level of general culture, with certain combinations of economic and social conditions (which it would be well worth while to explore), certain artistic and literary forms impose themselves. These forms the writer is almost compelled to accept, either because he relies on his writing for his living, or because he feels instinctively that he *must* embrace the means necessary to reaching the largest possible audience. When the fates are peculiarly kind, the writer will find himself naturally attracted to the predominant form of the age. I myself make no doubt that Shakespeare was fairly 'comfortable' with the drama; some of the Shakespearians, I think, were not. With the greatest master of English literature now living, Mr. Hardy, it went against the grain to accept the novel form: from the first (he has lately told us) he preferred poetry, and the sureness of his instinct has been abundantly shown by the astonishing poetical achievements of his later years, when the necessity of accepting the novel form no longer existed for him. George Gissing even more reluctantly accepted the novel, and won a minor triumph in a form he detested. In his work you can actually see inclination at war with destiny, and his style (which was naturally that of the scholar handling general ideas) suffered obviously as a result. On the other side, the history of English poetry in the nineteenth century might well be written as the history of an unsuccessful attempt to discover a poetic form that should be as natural to the age as the novel. The greatest poets of the period died while they were still experimenting—Keats, Shelley, and Wordsworth. Browning went farthest on the voyage of exploration. Keats, who realized what the problem was and by the richness of his natural genius had the greatest chance of reaching a conclusion, died at 25. In England the nineteenth century was an age which produced many fine poems, but no poetic finality; and, in my own opinion, we are no farther advanced to-day towards a solution of the difficulty than we were a century ago.

For if the writer cannot accept the form that is vital in his own time, he is confronted by the Herculean task of making a form vital by imposing it upon the contemporary taste. At the beginning of last century, poets could still persuade themselves—for the continuous tradition of the theatre had not been really broken since the Commonwealth—that the poetic drama might be resuscitated. On the one hand, they had a theatre where plays in verse were often accepted and occasionally applauded; on the other, all the enthusiasm of their rediscovery of the Elizabethans. The omens looked better than good. And a great deal was at stake. Ever since the Commonwealth, poetry had been dead—dead, I mean, in the most important sense; it had ceased to play an essential part in the social life of the nation as a whole. If it could have been restored in the first thirty years of last century, the history of English literature would, I believe, have been strangely different. You would not now see it culminating in huge, unwieldy works of genius like *The Dynasts* and *The Ring and the Book*; works which are characteristic of their century, because they show the true creative impulse working free from the discipline of an accepted form. We can see from *The Dynasts* that (in spite of its tremendous power of vision and language) Mr. Hardy, on the whole, did well to suppress his personal inclinations, and to submit himself to the convention of his time; he did well to write the Wessex novels to explicate his mode of experience, while using the lyric whenever his emotion offered the opportunity of complete concentration: Browning, likewise, would have done well had he buckled to the novel. But at the best there would have been waste.

It is, I know, idle to speculate on what would have happened if Keats had lived. The speculation is often indulged in; but it seems to me that it generally runs on less interesting lines than it might. A possible mature Keats is to be seen in relation to the century which followed him, in two ways. First, negatively: it seems to me that had he lived to set his work in true perspective, we should not have had Tennyson, Rossetti, and Morris founding their poetry on the passing phase in Keats's development which is represented by 'La Belle Dame sans Merci'. Second and positively, Keats was the one man who might have restored the poetic drama. His genius was sufficiently rich and humane; he had a springing vein of creative comedy—not the inferior stuff of 'Cap and Bells', but the ripe humour of his letters. And he not only had the gift, but he had the intention. His last considered declaration of his purpose was to write 'a few fine plays'. One can see why Coleridge and Shelley would not have succeeded; neither of them was sufficiently interested in humanity for its own sake. Yet the moment was apparently propitious: how propitious can be judged from the fact that even *Remorse* had a tolerable run, and brought Coleridge £400 in royalties. And in *The Cenci* Shelley had more nearly approached Elizabethan drama than anyone had done for two centuries. If Coleridge and Shelley could do so much, Keats could have done much more, and one cannot help thinking that he might even have reinstated the poetic drama as the natural satisfaction of a social need, and by so doing have made the most elastic and comprehensive of 'poetic' forms vital once more.

If England to-day needed the poetic drama as much as she needs the novel, we could prophesy a glorious future for our literature. For the difficulty with England is this: it is hardly possible for a writer of great creative genius to adapt himself to the form of the novel as wholeheartedly as, for instance, the great Russian writers did during the last century. The creative mind of Russia then poured itself completely into the novel, not because the Russian mind was less 'poetic' than the English mind during the same period, but because it was not hampered by the remnants of an old and venerable, but no longer truly living, tradition. *War and Peace* is in most valuable senses of the word just as poetic as *The Dynasts*, *The Brothers Karamazov* as *Hamlet*; but whereas the creative mind of Russia in the nineteenth century (like the English mind in the sixteenth) was concentrated into a single predominant form, in the nineteenth century the English mind was distracted between the obvious social predominance of the novel and the intellectual prestige of poetry. The possibilities of poetry and the novel are equally great; but at the present time there is this difference between them, that the popular taste for the novel is in the main a healthy taste, while the popular taste for poetry is not. I would gladly defend that rather provocative statement in detail, but this is not the occasion. My excursion has been long enough already. But another, and perhaps more convincing, way of stating the opinion is this: in the present condition of the general taste no really good novel will go under. The bad ones are the most successful, of course, but the good ones will never wholly fail. With poetry, however, the chances are heavy indeed that the good and original work will simply not be recognised at all. And the reason is that the novel-form is such that a good novel must contain certain elements which appeal to the consciousness at many levels of education; whereas poetry has no such testing form, now that the poetic drama has decayed; it no longer has to appeal to that complete cross-section of society which is represented in the gallery, the pit, and the stalls of the theatre, and to which the novel is addressed. The poetry-reading public is artificial in comparison; its interest and taste in poetry is largely artificial. Its approach to poetry is no longer direct. And, where the approach is not direct, the impact falls askew, and the reaction is erratic and unreliable.

The point of this discursive digression, which I have followed where it led, is in the rather fitful light that has been thrown upon the notion that the literary genius works itself out in the form of prose fiction or poetical fiction, indifferently, and that the form will largely depend upon the taste of the age. What is essential to literary genius of the highest kind is not the prose or the poetry, but the fiction—the imagined world peopled by characters sufficiently various to support that crystallization of a mode of experience which is the act of literary creation. And a criticism which deals in fundamentals, and works by the necessary method of comparison, finds itself moving easily among creative fiction and ignoring (until it comes to deal with the details of language) the difference which is so often regarded as absolute between the form of prose and the form of verse. For instance, the valuable reference of Dickens is to Marlowe and Ben Jonson, and of Mr. Hardy the novelist to Shakespeare: not of Dickens to Thackeray or Mr. Hardy to Meredith. Similarly, on a lower level, a rough equation can be established between the personal essayist and the lyric poet. Where the originating experience is predominantly emotional, there—I believe—it is largely a matter of accident or fashion whether prose or poetry is used for the expression, except that where the emotion is peculiarly intense and peculiarly personal the impulse to poetic expression is predominant. I cannot conceive Shakespeare's *Sonnets* in prose; but I can quite easily conceive some of his plays as novels—I can even imagine that *Hamlet* might have been more completely successful as a novel. In another degree Donne, though he had all the gifts for writing 'metaphysical' prose, was too intense and personal in his emotion to forgo the highly concentrated expression of poetry. For, where the emotion is intensely personal, poetry is the form which gives the maximum of control. Donne's sermons are splendid and in parts almost sublime, but they are curiously uncontrolled; their vehemence is seldom precisely marshalled. They will not really bear comparison with Bossuet's, perhaps not even with Jeremy Taylor's. Poetic expression was necessary to Donne if he was to get the best out of himself: in prose, *laxis effertur habenis*—he threw the reins on the neck of his personal horrors of Death and Eternity.

There may be something shocking in this doctrine of the interchangeability (within limits) of prose and poetry. Moreover, there is the obvious objection that it neglects the concrete individuality of works of literature. They are what they are, and to imagine them otherwise is to strive after a vain thing: *Hamlet* as a novel would simply not be *Hamlet*. I admit it freely. I am merely suggesting that a quite different *Hamlet* might, as a matter of fact, have given a more completely adequate expression to the emotional content of Shakespeare's mind. I am not urging that we should neglect the fascinating *Hamlet* we have, to 'fly to others that we know not of'; I am only trying to indicate a point of view from which we can get a comprehensive view of literature as a whole, and see the problem of style in its natural articulation instead of looking at it piecemeal. If you hold with conviction that all works of literature have, by some natural law, the form that is inevitable to them, then we are divided indeed; but I do not think that such a conviction will stand the test of our own reactions. The feeling that some even of the indisputably great works of literature are awkward and uncomfortable in their form is common enough. *Hamlet* is one, Wordsworth's *Prelude* is another; *The Ring and the Book* and *The Dynasts* I have already mentioned. But there are two small pieces of evidence worth considering.

The first is that poetry was the original form of literature, and prose a later development. This suggests the simple question: why was prose developed, if not to afford expression to a content which suffered by being thrust into metrical form? Quite early in the history of Greek literature it was felt that a metrical form could not follow with the proper exactness the forms of logical thought. The metaphysical hexameters of Parmenides are one of the earliest examples of a false form. And the whole huge crop of didactic poetry is really of the same hybrid kind—a sort of immense fungoid growth out of the small psychological fact that the best way to remember a word of practical wisdom is to have a jingle to remember it by. But a metaphysical argument is something different from the content of

> A woman, a dog, and a walnut-tree,
> The more you beat 'em, the better they be.

To force the form of the jingling proverb to hold a chain of discursive reasoning was merely one of the curious mistakes which literary evolution, like the other Evolution, is continually making. Apparently it took men a very long while to discover that the best mnemonic of an intellectual argument is the logical structure of the argument itself; and when the discovery had been made, it was continually forgotten.

The second point is this. Though the development of prose as the vehicle for argument—scientific, philosophical, and legal—was comparatively rapid, it was long centuries before it was adapted to a content primarily aesthetic. Even in Elizabethan times, though prose was nearly always lively and often splendid, it could not compare as an instrument of expression with Elizabethan blank verse. Bacon, for instance, makes a poor showing compared to Montaigne. Since the pre-eminent genius of Shakespeare was not applied to developing prose, another hundred years were needed to sweat the fat off English prose, and almost another hundred to give to it the grace and fertility of an organism in perfect condition. I am anxious not to be mistaken: the prose of the Authorized Version of the Bible is superb and majestic, but it is poetic prose, so is Milton's prose, so is Sir Thomas Browne's. It is prose that has glorious qualities that are not essential to prose, and has not other less striking qualities which *are* the specific qualities of prose; it has not that absolute precision of statement which is the mark of excellent prose; it has not the flexible, non-insistent rhythm that is proper to prose in the pink of condition; it has not the lithe glancing movement, swiftly and secretly advancing, which is characteristic of prose. It was not until the novel had become firmly established in England that prose could freely develop into a perfect instrument for creative art. Thus there was a whole period when in the absence of a proper instrument, the minor artist, who had not the strength to fashion one for himself, was compelled to use one that did not really suit him. Look at Massinger. His blank verse is nearer to the norm of plain, lucid prose than any actual prose written in his time. It must have been delivered quite conversationally, for to impose a blank verse rhythm upon it would be monstrous, except in the places where Massinger was deliberately ranting. Obviously,

Massinger would have been much happier, had he been freed from the obligation of cutting his prose up into lines. But there was no prose as simple and straightforward as Massinger's would have been, appearing as prose in his day. So he went on writing blank verse which is almost as remote from a true blank verse as was the prose of Congreve. Listen to this blank verse passage from a typical page of Massinger: [1]

> Sir, with your pardon, I'll offer my advice. I once observed in a tragedy of ours (in which a murder was acted to the life) a guilty hearer, forced by the terror of a wounded conscience, to make discovery of that which torture could not wring from him. Nor can it appear like an impossibility, but that your father, looking upon a covetous man presented on the stage, as in a mirror may see his own deformity and loathe it. Now, could you but persuade the emperor to see a comedy we have that's styled *The Cure of Avarice*, and to command your father to be a spectator of it, he shall be so anatomized in the scene, and see himself so personated, the baseness of a self-torturing miserable wretch truly described, that I much hope the object will work compunction in him.

The odd thing is that this blank verse is really excellent prose—lucid, well shaped, and sinewy. Massinger's sentence-management (as Coleridge noted) is beautiful: 'Mais que diable allait-il faire dans cette galère?'

I hope that these considerations will have diminished the apparent paradox of the conception that a writer's choice of prose or poetry for his expression is largely determined by accident, and depends on the fashion of the age in which he lives and the relative development of language in the two forms.

But these considerations themselves were preliminary to a further question. If, as I believe, the comprehensive and self-consistent experience which distinguishes the finest literature can be expressed almost indifferently in prose or poetry, is there a content which necessarily demands prose for its vehicle, and is there a content which necessarily demands poetry? I have already indicated the answer I should give to the second question by a passing reference to Shakespeare's *Sonnets* and to Donne. The first question concerns us now. Is there a content which is specifically the content of prose?

I imagine that it is obvious that exact thinking on any subject necessarily demands prose. The limitations of metre and rhythm and rhyme must be intolerable to it; to be forced to employ circumlocution and paraphrase, every word of which may be fertile in false suggestion, is practically for a logician or a scientist to be compelled to say 'the thing that is not'. Prose is the language of exact thinking; it was

[1] *Roman Actor*, ii. 1.

made for the purpose; and I suppose that a proposition in Euclid is an elementary example of good style, though in an absolutely non-creative kind.

But prose is the language not merely of exact thinking, but of exact description. A description, whether of a country, a wanted criminal, or the contents of a room, if it is to be exact, must be in prose. Give the botanist a posy of the flowers that Perdita longed for—

> Daffodils,
> That come before the swallow dares, and take
> The winds of March with beauty; violets dim,
> But sweeter than the lids of Juno's eyes
> Or Cytherea's breath; pale prime-roses,
> That die unmarried, ere they can behold
> Bright Phoebus in his strength, a malady
> Most incident to maids; bold oxlips and
> The crown imperial; lilies of all kinds,
> The flower-de-luce being one—

and he will give you a different description—a description that will enable you to recognize a daffodil and a violet when you see them. It may perhaps, if you are sufficiently familiar with his terms and the realities they stand for, enable you to visualize them, but nothing more. He is not in the least concerned with the emotional effects of which the flowers may be the occasion.

Prose of this kind is prose indeed; but it has no place in a discussion of style except as a type of the extreme, and a background against which to differentiate creative prose. But there are contents of other and more interesting kinds which seem positively to demand prose. Take, for instance, the passage from Massinger, which I deliberately read as prose, because it is to all intents and purposes prose. It is indeed a true prose period:

> I once observed in a tragedy of ours, in which a murder was acted to the life, a guilty hearer . . . make discovery of that which torture could not wring from him. Nor can it appear like an impossibility, but that your father, looking upon a covetous man presented on the stage, as in a mirror, may see his own deformity and loathe it. Now, could you but persuade the emperor to see a comedy we have that's styled *The Cure for Avarice*, and to command your father to be a spectator of it, he shall be so anatomized in the scene, and see himself so personated, the baseness of a self-torturing miserable wretch truly described, that I much hope the object will work compunction in him.

In order to distinguish the quality of this more precisely, compare the kindred passage in *Hamlet*:

> I have heard
> That guilty creatures sitting at a play
> Have by the very cunning of the scene
> Been struck so to the soul that presently
> They have proclaimed their malefactions;
> For murder, though it have no tongue, will speak
> With most miraculous organ. I'll have these players
> Play something like the murder of my father
> Before mine uncle. I'll observe his looks,
> I'll tent him to the quick: if he but blench
> I know my course.

The passage from Massinger has a perfect logical structure. Hamlet, who is using exactly the same argument, and laying the same plan, leaps the essential steps to the conclusion, and leaps back again. The difference is one of emotional temperature; the Shakespeare is at boiling-point, the Massinger a few degrees below blood-heat; one is the poetry of passion, the other the prose of calculation. The calculation I mean is in the mind of Massinger, not of his character. Iago calculates, more and more coolly by far than Hamlet, yet his speeches have not any of the deliberate common-sense of Massinger in them; the emotion behind the conception of Iago compels him, at his coldest, to speak with the inward speed of passion. On the other hand, the speech of Hamlet might perfectly well be in prose; but it would be a very different prose from Massinger's. It would not be necessarily and inevitably prose.

This prosaic quality of Massinger, which makes us feel so acutely that the form of his time was unsuited to him, is the direct result of the temperature of his mind. Naturally, he is never at boiling-point; sometimes he feels that he ought to look as though he were boiling, and he begins to rant: then he makes most uncomfortable reading. There was something in Massinger which compelled him to take things coolly; they made no very deep impression upon him. He spent most of his life writing tragedies, for the simple reason that his abilities as a writer were real and tragedy was the fashion. But he was far indeed from having that peculiar sense of the quality of life which makes tragedy a natural expression; his conception of tragedy is utterly artificial; his hero, for example, in *The Virgin Martyr,* is inhumanly and impossibly good. He could work out a tragedy, but he could not conceive one. In other words, his attitude to life was perfectly rational and sane. The standards to which he referred it were not those absolutely personal standards which are derived from the writer's own instinctive reactions, but standards partly inherited, partly derived from the social sense of his time. He responded not to the thing or the event in itself, but to its aberration from the normal.

This was the prosaic quality in Massinger, and it is not surprising to any one who has read his tragedies that his real achievement was in comedy. *A New Way to Pay Old Debts* and *A City Madam* are obviously the most natural form of expression for his talent that the age could give. They, too, happen to be written in verse; but they are really the purest prose. The versification is extremely practised, but quite mechanical. His comedy, as a recent critic has pointed out, has really very little connexion with Elizabethan comedy; it is the direct predecessor of the Restoration comedy. He hovers unsteadily between the old conventions which were unfitted to him and the new which were not yet shaped and which he himself had not the strength to shape; but we can see that his talent was for prose comedy.

The attitude of mind which expresses itself in the comedy of manners is one which demands prose. To see the social comedy at all, to distinguish the excrescences from the polite normality of an age, means that the writer must interpose between his sensitiveness and the world a neutralizing screen of rational judgement. He is not engaged in creating a universe but in readjusting one; the ordering principle of his world is a social convention which he accepts, and with which he identifies himself; he measures men and women by the standard of an ideal, but the ideal is not his own, it is that of the society in which he moves, and if it has become second nature in him, that is because he feels himself freest and most comfortable as a member of society. Not that delicate perceptions are not necessary to the writer of social comedy; but the principle by which those perceptions are ordered does not arise out of the perceptions themselves; the endorsement they receive comes not from the self-consistent attitude refined by the author out of his own impressions, but from an inherited accumulation of social experience. The comedian is the most social of all artists. For his central activity, his measurement of the aberration from an ideal that is not only possible for, but inherent in society, prose, the medium of exactness, is the appropriate instrument. Poetry has no reinforcement to give—the emotional appeal which poetry heightens would be merely a disturbing element, for the comedian's appeal is to the rational judgement of men. Of course, social comedy has been written in verse form as Massinger's was and Molière's, but in these the form is largely irrelevant. No one dreams of calling Molière primarily a poet, and Massinger keeps the name chiefly because he has slipped in among the sacrosanct Elizabethans; while Aristophanes and Ben Jonson are writers of farce, not social comedians at all. The ideal of the art as practised in England lies somewhere between Congreve and Jane Austen. Consider this passage from Jane Austen's earliest novel, *Sense and Sensibility:*

Marianne's performance was highly applauded. Sir John was loud in his admiration at the end of every song, and as loud in his conversation with the others while every song lasted. Lady Middleton frequently called him to order, wondered how any one's attention could be diverted from the music for a moment, and asked Marianne to sing a particular song which Marianne had just finished. Colonel Brandon alone of all the party heard her without being in raptures. He paid her only the compliment of attention; and she felt a respect for him on the occasion, which the others had reasonably forfeited by their shameless want of taste. His pleasure in music, though it amounted not to that ecstatic delight which alone could sympathize with her own, was estimable when contrasted against the horrible insensibility of the others; and she was reasonable enough to allow that a man of five and thirty might well have outlived all acuteness of feeling and every exquisite power of enjoyment. She was perfectly disposed to make every allowance for the Colonel's advanced state of life which humanity required.

That is, as sportsmen would say, a perfect right and left; the two quite different birds of aberration are beautifully dropped—the social humbug of Sir John and Lady Middleton, and the romantic sensibility of Marianne. The author's point of vantage is central, and for her purpose she personifies it in Colonel Brandon. The use of anything but prose for the expression of such cool perceptions would obviously be not merely an unnecessary but a positively hampering convention. One would simply risk blurring the keen edge. These effects of contrast between the appearance and the reality, between affectation and honesty, demand exactness of language; the rich reward of enhanced emotional suggestion which poetry gives in return for the judicial precision it takes away would only be an encumbrance. The style resides in the exactness with which the perceptions and the scheme to which they are referred are conveyed; these are given at the same moment—the reference to a self-consistent mode of experience is immediately perceptible. It fully satisfies our definition of a true individuality of style: the reason why it is *necessarily* prose is that the mode of experience is not predominantly emotional.

For reasons which are somewhat similar it seems to me that prose is the proper vehicle of satire. Here again the historical fact is that many of the most famous satires have been written in verse—Horace and Juvenal among the ancients, and plenty from Donne to Churchill in English. Nevertheless, the metrical form no more makes the satire of Horace or Hudibras poetry than it did the passage of Massinger which I quoted. The content is almost invariably prosaic, whatever the form may be. Still, there is a meaning in the well-known tag of Juvenal, *Facit indignatio versus,* which makes it worth while to consider for a moment the nature of satire. There is not much doubt that Juvenal was right in saying that the emotion of indignation is fundamental in the satirist; and there is no reason why this disturbance of the emotional being should not find expression in poetry. Indeed, if poetry is (as I have previously suggested) the natural expression of the more violent kinds of personal emotion, it is surely the natural vehicle of indignation. I think immediately of some of the most withering epigrams of Catullus—'Lesbia, illa Lesbia, quam Catullus unam'—to which the rhythmical form is as necessary and inevitable as to any of his love-lyrics. *Facit indignatio versus* is true enough. But personal indignation of this kind, though it is the basis of satire, does not suffice for the real satirical attitude. Satire is not a matter of personal resentment, but of impersonal condemnation. Partly by reason of the classical tradition, invective and true satire are often indiscriminately lumped together under the single name; but they ought to be distinguished. True satire implies the condemnation of a society by reference to an ideal; it differs from invective in that it is not an attack aimed by a particular at a particular —'Of these the false Achitophel was first' is not satire; while it differs from social comedy in that the ideal to which the reference is made is not practical and inherent in society. The comedian is not indignant, because the space between his ideal and the actual can without difficulty be bridged; the satirist is indignant because there is an impassable abyss between the reality and his dream.

Satire is, in short, a kind of metaphysical comedy; and, like comedy, it is based on a method of contrast. The satirist is engaged in measuring the monstrous aberration from the ideal. The aberration is now all on one side: the satirist does not hold a middle point of vantage like the comedian. Nevertheless, he has to keep equally cool, for his activity is predominantly intellectual. His ideal standard of reference was framed in accordance with his emotions, indeed, but the measurement of the aberration from it is an affair of unbiased calculation. The emotion of the satirist has to be suppressed and concealed: the *emportement* of the lampooner or the thundering preacher is impossible for him, for again his appeal is to the rational part of man; he is engaged in a demonstration, and his aim is so to arrange the facts that his hearers, in spite of themselves, are driven to refer them to his own ideal. The famous technical device of the satirist is to compel an ordinary member of society to explain the conventions, institutions, and morality of his country to a being of a superior morality to whom they are unknown: Swift, Voltaire, 'Erewhon' Butler, and of our own contemporaries, Anatole France and Mr. H. G. Wells, have employed it, and we may almost say that it is the necessary technique of the true satirist. And the conclusion of the superior being is always in much the same terms as the verdict of the King of Brobdingnag on Gulliver's exposition of English society:

My little friend Grildrig, you have made a most admirable panegyric on your country; you have clearly proved that ignorance, idleness, and vice may be sometimes the only ingredients for qualifying a legislator; that laws are best explained, interpreted, and applied by those whose interest and abilities lie in perverting, confounding, and eluding them. I observe among you some lines of an institution, which in its original might have been tolerable, but these half-erased, and the rest wholly blurred and blotted by corruptions. It doth not appear from all you have said, how any one virtue is required toward the procurement of any one station among you; much less that men are ennobled on account of their virtue, that priests are advanced for their piety and learning, soldiers for their conduct or valour, judges for their integrity, or counsellors for their wisdom. As for yourself (continued the king) who have spent the greatest part of your life in travelling, I am well disposed to hope you may hitherto have escaped many vices of your country. But by what I have gathered from your own relation, and the answers I have with much pains wringed and extorted from you, I cannot but conclude the bulk of your natives to be the most pernicious race of little odious vermin ever suffered to crawl upon the surface of the earth.

Such an effect is proper to prose, and possible only in prose; it depends upon absolute economy of statement, for where the appeal is made to reason, it cannot be heightened by being garnished with an appeal to emotion. Its force will be diminished. No barrister wastes his forensic oratory upon the Law Lords.

The specific virtue of prose is that it is judicial; and that is a virtue that poetry cannot have: if it has, it is not poetry, but prose in metre. Where the appeal is to the judgement, there the vehicle is prose: if the appeal is made with absolute economy, so that the movement is swift and certain to the conclusion, then it will give an aesthetic pleasure over and above its convincing force. Though it may be too much to say that the finest prose is of this kind, or that perfect prose is only possible when it has to convey a content that is specifically the content of prose, it is worth while to protest against the frequent habit of estimating prose according as it approaches the condition of poetry. I have in mind a recent anthology of English prose, which carries this mistaken notion so far that it gives twenty pages to Charles Lamb and two to Swift; moreover, the anthologist has been at infinite pains to ransack Swift for perhaps the only purple passage he ever permitted himself; and he has done the same for two modern and closely allied masters of plain prose, Samuel Butler and Bernard Shaw. Of such an anthology one can only say that its author is insensitive to some of the most peculiar beauties of prose. But the heresy that the more poetic prose is, the finer it is, is widespread; it should be deplored and combated, not only because it is a vice of taste, but because in practice there is nothing more dangerous to the formation of a prose style than the endeavour to make it poetic. The habit of plastering a plain exposition or a simple narration with empty poetical beauties is very easy to acquire and very hard to unlearn; on the other hand, if you can manage plain prose tolerably well—and that is *not* easy to acquire—you may be confident that you have a safeguard against false emotionalism. Only when the emotional content you have is so urgent that your plain style will not express it, will you be tempted to depart from it; and then you will not be tempted but compelled; and then you will be on the way to a style of your own.

That fine prose is necessarily poetic, that it makes its appeal directly to the emotions, by the apparatus of image and rhythm essential to that appeal, is a heresy; on the other hand, the few purists who maintain that what I have called judicial prose, because it has the virtues and achieves the effects that prose alone can possess or achieve, is therefore to be preferred to all other prose, seem to me quite wrong-headed. They are like those politicians who, in order to rectify injustice to the manual labourer, deny that other classes in the community have any rights at all. As though it were somehow illegitimate that prose, because it alone can appeal to the judgement, should presume to appeal to the emotions! Prose is an instrument whose range is infinite, and probably its possibilities have been less explored than those of poetry. If we look back on the last hundred years not merely of English, but of European literature, it seems to me fairly plain that the bulk of the creative work of the century has been in prose; the bias of the period is definitely towards prose; and this is not, I believe, because of any imagined superiority in prose as a medium—there is no reason to suppose the great writers of the nineteenth century so deluded—but simply because of the changed social conditions. With the rise in the general level of education, and the breakdown of the old semi-feudal aristocracy which accompanied it, came the closing of one economic channel by which literature was kept productive, and the opening of another. At one and the same time the old system of patronage and pensions disappeared, and it became possible for a writer to maintain himself (sometimes almost in opulence) by the sale of prose fiction. (In passing, may I suggest that an extremely valuable work might be done by any one who would devote himself to writing 'An Economic History of English Literature'? Not only is the subject fascinating in itself, but it would supply a most necessary counterpoise to those metaphysical critics who tacitly assume that all writers who have not private incomes live on air, and in virtue of this assumption are able to enjoy the truly Hegelian spectacle of forms evolving out of forms in everlasting self-generation. This History needs to be written; for economic causes are as operative in determining the course of literature as they are in turning the current of history.) I was saying that the last century of European literature opened with two decisive changes—the disappearance of patronage, and the possibility of making an independent livelihood from prose fiction; and, in spite of all the real and obvious dangers of the popular appeal, literature has benefited by the change. It is always good when a vital relation between a writer and his audience is established. From economic necessity first, and then more positively from the sense of exhilaration which a writer receives from a vital relation with his audience, the bias of the century has been towards prose fiction; and in that time it has been abundantly proved that prose fiction is an instrument at least as adequate to the needs of the great creative genius as the other supreme literary form, the poetic drama.

Possibly it may not be true to say that prose fiction can do all that poetry can do; it is sufficient for my purposes if we admit that it can do most of the things that poetry can do, and if we remember that prose fiction is still very young. But I want, if I can, to persuade you to conceive it as a medium analogous to the medium of poetry; as an instrument on which the experiences and emotions that lay behind *Antony and Cleopatra* could find a different, but no less complete, expression. The forms of literature change, but not the form of creative literary genius. A Shakespeare and a Chaucer would have been perfectly happy with our modern fashions and our modern tools; but they would have written things that looked, to the superficial eye at least, very different from the work we know them by. If you find this idea not intolerable, or perhaps even persuasive, you will discover a good reason to mistrust both those who declare that obviously 'poetic' prose is the finest prose, and those who maintain that judicial prose must have the pre-eminence: supreme effects are possible in both kinds. But our conception of prose as an analogous instrument will lead us to suspect that even these two kinds are not exhaustive, but that there are achievements in prose fiction, of description, of dialogue, of dramatic crisis, which fall under neither of these heads, and of course escape the attention of the anthologists; yet their style may satisfy all the requisites of perfection, if not in the same way as the passage from *Antony and Cleopatra* which we have already analysed, in almost the same degree as the passage from Chaucer's *Troilus and Cressida*.

3

STENDHAL

From John Clare and other studies *(Peter Nevill, 1950). This essay first appeared in 1920.*

No one has better described the impression made by Stendhal than Goethe, who wrote in 1818: 'Er zieht an, er stosst ab, interessiert und ärgert, und so kann man ihn nicht loswerden.' ('He attracts, repels, interests, irritates, and one can't get away from him.') That was written after reading *Rome, Naples, and Florence,* which M. Edouard Champion has republished in his superb edition of the complete works, and the description fits the particular book perhaps a little more exactly than any of the others. It so obviously ought to be a dull work, and it so obviously is not. It has neither system nor shape; it is concerned with a society that has passed out of mind; it is studded with the irrelevant, tangential speculations of a perpetually curious mind, with odd facts of history, with long and enthusiastic appreciations of forgotten Italian operas and unremembered singers. Yet we are held. Stendhal's facts are not like anybody else's facts. They are like objects looked at from a peculiar and unexpected angle. We only half recognize them. The proportions are queer. At first they are almost silly, then they become bizarre, then fascinating, and then—at least for a period in most literary lives—all-absorbing.

Stendhal was a man of many surfaces. There are bold men who call themselves *stendhaliens* and profess to be adept in *le beylisme*; but they are not to be trusted. It is true that Stendhal had an attitude to life, a philosophy of conduct, which might be imitated. But the man who actively followed Beyle's precepts would, by the mere fact, be very different from Beyle. For this seeming *rusé* realist was the embodiment of timidity; this amateur of the *amour-passion* was one of the most backward love-makers who ever existed. In M. Arbelet's admirable biography, *La Jeunesse de Stendhal*, which is published as part (and a worthy part) of the collected edition, you may read of the comedy or the tragedy of young Beyle's initiation into love at Milan. It is an unfamiliar but characteristic episode in the man's life, which was as it were stained through and through with a dye of some paradoxical uniqueness. One feels that he was born in a momentary interregnum of the *Zeitgeist*, just as in the actual world he happened to be educated in one of those strange schools which were the immediate product of the Revolution, where masters and pupils alike were fired by a passion for *la Raison*—schools which lasted barely three years, just long enough to give a unique impress to the one boy with a touch of genius who might, on merely statistical grounds, be expected to be born in the period.

If one were writing the book upon Beyle which has still to be written—it will be the work of the English critic, for no Frenchman could have sufficient detachment, or even sufficient understanding—one would begin by showing how a cornucopia of uniqueness was made ready to be emptied upon the head of the infant Henri Beyle. M. Arbelet has gathered most of the material for a study of his astonishing parents and relations, those bourgeois aristocrats (like the Rênals of *Le Rouge et le Noir*) who were so much more exclusive even than the *grands bourgeois* of modern France. When one comes to know them a little more closely, to see them a little more clearly, than is possible through the melodramatic kaleidoscope of *La Vie de Henri Brulard* one comes to look upon Beyle as a kind of infant Samuel dedicated to one knows not what deity of contrariety and paradox. One feels, rather than understands, the reason of the inevitability which imposes itself upon any one who attempts even in the scope of a brief essay to define the substance of Beyle, the man and the writer. Every comparison turns into paradox. The outward garment of his style suggests the influence of Voltaire; in fact, Beyle hated Voltaire, and the real influence was much rather Jean-Jacques. His whole manner is that of an aristocrat of aristocrats; he was, in fact, and most profoundly, a republican, a libertarian, and a radical. Most sincerely in the literary controversy of his age Beyle insisted that he was a romantic; in fact, he detested Chateaubriand, and he was pretty exactly what we call a realist. His lucid and exact psychological analysis recalls no dramatist in the French tradition so directly as Racine: in fact, Beyle could not abide Racine, and most honestly and for the most substantial reasons idolized Shakespeare. 'Adorava Shakespeare' was the alternative epitaph to the one which he finally chose: 'Arrigo Beyle Milanese: vissè, scrissè, amò.' The art of Shakespeare and the life of Italy—between Rivoli and the Risorgimento, be it understood—may fairly be said to have been the two passions whose rule over him endured throughout his life.

Beyle is, perhaps, the smallest of great men; but he is also one of the most compact, and his title to be called great is proved not least by the wholly peculiar persistence with which he seems to avoid all classification. He makes a queer final impression—how delighted he would have been to read it!—as of a miniature, desiccated Shakespeare, and, indeed, one can easily conceive a definition of him in terms which in a richer, riper world of perceptions would apply to Shakespeare. His universe of men was also blank between the aristocrat and the peasant, and it may be for the same reason. He confesses that because he was a bourgeois, the bourgeois had become as intolerable to him as the taste of oysters to a man who had a surfeit of them; he had supped too full of the horrors of the bourgeoisie in childhood ever to contemplate them again. The middle class were ciphers in his system of values, and even an ideal member of it remained a cipher, just as zero, raised to the *n*th power, remains zero. 'Ce qui est exactement raisonnable ne donne pas prise aux beaux-arts; j'estime un sage républicain des Etats-Unis, mais je l'oublie à tout jamais en quelques jours; ce n'est pas un homme pour moi, c'est une chose.' Therefore, although he was by impulse a realist, he was nevertheless a romantic because he had a theory of what was real. Not all that existed in the shape of human beings was real to him. This anti-bourgeois speck in his telescope, he wrote in *Henri Brulard*, had been very useful to him with the characters of his novels. It was true; but the word 'bourgeois' had by that time come to denote for him not so much a social class as a type of being. The reality of a man for Stendhal lay in his faculty of allowing all that is prudential and calculating in him to be swept aside by what is instinctive and passionate.

That is a fairly complete and coherent attitude towards life: it certainly has its counterpart in Shakespeare, it is, moreover, what we might call a very good working basis for a literary artist. But it does not in the least resemble that enlightened hedonism which the 'Beylistes' profess to find in their idol. Beyle, indeed, makes a poor showing as a hedonist. The overwhelming impulses of soul which he set highest, and counted most real among human capacities, the precious *élans d'âme*, were likely to prove annihilating to their vehicles. Indeed, they not only annihilated his heroes and heroines, Fabrice, Julien Sorel, Mademoiselle de la Môle, Clélia, and the rest, but they came near to being his own undoing at one or two points of his own career. To be interesting to Beyle people must be ready to surrender their lives at the summons of a *grande passion*; to be interesting to himself he had to believe that the same readiness lay in him. It is therefore inexact to call him a romantic, even though he called himself one. Your true romantic is ready to surrender himself only to his dreams; his *élan d'âme* has little or no repercussion in the visible world. The real world is altogether too sordid, and perhaps too difficult a place for him to be concerned with it. His passions are veritably passive. It was, however, the essence of Stendhal's conception of passion that it should issue, and issue immediately in act. Whether the act seems grandiose or ridiculous, momentous or merely bizarre, was of small account; it was precisely indifferent. He prefaces almost every one of his stories of *la vie passionelle* in *Rome, Naples et Florence* with the warning that it will seem ridiculous, but the implication behind the warning is that if you find it ridiculous, you are a poor creature. The faculty which he admired in men had two complementary aspects. Looked at from the inside it was passion, the *élan d'âme*, from the outside was *la force*. This is the meaning of his paradox: 'J'aime la force, et de la force que j'aime, une fourmi peut en montrer autant qu'un éléphant.'

Stendhal's attitude to life was not romantic, therefore; it was tragic. It falls in between the classical and the romantic attitudes. His ideal is neither the harmonious man of the Greeks nor the gesticulating, dreaming hero of romanticism; it is, really, the hero of a Shakespearean tragedy, a hero who plays his part in the active life of a real world. In order to give literary expression to this tragic hero-worship, Stendhal had to become what is generally called a realist. But just as the term 'romantic' has to be given an unfamiliar and improper meaning to fit him, 'realist' has also to be given a precise and particular sense. Realist in the proper critical meaning he was not. A good deal more than half human life was supremely uninteresting to him. But the part he was interested in had a sort of super-reality to compensate. The problem was how to convey and communicate this, how (in the expressive phrase of the working artist) 'to get it across.' An unobtrusive sentence in *Rome, Naples et Florence*—we are endeavouring to explain Stendhal on the evidence of this single book—gives us his solution. 'On n'a jamais du feu,' he writes, 'qu'en écrivant la langue qu'on parle à sa maîtresse et à ses rivaux.'

Now there is much more in Stendhal's style than is indicated here; but that dictum contains the solid basis of some of his most remarkable achievements—passionate episodes expressed in the natural language of passion. On the creative side one can think immediately of a dozen passages in the two great novels where the theory is superbly exemplified—for instance, the 'Qu'avez-vous dans la poche de côté de votre habit?' of Mathilde de la Môle—on the critical, it is a main count in his one-sided, but convincing case against Scott. 'Ses personnages passionnés semblant avoir honte d'eux-mêmes'; therefore they are unreal. This principle is the chief of the two tendencies that unite to form Stendhal's 'realism.' From his childhood upwards he was, in regard to literature, a dissatisfied rather than a disillusioned romantic. M. Arbelet has unearthed a singularly interesting passage from one of his unpublished notes which bears upon this. It was written before he was twenty:

Dans les romans on ne nous offre qu'une nature choisie: nous nous formons nos types de bonheur d'après les romans. Parvenus à l'âge où nous devons être heureux . . . nous nous étonnons de deux choses: la première, de ne pas éprouver du tout les sentiments auxquels nous nous attendions; la deuxième, si nous les éprouvons, de ne pas les sentir comme ils sont peints dans les romans.

Two years later he re-read his note, and added: 'Voilà l'histoire de ma vie; mon roman était les ouvrages de Rousseau.' Stendhal himself was destined to offer to future generations a *nature choisie*, more sedulously selected, perhaps, than that of any other considerable novelist. It was not the ignoring of half reality that shocked him, but the being unreal in the expression of the reality you choose. Because he was consistently and profoundly a 'romantic', he hated with a threefold hatred romantic falseness and pomposity; because he really had a tragic attitude to life, the high falutin' of French classical tragedy goaded him to a frenzy. It was making his heartfelt realities ridiculous. From this he directly derived his detestation of the phrase and the circumlocution, which remained with him all his life, and his at first sight strange desire, which lasted to middle age, to write a good comedy. An instinct told him that the drama was the most perfect vehicle for his tragic view of life; another instinct told him that a genre in which you had to write *coursier* for *cheval* and the precious word *pistolet* was taboo, was intolerable. To get natural speech on to the stage he must write comedy. It may seem a fantastic conclusion; fantastic it must seem if you have read the outline of any of his projected 'comedies'—irrefutable evidence that he had not a shred of a sense of humour—but yet it was inevitable.

The other component of his style, a bare and vigorous clarity of analytical exposition, came from two sources. He was, as we have said, a devout believer in the tragic attitude. Tragic heroes were real people; he had met plenty of them in the Italian society he loved. He wanted to prove that they existed, to take them to pieces, as it were, in the intervals when they were not expressing *élans d'âme* in the natural language of passion. Here the ideologists who had been triumphant in the French educational system for the three brief and impressionable years he spent at the Ecole Centrale at Grenoble lent him powerful aid. Those forgotten psychologists, Destutt de Tracy and Condillac, whose names recur so often in his pages, were indeed his masters of method here. Hence came the passion for *la lo-gique* which in his curious drawl he so often impressed upon Mérimée, and his recourse to the Code Napoléon as a model of descriptive style. His education and the demands of his theory of life and art worked together for good. His heroes, being heroes of action, were saved from perishing in a maze of super-subtle psychology; since their supreme moments had to be expressed in the natural language of passion, they were also saved from becoming 'desiccated.'

Stendhal, in brief, was a tragic realist. Tragic realism is, on the whole, an unusual kind; but some of the greatest works of literary art belong to it, the *Medea* and *Antony and Cleopatra, Anna Karenina,* and *The Possessed*. Stendhal differs from the writers called up by these names in that he held his faith a perceptible shade more naïvely than they. It was for him not merely the attitude of an artist towards life, not merely a philosophy which enabled the artist to express his vision of the truth and quality of life, it was also, and perhaps chiefly, a philosophy of conduct. Tragic heroes did not merely exist because their destiny was forced upon them; it was man's duty to be one. The first thing was to be *une âme supérieure* (his beloved phrase), the second to assert it in act, the third—and a bad third—was to write about it. And here is the reason why, although there is no real incongruity in naming Stendhal with Euripides and Shakespeare and Tolstoy and Dostoevsky, a vital difference remains. To a casual glance it presents itself as a constant amateurishness in Stendhal the artist. We must look deeper than that, however; and, looking deeper, we shall discover it to be a profound naïvety. What satisfies only a part of the great writer's mind satisfied the whole of his: in other words, Stendhal was even less a creator of heroes than a hero-worshipper.

4

CRIME AND PUNISHMENT

From Fyodor Dostoevsky, a critical study *(Secker, 1916), pages 102–122.*

Crime and Punishment is the first of Dostoevsky's great books. It is the first in which he dared really to state the doubt which tortured him. Hitherto he had been on the side of the law. In the sight of men he had done no more than to lift his head above the wall of the City of Good and observe the enemy. Perhaps he had approached it more closely than his fellow-citizens: he had drunk and eaten with the Adversary in the Morskaya café, but he had insisted on paying his own bill. He would carry that bill away with him if need be to establish his innocence from all complicity with the works of darkness.

Hitherto he had been content to state a simple antagonism, and to pronounce himself without reserve upon the side of the good. No doubt for those who read even *The Insulted and Injured* with clairvoyant eyes, he did protest too much. To them it may have seemed that he knew rather too much about the enemy, more than could be learned by a simple soldier in the cause of the simple good. At least he must have been a spy in the enemy's camp, they might have argued, and a spy to have wormed himself so deep into the enemy's confidence, must have subdued himself to that he worked in. The true saint flees the very approach of the evil one, and is affrighted by the faint and far-off murmur of his pinions in the air. He does not wait to look the Old Adversary full in the face, or pause to note the colour of his hair and the expression of his eyes.

But if there were any uneasy at the intimacy of Dostoevsky's knowledge of the dark power, they seem to have held their peace. Apparently the Russian world was well content with the new champion of the old morality. But if they were content, Dostoevsky himself was not. He could not suffer that his expression should so far run short of his knowledge. He must follow out his thought in the language of his imagination—and who knows how much actual experience went to the making of that imagination—wherever it would lead him, for he too was possessed with a devil that drove him to his own fulfilment.

And in the opening chapter of *Crime and Punishment* the gates of the City of Good clang together, and Dostoevsky is outside them. He is already an outlaw, but a timid outlaw, haunted still by the memory of the security which he has left behind him. ' "I want to do a thing *like that* and am frightened by these trifles," thought Rodion Raskolnikov with an odd smile.' A thing *like that*—perhaps it could never be defined more closely. Certain it is that there is a vague sense in the mind of frustrated expectation when the deed is made actual and Raskolnikov has murdered the old money-lender, Alyona Ivanovna, and her simple sister. In spite of all the tremendous power with which the imagined act is made real, the disquiet of vague disappointment remains, an uneasy feeling that even a dreadful murder, perhaps by the very fact of its being so present and so real, is in the nature of a parody of the intention, not of the murderer, so much as of his creator. But the mind cannot work freely any more; it is riveted to the concrete drama which is unrolled before the eyes. The crime is committed, the murder is done, and by an heroic accident so done that no suspicion can fall upon the murderer. He is beyond reach of punishment, if his will prove strong and constant in its first resolution.

But though Dostoevsky has escaped from the city and the gates have closed upon him, no one has seen him. He will not be the one to raise the hue and cry. If the citizens persist in seeing in him their most valiant warrior, the very champion of their morality, he will not take it upon him to open their eyes. He is content to be a moral writer, so long as they are content to believe him such. He has gone without the walls to reconnoitre the enemy once more, with the boldness of old experience, and he will bring back a knowledge that is as triple brass to the defenders. He will show that the power of their morality is set on foundations more eternal than the ordinances of man-made law; he will prove that it stands in the very nature of man himself. Even though Raskolnikov has placed himself beyond the reach of punishment, in a stronghold where the king's writ does not run, yet will he be forced to confess his crime by the torments of his own conscience, and to come forward and accept his punishment and his suffering.

Of course, a capable police-officer, like Porfiry Petrovitch in the novel, well versed in the psychology that cuts both ways, could have told them as much. But the lesson would have been less memorable. It is more comforting to have these assurances from the lips of genius; and there are no geniuses in Scotland Yard, but only clever men. They might be able to state the law, but they could not prove it in flesh and blood. A Dostoevsky can point the moral in the imperishable stuff of humanity, he can show the very pulses of the heart which drives the murderer to the stool of repentance. By his art they can have the inexpressible consolation of watching the sinner in his self-created agony, of seeing his lips move and hearing the words come 'softly and brokenly, but distinctly', from his lips:—*It was I killed the old pawnbroker woman and her sister Lizaveta with an axe and robbed them.*

That is enough. The Law is vindicated out of the inevitable workings of the human heart. Even though its officers may fail, conscience flings a wider net than theirs, into which the enemies of society are safely gathered. So can the citizens sleep quietly in their beds.

But Dostoevsky, though he deceived them, did not deceive himself. He knew that in Raskolnikov he had chosen a weak vessel, but one in whom, though the flesh was weak the spirit was willing. Not even Raskolnikov will confess himself repentant of his crime with his own lips. It was *reported* that on his trial 'to the question what led him to confess, he answered that it was his heartfelt repentance', and it was added that the audience felt that 'all this was almost coarse'. Dostoevsky knew that it was not almost, but quite coarse, quite crude and quite untrue; and having thrown this sop of the appearance of repentance to the anxious householders, he had the courage to express the truth without ambiguity. A year after his heartfelt repentance, in the solitude of his Siberian prison, Raskolnikov could confess his heart aloud.

If only fate would have sent him repentance—burning repentance that would have torn his heart and robbed him of sleep, that repentance the agony of which brings visions of hanging or drowning! Oh, he would have been glad of it. Tears and agonies would at least have been life. But he did not repent of his crime.

At least he might have found relief in raging at his stupidity as he had raged at the grotesque blunders that had brought him to prison. But now in prison, *in freedom*, he thought over and criticised all his actions again and by no means found them so blundering and grotesque as they had seemed at the fatal time.

'In what way,' he asked himself, 'was my theory stupider than others that have swarmed and clashed from the beginning of the world? One has only to look at the thing quite independently, broadly and uninfluenced by commonplace ideas and my idea will by no means seem so . . . strange. Oh, sceptics and halfpenny philosophers, why do you halt half-way?'

'Why does my action strike them as so horrible?' he said to himself. 'Is it because it was a crime? What is meant by crime? My conscience is at rest. Of course, it was a legal crime; of course, the letter of the law was broken and blood was shed. Well, punish me for the letter of the law . . .

and that's enough. Of course, in that case many of the benefactors of mankind who snatched power for themselves instead of inheriting it ought to have been punished at their first steps. But those men succeeded and so *they were right*, and I didn't, and so I had no right to have taken that step.'

It was only in that that he recognised his criminality, only in the fact that he had been unsuccessful and had confessed it. . . .

It is true that even that agony passed, as it could not but pass, away from him who loved life so dearly. He finds an ecstasy of forgetfulness in Sonia's love for him, we are told, and in that ecstasy the burden of his crime and his past suffering slipped silently away from him. His logic is forgotten and his will bent in his happiness: but neither the logic is recanted nor the will denied. There is no hint of repentance, and no more than the doubtful promise of his acceptance of Sonia's beliefs. 'Can her convictions not be mine now? her feelings, her aspirations at least. . . .' That gradual diminuendo, upon which the book closes, is of most dubious omen for the future. Perhaps Raskolnikov did wholly forget his old determination and his reasoning: but to forget is not to repent. Repentance demands an ever-present memory of the sin. The most we can hope for Raskolnikov is that he should be too happy in the present to remember the past, for, if he should remember, the old problem would face him still.

But, long before Raskolnikov had reached the security of calm, Dostoevsky had turned away from him. Raskolnikov was for Dostoevsky, as he was for himself, merely the victim of his unsuccess and of his weakness. He was not even an unsuccessful criminal, but an unsuccessful philanthropist. His will was a will to Good; he leaned upon a Right. There was no difficulty in winning the sympathies of the world for this youthful Don Quixote, who had ridden forth with the gage of humanity in his helmet, this Saint George who had gone forth to combat with the Dragon for the lives of all men. Did not Raskolnikov choose out with infinite precaution 'a louse', a vile insect that preyed upon mankind, and guarded a treasure of gold within its den that might be of bountiful service in the cause of the Good? In so doing did he do more than that which the very Law he defied may soon by its own ordinance accomplish? He rid, by murder, society of a pest. Had the victim been other than an old pawnbroker woman who lived by evil usury, Raskolnikov would never have lifted the axe; he would never have dreamed of the crime. It is in vain that he cries out:—

I wanted to murder without casuistry, to murder for my own sake, for myself alone! I didn't want to lie about it even to myself. It wasn't to help my mother I did the murder—that's nonsense—I didn't do the murder to gain wealth and power and become the benefactor of mankind. Nonsense!

But it is not nonsense. The very stones cry out, not that this was the only cause, but that it for him was a necessary consequence of his act. Only in the magniloquence of his own conceit, only in the intoxication of his own vision of himself as a Napoleon, could he dare to deny it. It is true that the motive was deeper than this, that he murdered because 'he wanted to have the daring'. But that was his fevered dream. He had already chosen the lesser part when he began to search for 'a louse' for his victim. He had dreamed of a will which should trample all things under foot, for the sake of its own pure assertion; but he knew that this was for him only a dream, he knew that even should he find the courage to kill the usurer, he would have proved nothing to himself.

What shows that I am utterly a louse is that I am perhaps viler and more loathsome than the louse I killed, and *I felt beforehand* that I should tell myself so *after* killing her. Could anything be compared to the horror of that! The vulgarity! The abjectness!

The magnificently triumphant will of which he had dreamed, had in the first moment of his conception of his plan, been degraded into a cowardly shivering caricature of itself, a little feeble thing that could not for one second stand alone but must lean upon Right. In the underworld Raskolnikov had dreamed of committing crime for its own sake; in the waking world he was one of the thousands who do evil that good may come. He had never for one moment ventured outside the walls of the City of Good: he was only a Schiller, as Porfiry Petrovitch told him, and a Schiller who was in heart and act the President of the City Committee for Social Reform.

Raskolnikov had done no crime. He had done no more than to transgress the Laws which are human institutions; like a timid child, who holds his nurse's hand, he invokes the Good of All for a sanction to his beneficent destruction. No wonder he does not repent, when he has done no sin. What defeats him is the never slumbering consciousness that he is at the mercy of the law. He surrenders to the dead weight of an enemy, not to any Right. Right is on his side, and that not merely his own right—that is a power he had not the courage to invoke—but a right which any clear-seeing man might recognise, and society itself at no far point in the future ratify.

And because he had done no crime, his punishment is beside the mark. Dostoevsky knew that the fate of a Raskolnikov is a baby-problem. Evil, at this phase, has not yet begun to be. 'What is crime?'

Raskolnikov asks himself in the Siberian prison; and that is indeed the question. If the killing of 'a louse' be crime, then crime is only a name, a convention as the laws by which it is defined are a convention. This was not the thing Raskolnikov had dreamed of attempting when he muttered: 'I want to attempt a thing *like that*'. Crime, as Raskolnikov knew, was crime for its own sake, the naked working of the evil will. Of this evil Raskolnikov is incapable and knows himself incapable. His loving friends will tell him that he cannot do evil because his nature is good. It may be so, but Raskolnikov, who sees clearly, suspects that it is because his will is weak.

But what of the man whose will is strong? Dostoevsky knew that the problem was here, and towards the end of *Crime and Punishment* he turns away from Raskolnikov, whom he has weighed in the balances and found wanting, to Svidrigailov. Svidrigailov is the real hero of the book. Raskolnikov himself acknowledges it, and makes way for him when, in spite of his horror of Svidrigailov, he cannot deny that there is something in common between them. The potentialities of Raskolnikov are made real in Svidrigailov; the dialectic of the student has been carried to its last conclusion in the person of the man. He enters the book first as the rumour of a sinister presence, of something less and more than man, who has outraged the virgin spirit of Raskolnikov's sister, and done violence to the virgin body of a child. This last is rumour, but he is a power to whom such rumours cling, for they are no more than symbols of the reality which is in him. And it is right that this embodied power should make his actual entrance upon the scene 'between a dream and a waking', at the moment when Raskolnikov is passing through the horror, the distorted, malignant horror, of his crime in a vision of sleep.

He drew a deep breath—but his dream seemed strangely to persist; his door was flung open and a man whom he had never seen stood in the doorway watching him intently.

Raskolnikov had hardly opened his eyes, and he instantly closed them again. He lay on his back without stirring.

'Is it still a dream?' he wondered, and again raised his eyelids hardly perceptibly: the stranger was still standing in the same place still watching him. . . .

Ten minutes passed. It was still light, but beginning to get dusk. There was complete silence in the room. Not a sound came from the stairs. Only a big fly buzzed and fluttered against the window-pane. It was unbearable at last. Raskolnikov suddenly got up and sat on the sofa.

'Come, tell me what you want.'

'I knew you were not asleep but only pretending,' the stranger answered oddly, laughing calmly. 'Arkady Ivanovitch Svidrigailov, allow me to introduce myself. . . .'

'Can this still be a dream?' begins the next chapter, for Svidrigailov is the incarnation of the evil will. In his creation Dostoevsky had left the city. He was no more a timid outlaw, but a man with the courage of his thought and his full imagination. And Svidrigailov is not only a Dream and a Will, but a Man. He is Raskolnikov grown old, but one who with advancing years has abated nothing of his resolution, that his will should compass all things. He has stood alone with the power which is in him, which is the will to know life to the uttermost, and by that will to triumph over life. He has passed beyond good and evil. He has willed that his will should be omnipotent. Nothing shall be forbidden him. He has taken his stand against the whole of life to wrest its secret from it. Svidrigailov is real, real even beyond reality, and he is also Raskolnikov's dream. To be a Svidrigailov and not a mere Napoleon—that was the vision which had haunted the murderer. But Svidrigailov does no murder before the law, for he knows that this is no question for him, nor will he deceive himself by having even the faint semblance of a right upon his side. He is his own right; another right can only take away from him and blunt the barb of his question.

And the question is this: Which shall prevail, the I, the self, which I know, or some power which I know not? Shall I be forced to recognise any will beyond my own? Though Svidrigailov appears chiefly to be a manifestation of the will to evil in act, he is far more than this. He appears to us first as evil, because the deliberate working of evil is portentous to our minds. Because he does evil things, he is a monster of depravity. Yet this monster does good with the same even hand; he spares Raskolnikov's sister, Dounia, whom he desires, when she is at his mercy; he cares for Sonia and the orphaned children of the Marmeladovs; he makes over a fortune to the girl bride whom he does not marry. In him both good and evil may be found side by side, yet he is neither a good man with evil impulses nor an evil man with reactions to the good. For all the appearance of contradiction, we feel that he is not divided against himself but one; and the secret of his singleness is his single will. This he has measured against life and the laws of life. He has done evil, not because he desired it, but because he desired to be beyond it. In the process of his complete assertion, every fetter upon the working of the will to be free must be broken, simply because it is a fetter. The things which he knew to be evil he has done simply because an instinct within him recoiled from the evil: therefore that instinct must be crushed. He, like Raskolnikov, had 'wanted to have the daring', and he had found it in himself.

In *The Journal of an Author* and his letters Dostoevsky returned again and again to the definition of literary genius as the power which should bring 'a new word' into literature. Svidrigailov was Dostoevsky's new word. The creation of this character marks the beginning of his own peculiar achievement. He was to develop this conception to heights and depths undreamed of, to refine it, to make it more and more actual until it should seem that the human and the inhuman were finally confounded.

Therefore we must understand Svidrigailov at all costs. He may be a monster, conjured out of the darkness, but he too is human, too human. Watch him when he has enticed Dounia, whom he loves with a passion of desire, into the solitary room, intending—to do her violence?—he does not know. But the gleam of the beast began to shine in his eyes, that light in them which months before 'had frightened Dounia, and had grown stronger and stronger and more unguarded till it was hateful to her'. To defend herself from the horror of this she draws a pistol and shoots at him. The first shot goes wide; he does not move. The second shot misses fire.

'You haven't loaded it properly. Never mind: you have another charge there. Get it ready, I'll wait.'

He stood facing her two paces away, waiting and gazing at her, with feverishly passionate, stubborn, set eyes. Dounia saw that he would rather die than let her go. 'And now of course she would kill him, at two paces!' Suddenly she flung away the revolver.

'She's dropped it!' said Svidrigailov with surprise, and he drew a deep breath. A weight seemed to have rolled from his heart—perhaps not only the fear of death; indeed he may scarcely have felt it at that moment. It was the deliverance from another feeling, darker and more bitter, which he could not himself have defined....

He went to Dounia and gently put his arm around her waist. She did not resist, but, trembling like a leaf, looked at him with suppliant eyes. He tried to say something, but his lips moved without being able to utter a sound.

'Let me go,' Dounia implored. Svidrigailov shuddered. Her voice was now quite different.

'Then you don't love me?' he asked softly. Dounia shook her head.

'And... and you can't? Never?' he whispered in despair.

'Never!'

There followed a moment of terrible dumb struggle in the heart of Svidrigailov. He looked at her with an indescribable gaze. Suddenly he withdrew his arm, turned quickly to the window and stood facing it. Another moment passed.

'Here's the key.'

What was the feeling, darker and more bitter even than fear of death, from which he was delivered? Dostoevsky knew, and perhaps we too can know. Svidrigailov has dared to face life alone, to measure his individual will against all things. And at the last he is broken.

He is conscious of his utter loneliness. He has dared to try the great issue. He has done that he knows to be evil, so that he might know whether there was some power beyond him that should punish. He does know: he has not been blasted. Yes, he would have had a flash of ecstatic happiness thrill his soul, if when he did evil he had been struck dead. But no, nothing. . . .

And that nothing means that there is nothing—nothing for that unconquerable will to will any more. He has put the great question, and the answer is silence, that dead silence in which he can hear every beat of his own weary heart, in which he knows himself eternally alone. And that silence and that loneliness is more than even his heroic spirit can bear. He turns to another being, knowing her loathing, yet hoping too that beyond that loathing there may be a spark if not of love, of some feeling that would show him not finally alone. Twice she fires at him. He does not move. His will remains to him, even though the desire to use it is gone from him. The third time she drops the pistol. Something then remains, one last gleam of hope is fired within him, and he asks in a fever of despairing passion if she loves him, or will ever love him. That hope too is destroyed. He is alone; he has crossed the bounds of all human experience, in his desire to find whether the burden of Life rests on his will alone, or whether there is something beyond, and he has found nothing. Now one thing remains. Death is untried. He tries it, for it lies in his destiny that he should will all things, and will that he should not be.

But to will his own annihilation is easier than to be assured of victory. A Svidrigailov is not deceived by mortal death. Had he known that self-destruction was the end of all, he would not have waited so long. But what if it should be only another question, and another silence, or something worse than silence.

'But what do you say to this argument (help me with it): ghosts are as it were shreds and fragments of other worlds, the beginning of them. A man in health has, of course, no reason to see them, because he is above all a man of this earth, and is bound for the sake of completeness and order to live only in this life. But as soon as one is ill, as soon as the normal earthly order of the organism is broken, one begins to realise the possibility of another world; and the more seriously ill one is, the closer becomes one's contact with that other world, so that as soon as the man dies he steps straight into that other world. I thought of that long ago. If you believe in a future life, you could believe in that, too.'

'I don't believe in a future life,' said Raskolnikov. Svidrigailov sat lost in thought.

'And what if there are only spiders there, or something of that sort?' he said suddenly.

'He is a madman,' thought Raskolnikov.

'We always imagine eternity as something beyond our conception, something vast, vast! But why must it be vast? Instead of all that, what if it's one little room, like a bath-house in the country, and that's all eternity is? Sometimes I fancy it like that.'

'Can it be you can imagine nothing juster and more comforting than that?' Raskolnikov cried, with a feeling of anguish.

'Juster? And how can we tell? Perhaps that is just, and do you know it's what I certainly would have made it,' answered Svidrigailov with a vague smile. . . .

Not even death has its answer to his question. It is only the one last issue, which, being untried, must be tried. Yet is it the most hopeless of all? The silence in which the great question echoes here, may there give back an echo of laughter, of vulgar, sordid, malignant laughter.

But a will which by willing its own omnipotence has nothing left to will, is a living death. Therefore Svidrigailov goes 'his journey', early in the morning, while a thick milky mist hangs over the town, in the presence of an official witness, a little Jew soldier, with a peevish look of dejection on his face and a copper Achilles helmet on his head.

Svidrigailov took out the revolver and cocked it. Achilles raised his eyebrows.

'I say, this isn't the place for that kind of joke!'

'Why isn't it the place?'

'Because it isn't.'

'Well, brother, I don't mind that. It's a good place. When they ask you, you just say he said he was off to America.'

He put the revolver to his right temple.

'You can't do it here, it's not the place,' cried Achilles, rousing himself, his eyes growing bigger and bigger.

Svidrigailov pulled the trigger.

'Is there Crime? Is there Punishment?' Not in the person of Raskolnikov does Dostoevsky ask these questions, but in that of Svidrigailov. Therefore Raskolnikov's repentance and regeneration is no reply, nor is the foolishly repeated panacea of 'Purification by Suffering'. Suffering may have been enough for Raskolnikov, though Dostoevsky leaves the proof of that to another story, which he never wrote. It would not have interested him enough to write. In Dostoevsky's eyes Raskolnikov could never have been more than an incomplete Svidrigailov, and once he had found in himself the courage and the genius to grapple with the imagination of Svidrigailov, Raskolnikov was no more than a puppet to him.

5

THOUGHTS ON TCHEHOV

These two pieces on Tchehov, written in 1919 and 1920 respectively, were published together in Aspects of Literature.

i

WE do not know if the stories collected in this volume[1] stand together in the Russian edition of Tchehov's works, or if the selection is due to Mrs. Constance Garnett. It is also possible that the juxtaposition is fortuitous. But the stories are united by a similarity of material. Whereas in the former volumes of this admirable series Tchehov is shown as preoccupied chiefly with the life of the *intelligentsia*, here he finds his subjects in priests and peasants, or (in the story *Uprooted*) in the half-educated.

Such a distinction is, indeed, irrelevant. As Tchehov presents them to our minds, the life of the country and the life of the town produce the same final impression, arouse in us an awareness of an identical quality; and thus, the distinction, by its very irrelevance, points us the more quickly to what is essential in Tchehov. It is that his attitude, to which he persuades us, is complete, not partial. His comprehension radiates from a steady centre, and is not capriciously kindled by a thousand accidental contacts. In other words, Tchehov is not what he is so often assumed to be, an impressionist. Consciously or unconsciously he had taken the step—the veritable *salto mortale*—by which the great literary artist moves out of the ranks of the minor writers. He had slowly shifted his angle of vision until he could discern a unity in multiplicity. Unity of this rare kind cannot be imposed as, for instance, Zola attempted to impose it. It is an emanation from life which can be distinguished only by the most sensitive contemplation.

The problem is to define this unity in the case of each great writer in whom it appears. To apprehend it is not so difficult. The mere sense of unity is so singular and compelling that it leaves room for few hesitations. The majority of writers, however excellent in their peculiar virtues, are not concerned with it: at one moment they

[1] *The Bishop, and Other Stories*, by Anton Tchehov. Translated by Constance Garnett (Chatto & Windus).

represent, at another they may philosophise, but the two activities have no organic connection, and their work, if it displays any evolution at all, displays it only in the minor accidents of the craft, such as style in the narrower and technical sense, or the obvious economy of construction. There is no danger of mistaking these for great writers. Nor, in the more peculiar case of writers who attempt to impose the illusion of unity, is the danger serious. The apparatus is always visible; they cannot afford to do without the paraphernalia of argument which supplies the place of what is lacking in their presentation. The obvious instance of this legerdemain is Zola; a less obvious, and therefore more interesting example is Balzac.

To attempt the more difficult problem. What is most peculiar to Tchehov's unity is that it is far more nakedly æsthetic than that of most of the great writers before him. Other writers of a rank equal to his—and there are not so very many—have felt the need to shift their angle of vision until they could perceive an all-embracing unity; but they were not satisfied with this. They felt, and obeyed, the further need of taking an attitude towards the unity they saw. They approved or disapproved, accepted or rejected it. It would be perhaps more accurate to say that they gave or refused their endorsement. They appealed to some other element than their own sense of beauty for the final verdict on their discovery; they asked whether it was just or good.

The distinguishing mark of Tchehov is that he is satisfied with the unity he discovers. Its uniqueness is sufficient for him. It does not occur to him to demand that it should be otherwise or better. The act of comprehension is accompanied by an instantaneous act of acceptance. He is like a man who contemplates a perfect work of art; but the work of creation has been his, and has consisted in the gradual adjustment of his vision until he could see the frustration of human destinies and the arbitrary infliction of pain as processes no less inevitable, natural, and beautiful than the flowering of a plant. Not that Tchehov is a greater artist than any of his great predecessors; he is merely more wholly an artist, which is a very different thing. There is in him less admixture of preoccupations that are not purely æsthetic, and probably for this reason he has less creative vigour than any other artist of equal rank. It seems as though artists, like cattle and fruit trees, need a good deal of crossing with substantial foreign elements, in order to be very vigorous and very fruitful. Tchehov has the virtues and the shortcomings of the pure case.

I do not wish to be understood as saying that Tchehov is a manifestation of *l'art pour l'art,* because in any commonly accepted sense of that phrase, he is not. Still, he might be considered as an exemplification of what the phrase might be made to mean. But instead of being diverted into a barren dispute over terminologies, one may endeavour to bring into prominence an aspect of Tchehov which has an immediate interest—his modernity. Again, the word is awkward. It suggests that he is fashionable, or up to date. Tchehov is, in fact, a good many phases in advance of all that is habitually described as modern in the art of literature. The artistic problem which he faced and solved is one that is, at most, partially present to the consciousness of the modern writer—to reconcile the greatest possible diversity of content with the greatest possible unity of æsthetic impression. Diversity of content we are beginning to find in profusion—Miss May Sinclair's latest experiment shows how this need is beginning to trouble a writer with a settled manner and a fixed reputation—but how rarely do we see even a glimmering recognition of the necessity of a unified æsthetic impression! The modern method is to assume that all that is, or has been, present to consciousness is *ipso facto* unified æsthetically. The result of such an assumption is an obvious distintegration both of language and artistic effort, a mere retrogression from the classical method.

The classical method consisted, essentially, in achieving æsthetic unity by a process of rigorous exclusion of all that was not germane to an arbitrary (because non-æsthetic) argument. This argument was let down like a string into the saturated solution of the consciousness until a unified crystalline structure congregated about it. Of all great artists of the past Shakespeare is the richest in his departures from this method. How much deliberate artistic purpose there was in his employment of songs and madmen and fools (an employment fundamentally different from that made by his contemporaries) is a subject far too big for a parenthesis. But he, too, is at bottom a classic artist. The modern problem—it has not yet been sufficiently solved for us to speak of a modern method—arises from a sense that the classical method produces over-simplification. It does not permit of a sufficient sense of multiplicity. One can think of a dozen half-treatments of the problem from Balzac to Dostoevsky, but they were all on the old lines. They might be called Shakespearian modifications of the classical method.

Tchehov, we believe, attempted a treatment radically new. To make use again of our former image, in his maturer writing he chose a different string to let down into the saturated solution of consciousness. In a sense he began at the other end. He had decided on the quality of æsthetic impression he wished to produce, not by an arbitrary decision, but by one which followed naturally from the contemplative unity of life which he had achieved. The essential quality he discerned and desired to represent was his argument, his string. Everything that heightened and completed this quality accumulated about it, quite independently of whether it would have been repelled by the old criterion of plot and argument. There is a magnificent example of his method in the longest story in this volume, 'The Steppe'. The quality is dominant throughout, and by some strange compulsion it makes heterogeneous things one; it is reinforced by the incident. Tiny events—the peasant who eats minnows alive, the Jewish innkeeper's brother who burned his six thousand roubles—take on a character of portent, except that the word is too harsh for so delicate a distortion of normal vision; rather it is a sense of incalculability that haunts us. The emphases have all been slightly shifted, but shifted according to a valid scheme. It is not while we are reading, but afterwards that we wonder how so much significance could attach to a little boy's questions in a remote village shop:

> 'How much are these cakes?'
> 'Two for a farthing.'
> Yegorushka took out of his pocket the cake given him the day before by the Jewess and asked him:
> 'And how much do you charge for cakes like this?'
> The shopman took the cake in his hands, looked at it from all sides, and raised one eyebrow.
> 'Like that?' he asked.
> Then he raised the other eyebrow, thought a minute, and answered:
> 'Two for three farthings. . . .'

It is foolish to quote it. It is like a golden pebble from the bed of a stream. The stream that flows over Tchehov's innumerable pebbles, infinitely diverse and heterogeneous, is the stream of a deliberately sublimated quality. The figure is inexact, as figures are. Not every pebble could be thus transmuted. But how they are chosen, what is the real nature of the relation which unites them, as we feel it does, is a secret which modern English writers need to explore. Till they have explored and mastered it Tchehov will remain a master in advance of them.

ii

The case of Tchehov is one to be investigated again and again because he is the only great modern artist in prose. Tolstoy was living throughout Tchehov's life, as Hardy has lived throughout our own, and these are great among the greatest. But they are not modern. It is an essential part of their greatness that they could not be; they have a simplicity and scope that manifestly belongs to all time rather than to this. Tchehov looked towards Tolstoy as we to Hardy. He saw in him a Colossus, one whose achievement was of another and a greater kind than his own.

I am afraid of Tolstoy's death. If he were to die there would be a big empty place in my life. To begin with, because I have never loved any man as much as him. . . . Secondly, while Tolstoy is in literature it is easy and pleasant to be a literary man; even recognising that one has done nothing and never will do anything is not so dreadful, since Tolstoy will do enough for all. His work is the justification of the enthusiasms and expectations built upon literature. Thirdly, Tolstoy takes a firm stand; he has an immense authority, and so long as he is alive, bad tastes in literature, vulgarity of every kind, insolent and lachrymose, all the bristling, exasperated vanities will be in the far background, in the shade. . . . —(January, 1900.)

Tchehov was aware of the gulf that separated him from the great men before him, and he knew that it yawned so deep that it could not be crossed. He belonged to a new generation, and he alone perhaps was fully conscious of it. 'We are lemonade,' he wrote in 1892.

Tell me honestly who of my contemporaries—that is, men between thirty and forty-five—have given the world one single drop of alcohol? . . . Science and technical knowledge are passing through a great period now, but for our sort it is a flabby stale, dull time. . . . The causes of this are not to be found in our stupidity, our lack of talent, or our insolence, but in a disease which for the artist is worse than syphilis or sexual exhaustion. We lack 'something', that is true, and that means that, lift the robe of our muse, and you will find within an empty void. Let me remind you that the writers who we say are for all time or are simply good, and who intoxicate us, have one common and very important characteristic: they are going towards something and are summoning you towards it, too, and you feel, not with your mind but with your whole being, that they have some object, just like the ghost of Hamlet's father, who did not come and disturb the imagination for nothing. . . . And we? We! We paint life as it is, but beyond that—nothing at all. . . . Flog us and we can do more! We have neither immediate nor remote aims, and in our soul there is a great empty space. We have no politics, we do not believe in revolution, we have no God, we are not afraid of ghosts, and I personally am not afraid even of death and blindness. One who wants nothing, hopes for nothing, and fears nothing cannot be an artist. . . .

. . . You think I am clever. Yes, I am at least so far clever as not to conceal from myself my disease and not to deceive myself, and not to cover up my own emptiness with other people's rags, such as the ideas of the 'sixties and so on.

That was written in 1892. When we remember all the strange literary effort gathered round about that year in the West—Symbolism, the *Yellow Book*, Art for Art's sake—and the limbo into which it has been thrust by now, we may realise how great a precursor, and, in his own despite, a leader, Anton Tchehov was. When Western literature was plunging with enthusiasm into one *cul de sac* after another, incapable of diagnosing its own disease, Tchehov in Russia, unknown to the West, had achieved a clear vision and a sense of perspective.

To-day we begin to feel how intimately Tchehov belongs to us; to-morrow we may feel how infinitely he is still in advance of us. A genius will always be in advance of a talent, and in so far as we are concerned with the genius of Tchehov we must accept the inevitable. We must analyse and seek to understand it; we must, above all, make up our minds that since Tchehov has written and his writings have been made accessible to us, a vast amount of our modern literary production is simply unpardonable. Writers who would be modern and ignore Tchehov's achievement are, however much they may persuade themselves that they are devoted artists, merely engaged in satisfying their vanity or in the exercise of a profession like any other; for Tchehov is a standard by which modern literary effort must be measured, and the writer of prose or poetry who is not sufficiently single-minded to apply the standard to himself is of no particular account.

Though Tchehov's genius is, strictly speaking, inimitable, it deserves a much exacter study than it has yet received. The publication of this volume of his letters[1] hardly affords the occasion for that; but it does afford an opportunity for the examination of some of the chief constituents of his perfect art. These touch us nearly because—we insist again—the supreme interest of Tchehov is that he is the only great modern artist in prose. He belongs, as we have said, to us. If he is great, then he is great not least in virtue of qualities which we may aspire to possess; if he is an ideal, he is an ideal to which we can refer ourselves. He had been saturated in all the disillusions which we regard as peculiarly our own, and every quality which is distinctive of the epoch of consciousness in which we are living now is reflected in him—and yet, miracle of miracles, he was a great artist. He did not rub his cheeks to produce a spurious colour of health; he did not profess beliefs which he could not maintain; he did not seek a reputation for universal wisdom, or indulge himself in self-gratifying dreams of a millennium which he alone had the ability to control. He was and wanted to be nothing in particular, and yet, as we read these letters of his, we feel gradually form within ourselves the conviction that he was a hero—more than that, *the* hero of our time.

It is significant that, in reading Tchehov's letters, we do not consider him under the aspect of an artist. We are inevitably fascinated

[1] *Letters of Anton Tchehov*, translated by Constance Garnett (Chatto & Windus).

by his character as a man, one who, by efforts which we have most frequently to divine for ourselves from his reticences, worked on the infinitely complex material of the modern mind and soul, and made it in himself a definite, positive, and most lovable thing. He did not throw in his hand in face of his manifold bewilderments; he did not fly for refuge to institutions in which he did not believe; he risked everything, in Russia, by having no particular faith in revolution and saying so. In every conjuncture of his life that we can trace in his letters he behaved squarely by himself, and, since he is our great exemplar, by us. He refused to march under any political banner—a thing, let it be remembered, of almost inconceivable courage in his country; he submitted to savagely hostile attacks for his political indifference; yet he spent more of his life and energy in doing active good to his neighbour than most of the high-souled professors of liberalism and social reform. He undertook an almost superhuman journey to Sahalin in 1890 to investigate the condition of the prisoners there; in 1892 he spent the best part of a year as a doctor devising preventive measures against the cholera in the country district where he lived, and, although he had no time for the writing on which his living depended, he refused the government pay in order to preserve his own independence of action; in another year he was the leading spirit in organising practical measures of famine relief about Nizhni-Novgorod. From his childhood to his death, moreover, he was the sole support of his family. Measured by the standards of Christian morality, Tchehov was a saint. His self-devotion was boundless.

Yet we know he was speaking nothing less than the truth of himself when he wrote: 'It is essential to be indifferent.' Tchehov was indifferent; but his indifference, as a mere catalogue of his secret philanthropies will show, was of a curious kind. He made of it, as it were, an axiomatic basis of his own self-discipline. Since life is what it is and men are what they are, he seems to have argued, everything depends upon the individual. The stars are hostile, but love is kind, and love is within the compass of any man if he will work to attain it. In one of his earliest letters he defines true culture for the benefit of his brother Nikolay, who lacked it. Cultivated persons, he said, respect human personality; they have sympathy not for beggars and cats only; they respect the property of others, and therefore pay their debts; they are sincere and dread lying like fire; they do not disparage themselves to arouse compassion; they have no shallow vanity; if they have a talent they respect it; they develop the æsthetic feeling in themselves . . . they seek as far as possible to restrain and ennoble the sexual instinct. The letter from which these chief points are taken is tremulous with sympathy and wit. Tchehov was twenty-six when he wrote it. He concludes with the words: 'What is needed is constant work day and night, constant reading, study, will. Every hour is precious for it.'

In that letter are given all the elements of Tchehov the man. He set himself to achieve a new humanity, and he achieved it. The indifference upon which Tchehov's humanity was built was not therefore a moral indifference; it was, in the main, the recognition and acceptance of the fact that life itself is indifferent. To that he held fast to the end. But the conclusion which he drew from it was not that it made no particular difference what anyone did, but that the attitude and character of the individual were all-important. There was, indeed, no panacea, political or religious, for the ills of humanity; but there could be a mitigation in men's souls. But the new asceticism must not be negative. It must not cast away the goods of civilisation because civilisation is largely a sham.

> Alas! I shall never be a Tolstoyan. In women I love beauty above all things, and in the history of mankind, culture expressed in carpets, carriages with springs, and keenness of wit. Ach! To make haste and become an old man and sit at a big table!

Not that there is a trace of the hedonist in Tchehov, who voluntarily endured every imaginable hardship if he thought he could be of service to his fellow men, but, as he wrote elsewhere, 'we are concerned with pluses alone.' Since life is what it is, its amenities are doubly precious. Only they must be amenities without humbug.

> Pharisaism, stupidity, and despotism reign not in bourgeois houses and prisons alone. I see them in science, in literature, in the younger generation. . . . That is why I have no preference either for gendarmes, or for butchers, or for scientists, or for writers, or for the younger generation. I regard trade marks and labels as a superstition. My holy of holies is the human body, health, intelligence, talent, inspiration, love, and the most absolute freedom—freedom from violence and lying, whatever forms they may take. This is the programme I would follow if I were a great artist.

What 'the most absolute freedom' meant to Tchehov his whole life is witness. It was a liberty of a purely moral kind, a liberty, that is, achieved at the cost of a great effort in self-discipline and self-refinement. In one letter he says he is going to write a story about the son of a serf—Tchehov was the son of a serf—who 'squeezed the slave out of himself'. Whether the story was ever written we do not know, but the process is one to which Tchehov applied himself all his life long. He waged a war of extermination against the lie in the soul in himself, and by necessary implication in others also.

He was, thus, in all things a humanist. He faced the universe, but he did not deny his own soul. There could be for him no antagonism between science and literature, or science and humanity. They were all pluses; it was men who quarrelled among themselves. If men would only develop a little more loving-kindness, things would be better. The first duty of the artist was to be a decent man.

> Solidarity among young writers is impossible and unnecessary. . . . We cannot feel and think in the same way, our aims are different, or we have no aims whatever, we know each other little or not at all, and so there is nothing on to which this solidarity could be securely hooked. . . . And is there any need for it? No, in order to help a colleague, to respect his personality and work, to refrain from gossiping about him, envying him, telling him lies and being hypocritical, one does not need so much to be a young writer as simply a man. . . . Let us be ordinary people, let us treat everybody alike, and then we shall not need any artificially worked-up solidarity.

It seems a simple discipline, this moral and intellectual honesty of Tchehov's, yet in these days of conceit and coterie his letters strike us as more than strange. One predominant impression remains: it is that of Tchehov's candour of soul. Somehow he has achieved with open eyes the mystery of pureness of heart; and in that, though we dare not analyse it further, lies the secret of his greatness as a writer and of his present importance to ourselves.

6

MARCEL PROUST

From John Clare and other studies, *pages 67–72. This is part of an essay written in 1921, when only the first four parts of* A la Recherche du Temps Perdu *had appeared.*

. . . We live in perpetual illusion; the imagined friend, the imagined lover, the imagined society, the imagined reality, are never real. Suddenly, by a devious way, we hear of something said or done which cannot enter into our picture: we are shocked and pained, then we rebuild another picture, no less illusory, and imagine that this at least is true. This recurrent theme of perpetual disillusion, of impotent encounter with the unknown, may be called the philosophical background of the book, and from this angle we might regard it as a philosophical justification of the art of writing, presented through the history of a consciousness. For as the growing man turns away from the continual disillusion which is the only result of his attempt to penetrate the reality beyond himself, he more clearly sees that the only reality he can hope to master is his own experience. Thus to enter into complete possession of the past by the method of which *Du Côté de chez Swann* is an example is presented not only as the goal to which an 'invisible vocation' was calling a particular person, but in fact also as the highest end of man, *la vraie vie* indeed. In so far as literature is based upon that method of evoking the past through an associated symbol (and it certainly is one very important element in literary creation) it is, according to this underlying philosophy, the supreme activity of life.

This concealed motive it is which differentiates M. Proust's book from all that have gone before. The metaphysician might call it the history of a solipsist. But such a definition would be as misleading as all other attempts to find a philosophical definition for a particular work of literature. For, though M. Proust is in a sense applying a theory to experience, he is doing so by the strikingly novel method of describing the process by which the theory was gradually and inevitably formed in the consciousness which applies it. If, therefore, M. Proust's book ends, as we believe it will end, in its own beginning, it will have a unity—in spite of the apparent discrepancy of certain of the parts—of a kind which has never been achieved in a work of literature before: it will be the first book which has been the psychological history of its own creation and a philosophical justification of its own necessity. It will belong in this respect to a new order of literature. And that is what we already vaguely feel as we read it. It is something more than a book in an unfamiliar language, more than a fiction of greater psychological subtlety than we are accustomed to. For better or worse, it marks the emergence of a new kind, the arrival of a new sensibility.

That is its uncommon significance. To find an approximate parallel in the history of modern literature we should probably have to go back to Rousseau. There we should discover the paradox of a man not primarily a literary artist whose work revolutionised the literature of the next hundred years. M. Proust likewise is not primarily a literary artist. Nothing could be more significant than the length of the process of his finding his 'invisible vocation'. Like Rousseau, he is ultimately compelled to writing as a satisfaction for his sensibility The chief point of difference is that where Rousseau was compelled to express his sensibility upon alien themes, M. Proust has been in the privileged position of one who could afford to wait for the truly inevitable occasion. Still, the only work of literature with which *A la Recherche du Temps Perdu* could profitably be compared is the *Confessions* of Jean-Jacques. There is a real likeness between the driving impulses at work in these books, and a careful comparison might enable us to determine the more important differences between the new sensibility of the eighteenth, and the new sensibility of the twentieth century. At all events, a century of science has passed between. M. Proust is not preoccupied with finding God, but with finding *la vraie vie*, though a previous quotation shows that where Rousseau always did, he sometimes does identify them. But more apparently still, a century of scientific psychology, of astronomical physics, of the biology of Natural Selection, has intervened. The last shreds of anthropocentrism have been worn away. Where Rousseau felt his own isolation and was tormented by the discrepancy between his dream and the reality, and could not reconcile himself to his isolation or his torment, M. Proust can. He accepts these conditions, he formulates them as an actual law of human existence; and the acceptance has been incorporated into the very mechanism of his sensibility. He discerns in the world that which he feels in himself; he is a Rousseau to whom some of the hidden causes of his perplexity have been made plain.

And the detailed knowledge of a century of applied science is at his fingers' ends to help him refine and express his sensibility. How many times does he use the simile of a camera to make more apparent the working of two planes of consciousness! 'Ce qu'on prend en présence de l'être aimé n'est qu'un cliché négatif, on le developpe plus tard.' By that means he expresses in a sentence a truth which lies behind a whole section of the fifth volume, 'Les Intermittences du Cœur', where for the first time realising the loss of his beloved grandmother, months after her death, the young man learns that the uniqueness of our most precious experience eludes us till the opportunity of it is lost for ever. Again, when the boy, occupied with the anxiety of obtaining his mother's kiss, waits nervously at the dinner table—'comme un malade, grâce à un anésthésique, assiste avec pleine lucidité à l'operation qu'on pratique sur lui, mais sans rien sentir, je pouvais me réciter des vers que j'aimais ou observer les efforts que mon grand'père faisait pour parler à Swann du duc d'Audiffret-Pasquier, sans que les premiers me fissent éprouver aucune émotion, les seconds aucune gaîté.' And on the same occasion, having to take the kiss in public, he had not even the time or the freedom of mind necessary 'pour porter à ce que je faisais cette attention des maniaques qui s'efforcent de ne pas penser à autre chose pendant qu'ils ferment une porte, pour pouvoir, quand l'incertitude maladive leur revient, lui opposer victorieusement le souvenir du moment où ils l'ont fermée.' And for a final example we may choose the part played by the Duchesse de Guermantes' tree, which needs to be fertilised by an insect, in the explication of the psychology of the closing pages of *Du Côté de Guermantes*, and the writer's declaration: 'Mes réflexions, avaient suivi une pente que je décrirai plus tard et j'avais déjà tiré de la ruse apparente des fleurs une conséquence sur toute une partie inconsciente de l'œuvre littéraire.' Such are some of the typical contributions of the science of the nineteenth century towards the expression of a sensibility shaped by its larger knowledge.

But in endeavouring to analyse the singular impression which M. Proust's work makes upon us and to isolate the elements which produce the effect of novelty, in trying to investigate and assess its deeply-rooted originality, we are in danger of neglecting the more obvious qualities of a book which exhibits at least as many beauties as it conceals. It needs no second reading to appreciate the subtlety of psychological observation, the ironic detachment of the writer's vision of high Parisian society. If the dinner-party at the Guermantes is a masterpiece in a not wholly unfamiliar genre, in the description of the musical evening at Mme de St. Euverte's the same lucid irony is perceptibly lifted to a higher plane and made to subserve a complex emotional effect. And though the biting wit which flashes home again and again through the narrative of *Du Côté de Guermantes* is of the very highest order in its kind, though the semi-satirical portrait of the *bien pensant* ambassador, M. de Norpois, at the beginning of *A l'Ombre des Jeunes filles* is perfect, they yield in impressiveness to the certainty of the single touch with which, in the description of the grandmother's illness, M. Proust sounds the note of the tragedy of death. When the grandmother has had a paralytic stroke in the Champs Elysées, and the boy suddenly sees 'son chapeau, son visage, son manteau dérangés par la main de l'ange invisible avec lequel elle avait lutté', we feel we are in the presence of a great writer indeed. And besides the command of tragic simplicity and wit, M. Proust has also the gift of humour. To appreciate this picture of life in the kitchen it is necessary to know that it was an established convention that the servants should not be disturbed at their lunch.

Déjà depuis un quart d'heure, ma mère qui n'usait probablement pas des mêmes mesures que Françoise pour apprécier la longueur du déjeûner de celle-ci, disait:

'Mais qu'est-ce qu'ils peuvent bien faire, voilà plus de deux heures qu'ils sont à table.'

Et elle sonnait timidement trois ou quatre fois. Françoise, son valet de pied, le maître d'hôtel entendaient les coups de sonnette comme un appel et sans songer à venir, mais pourtant comme les premiers sons des instruments qui s'accordent quand un concert va bientôt recommencer et qu'on sent qu'il n'y aura plus que quelques minutes d'entr'acte. Aussi quand les coups commençant à se répéter et à devenir plus insistants, nos domestisques se mettaient à y prendre garde et estimant qu'ils n'avaient plus beaucoup de temps devant eux et que la reprise du travail était proche, à un tintement de sonnette un peu plus sonore que les autres, ils poussaient un soupir et prenant leur parti, le valet de pied descendait fumer une cigarette devant la porte, Françoise, après quelques réflexions sur nous, telles que 'ils ont surement la bougeotte', montait ranger ses affaires dans son sixième, et le maître d'hôtel ayant été chercher du papier à lettres dans ma chambre expédiait rapidement sa correspondance privée.

But it is not these qualities, rare and valuable as they are, which make *A la Recherche du Temps Perdu* one of the most significant of contemporary works of literature. They are precious qualities, but they are in a sense superficial, and they might be outweighed by the undoubted obscurity, the awkward complication of language, in large portions of the book. It is something much more than a dark narrative with frequent gleams of beauty; it is a book with at least one of the qualities of permanence, an animating soul. It is maintained by a high and subtle purpose, informed by a view of life as a whole, and because this secret fire glows steadily within it, we feel the radiance through the most forbidding pages long before we are able to detect its source. One consequence of this is that though M. Proust's language is sometimes alembicated to a point of grotesqueness, he has style; we might more exactly apply to him a phrase which he himself has aptly used of a great predecessor, Stendhal, and say that his work has *la grande ossature du style*, a thing of infinitely more importance than limpidity or beauty in the detail of expression. M. Proust's style, in this larger meaning, is as new and original as is the sensibility to which it owes its being.

7

D. H. LAWRENCE

This review of Fantasia of the Unconscious *appeared in the 'Algemeen Handelsblad' in 1923. It was reprinted in* Reminiscences of D. H. Lawrence *(Cape, 1933).*

About two years ago I wrote in an essay in an English review that 'Mr. D. H. Lawrence is the outlaw of English literature, and he is the most interesting figure in it'. In substance that opinion of mine may still stand. But a nuance of modification is necessary. Mr. Lawrence during the last two years has become a little less of the outlaw, and a little more perceptibly the most interesting figure among the writers of his generation. The cultivated people who wagged their heads and called him 'mad' a year or two ago, now nod their heads and murmur 'genius'. Their real feeling is, of course, unchanged. They cannot get on with Mr. Lawrence any more now than they could then; but they feel themselves compelled to pay at least lip-service to the growing and only half conscious recognition that Mr. Lawrence is of a quite different order from his contemporaries.

Lawrence—with whom we are quickly compelled to drop the polite prefix—is primarily a novelist. As such his work falls outside the province of my criticism in the *Handelsblad*. He is also a notable poet; but it is a long while now since he published a volume of verses. In the last year, however, he has presented to the world two volumes which contain an exposition of his beliefs. Of these, the more important by far is the latter one, *Fantasia of the Unconscious*, which has just fallen into my hands.

There are many things which might be said of *Fantasia of the Unconscious*—things most pertinent and necessary to be said, for which there will, alas, be no room in this brief article. I must content myself for the moment with pointing out the significance and indicating the context of two perfectly commonplace facts concerning this remarkable book. The first of these may seem almost puerile. The book has been published in America, and not in England. For the time being, if we desire to read it, we have to procure it from the United States. And the meaning of this is that Lawrence—an

Englishman of the English, born in a Midland mining village, where the grim Black Country fades into some of the most beautiful rural scenery that England possesses—is, or has been, in a state of rebellion against his native land. By a monstrous abuse of the law in 1915 one of the most significant of his novels, *The Rainbow*, was suppressed on a fantastic charge of immorality. Shortly after, so soon, in fact, as the material opportunity offered—the suppression of the one book made publishers fearful of accepting work from him—he shook the dust of England from his feet and began a slow and haphazard journey round the world, which has ended temporarily in the south of the United States. This was the period of his outlawry in spirit and in fact. He was anathema to English criticism. Even I myself—let me admit it freely—though I had been his intimate friend for many years, attacked him violently in the very article in which I declared that 'he was the outlaw of English literature, and the most interesting figure in it'.

I felt, and I said, that he was an enemy of civilisation. It was perfectly true. He is the conscious and deliberate, yet passionate and potent, enemy of modern civilisation. If our modern life, our modern civilisation, is fundamentally good and true and valuable, then indeed the cry must be raised against Lawrence: 'Écrasez l'infâme!' It is war to the knife between them, and two years ago the attack and the defence were alike angry and embittered. I do not wish to suggest that, at that or any other time, I was the equal antagonist of Lawrence. He has a sheer creative power that is completely beyond my range. But at that time I was the only English critic who took Lawrence with the impassioned seriousness he deserved: the rest had washed their hands of him long ago, or, if they wrote of him at all, wrote only of his early novels and poems in a tone of mild regret that he should wilfully have forsaken such comparatively mild and flowery paths. At all events it so happened that I was the only English critic who took up his challenge with a vehemence comparable to that with which he had flung it down. After all, it was not surprising. I had known Lawrence intimately. I had realised, beyond any faint shadow of doubt, that he was the most real and powerful personality, the most naturally gifted man, among all my coevals. And perhaps I knew what Lawrence *meant* by his writing far better than other men. Therefore I cried, with vehemence and passionate sincerity, over the débris of a broken friendship: 'Écrasez l'infâme!'

Well, I changed. I came to believe that Lawrence was right and I was wrong. In reviewing his next novel, *Aaron's Rod*, I published my recantation, with these words: '*Aaron's Rod* is the most important thing that has happened to English literature since the war. . . . To read it is to drink of a fountain of life.' For the bitterness had gone out of Lawrence's hostility to modern life. No less, nay, even more profoundly the enemy of modern 'civilisation', he was no longer an angry and venomous enemy. He had reached the gaiety and serenity of a man who has come, through bitter struggles, into the secure possession of his truth. He had lived out life to an issue.

That brings me to the second of my simple facts, in order to explain, as briefly as I can, the nature of Lawrence's challenge to modern life. Both of Lawrence's expository or philosophical volumes start from a psycho-analytical basis. Lawrence was the first man in England, and I believe the first man in Europe, truly to realise the scope, the *envergure*, of the problems of which psycho-analysis has touched the fringe. This knowledge he had not as a student of Freud or Jung, but directly and instinctively by his own intuitive apprehension of life. The language and conceptions of the psycho-analysts were useful to him sometimes in giving expression to his own discoveries; but his discoveries were his own: they were also far in advance of anything the professional psycho-analysts had reached. For Lawrence knew, as a creative artist delving into his own depths for the life of his characters, what the professional psycho-analysts even now are only dimly aware of, that the problem they have (almost inadvertently and almost ignorantly) touched is the central problem of life—the problem to which all religions are in some sort attempted answers: 'What shall a man live by?'

The professional psycho-analysts had discovered that in modern 'civilisation' some great primal urge—'Sex' for Freud, something less simple, *Libido*, for Jung—was thwarted and contorted with disastrous results to the individual. They began, clinically, to elaborate a subtle technique for liberating these suppressions. They have only just begun to see that when the suppressions are liberated, the problem of life remains, only more conscious and urgent than before. For the victim of neurosis, the man who cannot live in modern life, has at least a *modus vivendi* in the framework and among the compulsions of our industrial 'civilisation'. If he becomes a machine, he also acquires some of the numbness of a machine. To make him aware of his own deep discomfiture, his lack of true satisfaction, his poverty of being, is only to increase his pain and his impotence, unless you can give him something new and true to live by. Psycho-analysis, without knowing what it is doing, has assumed the responsibilities of a religion without having religious duties to impose or religious satisfactions to offer.

This then is the cardinal issue which Lawrence has faced continuously and unflinchingly during his life as a writer, in moods that have passed through anger, embitterment, dismay, to a final serenity and insouciance. Men must enter into a new order of being. It is the conclusion of the great minds of modern times—of Dostoevsky, of Tolstoy, of Nietzsche, of Whitman. But how? In *Fantasia of the Unconscious* Lawrence gives, with a joyful spontaneity of language which is itself an augury of the newness of life he proclaims, his answer to the question. And, for my own part, I will declare my faith that it is essentially a true one; that D. H. Lawrence is the only writer of modern England who has something profoundly new to say; and finally that he must inevitably become a figure of European significance.

8

SERIOUSNESS

From Pencillings *(Collins, 1923). This article first appeared in a weekly column in* The Times *in 1922.*

It is becoming a habit with modern critics to talk much of artistic 'seriousness'. Matthew Arnold set the fashion originally, and he picked it up from Aristotle. Arnold admirably translated 'spoudaiotês' as 'high seriousness', and since then seriousness has become one of the shibboleths of serious criticism. I am myself no small offender. I am continually demanding seriousness. But my conscience has begun to prick me, and I have begun to wonder what it means.

I imagine that when we say a writer is serious, we mean that he has a morality, that he is communicating to us the profoundest truth that he feels about human life. This truth of the writer cannot be formulated as an intellectual judgment; it is an intuitional, emotional, qualitative certainty, which cannot be summed up in a verdict, but only communicated through a work of literature. In other words a serious piece of literature is one which has validity. It illuminates our human experience. It puts us in a position whence a clearer view of human life is possible. When we have read *Don Quixote* we seem to see the double thread of ideal and actual that is entwined in all human action. We receive a like vision from *Le Misanthrope*; we see the hopelessness of demanding that human beings should be ideal.

That these two works immediately suggest themselves as examples of seriousness in literature shows plainly that fine comedy is just as serious as fine tragedy. Instinctively we know that is true, and yet the ordinary implications of the word serious seem to prevent us from realising it. At least I can see no other way of accounting for a curious 'might have been' in that stimulating volume, *The Sacred Wood*. 'How astonishing,' Mr. Eliot wrote in it, 'if Arnold had shown his contemporaries exactly *why* the author of *Amos Barton* was a more serious writer than Dickens, and *why* the author of *La Chartreuse de Parme* is more serious than either.' Astonishing indeed! is the immediate reply—astonishing as any other murder of impossibility. But Mr. Eliot, though he noticeably refrains from telling us 'exactly why', most evidently does believe that George Eliot is a more serious writer than Dickens. And that is odd. One can only suggest that the word serious has proved a pitfall for Mr. Eliot's careful feet, and that he has come to believe that George Eliot was a more serious writer than Dickens, because his creation was mainly comic, while hers was mainly tragic.

One suspects also the influence of another word-suggestion; namely that the writer is pre-eminently serious who takes himself seriously. George Eliot, under Lewes's inspiration, came to take herself seriously indeed, and the result was *Romola*, in fact disastrous. Doubly disastrous, because *Romola* is as dead as *Salammbô*, and because (as her husband said) she began it a young woman and finished it an old one. George Eliot was a great writer, but she was born with enough seriousness to last her a lifetime. Her chief need was to keep herself unbent, instead of making herself taut and old in the effort to achieve a serious masterpiece. And, great writer as she is, she is a small one beside Dickens. So for the matter of that is Stendhal, and Dickens is, in any valuable critical sense of the word, more serious than either. His comic vision was the fiercest that has ever been in English literature, so savage as to be sometimes all but unbearable. What could be more terrifying than the final quarrel between Sarah Gamp and Betsy Prig? Dickens probably roared with laughter when he wrote it, we do when we read it; but if we happen to stop laughing and get a clear sight of what he is showing us, we do not laugh again.

Seriousness, yes. It is the vital quality of enduring literature. But for heaven's sake let us not begin to confuse it with tragedy or solemnness. When Mr. Wells wrote *Mr. Polly*, he was a serious writer, though he laughed all the while; when he wrote *The Secret Places of the Heart*, he was not, though he pulled a long face over it. Seriousness comes from a keen vision of life and a deep feeling about it. And that is not altered by laughter or tears. Great comedy is terrible; we laugh at it, it sometimes seems, only to prevent ourselves from seeing it, and when we do see it we flinch as we never do from tragedy, because it is more sudden and more cruel.

There is yet another alien nuance to be traced in this word seriousness. It is often ascribed to the work of a writer who is very serious about the technique of his craft. Dickens is sometimes a careless writer, more careless of the build of his sentences than George Eliot, though hardly more careless than Stendhal. In this sense Flaubert is *the* serious writer. But though we may freely admit that it is a good thing to be serious in Flaubert's way, we must also admit that it is incompatible with a great creative energy. A man from whose brain Squeers is pushing out Micawber and Pecksniff being jostled by

Podsnap cannot spend years over a single book, or days over a single page; he simply hasn't the time. This kind of seriousness is a minor virtue, but no amount of it will replace the seriousness that is vital.

We must not confuse it, neither must we despise it. We may legitimately share the contempt of a famous novelist for 'holiday authors', for the men 'who sit down to write a book as they would sit down to a game of cards—leisurely—living people who coolly select as an amusement to kill time, an occupation which can only be pursued, even creditably, by the patient, uncompromising reverent devotion of every intelligent faculty, more or less, which a human being has to give.' Noble words! And the novelist who wrote them was not Flaubert, nor George Eliot, nor Stendhal, nor Balzac, nor Dickens, nor Hardy—but Wilkie Collins. What shall we say then? Beware of seriousness? Probably that is safer advice than 'Be serious!' For the seriousness that matters cannot be won by pains; while the seriousnesses that do not matter may lead to *The Moonstone* and perhaps to *The Law and the Lady*.

9

CONGREVE AND MOLIÈRE

From Pencillings. *This article first appeared in a weekly column in* The Times *in 1922.*

Fashion in reading, as in all things else, is fickle. Ibsen is not read nowadays half so much as he was fifteen or twenty years ago when earnest young men cut their wisdom teeth on *Hedda Gabler* and *The Master-Builder*. For some reason he is now become almost as dowdy as the suburban society which he depicted in his plays. And this year the Molière tercentenary came to remind us that the great French dramatist is not so much regarded as he was. There were a dozen perfunctory articles and one good one; conscience-stricken people said 'they must read Molière again' in an unconvincing, parenthetical way which suggested that they had not read him once; and the big sleeping dog was let lie. An older generation which had Molière at its finger-ends has been succeeded by one which has barely touched him with its finger-tips.

It was not, therefore, altogether surprising to find one of the leaders of the moderns, Mr. Clive Bell, lately declaring in his provocative way: 'Yes: I put Congreve above Molière.' Whether the challenge has been taken up I do not know. It is, perhaps, a statement to which the older generation would not deign, and the younger would not care, to reply. Nevertheless, it would be a pity if in this year of nominal piety to the master of comedy a judgment so uncompromising were allowed to go by default.

Mr. Clive Bell, who does not fire off his thunderbolts unadvisedly, gives two reasons for his verdict. First, Molière's attitude to life 'reminds him too often of the attitude of *Punch*'—not the famous figure of Guignol, I imagine, but our own comic weekly—and he thinks that

> 'La Parfaite raison fuit toute extremité
> Et veut que l'on soit sage avec sobriété.

really means, in the long run, that the *bourgeoisie* knows best.' It would need a very long run indeed: but of that later. The second argument is an argument from style. 'Molière wrote perfectly adequate French verse, whereas Congreve wrote prose which is always dazzlingly brilliant and sometimes exquisite.' No one would dispute the description of Congreve's prose, or deny that Molière's verse *is* perfectly adequate. But whereas Molière's verse is always adequate, it is very doubtful whether Congreve's prose is. Is not the chief reason why *The Way of the World* has always failed on the stage the excessive brilliance of a dialogue which obscures the action and does not allow us to see the wood for the trees? And when it comes to comparing the two comic dramatists, surely the fact that Molière is infinitely the better dramatist should count for something. His plays are as actor-proof as Shakespeare's.

The antithesis, moreover, between the adequacy of Molière's verse and the exquisiteness of Congreve's prose is meant to imply that Molière's verse was never exquisite. That is an odd idea. Take, for a single instance, Agnès's speech in *L'École des Femmes:*

J'étois sur le balcon à travailler au frais
Lorsque je vis passer sous les arbres d'auprès
Un jeune homme bien fait, qui rencontrant ma vue,
D'une humble révérence aussitôt me salue:
Moi, pour ne point manquer à la civilité,
Je fis la révérence aussi de mon côté.
Soudain il me refait une autre révérence:
Moi, j'en refais de même une autre en diligence;
Et lui d'une troisième aussitôt repartant,
D'une troisième aussi j'y repars à l'instant.
Il passe, vient, repasse, et toujours de plus belle
Me fait à chaque fois révérence nouvelle;
Et moi, qui tous ces tours fixement regardois,
Nouvelle révérence aussi je lui rendois:
Tant que, si sur ce point la nuit ne fût venue,
Toujours comme cela je me serois tenue,
Ne voulant point céder, et recevoir l'ennui
Qu'il me pût estimer moins civile que lui.

If that is not exquisite verse, I do not know the meaning of the phrase. The real difference between Molière and Congreve in this particular matter is that Molière's verse is always exquisite when exquisiteness is necessary, while Congreve's prose is often exquisite when something more straightforward would serve his purposes better. Millamant is wonderful and speaks divinely: but Agnès is just as wonderful, she speaks just as divinely, and she is firm in outline and as clear as a crystal.

L'École des Femmes, for all its purity and completeness, is but a minor comedy of Molière's, yet it is equal to anything of Congreve's.

With *Le Misanthrope* or *Tartuffe* we pass into a realm of profound comic reality which Congreve with all his genius could not enter. Put the equation grossly: Celimène is at least the equivalent of Millamant, and what has Congreve to show for Alceste? Congreve's graceful yacht is dwarfed by the side of Molière's splendid schooner. Congreve's draught, his weight, his substance is smaller, and so is his beauty. *Le Misanthrope* is one of the most perfect things in all literature: it is also one of the most substantial. To pit Congreve's exquisiteness against Molière's adequacy is to make a false antithesis and to mistake the accidents for the essentials of style.

But strangest of all is the paradoxical opinion that Molière's attitude, 'in the long run', meant that the *bourgeoisie* knows best. Since when has harmony of the faculties been a bourgeois virtue? Does the bourgeois Arnolphe (de la Source), to take *L'École des Femmes* again, know best? Is Orgon infallible, or Georges Dandin the fountain of mundane wisdom? No doubt, Molière did not possess the common element which Mr. Bell so curiously finds in Flaubert and Machiavelli, and no less curiously calls their 'fine intellectuality'. He had something better, a point of view which would have enabled him to see the comic side of Flaubert's anti-bourgeois *emportement*, and to savour the aridity of Machiavelli's intellectualism. Molière may not have been an intellectual, but he was reasonable, and that is a much more difficult thing to be. Harmonious rationality is not generally supposed to be a bourgeois attribute, and certainly Molière did not represent it as one: it is more often ascribed to Greek civilisation in its brief maturity. To call Molière's attitude bourgeois beside Congreve's is not to criticise Molière, but Congreve himself. Molière is central, Congreve is eccentric. Molière's light is steady, Congreve's, with all its dazzling brilliance, flickers. Molière's vision is searching, Congreve's is superficial. We read Congreve for his verbal wit and the delicate beauty of one splendid scene, we read Molière for his wisdom and his truth, and it is only when he is challenged that we worry to point out the high and exquisite perfection of his art.

10

METAPHOR

From John Clare and other studies. *This essay was written in 1927.*

Discussions of metaphor—there are not many of them—often strike us at first as superficial. Not until we have ourselves made the attempt to get further do we begin to realize that the investigation of metaphor is curiously like the investigation of any of the primary data of consciousness: it cannot be pursued very far without our being led to the borderline of sanity. Metaphor is as ultimate as speech itself, and speech as ultimate as thought. If we try to penetrate them beyond a certain point, we find ourselves questioning the very faculty and instrument with which we are trying to penetrate them. The earth trembles and yawns beneath the explorer's feet. *Medio tutissimus ibis*; but the middle way is hard to find.

Suppose we take a familiar metaphor, as that the fiery spirit of Emily Brontë burned up her body. It cannot fairly be called *cliché*; it is rather a familiar and necessary idiom. Necessary, because we find that there is no way of saying what we want to say about Emily Brontë save by this metaphor or one of its variations. This obvious necessity of the metaphor, this absence of genuine alternatives, seems to make it clear that so soon as one person perceived in another and sought to describe such a quality as Emily Brontë's, a kindred metaphor was forced upon him. We may even say that the quality could not have been perceived without the metaphor. The imagination that the soul inhabits the body as fire inhabits the material which it burns must surely go back to the moment when the existence of the soul was first surmised; for only by such an image could the nature of the soul's existence be at all apprehended. And we may leave it undecided, or as impossible of decision, whether the creation of the metaphor was the result of a search for a description of the previously felt existence of the soul, or the existence of the soul was suggested by the manner of the flame's existence.

For, whichever it may have been, and perhaps the processes were equally prevalent, metaphor appears as the instinctive and necessary act of the mind exploring reality and ordering experience. It is the means by which the less familiar is assimilated to the more familiar, the unknown to the known: it 'gives to airy nothing a local habitation and a name', so that it ceases to be airy nothing. To attempt a fundamental examination of metaphor would be nothing less than an investigation of the genesis of thought itself—a dangerous enterprise. Therefore we instinctively seek to circumscribe our own inquiries by leaving out of account as far as may be the countless host of dead or dormant metaphors of which the most part of language is composed, and concentrating on the living ones. We take for granted the past exploration of reality of which dead and dormant metaphors are the record, and try to focus our minds on the present, hazardous, incomplete, and thrilling exploration of reality which is represented by metaphors which still retain their vitality.

Such are the metaphors of what we call creative literature. These remain alive because they are the records of an exploration of reality by men who stood head and shoulders above their fellows, who discerned resemblances between the unknown and the known which the generality could not accept nor common speech assimilate. Their metaphors are felt still to be the vehicle of some immediate revelation to those who attend to them. As Aristotle said, 'But the greatest thing of all by far is to be a master of metaphor. It is the one thing that can not be learned from others; and it is also a sign of original genius, since a good metaphor implies the intuitive perception of the similarity in dissimilars'. The statement, made so long ago, seems final still.

But before we hazard a small attempt to advance from it towards Coleridge's discussion of imagery, we need to inquire, for the sake of clarity, whether there is any but a formal difference between metaphor and simile and image. 'Far out, as though idly, listlessly, gulls were flying. Now they settled on the waves, now they beat up into the rainy air, *and shone against the pale sky like the lights within a pearl.*' The last words would be called indifferently an image or a simile. Change them to 'shining lights in the pale pearl of sky', it becomes—not by any means to its advantage, for a reason we may discover—a metaphor. But the act of creative perception remains the same. And it seems impossible to regard metaphors and similes as different in any essential property: metaphor is compressed simile. The word 'image' however, which has come to usurp a prominent place in these discussions, is more recalcitrant. It not only narrows the content of the word 'simile', but tends to force unduly into the foreground the part played by the visual image. In the beautiful simile quoted above the visual image is preponderant; in Baudelaire's agonizing one:

Ces affreuses nuits
Qui compriment le cœur comme un papier qu'on froisse,

the visual image has no part at all. Again, it is obvious foolishness to persuade oneself that any visual image underlies the magnificent metaphors—

Thou still unravish'd bride of quietness:
Thou foster-child of Silence and slow Time.

Yet though the suggestion of the word 'image' is dangerous, the word is necessary. For metaphor and simile belong to formal classification. The word 'image', precisely because it is used to cover both metaphor and simile, can be used to point towards their fundamental identity; and if we resolutely exclude from our minds the suggestion that the image is solely or even predominantly visual, and allow the word to share in the heightened and comprehensive significance with which its derivative 'imagination' has perforce been endowed—if we conceive the 'image' not as primary and independent, but as the most singular and potent instrument of the faculty of imagination—it is a more valuable word than those which it subsumes: metaphor and simile. To them clings something worse than false suggestion: a logical taint, an aura of irrelevancy.

The image may be visual, may be auditory, may refer back to any primary physical experience—as those hoary metaphors which describe the process of thought itself as a grasping or apprehension—or it may be wholly psychological, the reference of one emotional or intellectual experience to another, as

Then felt I like some watcher of the skies
When a new planet swims into his ken . . .

The essential is simply that there should be that intuitive perception of similarity between dissimilars of which Aristotle speaks. What we primarily demand is that the similarity should be a true similarity and that it should have lain hitherto unperceived, or but rarely perceived by us, so that it comes to us with an effect of revelation: something hitherto unknown is suddenly made known. To that extent the image is truly creative: it marks an advance, for the writer who perceives and the reader who receives it, in the conquest of some reality.

We also in our inquiry may take a step forward. That we demand more of imagery than this may be seen in our instinctive refusal of the image of a modern prose-writer, who speaks of the 'churches, like shapes of grey paper, breasting the stream of the Strand'. There are two images, and they war with each other. If the churches really breasted the stream of the Strand, they were not at that moment like shapes of grey paper. Possibly both perceptions are valid in isolation; in association they nullify one another. Yet how often does Shakespeare seem to commit the same offence.

> It is great
> To do that thing that ends all other deeds:
> Which shackles accident, and bolts up change;
> Which sleeps, and never palates more the dug,
> The beggar's nurse and Caesar's.

Yet the offence is only apparent. The images do not in fact disturb each other, whereas the modern writer's images do. This is partly because in the modern writer's imagery the stress lies wholly upon the visual: if we do not see what we are required to see, the sentence fails of its effect; and partly because of the characteristic swiftness of Shakespeare's language. We have not, and we are not intended to have, time to unfold his metaphors; and, moreover, the boldest and most abrupt transition among them is in its effect the smoothest. For the rhythm leaves no doubt that it is not 'the dug' but Death that is 'the beggar's nurse and Caesar's'. Death, which in the previous line was the child sleeping against the heart, becomes the bosom that receives mankind. We may say it is the mere verbal suggestion that links the metaphors. Yet, though it is true that verbal 'self-suggestion' is potent in high poetry ('Forlorn! the very word is like a knell . . .'), it seems truer in this case to say that the one metaphor grows immediately out of the other. It is as though the vague 'thing', from which the images take their rise, swiftly groped after shapes before our mind's eye, and finally achieved a full realization—'the beggar's nurse and Caesar's'.

This is the work of the greatest of all masters of metaphor, and it would be preposterous to try others' achievement by its standard. The self-creative progress of Shakespeare's imagery is a thing apart. But by comparing small things with great we may see that the internal harmony which the modern writer fails to secure is a necessary quality of true imagery. Shakespeare's methods of securing it are indeed startling; he takes what seem to be impossible risks, and wins with ease. His success, when we examine it, is not really so surprising, for the extent to which images are discordant depends upon the extent we unfold them, and that is wholly within the great poet's control, for it in turn depends primarily upon the rhythm and tempo of his writing. And this, more than any other, is the reason why the successful use of metaphor is very much bolder in poetry than in prose. The poet's means of control—that is to say, the possibilities of tempo and rhythm in poetry—are much richer and more flexible than in prose. He has our sensibilities, our powers of realization and comparison, far more completely under his thumb than the prose-writer. So that we may hazard a generalization and say that the creative simile is by nature more appropriate to prose than the creative metaphor. Prose gives us time to bear upon the comparison, which if it be exact and revealing, will stand the strain of our attention, and is better frankly exposed to the inquiry it must receive. And, again, the function of imagery in poetry differs perceptibly from the function of imagery in prose. In poetry metaphor is chiefly a means to excite in us a vague and heightened awareness of qualities we can best call spiritual. Exactness and precision are seldom sought, and, if they are, are seldom valuable; and often where an apparent exactness exists, as in the Homeric simile, it is an incidental exactness and does not reinforce the point of specific analogy. Set two equally famous heroic portraits by great poets against each other.

His legs bestrid the ocean; his rear'd arm
Crested the world: his voice was propertied
As all the tunèd spheres, and that to friends;
But when he meant to quail, and shake the orb,
He was as rattling thunder. For his bounty,
There was no winter in 't; an autumn 'twas
That grew the more by reaping: his delights
Were dolphin-like; they show'd his back above
The element they liv'd in: in his livery
Walk'd crowns and crownets; realms and islands were
As plates dropp'd from his pocket . . .

He above the rest
In shape and gesture proudly eminent
Stood like a Tower, his form had not yet lost
All her original brightness, nor appear'd
Less than archangel ruin'd, and th' excess
Of glory obscur'd, as when the sun new risen
Looks through the horizontal misty air
Shorn of his beams; or from behind the moon
In dim eclipse disastrous twilight sheds
On half the nations; and with fear of change
Perplexes monarchs.

The Miltonic tempo, as ever, is far slower than Shakespeare's; therefore we bear more heavily upon his comparisons, and in sufficient measure they stand the strain; but the whole effect is not precise, but rather vague, vast, and foreboding. So also, in its totally different kind, the picture of Antony that is impressed upon our minds is of some thing (rather than some one) immense, generous, genial, a careless and overflowing force of nature—a dynamic phenomenon as peculiar to Shakespeare's view of the universe as the static figure of Satan to Milton's. Exactness of this kind there is in both; but it comes not from the exactness of the particular comparisons, it is a total effect of many comparisons, as it were a painting of one great and indefinable quality by many strokes of minor yet allied analogies. To evoke such elemental spirits is seldom the purpose of prose, nor of the imagery proper to it. It also seizes, in so far as it is creative, indefinable qualities, but they are more specific and more local.

> Soon after daybreak we were steaming down the arrowy Rhone, at the rate of twenty miles an hour, in a very dirty vessel full of merchandise, and with only three or four other passengers for our companions: among whom the most remarkable was a silly old, meek-faced, garlic-eating, immeasurably polite Chevalier, with a dirty scrap of red ribbon at his buttonhole, *as if he had tied it there to remind him of something.*

It is perfect, it gives us the man—an individual and comic inhabitant of earth. Perhaps as an example it suggests that the prose use of simile must be more prosaic than we mean to imply. We have quoted solely to point an essential difference between the imagery of prose and poetry. The imagery of poetry is in the main complex and suggestive; the imagery of prose single and explicit.

But the three examples serve also to illustrate what is the highest function of imagery—namely, to define indefinable spiritual qualities. All metaphor and simile can be described as the analogy by which the human mind explores the universe of quality and charts the non-measurable world. Of these indefinite qualities some are capable of direct sensuous apprehension, while others can be grasped only by a faculty which, though obviously akin to sensuous apprehension, yet differs from it. Sensuous perception is of the qualities of the visible, audible, tangible world; of the spiritual qualities of the more recondite world of human personality and its creations there is intuition. Both faculties are necessary to the great poet, but there have been many who, though richly gifted with sensuous perception, have been deficient or altogether lacking in spiritual intuition. To the great poet his constant accumulation of vivid sense-perceptions supplies the most potent means by which he articulates his spiritual intuitions, for recognitions of spiritual quality can be most forcefully and swiftly conveyed through analogous recognitions of sensuous quality. One has only to imagine how much, and how much in vain, another writer might toil to render the quality of Antony that is given once for all in the words, grammatically confused though they are:—

> . . . his delights
> Were dolphin-like; they show'd his back above
> The element they lived in . . .

or to consider the pregnant subtlety of these two kindred images:

> This common body,
> Like to a vagabond flag upon the stream,
> Goes to and back, lackeying the varying tide,
> To rot itself with motion. . . .
>
> Her tongue will not obey her heart, nor can
> Her heart inform her tongue,—the swan's down-feather,
> That stands upon the swell at full of tide
> And neither way inclines . . .

to realize the enormous resources for describing the subtlest nuances of emotion and character which a vivid percipience of the sensuous world can give.

But the greatest mastery of imagery does not lie in the use, however beautiful and revealing, of isolated images, but in the harmonious total impression produced by a succession of subtly related images. In such cases the images appear to grow out of one another and to be fulfilling an independent life of their own. Yet this apparent autonomy is as strictly subordinated to a final impression as the steps of a logical argument are to their conclusion. Such triumphs of imagery are to be conceived as a swift and continuous act of exploration of the world of imagination—though an obvious metaphor is in that phrase. A magnificent example of this peculiar movement of mind on a scale so large that it can be carefully examined is Keats's *Ode to a Nightingale*. The strange combination of imaginative autonomy and profound total harmony in that poem is characteristic of the movement of creative imagery in its highest forms. We can perhaps get a clear glimpse of the nature of this contradictory process of creative imagery—the maximum of independence combined with the most complete and pervasive subordination—in one of the rare moments when we can honestly claim to be able to look over Shakespeare's shoulder. The famous picture of Cleopatra on Cydnus comes substantially from North's Plutarch, of which the following sentence is the original of Shakespeare's first seven lines:

> She disdained to set forward otherwise, but to take her barge in the river of Cydnus, the poope whereof was of gold, the sails of purple, and the owers of silver, which kept stroke in rowing after the sound of flutes, howboys, cytherns, violls, and such other instruments as they played upon the barge . . .

It is often said that Shakespeare followed North as closely as he could, with the minimum of original effort. It is not true. North's sentence would fall quite easily into good blank verse, but it would be nothing like—

> *The barge she sat in, like a burnish'd throne,*
> *Burn'd on the water*: the poop was beaten gold;
> Purple the sails, *and so perfuméd that*
> *The winds were love-sick with them;* the oars were silver,
> Which to the tune of flutes, kept stroke, *and made*
> *The water which they beat to follow faster,*
> *As amorous of their strokes . . .*

The phrases in italics are Shakespeare's additions: afterwards he keeps more closely to North until he comes to the climax. North has it:

> Others also rann out of the city to see her coming in. So that in the end, there rann such multitudes of people one after another, that *Antonius* was left post alone in the market-place, in his Imperiall seate to give audience.

Which is transformed into:

> The city cast
> Her people out upon her, and Antony,
> Enthron'd in the market-place, did sit alone,
> *Whistling to the air: which, but for vacancy,*
> *Had gone to gaze on Cleopatra too*
> *And made a gap in nature.*

The additions are worth attention. North's somewhat amorphous prose is given a beginning and an end. The additions are all, in spite of formal differences, essentially similes and metaphors; and, after the first, which gathers the vision into one whole which it puts imperishably before the mind's eye, the second and third develop the theme which is clinched in climax by the fourth. In them the successive elements—the winds, the water, the air—are represented all as succumbing to the enchantment of love which breathes from the great Queen and her burning barge; and by this varied return on a single motive North's inconsequential panorama is given an organic unity. It is quite impossible to conceive Shakespeare as dovetailing old and new together. Before his mind's eye as he read North had risen a picture half visible, half spiritual, in short, truly imaginative—the manifestation of Egypt, before whom the elements made obeisance. All of North that was congruous with his enchanted vision he incorporated with a flowing pen into his new creation. And the added imagery, about which he probably took no second thought, grew naturally into harmony with itself and with the whole.

To this strange but strangely natural process Coleridge was referring in his often-quoted and sometimes violently interpreted words:

> Images, however beautiful, though faithfully copied from nature, and as accurately represented in words, do not of themselves characterize the poet. They become proofs of original genius only in so far as they are modified by a predominant passion, or by associated thoughts and images awakened by that passion; or when they have the effect of reducing multitude to unity, or succession to an instant; or lastly when a human and intellectual life is transferred to them from the poet's own spirit.

Instances, and better instances than Coleridge himself gives, of all the qualities which he demands of truly creative imagery are to be found in the picture of Cleopatra. 'Multitude is reduced to unity' by the first of the added images; and in the other three a human and intellectual life is transferred to the images (Coleridge should perhaps have said, to the objects of the images) from the poet's own spirit. This last desideratum had been put forward long before by Aristotle in his discussion of 'vividness' in the *Rhetoric*. Vividness, he there says, depends upon metaphor and on 'setting things before the eyes'; but 'setting things before the eyes' turns out itself to be a metaphor, and not, as one might imagine, a demand for the visual image. 'This is my definition,' says Aristotle:

> Those words set a thing before the eyes which describe it in an active state . . . Or we may use the device often employed by Homer of giving life to lifeless things by means of metaphor. In all such cases he wins applause by describing an active state, as in the line
>
> Back to the plain rolled the shameless stone.

Whether the process is described thus dryly as by Aristotle, or more transcendentally by Coleridge, as the working of the poetic spirit 'which shoots its being through earth, sea, and air', the fact is indubitable. It seems to be an imperious need of the creative spirit of the poet to impart life to the apparently lifeless. This may appear a 'device' in the cold light of analysis; but nothing is more certain than that when it is used as a device it is intolerable. No conscious contrivance produced 'Thou still unravish'd bride of quietness', or 'Joy, whose hand is ever at his lips, Bidding adieu'. Such things as these —and how many of the most magnificently natural achievements of poetry belong to this kind—are, beyond all doubt, the effect of some 'silent working of the spirit'. By the intensity of the poet's contemplation the lifeless thing lives indeed.

Probably the world of true imagination of which these miracles are the common substance is for ever inviolable by intellectual analysis.

Even to apprehend its subject-matter the intellect must suffer a sea-change, so that it is no longer itself and cannot perform its proper function. Restore its power to the intellect again, and that which it seeks to understand has ceased to exist as what it really is. This world of imagination is a universe wherein quality leaps to cohere with quality across the abysms of classification that divide and categorize the universe of intellectual apprehension. Its true citizens are few and far between; they are the masters of metaphor, and the authentic messages they bring from that near yet distant country perplex our brains and comfort our souls with the half-assurance that the things that are may be otherwise than as we know them.

Towards this exalted region, as to the sole reality, Coleridge was ever groping; and what he meant by the 'predominant passion' which modifies the images of original genius is the power by which genius comprehends its chosen region of this world of qualitative interpenetration. The passion is a passionate contemplation of the unity which pervades the chosen region: a creative passion to correspond with an organic unity. Whether the unity proceeds from the passion, or the passion from the unity, it would be profitless to inquire. They are knit together, as knower and known, in one act of creative comprehension. But if we are shy of the notion of Coleridge which seems to give the poetic spirit an actually plastic power over the material world, we have only to reflect that the predominant passion of the poet's mind is but the counterpart of a predominant quality of the region of the universe which he contemplates. His passion roused by the quality is reflected back upon the quality, and gives it redoubled power; so that it begins to dominate all other qualities and properties, to suffuse them with itself till it becomes as it were the living and governing soul of that which the poet contemplates. By means of his passion the actual realizes its own idea.

However much we struggle, we cannot avoid transcendentalism, for we are seeking to approximate to a universe of quality with analogy for its most essential language through a universe of quantity with a language of identities. Sooner or later, a transcendentalism (which is only the name for a prodigious metaphor) is inevitable. But the process may be brought a little closer to the light of common day if we take once more that region of the qualitative universe which Shakespeare embodied in Cleopatra. She was, we may say, the incarnation of love: the mighty, elemental power which, in Shakespeare's experience, was love, was made corporeal in her. She is possessed by it; from her it radiates and compels obeisance from the elements. But she is not merely a contemplated but a self-uttering thing; and this power that informs her body informs her soul also.

All her thoughts are shaped by it. Without her love she will die, she must die; but when she imagines death, she imagines it as a consummation of love, as the thing

> Which sleeps, and never palates more the dug,
> The beggar's nurse and Caesar's . . .

She dies, and her dying she imagines as a reliving of her triumph on Cydnus. 'I am again for Cydnus, to meet Mark Antony.' And it is a more wonderful triumph. 'Yare, yare, good Iras.' The flower-soft hands that yarely framed the office frame one last office more; and at the aspic's touch the Queen is wholly dedicate to the love she is and serves. The winds, the water, the air obeyed on Cydnus; now the most fickle element of all obeys—her own secret self, from which well up the images of love in death, and death in love:

> The stroke of death is as a lover's pinch
> That hurts and is desired . . .
> Peace, peace!
> Dost thou not see my baby at my breast
> That sucks the nurse asleep?

In the intensity of Shakespeare's imagination the great property takes utter and complete possession of that it dwells in. By the alchemy of Cleopatra's images death is transmuted into a sleep of love. But her thoughts are Shakespeare's thoughts, her predominant passion his. Therefore it is not strange that Caesar, who in the waking world knows nothing of her dying words, should echo them, and prolong her triumph beyond her death.

> She looks like sleep,
> As she would catch another Antony
> In her strong toil of grace.

But Caesar did not know what Shakespeare knew, that it was the selfsame Antony whom she had taken.

11

THE POETS' POET

From John Clare and other studies. *This essay was written in 1930.*

WHEN Charles Lamb gave Edmund Spenser the title he has borne ever since, of 'the poet's poet', he was not merely recording the simple fact that most of the English poets since Spenser's time had been deeply read in his work; he was also asserting that there was a very good reason why Spenser has always been beloved of his similars.

But since what was simple fact in Charles Lamb's day is simple fact no longer, we may refresh our memories. When Wordsworth heard, with his mind's ear, old Triton blow his wreathèd horn, the sound came to him through Spenser; when Keats sat down to write a new 'romance' and began—

Fair Isabel, poor simple Isabel . . .

he was, whether he remembered it or not, singing over again a tune he had learned from Spenser—

To Philemon, false faytour Philemon.

Again, even the very terms of that advice of Keats to Shelley, which some have found so harsh, that 'an artist must serve Mammon . . .' were derived from Spenser; nor can they be properly understood without a memory of the Cave of Mammon similar to that upon which Keats himself, consciously or unconsciously, was drawing. 'You will forgive me,' he said to Shelley, 'for sincerely remarking that you might curb your magnanimity, . . . and load every rift of your subject with ore.' What was in his mind was the house of Mammon.

That house's forme within was rude and strong,
Like an huge cave hewne out of rocky clifte,
From whose rough vaut the ragged breaches hong
Embost with massy gold of glorious guifte
And with rich metall loaded every rifte. . . .

Keats's mind, indeed, was saturated with Spenser, whose influence upon him was second only to the more subtle and more intimate, and in a sense less scrutable, influence of Shakespeare. From Spenser, one might say, he learned to be a poet; from Shakespeare to be a great one.

Assuredly in Lamb's day Spenser was the poets' poet, as he had been Milton's poet, and probably at one time Shakespeare's also. But to-day things are different. True, Charles Doughty could proclaim 'Edmund my lodestar' but Doughty was writing an epic of England, in twenty-four books, and who can pay attention to-day to an epic in twenty-four books? Obviously, the same sort of people who can read *The Faerie Queene*—antediluvians manifest. For Spenser is, for the practical purposes of modern poetry, sadly out of fashion. And this is not because he is ancient simply; for one of the most accomplished of our modern poets can recommend his contemporary poets to seek in Dante their sustenance and the pattern of their skill. But Spenser belongs to the archaeology of literature.

This is strange, and worth consideration; for the tradition of English poetry is rooted in Spenser. And it is a very real question whether, if these roots are severed, English poetry will flourish again. Charles Doughty thought not. It is a pity that he never argued his opinion; he was content to assert it in the text of his epic from time to time, and get on with the writing. But, if he had argued it, he would have argued it, we may suppose, in this fashion. Spenser, he would have said, is the great 'maker' of English poetry; he is the man who, by his learning, his passion, his exquisite sense of form and his delicate ear, was able to establish in the English tongue all that the English language would admit of the tunes and technique accumulated during the fifteen hundred years that European poetry had been extant. This was Spenser's service, done to English poetry, once for all; for what Spenser did not transmit to his poetic successors was not transmissible. It was not, so to say, poetic 'material'; it was idiosyncrasy, the ungovernable, incalculable and inimitable personal element—that which a poet cannot learn, but can only learn how to express. This fundamental distinction, between poetic commonplace and poetic idiosyncrasy, between impersonal and personal style, is itself alien to modern criticism. Whether it calls itself classical or romantic, modern criticism is on this essential point altogether romantic. It unquestioningly accepts the principle that 'le style, c'est l'homme même'; and almost as unquestioningly it accepts the converse of the dictum: 'l'homme même, c'est le style'. But the English romantics themselves, from whom this opinion ostensibly is derived, were not at all of this mind. They were conscious that their art was inherited; they conceived it as an acquisition, and they practised to acquire it. In their own view—surely a true one—they were not men who broke with the poetical tradition, but men who reasserted it. Since they were fine critics—indeed, their whole effort, like Spenser's own, was grounded on a deliberate critical realization—they distinguished without difficulty, between the personal and the impersonal elements in the style of their great predecessors. For the impersonal element, which they might reasonably hope to acquire, they went chiefly to Spenser.

The reason why their example was not followed in the nineteenth century was partly, no doubt, because their practice was not understood; partly, also, because it was the inimitable, even the accidental, elements in their achievement which chiefly fascinated their successors. How great a mass of mid-nineteenth-century poetry and art, for instance, grew out of a single casual poem by Keats which he did not think worthy to be included in his last volume: *La Belle Dame sans Merci*! But certainly more important than either of these causes was the change that was taking place in the structure of English society. Democracy was establishing itself, and with democracy the democratic art of literature—the Novel. Whatever optimists may believe, poetry is not a democratic art; it has never been, and never will be unless the day shall arrive when democracy becomes itself aristocracy. It is futile to appeal to the example of the Ballads, which, however beautiful, do not at all belong to the kind of great poetry: or to the example of Shakespeare, whose *Hamlet* succeeded rather because it contained twenty-seven good pieces of stage-business than by reason of the poetry which Shakespeare could not keep out of it. The truth is that Keats himself was probably the last relatively poor man in England who was able honestly to believe that he might make a living by serving a full apprenticeship to the art of poetry. When at the beginning of *Endymion* he sat down to write to Haydon, quoting Spenser again,

> The noble hart that harbours vertuous thought,
> And is with childe of glorious great intent,
> Can never rest, untill it forth have brought
> Th' eternal brood of glorie excellent . . .

he really believed that by bringing forth that brood in the form of poetry he could achieve livelihood and fame. Nor was it an unreasonable illusion. His friends, some of them well-tried journalists, believed it. Yet more, his publisher believed it. Mr. Abbey, tea merchant and guardian did not. Mr. Abbey was right.

There were popular poets in Keats's time: there was Scott, there was Byron, there was Moore. Whatever qualities they had, they had not the qualities of great poets. Thinking of them in 1864, Walter Bagehot wrote:

> Almost the sole result of the poetry of that time is the harm which it has done. It degraded for a time the whole character of the art. It fixed upon

the minds of a whole generation, it engraved in popular memory and tradition, a vague conviction that poetry is but one of the many *amusements* for the enjoying classes, for the lighter hours of all classes. The mere notion, the bare idea, that poetry is a deep thing, a teaching thing, the most surely and wisely elevating of human things, is even now to the coarse public mind nearly unknown.

Bagehot was expecting a change; but what was true of England in 1864 is equally true of England to-day. Our poetry is slight, occasional, indisputably minor. Only by thus circumscribing its intentions does it exist at all. The 'mere notion, the bare idea' that a man should, from the beginning, devote his life to poetry, to expressing through the medium of poetry the thought that is born of a lifetime's full experience, is become almost fantastic.

The position of Spenser, the great teacher of English poets, is therefore now anomalous. There is nobody for him to teach. All that he has to teach is precisely all which is most irrelevant to the pursuit of literature to-day—the veritable 'art' of poetry, the specific skill by which a poet is a poet and not something else. Whether that situation is in itself deplorable or not, the consequence of the situation, with which we are here concerned, is a simple one—namely, that Spenser is not appreciated for the qualities that are peculiarly his own. He is judged, if judged at all, by standards which are not really germane to his intentions or his achievement; he is required to stand or fall by his intrinsic interestingness.

To require this of Spenser is unreasonable. But what seems unreasonable, to-day, is the assertion that the work of a great poet should be absolved from the application of a standard so obviously natural. If Spenser fails to interest, he fails in everything. But interestingness is relative. The criterion of interestingness which prevails under democratic conditions is that described by Dr. Johnson: 'Nothing can please many and please long but just representations of human nature.' It is, no doubt the most essential kind of interestingness. Chaucer and Shakespeare both possess it in abundance; Spenser scarcely at all. But Spenser, though he aimed at pleasing long, did not aim at pleasing many. He was not even very much concerned with his own subject matter, or at any rate he was concerned with it in a manner quite different from that in which he professed to be concerned with it. Its intrinsic interest for him, we may be sure, was very small. Provided that it was a subject-matter appropriate (by traditional canons) to a great poem in the English language; it could be about—anything that great poems were about.

Much is sometimes made of Spenser's moral intention in composing *The Faerie Queene*; and, indeed, Spenser rather paraded it himself. But in reality this moral intention amounts to little. We have only to read, with an advised ear, the passage of most sustained and various beauty in *The Faerie Queene*—the adventure of Sir Guyon in the Gardens of Acrasia—to be certain that Spenser's heart was not in his morality. When, as in this episode, it came to a struggle between his morality and his sense of beauty, the sense of beauty, very properly, triumphed. The sense of beauty did with Spenser precisely what it did with his pupil Keats, 'it obliterated all consideration'. Spenser as a philosopher was hopelessly inconsistent, as a moralist hopelessly divided. He was fairly caught between the old ascetic morality and the new enthusiasm for Beauty for its own sake. He did not know whether Beauty was from God or the Devil; but it would not be true to say of him (as it would be true to say it of Marlowe or Shakespeare) that he did not care: he was, in this respect, a divided man. There was that in him which cared, and there was that in him —call it, with Coleridge, the genius in the man of genius—which did not care. This half-conscious, instinctive or intuitive part of him was content to suffer the sense of beauty to 'obliterate all consideration'. This was his destiny and he must follow it, even when it played havoc with his allegory and his conscious morality. Essentially, he was in much the same case as Keats when he wrote *Endymion*, inwardly impelled to trust to his sense of beauty, yet with his consciousness mistrusting his own faith, ostensibly even disowning it. Keats did not do this; but Spenser was near to the Middle Ages and Keats was far away. Keats was committed to find an individual solution for an individual problem, where Spenser could still, in consciousness at least, support himself with authority. Besides, Keats had time to think, where Spenser had not. The business in hand was too tremendous, too urgent, and too exciting to allow him to be turmoiled with its implications. The business in hand was making a great poem and laying the foundations of English poetry.

That English poetry should be beautiful, subtle, and inexhaustibly capable: that the instrument should hence forward have the capacity of 'divine respondence meet': that the language and the forms of English verse should become sensitive like that fair almond tree on Selinus, by whose vision Marlowe was entranced—

> Like to an almond tree ymounted hye
> On top of greene Selinis all alone,
> With blossoms brave bedecked daintily;
> Whose tender locks do tremble every one
> At everie little breath that under heaven is blowne—

this was the aim after which Spenser laboured as no English poet has laboured, nor needed to labour, since. The instrument which he devised, and shaped, and inlaid and polished is still *the* instrument of

English poetry. Strings were added, like the blank verse of Shakespeare and Milton, or the rich stanza of Keats's odes; or strings were taken away to make the heroic couplet of Dryden or of Pope. But the *sermo communis* of English poetry was settled: the themes, the tunes, the immense liberty of absolute and intricate formality, were won. All the great poets of England have known by simple instinct to whom they must go to learn their craft.

And surely, for those who have ears to hear, the sheer patterning of Spenser's 'music' has never been surpassed. Take these few passages which follow hard upon one another:

Her wanton palfrey all was overspred
With tinsel trappings woven like a wave
Whose bridle hung with golden bells and bosses brave . . .
Ah, deare Sansjoy, next dearest to Sansfoy,
Cause of my new griefe, cause of my new joy . . .

or this to link one stanza with another:

Then turning to his Lady, dead with feare her found.
Her seeming dead he found with feigned feare . . .

or this whole stanza:

One day, nigh wearie of the yrksome way,
From her unhastie beast she did alight;
And on the grasse her dainty limbs did lay
In secrete shadow, far from all men's sight:
From her fayre head her fillet she undight
And layd her stole aside. Her angel's face,
As the great eye of heaven, shyned bright,
And made a sunshine in the shady place;
Did never mortall eye behold such heavenly grace.

But to attempt to exhibit the infinitely various modulations of Spenser's verse is a fantastic enterprise. Do we seek the characteristic music of Pope's heroic couplet? Here it is:

Flesh without blood, a person without spright
Wounds without hurt, a body without might,
That could doe harme, yet could not harmèd bee,
That could not die, yet seemd a mortall wight,
That was most strong in most infirmitee.

or take these two single lines from neighbouring stanzas and recollect what Keats made of them:

What hevens? what altars? what enraged heats? . . .
And precious odours fetched from far away . . .

or the subsequent history of these:

> Come then; come soone; come sweetest death to me
> And take away this long lent loathed light:
> Sharp be thy wounds, but sweet the medicines be
> That long captived souls from weary thraldom free.

or this, for its own perfect felicity:

> Withall she laughed, and she blushed withall,
> That blushing to her laughter gave more grace,
> And laughter to her blushing, as did fall.

or—to make an end of the endless—this single line:

> Deep in the bottom of an huge great rock . . .

Lost in our admiration of this unbounded store of riches, we can only say, in Spenser's own words of the painter of Leda and the swan, 'O wondrous skill and sweet wit of the man!'

By common consent there is one perfect poem of Spenser's—'one entire and perfect chrysolite'—the *Epithalamion*. The reason of its universally recognised appeal is not far to seek: it lies in that which is, for the reader of Spenser as a whole, the subtle but immediately felt difference between this and all his other work save the Sixth Book of *The Faerie Queene*—the contained tremor of an intimately personal emotion. It is but natural that those who have been rapt by the intoxication of this silver music should feel a faint sense of disappointment when they turn afterwards to his other work. But, rightly regarded, the *Epithalamion* is not an introduction to, but a culmination of, Spenser's poetry; it is the accidental triumph which he might easily never have had, but which none but himself could have won. Twenty-five years of toil at the sheer craft of poetry went to make that love-poem. And how many times in the history of a nation's literature does it happen that a mature and perfect poetic craftsman falls in love? Great poets have fallen in love often enough, and often enough have become great poets in part through that experience; but Spenser was complete when the experience came to him. If he himself was disturbed, his poetry could not be; it was immune from perturbation, for it was an impersonal thing.

Impersonal, in the strictest sense, no form of art can be; but the difference is immense between a form of art which is sustained by a pure aesthetic emotion and one which is primarily the expression of ordinary emotional and intellectual experience. The object in the one case is the making of a beautiful thing, in the other the communication of experience. No doubt these two distinct aims have been variously mingled in various poets, and in the same poet at various times;

but in no English poet has the former aim been so completely dominant as in Spenser. He appears deliberately to have sacrificed to his ideal of formal poetic beauty a genuine personal emotion, even when the influence of that personal emotion was relevant and appropriate and even necessary. We have no reason to doubt that his grief over Sidney's death was sincere; *Astrophel*, nevertheless, is completely frigid. Matthew Roydon's companion elegy is simple and affecting beside it. And as this apparently deliberate sacrifice of personal emotion may be explained by the excessive strength of Spenser's passion for formal beauty, so the excessive strength of the passion itself may be explained by the evident difficulty which Spenser found in controlling his patterns. The lack of balance and proportion in a poem relatively so personal as *Colin Clout's Come Home Again* is very notable; so it is in *The Ruines of Time*. One feels that Spenser had always to keep a tight rein on himself, and that the apparent ease of his formal patterning was achieved only by a rigorous concentration.

We might put it that he could afford to run no risks by entertaining other emotions than those aroused by the pure pursuit of form and formal beauty. In such a statement there is inevitable exaggeration. But it is remarkable that both the morality and the imagery of *The Faerie Queene* are largely formal. In another, and perhaps a greater, kind of poet precisely these two elements are impassioned; his morality is what he intimately is, and his imagery is subdued to the urgency of his utterance. But in Spenser the morality is a mere convenience or a useful theme, and the imagery quite often mere decorative fantasy. The meetings of a lion and a unicorn, or a gryphon and a dragon, provide poor similes: they are there not from any inherent necessity, but because images are formally required. It is only when he leaves for the time being the company of his patterns of virtue and comes nearer to the actual world of men that his imagery is more than abstract decoration. And in this regard one can mark a sort of progress towards reality. When Paridel has cast off Hellenore,

> Alone he rode without his Paragone;
> For, having filcht her bells, her up he cast
> To the wide world, and left her fly alone:
> He nould be clogd. So had he served many one,—

when Trompart lays his snare for Malbecco,

> Yet stoupt he not, but lay still in the winde,
> Waiting advantage on his pray to sease . . .

the images do more than decorate, they define; and by the time we have reached the pastoral loveliness of the Sixth Book we are scarcely surprised by the simple perfection of what is surely the most dramatically appropriate image in all Spenser, when Calidore makes the enchanting Tristram his squire:

> So he him dubbed, and his Squire did call.
> Full glad and joyous then young Tristram grew;
> Like as a flowre, whose silken leaves small
> Long shut up in the bud from heavens vew,
> At length breakes forth, and brode displays his smyling hew.

The Sixth Book is perhaps no more truly characteristic of Spenser than the *Epithalamion*, with which it is probably contemporary; into both alike enters a warm fragrance of reality. In Calidore morality steps down from the abstract empyrean and is incarnate and humane, wayward and lovely. In Calidore, as in young Tristram, it veritably flowers. And being humane, it does not even pretend to stifle in itself the lust of the eye and the pride of life. No whisper of conscience, nor monition of Palmer, warns Calidore that he is on the road to damnation when he peeps from the covert of the wood:

> There did he see that pleased much his sight
> That even he him selfe his eies envyde,
> An hundred naked maidens lily white
> All raunged in a ring and dauncing in delight.

And since Colin Clout ('who knows not Colin Clout?') was in the midst of them, piping so merrily as never none, it is clear Calidore was not in temptation, but in Elysium. It is woefully inconsistent with all that had gone before. Poor harried Acrasia and her lovely maidens, in sober justice, should have burst like a troop of Maenads into that naked conclave, for revenge. But the writ of sober justice does not run in the world of imagination. Colin Clout had no need to be abashed by the invasion; he had only to trust his genius and let it speak for him. 'It was I,' his genius would have said to Acrasia and her maidens, 'who called you out of nothingness and made you lovely; it was not I who destroyed you. For I am Imagination, who, having once created beauty, can never destroy it again. Join in the dance.' And the enchantment of the Sixth Book is that we feel that Acrasia and her maidens have joined in the dance in virtue of that title which Keats proclaimed: 'What the Imagination seizes as Beauty must be Truth.'

It is an old problem, this of Art and Morality, solved in fact easily enough by those who have the strength to make either a morality of their art or an art of their morality, but a cause of incessant perplexity to those without the courage to do either. Spenser, we know, did the former; and few who read him well will not be inwardly convinced that he did the latter also. The poet who conceived his ideal in the semblance of Sir Calidore, it is true, may not himself have been much like him; and perhaps that perfection of grace in conduct was no more the gift of the gods to Spenser than the perfection of grace in his poetry. After all, he half-confesses as much when he speaks of Sir Calidore's courtesy:

> Thereto great help Dame Nature selfe doth lend;
> For some so goodly gratious are by kind,
> That every action doth them much commend
> And in the eyes of men great liking find;
> Which others that have greater skill in mind,
> Though they enforce themselves, cannot attain;
> For everie thing to which one is inclin'd
> Doth best become and greatest grace doth gaine:
> Yet praise likewise deserve good thewes enforst with paine.

'Good thewes enforst with paine'—that is certainly the chief secret of Spenser's great and enduring achievement in poetry; quite possibly it was also the cause of his long wooing of his wife.

But the long wooing had a happy ending; and something of Spenser's moment of felicity is suffused through the Sixth Book, as it is through the *Epithalamion*. The five books which precede it are romance; the sixth is simply romantic, in the sense in which *As You Like it* and *A Winter's Tale* are romantic. The characters are real, their virtue and their love both credible and charming. We enter into a different world which, if it is not the world of every day, is at least a world into which if the fates were propitious and the stars dancing, the world of every day might be transmuted. And the tense atmosphere of derring-do is so mightily relaxed in this happy kingdom that nobody cares, though Sir Calidore forgets all about his blatant enemy for long months on end. The air is kindly here; the savage man discovers himself the pattern of courtesy, cruel ladies learn to be kind, and tyrannous husbands are taught to be gentle. *Redeunt Saturnia regna.*

12

REASON AND CRITICISM

From Countries of the Mind, Second Series *(Oxford University Press, 1931). This essay was written in 1926.*

THE comparative quiescence of the creative spirit in our literature of recent years has found a certain compensation in the increased activity of the critical. That the body of serious criticism has grown in the last dozen years is evident to a sober survey. Criticism may be less popular, but it is more critical; and to that extent may fairly be held to supply a counterpoise to creative barrenness. For criticism that is critical is the expression of a real spiritual energy and the satisfaction of a real spiritual need. It is autonomous. That is not to say merely that criticism is the satisfaction of an individual's need for self-expression, which is obvious enough, but that it is not a secondary and derivative means of self-expression. In creative periods it may be apparently true that, as Dryden said, the corruption of a poet is the generation of a critic; but the reality, as Dryden himself signally proved, is that in a creative period the poet himself is the best critic.

If we may talk of periods at all, we are now in a critical period. The most forceful, the most creative literary intelligences of to-day have a bias towards criticism. It may be true that they are also lacking in energy; but their critical preoccupations derive most directly from their own awareness of this lack of energy, and of the extraordinary demands upon their fund of energy made by the social and spiritual disintegration of the age. To create significantly, Tolstoy once said, an artist must be on a level with the highest life-conception of his age. That position was not so hard to achieve fifty, even twenty, years ago; the artist could acquire it almost unconsciously. But to-day the situation is very different: there is no predominant life-conception which commands the adherence of the spiritual *élite*, if a snobbish expression may be used without snobbish intention. The artist who would be significant has first painfully to work out his own synthesis of experience, beginning from utter nakedness; nothing is *given* to him. What wonder if all his energies are employed in making a garment for himself when he has to build his loom and spin his thread?

Creation there is, of course, and creation in plenty, but it is seldom significant. It is based on either a naïve and ignorant, or a deliberate and labour-saving, exclusion of significant experience. For this sufficient reason contemporary criticism is but little concerned with contemporary creation, which it criticizes implicitly by ignoring; and that is a sufficient reply to those who inveigh against contemporary criticism for its lack of interest in the present. Because it is really interested in the present, and the future in the present, it turns aside from the irrelevance of so much contemporary creation. It has positive work to do; and to confuse positiveness with actuality, or 'news-value', is one of the most alarming symptoms of that disintegration against which modern criticism is dispersedly but pertinaciously striving. To justify literature—this is the object and aim of modern criticism. Thus stated, it seems either quixotic or otiose. It may be said, literature happens. That nowadays it does very little else is the gravamen common to all serious criticism. This criticism is well aware that no possible legislation can control the birth of the *εὐφυὴς ἢ μανικός*; but it insists that something can be done to make him *εὐφυής* rather than *μανικός* when once he has been born. This possible something is the re-elaboration of a system of values, the determination of the question whether literature is a sort of pastime or at best a private and esoteric religion—and eventually the creation of a common consciousness of literary responsibility which may serve as a palaestra for the right exercise of genius in happier days to come.

To this work Mr. Herbert Read has made a valuable contribution in his book of essays.[1] The scope and purpose is not quite adequately indicated in the title *Reason and Romanticism*, which may suggest that the author is engaged is positing anew the old and barren opposition between classicism and romanticism. Though there are moments when Mr. Read himself seems to give colour to this view of his undertaking, most of his pages are animated by a more generous breath, and are made exciting, and perhaps also a little elusive, by his effort towards a new synthesis. He avowedly finds the pattern of it in an old one, in the system of St. Thomas Aquinas, though we wonder sometimes whether his nearer inspiration should not be sought in Mr. Santayana, of whom, to our surprise, Mr. Read has little to say.

A new synthesis is a vague and, as used in late years, an ultra-romantic expression. We had best establish as clearly as we can the elements Mr. Read seeks to synthesize. He holds, in common with

1 *Reason and Romanticism:* Essays in Literary Criticism, by Herbert Read (Faber and Gwyer).

many others, that the old religious nexus of European civilization has been finally destroyed:

> The criticism of revealed religion has been operative not only on the empirical plane (which matters little) but also on the psychological plane. A religion like Christianity is built up largely of unconscious symbols: it finds its most powerful forces in subconscious processes, like prayer, grace, and faith. The effect of experimental science has been to destroy the unconsciousness of these symbols: it understands them and therefore equates them with conscious equivalents, which are no longer symbols, and which on that account no longer compel the imagination.

It may be remarked in passing that the word 'subconscious' in the second of these sentences come strangely from the pen of a Thomist. Perhaps it is a little more difficult than Mr. Read imagines to be a Thomist when you have abolished one term of the Thomist synthesis, which was between religion and science. For some cause, moreover, Mr. Read is a little shy of stating explicitly what is to take the place of religion in the new synthesis. It is, of course, literature. 'Science and Poetry have but one ideal, which is the satisfaction of the Reason.' At which the scientist, at least, will prick up his ears. What does Mr. Read mean by reason? It is, as he truly says, 'a very difficult word to use without confusion'.

> It is often used as a synonym for rationality, or even for a mechanistic logic. Reason should rather connote the widest evidence of the senses, and of all processes and instincts developed in the long history of man. It is the sum total of awareness, ordained and ordered to some specific end or object of attention.

The logician may make merry over that definition, not we. On the contrary, we heartily approve of the breadth of connotation Mr. Read seeks to give to the much-disputed word. However much he may abjure the epithet, we welcome him as a true humanist, for whom reason is rather a condition than a faculty. To possess reason is to have achieved an ordered and comprehensive experience. To this ordered and comprehensive experience science and poetry alike make their appeal, and by it they are judged.

But, it may be asked, why should the religious experience be denied a place in this ordered sum total of human awareness which is reason? Even if we accept Mr. Read's contention that the Christian symbolism has ceased to be valid, how does it follow that the mode of experience which found satisfaction in these symbols has ceased to exist? Are the experiences that were once called prayer and grace and faith no longer realities for the enlightened mind because it has reduced them, or believes it has reduced them, to subjective attitudes? It is just at this point that we should be grateful for a little more clarity in Mr. Read's exposition. We surmise, but we cannot be sure, that his aim is to transfer the religious response to literature and art. The religious experience, criticized and ordered by the intellect, will still hold its place in reason, but its mode of expression is changed. Into what, again we cannot precisely determine; but it seems that Mr. Read's solution is adumbrated in his interesting essay on 'The Nature of Metaphysical Poetry', which he describes as 'the emotional apprehension of thought'. Whether or not this description is too wide (for it would cover a good deal of poetry which Mr. Read would not, or would not yet, admit to be 'metaphysical'), it suggests that his ideal reconciliation of religion and science and poetry is in a sort of Aristotelian *θεωρία*. We should have to go to Mr. Santayana for a lucid statement of the ideal.

> In philosophy investigation and reasoning are only preparatory and servile parts, means to an end. They terminate in insight, or what in the noblest sense of the word may be called 'theory', *θεωρία*—a steady contemplation of all things in their order and worth. Such contemplation is imaginative. No one can reach it who has not enlarged his mind and tamed his heart. A philosopher who attains it is, for the moment, a poet; and a poet who turns his trained and practised imagination on the order of all things, or on anything in the light of the whole, is for the moment a philosopher.

Such a contemplation could be called indifferently poetic, philosophic, or religious. The essential of its attainment is that process of self-discipline which Mr. Santayana describes as an enlargement of the mind and a taming of the heart—or, in more schematic terms, that the man whose nature it is to advance by one of the three paths should at all times be mindful of the existence of the other two and accustom himself to reach the same position by working along them.

Mr. Read himself comes nearest to an explicit formulation of this ideal in some admirable words on the 'universal mind', which he puts forward as the ideal type of the critical mind.

> It has been a common saying, since Pope first said it, that a little learning is a dangerous thing. But far more dangerous is the learning which, though not little, is limited. It is idle to think that any good can come of a specialization that is not linked to some wider ethos, itself the product of a versatile intelligence, or that is not subordinate to general wisdom. And this applies not only to the scientist whom we regard rather rashly as the only specialist, but equally to the critic and the poet. A general idea, whether it be a new image or a new hypothesis, invariably springs across two hitherto widely separated concepts: it is the electric spark that plays suddenly *before* contact is made between approaching poles of magnetism. Only a universal mind is likely to contain these pairs of opposites, and for that single reason (and apart from the question of general wisdom) the

universal mind alone is capable of 'creative' thought. It may be said that this is an impossible ideal: that the rare occurrence of a universal mind, as in Aristotle, Dante, Leibniz, or Goethe, is the definite result of a *lusus naturae*—of chance, in fact. But the universal mind is not necessarily of this order, and universality is a quality possessed by all the rarer spirits of any age: it is a quality I would ascribe, not merely to Aristotle and Leibniz, but to Lucian, Diderot, and Ruskin, as well as to Emily Brontë. It does not mean the possession of all knowledge, or even, necessarily, of any knowledge at all. It does imply a capacity *to receive* all knowledge and events with equanimity and unprejudiced percipience; and to build up a positive attitude on this clear and serene perceptual basis.

That is excellently said; and it is to be remarked how close this ideal of the critical mind is to the ideal of the creative mind. Indeed, Mr. Read has already identified them by saying that the universal mind alone is capable of creative thought; and when he passes on to describe the potentially universal mind he comes as near as he may to identifying it with that 'experiencing nature' which Bagehot posited as the primary endowment of the creative writer. Yet, strangely enough, among the names which Mr. Read singles out we do not find Shakespeare, to whom Goethe of the universal mind ascribed a universality immeasurably greater than his own. And the omission, set beside the inclusion of Dante, is surely deliberate.

It is significant that this striking omission should correspond with what we can only call a bias towards intellectualism which, in spite of intermittent repression, emerges continually through this book. In the abstract Mr. Read sees clearly enough that the reason which he champions is of a higher order than any intellectualism; more remarkably still, when he comes to the specific exercise of his critical powers, as in the brilliant essays on Smollett and on Charlotte and Emily Brontë, his judgement is quite free from this bias. Nevertheless, in his more general discussions his comprehensive and creative conception of reason tends steadily to narrow in scope and to become purely discursive and conceptual. In his essay on metaphysical poetry he manages to superinduce in himself that uncritical frame of mind for which verse that contains a maximum of explicit conceptual thought becomes superior to poetry that is mindful of its proper function and excellence—namely, to pursue its rhythmic progress through an identity of image and idea. He becomes for the moment unable to distinguish between a mere transposition of discursive thinking into the form of poetry and the organic sequence of embodied intuitions which gives to great poetry its peculiar and inimitable design. This leads him greatly to overpraise Donne and to fail to recognize that Donne's glaring deficiencies in 'architectonic' are the confession of failure of a mind that was almost as undisciplined as it was active. 'Exactitude and all the last conditions of form,' said Goethe, 'can just as well accompany the formless, as the truly formed.' And Donne's exactitude is of this deceptive kind.

In spite, therefore, of his clear theoretic appreciation of the distinction, Mr. Read comes very near to confusing reason with intelligence. His own search for a precise terminology has had the unexpected effect of making him more liable to the error than of safeguarding him against it. Poetry, he says at the end of a rather caustic criticism of Mr. George Moore's anthology of 'Pure Poetry', is to be judged 'by the quality of intelligence inherent in the poem'. 'But what,' he rightly anticipates our asking, 'is intelligence?' And he replies:

> It is a question I have tried to answer generally in this book; here it will be sufficient to say that it is the same faculty of 'direct apprehension' already distinguished by mediaeval philosophy, and since then somewhat compromised, in differing degrees, by Descartes, Spinoza, and Bergson. It is dangerous perhaps to describe it as a 'faculty', for it is in reality but one aspect of the single faculty of apprehension. It is perhaps only the distinction between reason which is concentrated on a single object and reason which is discursive. It is a distinction clearly and for all time made by no less an authority than St. Thomas Aquinas: 'intelligere enim est simpliciter veritatem intelligibilem apprehendere: ratiocinari autem est procedere de uno intellecto ad aliud, ad veritatem intelligibilem cognoscendam.'

The distinction may have been made clearly and for all time, but to a modern mind the word 'intelligence' does not connote the faculty or act of 'simple apprehension of truth'. To a modern mind that act or faculty is 'intuition'. Whether we know as much as we ought to know about intuition may be doubted, but we shall not increase our knowledge by calling it intelligence. We shall only wander in a maze of misunderstandings. Synthesis is certainly desirable, but we shall pay too heavy a price for it if we are to be required to confound realities which are different.

Mr. Read's problem, which he has not solved but has rather concealed from himself, is to determine the nature of 'intuition'. His reference to the statement and authority of St. Thomas settles nothing; in fact it brings him only to a position identical with that of Signor Croce, for whom intuitions are primary perceptions—the elements of thought. But such intuitions are obviously not the intuitions with which we are concerned in a great poem. These are not primary and direct perceptions, but complex and elaborate attitudes to whose formation both sense-perceptions and thought-intuitions have contributed; and, though it would be true to say that the validity and worth of the work depend upon the degree to which it satisfies the reason, in Mr. Read's largest interpretation of the word, it is not to be forgotten that this satisfaction of the reason (in the case of a true work of art) is discovered well after the experience. The great poem acts like a magnet on the paper of iron filings; it *creates* a new order in our experience, and itself enlarges our conception of reason. It may give some small stay to our hunger for schematism to assimilate this mysterious operation of the work of literature to the direct and simple apprehension of the truth of an axiom of Euclid, but in reality they are very different; and by insisting upon this premature identification we run a serious risk of exaggerating the purely intellectual element in the work of literature and of demanding from it a quality that it does not, and ought not to, possess.

For if, as we with Mr. Read believe, reason is ordered experience and the highest reason is the most comprehensive experience rightly ordered, what grounds have we for supposing that this order is an intellectual order? There is observable in the great province of life to which we human beings belong another kind of order than the geometric or intellectual; there is organic order. And that is the kind of order we should naturally suppose to be appropriate to human experience. That also is the kind of order we find in the highest literature. We cannot say, even in the simplest instance, that we 'understand' an organism; neither ought we to say that we must abjure our understanding ('plunge into the life-stream') to apprehend it; rather, perhaps, that we must transcend our understanding. Transcend is a dangerous word; but we are forced to use some term to designate the middle path between understanding and nescience. The middle path exists; it is positive and autonomous. It is that which Pascal strove to distinguish when he contrasted the *esprit de finesse* with the *esprit de géométrie*. May we not hazard the conjecture that it alone can truly be called the path of reason? It is not easy to discover or to tread. The temptation to reduce reason to understanding is persistent, and the consequences of surrendering to it, for the individual and for society alike, pernicious. For the feelings, as Coleridge said, 'will set up their standard against the understanding, whenever the understanding has renounced its allegiance to the reason'. That is the explanation of the extravagances of romanticism in the large history of the human spirit. But the function of the individual is to overcome this secular antinomy in himself. The insurgence of feeling against the understanding, the war of the romantic against the classic, is no less an individual than a social condition. But neither side will ever gain a victory that is permanent; the true, the positive, the creative outcome of the struggle is a harmonious unity. The intelligence as such will never succeed in controlling the emotions, only in killing them: 'le cœur a ses raisons . . .' It is reason that should control both.

Yet the notion of control is itself misleading and irrelevant. Reason is born of the pregnant opposition between intelligence and feeling, Mind and Heart; and they exist no longer in themselves, but in their offspring.[1] There is a complete interfusion of understanding and emotion, so that both are different in nature from what they were before. This organic evolution of the consciousness which both Goethe and Coleridge strove, not wholly in vain, to describe and to communicate finds its appropriate object of contemplation in an organic universe: to this end indeed was it born, and from the failure of the effort to accommodate emotional experience of the living world, within and without, to intellectual categories, it took its origin. Reason is the understanding of life.

Of this possible condition wherein, by virtue of the organic order achieved within the individual consciousness, a comprehension of the organic order of human experience is attained, the manifold complex and harmonious satisfactions of the great work of literature are, as it were, premonitory. More than that, they are directly creative of it. A great work of literature does not so much satisfy the reason as bring it to birth within ourselves. We experience its potency long before we can appreciate the worth and significance of the experience; it works in ways beyond our conscious control. To seek consciously to control it is a temptation and an error: we succeed only in making ourselves immune from its beneficent operation. But once we know, by subtle and unmistakable signs, that a creative contact has been established, that our experience has become, in a single moment, both richer and more serene, then it is our manifest

[1] Those who have had the patience to make themselves familiar with Blake's symbols—a patience most richly rewarded, notwithstanding the contrary opinion of Mr. J. C. Squire—will know a more precise and more satisfying language than mine for expressing the distinctions and relations adumbrated in this essay. Reason, in the sense in which I use it in this essay, is the creative harmony of Blake's fourfold man. And the usurpation of control by the Intelligence is precisely that Tyranny of Urizen which is one of the main themes of his prophetic books. What I have tried to say in the concluding pages of this essay is said, more pregnantly, by Blake in seven lines of *Milton* (p. 46):

> All that can be annihilated must be annihilated
> That the Children of Jerusalem may be saved from slavery.
> There is a Negation, & there is a Contrary:
> The Negation must be destroy'd to redeem the Contraries.
> The Negation is the Spectre, the Reasoning Power in Man:
> This is a false Body, an Incrustation over my Immortal
> Spirit, a Selfhood which must be put off & annihilated alway.

This work of liberation is, for Blake, the work of the Poetic Genius. And it is a principle with Blake that 'the Poetic Genius is the true Man, and that the body or outward form of Man is derived from the Poetic Genius' (*All Religions are One*). This truth Blake afterward expressed by saying 'The imagination is not a State: it is the Human Existence itself' (*Milton*, p. 35).

duty to bring the details of the strange process into the full light of our consciousness. Only thus can we consolidate our position on the heights that genius has won for us. The man who leaves the poetic experience as an isolated miracle is not merely uncritical, he is not truly alive. He must, for his own sake, co-ordinate it. But this co-ordination cannot be accomplished by reducing the experience to an intellectual category which it transcended. We have been granted a moment of the pure life of Reason; it is our duty not to degrade it into a function of our ordinary consciousness, but to seek a way to lift our ordinary consciousness to the condition we have been privileged to share. It is, after all, not an alien condition, but our own, because we have been proved capable of it.

13

LESSING

From Countries of the Mind, Second Series.

Gotthold Ephraim Lessing made one serious attempt to advance his worldly fortunes. In 1760, during the Seven Years War, he became Secretary to General Tauentzien, the military governor of Breslau, one of whose duties was to restore his master Frederick's finances in the good old way by calling in the sound Saxon money and issuing a debased coinage in its stead. Such profitable operations being full of pickings, Lessing had his chance, and took it, though not so well as the morality of the day demanded. But having money and being unused to it, he felt that it burned his pockets. Part he spent in collecting a magnificent library (which was sensible), part in playing faro for high stakes (which he said was hygienic). The hours he kept were in themselves deplorable; and they were vexatious to the good baker with whom he lodged. The baker took an odd revenge. He made a new mould for his gingerbread cakes, and had it carved with a caricature of Lessing dressed as a night-watchman, and his name in full—Gotthold Ephraim Lessing—below the effigy. Long after his death the gingerbread Lessing was still being eaten by the small boys of Breslau.

So runs the story: and it is symbolic. Not many men of letters have lent themselves to a gingerbread revenge, or achieved so queer an immortality. But in Lessing there was something of which gingerbread pictures, clay-pipe figureheads, or Toby-jugs could, not inappropriately, be made. He was solid. Between him and common reality there was a force of mutual attraction like gravity. He reminds one, in some essentials, of Dr. Johnson. He might have refuted Berkeley by kicking a stone; and the sweat that ran down his face while he sat at the faro table has a sort of kinship with the knotted veins of Johnson's forehead when he sat down to one of his voracious meals. They had their feet not of clay, but on it; they were great men of letters, but we remember them as great men.

That is, if we remember Lessing at all. Even the *Laokoon* seems to be out of fashion nowadays, and to have become demoded like the piece of statuary from which it arose. We suspect that Mr. Irving Babbitt's *New Laokoon* is more familiar to the present generation than Lessing's old one. His discoveries have become commonplaces, his boundaries are landmarks. So also have Aristotle's; to whom, nevertheless, we pay lip-homage. But not to Lessing. Yet he was, of all the critics since Aristotle, the most truly Aristotelian; if Aristotle deserves our homage, as he surely does, so does Lessing—and in one sense even more than Aristotle himself, for he first showed the world how to see Aristotle as a master of method, not a mine of maxims. Since it is not an easy lesson to learn, we need not wonder that criticism has not greatly profited by his example. To use Aristotle's method one needs to be almost an Aristotle—and Lessing was.

He was, in short, a very great critic. Probably the greatest literary critic we have had in Europe—not in virtue of the *Laokoon*, though that is possibly his masterpiece, but in virtue of his qualities which are to be discovered everywhere in his work—in his *Dramaturgie*, and in those *Kleine Schriften* which Coleridge (to one's surprise) declared he read every year as a model of critical prose—and are so finely manifest in the *Laokoon*. The chief of these qualities are two. One, which we expect naturally from so great a disciple of Aristotle, is a passion for clear distinction that never loses sight of the particulars to be distinguished. Drama and Art never become abstract for Lessing; they are always these dramas—and he seems to know all of them—and these works of art—and he seems to know a prodigious number even of them. He never talks by hearsay. The second quality is one which we do not naturally expect from a great disciple of Aristotle, not because it is not in Aristotle—it is in him abundantly—but because it is not obvious in the Aristotle expurgated by orthodoxy who is usually put forward for admiration to-day. It is a sense of the genetic and organic in things, and in the mind which strives to master them—of a creative *φύσις*; an attitude not at all to be confused with what is vaguely called the evolutionary outlook, or at least not to be equated with any facile version of Darwinism, but an instinctive or intuitive aversion from absolutes—a feeling that truth is as much a quality of the minds that seek it as of the things wherein they find it. The search is as important as the discovery, the method as the matter. 'The manner in which one has come to a matter is as valuable', Lessing wrote in the *Kleine Schriften,* 'and even as instructive as the matter itself.' And it was this sense of a dynamic governing the motions of the mind which made him so masterly an interpreter of Aristotle. He had, what Aristotle had, a mind so naturally comprehensive that it could, so to speak, begin anywhere; he was aware that approaches to the truth are many, and that all statements of it have an element of approximation. He held that it is by our power to hold various approximations together in a single act of apprehension that we show our capacity for truth. In this spirit he interpreted Aristotle, not in accordance with the demands of an impossible and unnatural clarity, but by himself; he did not regard the Poetics as an inviolable Scripture, but sought to learn how to understand them by studying the Rhetoric and the Ethics. It was the mind not the maxims of the master that fascinated him. He might have said of him what he said of Shakespeare, that he 'demands to be studied, not be plundered'. But the mind and the maxims of Aristotle were not to be separated; they were interdependent.

I would seem to set aside Aristotle's authority [he wrote in the *Dramaturgie*] if only I could set aside his reasons. I have my own ideas about the origin and basis of this philosopher's Poetics, which I have not space to give here, yet I do not hesitate to declare (even at the cost of being laughed at in these enlightened times) that I consider them infallible as Euclid's Elements. Their fundamental principles are just as true and certain, only not so definite, and therefore were exposed to misconstruction. I trust to prove incontrovertibly, of tragedy in particular, that it cannot depart a step from the rules of Aristotle without departing just so far from perfection.

There speaks not so much of the opposite as the superior of the dogmatic mind. The dogmatic mind reveres principles without understanding them; its opposite rejects principles without understanding them. Lessing was never, like the mere anarchist, afraid of dogma; he only insisted on understanding it, so that it was for him no longer dogma. This quality of mind is strikingly displayed in the *Laokoon*. To the casual glance, which is all he gets to-day, he appears to be reverential to classical authority. The matter in which his argument moves is wholly classical. It is only when we have begun to wrestle with the substance of his book that we discern that he is moving amongst the writers of antiquity as a man amongst men, discriminating, deciding values, accepting this as true, rejecting that as false, allowing nothing that he does not understand. 'We read fine things,' said Keats, 'but we do not understand them till we have gone the same steps as the author.' Lessing's ratification of classical values by his own experience is of this kind. He reanimates, and is reanimated by, the mind of antiquity.

That is why the *Laokoon* is a living book. The breath of life is in its style—swift, clear, colloquial, pungent—the style of a real experience, cutting easily and with a laugh through the tangled confusions of pedantic criticism. Virgil's Laocoon wears his priestly robe; the figure in the statue is naked. Why, asked the critics, this offence against the decorum? Because, they said, statuary cannot imitate drapery. 'The old artists might have laughed at the objection, but I know not what they would have said to this manner of answering it.' Then from his silver bow, Lessing lets fly his real shaft:

> In poetry a robe is no robe. It conceals nothing. Our imagination sees through it in every part. Whether Virgil's Laocoon be clothed or not, the agony in every fibre of his body is equally visible.

How obvious! Yet no one had thought of it before. Nor even to-day is it by any means as obvious to criticism as it was to Lessing, that the application of the words 'imagery' and 'picture' to a work of literature is almost wholly a metaphor.

> A picture in poetry is not necessarily one that can be transferred to canvas. But every touch, or combination of touches, by means of which the poet brings his subject so vividly before us that we are more conscious of the subject than of his words, is picturesque and makes what we call a picture; that is, it produces that degree of illusion which a painted picture is peculiarly qualified to excite, and which we in fact most frequently and naturally experience in the contemplation of the painted canvas.
>
> Experience shows that the poet can produce this degree of illusion by the representation of other than visible objects. He therefore has at his command whole classes of subjects which elude the artist. Dryden's 'Ode on St. Cecilia's Day' is full of musical pictures, but gives no employment to the brush. But I will not lose myself in examples of this kind; after all they teach us little more than that colours are not tones, and ears not eyes.

That is, or it should be, one of the great commonplaces of literary criticism; even in translation it shows the easy vigour of Lessing's prose. Reading it, one can hardly believe that 'Ut pictura poesis' had reigned unchallenged for a century before it, or that it would have been possible after it for the confusion to lift its head again.

Lessing wrote plays. *Minna von Barnhelm* and *Nathan der Weise* have become classics of the German theatre. But he knew the real nature of his own eminence. He was, first and foremost and all his life long, a critic. Even *Minna von Barnhelm* was written rather to show the nugatory German drama how it might advance to some contact with reality than from autonomous impulse; and *Nathan der Weise* was deliberate propaganda for the cause which in his later life he had most deeply at heart. At the end of the *Dramaturgie* he explained himself and vindicated his own calling:

> I am neither actor not poet. It is true I have sometimes had the honour of being regarded as a poet, but only because I have been misunderstood. It is wrong to draw such generous inferences from the few dramatic attempts I have ventured. Not everyone who picks up a brush and lays on colours is a painter. My earliest attempts were made at that time of life when we are only too ready to regard inclination and facility as genius.

What is tolerable in my later attempts is due, I know well, simply and solely to criticism. I have always felt ashamed and annoyed when I have read or heard anything in disparagement of criticism. It is said to suppress genius; but I flatter myself that I have gained from it something very nearly approaching genius. I am a lame man who cannot possibly be edified by abuse of his crutch.

Criticism, as Lessing understood and practised it, was comprehensive and conscious of itself. It therefore passed continually into history, into philosophy and into religion. Yet he was, for most of his life, an ill-paid journeyman of letters; a journalist he would be called to-day, though it is difficult to conceive how a mind so universal would find expression under modern conditions of journalism. His fighting prose might be popular, but his seriousness and profundity would not. One can imagine well enough the general applause at some of his sallies. It had been written: Nobody will deny that the German theatre owes much of its improvement to Professor Gottsched. 'I am that Nobody,' says Lessing. 'I deny it entirely.' There seems nothing more to say.

But Lessing had another fling at Gottsched in the then new pages of the *Vossische Zeitung*, where he inserted this brief review of Gottsched's poems:

> The outside is so excellent that we hope it will do the bookseller's shop great credit, and we wish it will long do so. To give an adequate idea of the inside is beyond our powers. These poems cost 2 thalers, 4 groschen. Two thalers pay for the absurd, and four groschen about cover the useful.

It would be cruel, had it not been so just and so necessary. The dilettante professors who composed cultivated Germany when Lessing entered the arena had to be smitten hip and thigh if a genuine German culture was to have room to grow. Lessing the journalist made fun of them, Lessing the scholar confuted them; and though a professorship was his only hope of security, he refused to join their ranks. The sheer strength of the man who thus, practically single-handed, cleared the path for German literature was prodigious. He created a public and imposed himself upon it; instead of the professor of a university, he made himself the teacher of Germany. 'What would you?' he replied to his friends who remonstrated with him for turning to hack translation, when the outbreak of the Seven Years War brought him once more to hardship. 'My writings are the productions of a man who is an author partly by inclination, partly by force. I cannot study at my own expense, so I try to do so at the expense of the public.' In this spirit, and by this method, Lessing pursued his task. He conducted his search for truth at the expense, and in the eyes, of the public.

But it was not until he was forty and had obtained the small security of a post as Librarian to the Duke of Brunswick at Wolfenbüttel that his dominant interest could fully reveal itself. This was religion. From early youth Lessing had been dissatisfied alike with orthodoxy, both Catholic and Lutheran, and with Voltairian rationalism. He had been educated to be, like his father, a Lutheran pastor, and he had very firmly refused. He had no patience with a nominal Christianity, and no intention of joining its *corps de garde*. 'So long as I do not see', he wrote to his father at twenty, 'the foremost command of the Christian religion, to love our enemies, better observed, so long shall I doubt whether those are Christians who profess themselves such. . . .' From that bad beginning he never returned; but his interest in religion grew steadily deeper. He had only just begun to make his mark in Berlin when he went off to Wittenberg for two years, mainly to study the history of Christianity; and in his writings of that time the main lines of his future thinking already emerge. Heresies began to fascinate him, on the principle that, as he said later concerning Berengarius, 'the thing we call heretic has one very good side. It means a person who has at least wished to see with his own eyes.' And Lessing set about a series of rehabilitations (*Rettungen*). It was an unusual enterprise; but Lessing was an unusual man. He was himself rooted in and detached from Christianity. He could understand, experience, and sympathize with religious impulse and religious conviction: it never seemed to him, as it did to the fashionable scepticism of his age, an unintelligible aberration of the human mind. To such an attitude, a heresy was as interesting and as valuable as an orthodoxy, and from his study of the heresies Lessing gained, what subsequent students of Church history have sometimes gained, a passionate hatred of religious intolerance. But he was a wiser man than Voltaire; he never indulged the fancy that the way to extirpate religious intolerance was to extirpate religion. It was to purify religion—and this chiefly by two means; by insisting that the centre of gravity of religion lay not in theology, but in conduct, and by giving religion the courage to look fearlessly at its own history.

By these means he believed he was contributing to a development of Christianity that was inevitable. That the nominally Christian mind should be made to appreciate that an intolerant Christianity was no Christianity at all was an obvious moral preliminary to a religious or philosophical attitude perhaps not so obvious, but in Lessing's view no less necessary. This was to regard the history of Christianity genetically, and to be ever mindful of the fact that it had been manifested through fallible and imperfect human instruments. Already at Wittenberg, in a rehabilitation of Lemnius, he had applied this humanistic calculus to Luther. Lemnius had been, he discovered, the victim of Luther's violent temper, and historical truth had been distorted in order that Luther's glory might not be tarnished.

> I reverence Luther so highly that on consideration I am heartily glad to have discovered a few failings in him, otherwise I should have been in danger of deifying him. The traces of common humanity I find in him are as precious to me as his most dazzling perfections: they are even more instructive than all these taken together. God! What a fearful lesson for our pride! How anger and revenge may degrade the holiest! But would a less vehement spirit have been capable of Luther's achievements? Certainly not. Let us therefore admire the wise Providence that can use even imperfections for its instrument. . . . In fact what does it matter what instruments God has employed? He does not always use the most blameless, but the most convenient. If envy was the source of the Reformation, would to God all envy might have such fortunate consequences.

At the end of this essay was the sting. Since Luther was but a man, he concluded, there was no reason why Protestantism should remain for ever at the point of enlightenment where Luther had left it.

This early essay, with its dangerous or pregnant principle that all history is significant of the Divine purpose, provided it be read with eyes as free from bias as contemporary knowledge will allow, was itself a contribution to the further enlightenment of Protestantism. If that be granted of the past, Lessing was well aware, it must be granted also of the present which knows the past; and all that the human mind can do in the way of realizing the past is a necessary furtherance of the Divine economy. This effort to realize the past is the effort which gives unity to all Lessing's work. It is as manifest in his *Laokoon*, in the recurrent discussion of Aristotle in his *Dramaturgie*, in the archaeological studies of his *Contributions*, as it is in the religious and theological writing which wholly occupied the later years of his life. But to realize the past, for Lessing, was not to rationalize it; hence he was a baffling figure to contemporary rationalists. Reason and rationalism were for him two different things. Reason was nourished by the imaginative apprehension which elicited truth from facts; it was essentially a submission to facts: whereas rationalism was an attempt to tyrannize over them. Thus historical criticism, of which Lessing was virtually the discoverer, was the most appropriate field for the exercise of reason. Of true historical criticism rationalism was incapable, because it denied the validity, and even the existence, of many of the profoundest impulses at work in history. Reason was not afraid of mystery; nor did it demand absolute truth. Its delight was in the search for truth, and in the comprehensiveness with which it was pursued. Again it was at

Wittenberg, that is when Lessing was only twenty-two, that he outlined his own ideal, in a criticism of the specialist mind:

> Everything outside his own specialism is small to him, not because it really looks small to him, but because he does not see it at all: it lies entirely outside his vision. His eyes may be as sharp as they please: one quality is wanting to make them really good eyes. They are as immovable on his head, as his head is immovable on his body. Therefore he can see only those objects before which his whole body is planted. He knows nothing of the rapid side-glances so necessary to the survey of a great whole.

No single sentence better than the last could convey the distinctive quality of Lessing's mind, or his conception of the training and the use of reason.

The full employment of this reason he held, very definitely, to be a religious duty of man: *vitai lampada tradit*. In the religious discussion and polemic to which he devoted all the last years of his life, he came inevitably to hold a position unintelligible to nearly all his contemporaries. He had been, and he always remained, an admirer of Luther; but for Lutheran orthodoxy he felt a contempt which he was quite willing to express. On the other hand, with Catholic orthodoxy he felt the genuine sympathy that it could not fail to arouse in a man of his historical imagination. Such an attitude appeared merely capricious; and his bewildered Lutheran opponents ascribed it to a subtle diplomacy by which Lessing aimed at dividing Catholic against Protestant on the Aulic Council, and so avoiding suppression by the censorship. They could not see that an admiration of Lutheran orthodoxy was really incompatible with a genuine admiration of Luther. Lessing's perfectly reasonable claim that he himself was the genuine Lutheran infuriated them:

> The true Lutheran [he wrote in *Anti-Göeze*] does not wish to be defended by Luther's writings, but by Luther's spirit; and Luther's spirit absolutely demands that no man be hindered from advancing in his own manner towards the knowledge of truth. But *all* are hindered if one be forbidden to impart his progress to others. Reverend Sir, if you cause our Lutheran pastors to become our popes, to prescribe to us where we must stop in our investigation of Scriptures, to place limits to our investigation and to the publication of our results: then I am the first to exchange these little popes for the big one.

That was written in reply to Goeze's appeal that the censor should forbid Lessing's publication of the famous Wolfenbüttel Fragments, the analysis of Christian origins which Reimarus, the Hamburg physician, had left behind in manuscript. With the publication of these fragments historical criticism of the New Testament began. Lessing did not identify himself with the theses of Reimarus, but he fought, in his most brilliant manner, for a hearing for them; and when he had reduced his adversary Goeze to silence, a great victory had been won for free inquiry, and a clear demonstration made that there can be no reasonable halting-place on the slippery slope of dogmatic Protestantism.

It was Lessing's clear perception of this which brought him into seeming alliance with Catholic orthodoxy, which has an equally clear perception of the ultimate destiny of dogmatic Protestantism, the difference being that Catholic orthodoxy regards as a danger what Lessing regarded as a destiny. The difference is great, but it is a difference of a kind that permits a clear understanding between the differing parties:

> I am more concerned [he wrote to his brother Karl] about sound reason than about theology, and I prefer the old orthodox theology, which is tolerant at bottom, because it is at open warfare with sound reason, whereas the new theology tries to bribe it. I make peace with my open enemies so that I may be better on my guard against my secret ones.

Though in one sense Lessing was the father of the Modernists, it is easy to see from this statement of the situation that he would have disowned his children. On the other hand, he would never have admitted the cogency of the dilemma put forward by those who maintain that the only alternative to orthodoxy is atheism. He would never have admitted that he himself was an atheist, and no reasonable student of his life and work could imagine he was.

Nor was he a Deist. What he was cannot be easily defined. But the most memorable of his later works, *Nathan the Wise* and *The Education of the Human Race*, were devoted to making his position unmistakable. The main thesis of *The Education* was that revelation, in the history of the Christian religion, was an anticipation of reason—the means employed by the divine economy for inculcating truths too difficult for the unripe understanding of the race. The religious progress of the race therefore consisted in outgrowing the need of revelation. In more modern language, Lessing held that the great religious intuitions were prophetic of truths to be apprehended by reason. The final purpose of Christianity was to become unnecessary. With the greater freedom allowed him by the dramatic form, he drove home his point in *Nathan the Wise*. In the play the one genuine Christian is the lay-brother, noble-hearted and simple-minded. The Patriarch is a mere unscrupulous schemer, while the Templar passes beyond Christianity to an apprehension of universal truth, and touches the wisdom of Nathan. The bitter criticism of conventional Christianity comes from a Moslem, Saladin's sister, Sittah.

Their pride is to be Christians, never men.
Ay, even that which since their Founder's time
Hath tinged their superstition with a touch
Of pure humanity, is prized by them
Never because 'tis human, but because
'Twas preached and practised by their Jesus Christ.
'Tis well for them he was so rare a man;
Well that they take his virtues upon trust;
But what to them the virtues of their Christ?
'Tis not his virtue, but his name alone
They seek to spread, that it may dominate
And cloud the names of other noble men.

'Never because 'tis human.' Lessing was, indeed, a humanist; and being a true humanist he was also perforce a naturalist. To the Christian piety of Daya, who must see a miracle in the rescue of Recha by the Templar, Nathan replies:

To me the greatest miracle is this,
That many a veritable miracle
By use and wont grows stale and commonplace.
But for this universal miracle
A thinking man had ne'er confined the name
To those reputed miracles alone
Which startle children, ay and older fools
Ever agape for what is strange and new
And out of Nature's course.

And when Daya demands to know what harm there is in their thinking that an angel rescued Recha, since with such a belief they feel themselves nearer to 'the great inscrutable first Cause of their deliverance', Nathan replies that it is

Pride, and only pride!
The iron pot longs to be lifted up
By tongs of silver from the kitchen fire
That it may think itself a silver urn.

A true humility was inseparable from Lessing's ideal of a religion from which all superstition had been eliminated. He detected—and his eyes were keen—a false humility in the apparent sacrifice of reason made by orthodoxy. True humility lay in the patient submission to Nature, of which man also was a part, and the illumination of reason which attended upon that submission. Religion, which cannot be reconciled with the intelligence, would have no difficulty in reconciliation with reason, for these were one. Lessing's life was a hard one, but it had the beauty which comes of deep inward coherence.

He never took the easy way when one more difficult led straighter to the truth he sought. His work is a monument to the validity of his own unshakable conviction that not the possession of truth but the passion, the sincerity, and the tolerance with which it is sought, is the noblest achievement of humanity.

14

'BEAUTY IN ALL THINGS'

From Keats and Shakespeare *(Oxford University Press, 1925), pages 69–75.*

THE greatest of all Keats' long poems is to me undoubtedly *Hyperion*, whether we consider it in its original and familiar form, as it appeared in the 1820 volume, or in the revised form as *The Fall of Hyperion: a Dream*. But in neither form is *Hyperion* as perfect as the *Odes*. They have the same deep sufficiency of inspiration and the same wealth of profound experience as *Hyperion*, and they have a perfection of form which *Hyperion* has not. Still, *Hyperion* is the greater achievement. It was begun in the autumn of this year 1818, when Keats had returned ill from his Scottish tour and was spending painful days at the bedside of his dying brother, dying of the same disease of which Keats' obstinate sore-throat was a premonitory symptom.

Hyperion differs from all Keats' other poems in one important respect. Its composition was frequently interrupted and abandoned and resumed. *Endymion, Isabella, The Eve of St. Agnes, Lamia* were all written straight ahead. The *Odes*—so far as we can tell—were each written in one piece. But *Hyperion* was composed quite differently. It is impossible to say with the certainty of external evidence when many parts of it were written. We know that it was begun in the September of 1818, that it was taken up again in January and the early spring of 1819, that a complete recast of the poem was begun in the summer, and finally that the poem was abandoned altogether in both forms in September 1819. In this book the attempt is made to prove by internal evidence that the first two books of *Hyperion* were written before the end of 1819; but that the main portion of the third book belongs to a different and later period of Keats' development.

A consideration of the causes why *Hyperion* was abandoned does not belong to this year 1818, but only a consideration of the causes why it was begun. We may say that Keats had fallen under the spell of Milton: and, if we remember the nature of the man of whom we are speaking, the phrase will pass. But few of those who use the phrase do remember the nature of the man of whom they use it, and therefore they forget that the kind of spell which Milton had for Keats was in the nature of things limited and circumscribed. We need only to remember the letter to Reynolds, in which Keats compares Milton with Wordsworth, and decides that Wordsworth 'thinks deeper into the human heart' to see that Milton could not finally satisfy Keats, and to understand the nature of the spell which Milton exerted upon him. It was the spell of a great technique and a prodigious art; and, more potent than this, it was the spell of a verse which could be constructed by a man of genius in abstraction from the torment of experience. Milton held for Keats the promise of a release from the pain of life, of a world of abstractions into which he could enter and be free, where his poetic genius would be nobly occupied and his overstrained nerves relaxed. Towards the end of September, when the work on *Hyperion* was well begun, he wrote to Reynolds, who was about to be married:

> I conjure you to think at present of nothing but pleasure. . . . I pity you as much that it cannot last for ever, as I do myself now drinking bitters. . . . This morning Poetry has conquered—I have relapsed into those abstractions which are my only life. . . .

On the same day he wrote to Dilke:

> I wish I could say Tom was any better. His identity presses on me so all day that I am obliged to go out—and although I intended to have given some time to study alone, I am obliged to plunge into abstract images to ease myself of his countenance, his voice, and feebleness.

Hyperion and Miltonics were a refuge of abstractions that Keats was building for himself to shut out the concrete world. But the hiding place which an architect of genius builds for himself is a palace. I am not, as I hope to prove abundantly, trying to diminish by a single scruple the sublime beauty of *Hyperion*. For me, taken together with its recast induction, it is the pinnacle of Keats' actual achievement; but because I wish to show that Keats was greater, far greater, than his actual achievement, because I wish to present him as the perfect type of the great poet, as a poetic genius second only to Shakespeare in our literature, and of the same pattern as Shakespeare, I am concerned at this moment to show that *Hyperion* was not central to Keats' poetic purposes. Those purposes were persistent, and I have tried to show their inward nature. They had a definite outward embodiment also. Keats' purpose was not to write epics, or even odes, but to write plays; all the poems he wrote from *Endymion* onwards were but a step towards his 'chief attempt in the drama'; he desired to reveal the truth of human life, not through abstractions, but in a mirrored reflection of life itself. The drama as the supreme height of literature was a necessary part of Keats' 'vast idea'; it was in the hierarchy of literary forms that alone which permitted the identification of the poet with every manifestation of the human universe, which as he had told Woodhouse in a letter of this time (27th October) was fundamental to the poetical character.

> As to the poetical character itself [he wrote]—I mean that sort, of which, if I am anything, I am a member; that sort distinguished from the Wordsworthian or egotistical Sublime— . . . it is not itself—it has no self.—It is everything and nothing.—It has no character—it enjoys light and shade; it lives in gusto, be it foul or fair, high or low, rich or poor, mean or elevated. It has as much delight in conceiving an Iago as an Imogen. What shocks the virtuous philosopher delights the chameleon poet. . . . A poet is the most unpoetical of any thing in existence, because he has no Identity—he is continually in for and filling some other body.

Keats saw truly into the nature of his own genius. It was, as we say nowadays, objective; it was concrete; it moved not in a world of philosophic thought and abstraction, but in a world of imaginative realizations. It was purely and truly poetic; and it turned towards the drama as the form which offered the most complete fulfilment of its own nature. At the beginning of this year (30th January) he had written to Taylor, his publisher, concerning the passage of *Endymion*, beginning 'Wherein lies happiness, Peona', that his having written that argument would perhaps be of the greatest service to him of anything he ever did.

> It set before me the gradations of happiness, even like a kind of pleasure thermometer, and is my first step towards the chief attempt in the drama. The playing of different natures with joy and Sorrow.

The drama, then, as the necessary form of 'the vast idea', was already an essential part of Keats' intention; and perhaps we have gained some perception of what was to be embodied in it—the apprehension of Beauty as Truth, the high reason which brings with it 'the love of good and ill', the acceptance of the burden of the mystery as a thing not to be dissipated by some trick of the intellect, or by some self-delusion imposed by 'an irritable reaching after fact and reason'. But we shall find no deeper, nor any more transparent, phrase for the content of Keats' ideal poetry than his own familiar words: 'the principle of beauty in all things'.

This phrase is usually and rightly remembered in the form in which Keats wrote it to Fanny Brawne soon after the haemorrhage which told him of his inevitable end. 'If I should die, said I to myself, I have left no immortal work behind me, nothing to make my friends proud of my memory, but I have loved the principle of beauty in all things, and if I had had time, I would have made myself remembered.' It seems almost a sacrilege to anatomize words so poignant, so lovely. They are locked up in men's hearts for ever, as the voice of one of the bravest and wisest and most beautiful spirits this England has been privileged to engender—the voice of one who is passed beyond pride and beyond humility. But because they are so precious and so haunting, it is our duty to know what they mean.

The meaning of the words 'I have loved the principle of beauty in all things' is not obvious. Of course, if they are taken vaguely as meaning 'I have loved beauty', there is no difficulty; and since I have never seen an admission that a difficulty exists, I suppose that this vague sense is the one that is usually given to them. It seems clear to me that they mean more than this; but when we try to extract the further meaning from them, by giving each words its full weight, the difficulty begins. For we can read them in two ways, thus: 'I have loved the principle of beauty—in all things', or, 'I have loved the principle—of beauty in all things'. Between these two interpretations there is a vital difference. In the first case 'principle' means 'element': it is the old *principium* of the scholastic philosophers which survives in such a phrase as 'the vital principle': and Keats' sentence will run 'I have loved the element of beauty—in all things.' And, again, even this is not quite clear: he may be saying that he has loved this element of beauty, in whatsoever things he has found it, or he may be saying that he has loved this element of beauty, and he has found it in all things. Even there the difference is important: but whichever of these interpretations we choose, the underlying thought is the famous thought of Plato: that there is an ideal and perfect Beauty which is partially manifested, as a shadow is a manifestation of the object which casts it, in the beautiful things of earth. 'This ideal beauty,' Keats will then be saying, 'I have loved'; and there is no means of telling whether he is saying further that he has loved it in whatsoever thing he has found it, or that he has found it in everything.

This may appear a singularly abstruse sort of quibbling. I ask those who shrink from it to remember that we are dealing with Keats' central thought, and that the central thought of a poetic genius such as his is not likely to be simple to understand; I ask them also to realize that there is all the difference in the world between the statement 'I have loved beauty, and beauty is in all things' and the statment 'I have loved all beautiful things'. The one implies acceptance, the other, rejection. With a sense of that difference in our minds, and a sense also of the importance of deciding which was Keats' belief, let us read the sentence as I believe it should be read, not as 'I have loved the principle of beauty—in all things', but as 'I have loved the principle—of beauty in all things'. 'Principle' now does not mean 'element', it means 'idea'; and Keats is saying 'I have loved the idea, that there is beauty in all things'. Now, I admit that if I had that single sentence alone to interpret: 'I have loved the principle of beauty in all things', I should hesitate to read it 'I have loved the principle—of beauty in all things', even though I am convinced that Keats meant by his sentence not that he had loved all beautiful things; but that he had loved beauty and beauty is in all things.

But the sentence does not stand alone. The phrase 'the principle of Beauty' occurs elsewhere in Keats' letters; so does the phrase 'Beauty in all things'. In the spring of this year, 1818, he had written to Reynolds (9th April): 'I have not the slightest feel of humility towards the public—or to anything in existence—but the eternal Being, the principle of Beauty, and the Memory of great Men.' That absolute use of the phrase would settle the question, were it not that six months later (October 1818) we find him writing to his brother George, then in America: 'The mighty abstract idea I have of Beauty in all things stifles the more divided and minute domestic happiness.'

Those two sentences, in their sequence, the first in the spring, the second in the autumn of this year of 'purgatory blind', are of cardinal importance. They establish the real meaning of 'I have loved the principle—of Beauty in all things': that love is essentially the same as 'the love of good and ill' for which he had striven. They reveal the intimate connection between 'the principle—of Beauty in all things' and 'the vast idea' which came to Keats in *Sleep and Poetry*; it was 'the mighty abstract idea of Beauty in all things'. And above all they reveal, in the history of a single phrase, the secret movement of Keats' mind. The 'vast idea' of *Sleep and Poetry* had involved the poet's passing beyond 'the realm of Flora and old Pan', that is away from the realm of beautiful things. He had asked

> And can I ever bid these joys farewell?

And he had answered:

> Yes, I must pass them for a nobler life
> Where I may find the agonies, the strife
> Of human hearts.

He had thus, in that prophetic poem, seen beyond the principle of beauty to the principle of beauty in all things. But in *Endymion*, for all his efforts, he had remained almost wholly within 'the realm of Flora and old Pan'. The principle of beauty had triumphed over the principle of beauty in all things. For many reasons, but for one in chief: Keats was a truly natural poet who could not write save out of that which he had proved upon his pulses: 'The agonies, the strife of human hearts' had not yet touched him directly. Ecstatic contemplation of beauty, the being thrown 'into a sort of oneness'—that he knew by direct experience; but the pain of life he did not know. He knew that he had to triumph over pain, but the pain had not yet come, and he was not one to invoke it intellectually. A merely intellectual reality was no reality at all to him; even 'a proverb was no proverb to him until his life had illustrated it'. And so in April 1818, when he is writing to Reynolds with *Endymion* in his mind, regarding the preface to *Endymion*, it is simply 'the principle of beauty' of which he speaks. He has just been putting his loyalty to the principle again to the proof by writing *Isabella*, which is pre-eminently a romantic tale in the sense of being devoid of all substance of actual life-experience.

At this very moment, when he was proclaiming the principle of beauty thus absolutely, pain had approached him: he was condemned to watch his brother die. He knew that in his actual life he was to be called upon to bid a long farewell to the principle of beauty. It was then that he was convinced upon his nerves of the pain and misery and heartbreak in the world, and confessed his despair of attaining to the love of good *and* ill. It was then that he told Taylor (24th April) that he 'had been hovering for some time between an exquisite sense of the luxurious and a love for philosophy'. The exquisite sense of the luxurious is the homage to the principle of beauty; philosophy is to Keats the apprehension of the principle of beauty in *all* things. Now he is caught midway between the two: he has lost hold of the one, he has not laid hold of the other. This is the condition he describes in the *Epistle to Reynolds:*

> Or is it that Imagination brought
> Beyond its proper bound, yet still confin'd,
> Lost in a sort of Purgatory blind
> Cannot refer to any standard law
> Of either earth or heaven? It is a flaw
> In happiness to see beyond our bourn.

This 'purgatory blind' is the condition which lies between allegiance to the principle of beauty and discovery of the principle of beauty in all things. This year 1818 had been a year of such a purgatory. After *Isabella* Keats wrote nothing until he began *Hyperion*, and in that poem the principle of beauty changes to the principle of beauty in all things. It is, as he tells his brother George, still a mighty *abstract* idea; he speaks, as ever, truly, for in *Hyperion* the 'vast idea' *is* abstract; but it is there—and the remainder of Keats' life was to be burned away in the process of its becoming concrete in and through him.

'Beauty in all things.' This was Keats' great poetic intuition, and the revelation of this beauty the great human purpose to which he dedicated himself and for which he was prepared to die. It sounds simple; it is tremendous. It involves a profound acceptance of life as it is, a passing beyond all rebellion, not into the apathy of stoic resignation, but into a condition of soul to which the sum of things —'foul or fair, high or low, rich or poor'—is revealed as necessary and true and beautiful: and for the creative genius of the poet it means not only to have this vision, not only to have attained 'high reason, and the love of good and ill', but to have the purpose and the power to reveal to men that good and ill are to be loved; not only the faculty to see that the sum of things is supremely beautiful, but the faculty to show to other men that it is supremely beautiful.

Such an achievement, Keats knew, was possible only in the form in which Shakespeare had achieved it, in the drama, in the poetry of representation, which in the hands of great genius, does perform this manifest miracle of revealing the secret harmony and high design which lie behind all human discomfiture. This consummate poetry which represents and reveals was, as Keats had already confessed to Taylor, and as he was to confess to him more fully hereafter, his poetic goal: it was one which he never attained. It was in the despairing vision of this unattained ideal that, when he wrote to Fanny Brawne, all his glorious poetic achievement dissolved away and he said that he had left no immortal work behind him, but if he had had time he would have made himself remembered. He is remembered; he will never be forgotten: but he is remembered, too often, and even by those who have devoted themselves to his memory, as something of a weakling, as a boy of genius in whose soul there was an element of sickness and sickliness, as someone who can be patronized, and be told that he was wrong to love with a passion so devouring, misguided to reject the influence of Milton, peevish and morbid to spoil his beautiful *Hyperion* by adding to it an opening in a different tone and manner.

15

SOUL-MAKING

From Keats and Shakespeare, *pages 132–143.*

AT the beginning of the month of silence, out of which he emerged with mastery of his art and in possession of the knowledge which he expressed by its means, Keats had made in his 'indolent' letter two discoveries at the same moment. He had discovered that the truth of human life was beautiful, and that its truth was its beauty; and he had discovered that poetry consisted in that instinctive and spontaneous attitude taken by his mind in making that discovery. These discoveries were made by flashes of sudden vision. The tormenting question which confronted him was how to make his knowledge of the truth he had glimpsed secure. He had for a moment become a 'Superior Being' and seen himself and his searchings as a part of the organic beauty of life. How was he, who had seen so much, who had by the very fact of his seeing been lifted out of that pattern of life of which he saw the beauty and the truth, to remain within it? Were not those gnawing thoughts of his own ineffectuality, his own unsatisfied hunger for the happiness of Love, of Fame and of Poetry, part of himself? How could he submit them to the vision? He had seen the beauty and the truth of life; but how could he declare it, when his soul was divided within him? Unless he could accept it in his own soul, for himself, and could believe that his own menacing destiny was beautiful and true, what he had seen was a lie, and he could not declare it.

There was the beauty, there was the truth: but something in him rebelled against it, and so long as he rebelled he betrayed the vision. He was a poet, and he had seen that poetry essentially consisted in a spontaneous attitude of his being. How, with all his knowledge, was he to remain spontaneous? Spontaneous, faced by a vision that all his most agonizing pains were endorsed by the universe? Spontaneous, when life was robbing him of all he held most dear? No, it was too much. Too much was asked of him: he could not pay that price for remaining a poet. And surely there is no man in the world who has the imagination to realize what Keats suffered but would say: The price *is* too great. He cannot be asked to accept *his* destiny. If the cup will not pass from him, then he must rebel; he must arraign for ever, in words that shall be immortal, the injustice and cruelty of whatever gods there be.

And what every man in the world must feel, if he has the power to feel anything at all, Keats must have felt a thousand times more deeply in that month of silence and fever. Yet he emerged from it with these words:

> How fever'd is that man who cannot look
> Upon his mortal days with temperate blood!

and with these words spoken by 'the friend to man':

> 'Beauty is truth, truth beauty',—that is all
> Ye know on earth, and all ye need to know.

Somehow the victory was accomplished; he had accepted his destiny, he had put away the fever, he had not 'spoiled his salvation by a fierce miscreed'.

The sonnet *On Fame* which marks the victory, not by asserting it but by being it, was written in the long journal-letter to his brother on 30th April. It follows immediately after the most astonishing portion of this, the greatest of all Keats' letters. Probably the sonnet was composed in the morning following the night on which the letter was written; it came into his head as the truer, because purely poetic, utterance of a thought which he had been struggling to convey in other terms to his brother.

This portion of the letter has become famous; it has been quoted many times, but I have never seen any attempt to grapple with the thought which it contains. It is famous and quoted and remembered, I suppose, for the same reason that many of the greatest things in poetry are famous and quoted and remembered. They contain some haunting beauty that is mysteriously knit up with some vaguely apprehended truth. It is not so much that we remember them, as that they cling to our minds in our own despite. They are not merely beautiful, or they could be admired and let us go; they are not merely true, or they could be understood and put away. But with such things as these we cannot have done, nor they have done with us.

Let us try to follow this one, if only because it comes at the crucial moment of Keats' inward growth, to the last verge of implication, no matter where it leads. The letter opens quite gently and simply. Keats has been reading two books of history.

> I have been reading lately two very different books, Robertson's America and Voltaire's 'Siècle de Louis XIV'. It is like walking arm in arm between Pizarro and the great-little Monarch. In how lamentable a

case do we see the great body of men in both instances; in the first when Men might seem to inherit quiet of Mind from unsophisticated senses; from uncontamination of civilization and especially from their being as it were estranged from the mutual helps of Society and its mutual injuries —and thereby more immediately under the Protection of Providence— even there they had pains to bear as bad, or even worse than Bailiffs, Debts and Poverties of civilized life.

The whole appears to resolve itself into this: that Man is originally a poor forked creature subject to the same mischances as the beasts of the forest, destined to hardships and disquietude of some kind or another. If he improves by degrees his bodily accommodations and comforts—at each stage, at each ascent there are waiting for him a fresh set of annoyances— he is mortal and there is still a heaven with its Stars above his head.

The thought is clear: the pains of humanity keep pace with its progress in the mechanics of civilization. To each advance in outward civilization a new pain corresponds:

The most interesting question [Keats continues] that can come before us is, How far by the persevering efforts of a seldom-appearing Socrates Mankind may be made happy—I can imagine such happiness carried to an extreme—but what must it end in? Death—and who could in such a case bear with death? The whole troubles of life which are now frittered away in a series of years, would then be accumulated for the last days of a being who instead of hailing its approach would leave this world as Eve left Paradise.

Again the thought is clear. Human happiness to be perfect must include the abolition of death. If pain were to be blotted out of the world, the result would merely be that death would be a thousand times greater agony than it is. For now the pains of life are such that we are prepared for death and accustomed to the thought of death. But it is surely of himself alone that Keats is thinking when he speaks of 'hailing its approach'.

But in truth [he goes on] I do not at all believe in this sort of perfectibility—the nature of the world will not admit of it—the inhabitants of the world will correspond with itself. Let the fish Philosophise the ice away from the Rivers in winter time and they shall be at continual play in the tepid delight of summer. Look at the Poles and the Sands of Africa, whirlpools and volcanoes. Let men exterminate them and I will say that they may arrive at earthly Happiness. The point at which Man may arrive is the parallel state in inanimate nature and no further. For instance suppose a rose to have sensation, it blooms on a beautiful morning, it enjoys itself, but then comes a cold wind, a hot sun—it cannot escape, it cannot destroy its annoyances—they are as native to the world as itself —no more can man be happy in spite, the worldly elements will prey upon his nature.

This is yet another example of the pure poetic thought of Keats, of his attainment of truth through the recognition of beauty. Keats mind is once more elucidating a harmony in the world; he is discerning a pattern and divining that man also must obey the pattern and be of one nature with the world which he inhabits. If the condition of man were perfectible, he would become a discordant element in the harmony.

If we were to analyse thought of this peculiar kind from the point of view of the logician, we should have to say that it was based upon an assumption; and that the assumption was that reality is harmonious. It is true: this is the fundamental assumption that the pure poetic mind does make; this is the central axiom of all poetic thought. It is made for the most part unconsciously, and can be discovered only by analysis of such primary acts of poetic thought as the seizing of images and making of metaphors; in other and higher forms of poetic thought it is made with knowledge. This is what Keats meant when he said to Bailey in November 1817: 'I have never yet been able to perceive how anything can be known for truth by consecutive reasoning', and when he reaffirmed this perception of the nature of his own mind at the beginning of 1819 by saying to George: 'I can never feel certain of any truth but from a clear perception of its beauty.' This is what one who is among the greatest of all French poets, Charles Baudelaire, meant when he said: 'La première condition nécessaire pour faire un art sain est la croyance à l'unité intégrale.' The process of poetic comprehension moves from the perception of harmony to the perception of harmony, and these successive harmonies are its truths.

That may sound singularly irrational, and indeed it is completely irrational. But we have to make the simple, though difficult, sideway leap with our minds, and see that rational thought is based, not one whit less than poetic thought, upon an assumption which is also for the most part unconscious. Rational thought *assumes* that reality is rational. Once we have seen that this is an assumption, we shall also see the futility of criticizing poetic thought because it is irrational. One might as well criticize rational thought for being unpoetic. What we have to understand and to accept is the fact that there are two orders or kinds of thinking, and that the only means of deciding which of them brings us nearer to reality is by the completeness of the ultimate satisfaction which they bring. There is absolutely no objective criterion by which one can be preferred to the other. They exist, each in its own right. It is for us to choose between them; and probably our choice will not be deliberate, but will be determined by some instinctive and unconscious inclination towards one or the other.[1]

[1] See notes, page 125.

Keats offers an almost pure case of poetic thought. Apprehension of truth was for him always apprehension of harmony. We have been watching his faculty at work in the contemplation of the human universe: he now advances further to the discovery of a more comprehensive harmony still.

> The common cognomen of this world among the misguided and superstitious is 'a vale of tears', from which we are to be redeemed by a certain arbitrary interposition of God and taken to Heaven. What a little circumscribed straightened notion! Call the world if you please 'The vale of Soul-making'. Then you will find out the use of the world (I am speaking now in the highest terms for human nature admitting it to be immortal which I will here take for granted for the purpose of showing a thought which has struck me concerning it). I say *'Soul-making'*—Soul as distinguished from an Intelligence. There may be intelligences or sparks of the Divinity in millions—but they are not Souls until they acquire identities, till each one is personally itself. Intelligences are atoms of perception—they know and they see and they are pure, in short they are God.
>
> How then are Souls to be made? How then are these sparks which are God to have identity given them—so as ever to possess a bliss peculiar to each one's individual existence? How but by the medium of a world like this? This point I sincerely wish to consider because I think it a grander system of salvation than the Christian religion—or rather it is a system of Spirit creation. This is effected by three grand materials acting the one upon the other for a series of years. These three materials are the *Intelligence*—the *human heart* (as distinguished from intelligence or Mind) and the *World*, or *Elemental space* suited for the proper action of *Mind and Heart* upon each other for the purpose of forming the *Soul* or *Intelligence destined to possess the sense of Identity*. I can scarcely express what I but dimly perceive—and yet I think I perceive it—that you may judge the more clearly I will put it in the most homely form possible.
>
> I will call the *world* a School instituted for the purpose of teaching little children to read. I will call the *human heart* the *horn Book* read in that School. And I will call the *Child able to read, the Soul* made from that *School* and its *horn book*. Do you not see how necessary a World of Pains and troubles is to school an Intelligence and make it a Soul? A Place where the heart must feel and suffer in a thousand diverse ways. Not merely is the Heart a Hornbook. It is the Mind's Bible, it is the Mind's experience, it is the test from which the Mind or Intelligence sucks its identity. As various as the Lives of Men are, so various become their Souls, and thus does God make individual beings, Souls, Identical Souls of the sparks of his own essence. . . .

In this remarkable passage Keats is discovering a harmony in the world within man which completes the harmony he had previously discovered in the world without him. There is, as ever, a deceptive simplicity about his statement. That it is not really simple, or rather that its simplicity is the simplicity of a directly apprehended mystery, will quickly be apparent to anyone who sincerely tries to grasp his thought. And that this is so is proven by his own words: 'I can scarcely express what I dimly perceive, and yet I think I perceive it.' Keats was making a supreme effort at comprehension; it stands to reason that what cost Keats so great an effort to comprehend and express will cost us no small one.

Let us return for a moment to Keats' 'indolent' letter. In it he had seen the world of men and women as forming a harmony with the animal world. Essentially all human beings are instinctive as animals, and if they are so seen, they have the grace and beauty of animals. When a man's mind works with the same instinctiveness, when instead of working in a vacuum of abstract thought it retains this spontaneity, when, in short, man's mind is in harmony with his instinctive being, then you have the essential condition of poetry.

But there remained an urgent problem, which Keats had left unsolved save by implication. How was this harmony of the mind with the instinctive being to be achieved? Keats was indeed achieving it as he wrote his 'indolent' letter, and he was aware of it. But how was he achieving it? Was it merely an accident? How was this spontaneity of the mind to be made a permanent possession, when his mind seemed for the most part to have an existence of its own which it spent in vexing his spirit and gnawing at his life with tormenting and impossible questions? For we must remember that the day on which he wrote his letter was a day of respite and peace. His words are perfectly clear. 'In this state of effeminacy the fibres of the brain are relaxed in common with the rest of the body, and to such a happy degree that pleasure has no show of enticement and pain no unbearable power. Neither Poetry, nor Ambition, nor Love have any alertness of countenance as they pass by me. . . .' That is to say, the mind had sunk back into harmony with the instinctive being, and the three most agonizing thoughts with which Keats' mind was torturing him had lost their power to pain. But such felicity was rare, and accidental. Keats says so. 'This is the only happiness, and is a rare instance of the advantage of the body overpowering the mind.'

It is clear that this condition was very far indeed from being a condition of laziness or effeminacy. Out of it directly sprang one of the two profoundest of all Keats' letters; and Keats himself was aware that the condition was truly creative. It is precisely this condition of subordination of the mind to the instinctive being, which, at the climax of his letter, he declares to be 'the very thing in which consists Poetry'. This is the condition in which the faculty of pure poetic perception can work, and it works in that letter with a sovereign power.[2]

[2] See notes, page 126.

But the condition was accidental and rare; it was an oasis in the desert of agonizing thought. How could it be made his own for ever? That and no other is the question Keats is answering in his letter on 'Soul-making'. It was the most urgent and vital question of all. Everything depended upon it, and above all else the question whether Keats could remain a poet. Poetry, for him, must come naturally as the leaves to a tree, or it had better not come at all; it was the natural product of a spontaneous attitude of the complete being. If he was to depend upon accident for the submission of rebellious mind to instinctive being, then it was better not to be a poet at all. Keats was above all things else, a man; and a man does not trust to accident to possess his own being.

One need not enlarge upon the implications of this problem, over which Keats was brooding during his month of silence. It is the deepest of all problems, and everything depends upon it, not only for Keats, but for mankind at large. The burden of consciousness, the burden of the mystery, is upon us all: Keats shows us the way to face it and conquer.

He has brushed aside, with sovereign ease, all shallow notions of the perfectibility of the conditions of human life. Were there to be realized conditions in which the human universe were freed from pain, death would become intolerable and, more than this, man would become a discordant element in the great harmony of which he is a part. No, Keats says, not the conditions of human life but the individual man is perfectible. Man has it in him to become a complete man, by possessing his own soul. This, and this alone, is the purpose of human life, and he tries to declare the way by which the purpose can be achieved.

He makes a threefold division of man's being: into Heart and Mind and Soul. The Soul exists only as a potentiality; it has to be created in the process of man's life. The original elements are only two: Mind and Heart. Mind is both 'an atom of intelligence' and, more strangely, 'a spark of the Divinity'; these atoms of intelligence —to use Keats' own simple and mysterious words—'know and see and are pure, in short they are God.'[3] Let us not pause over the stranger part of this definition for the moment, but remember only that it has been stated so. Mind shall be simply 'an atom of intelligence'. Heart is defined by Keats further on in this letter as 'the seat of the Human Passions'. We might call it Body; it is, in the widest sense, man's instinctive being. It is the instrument of all immediate knowledge, whether through sensation or intuition. In the language of modern psychology, Mind is 'consciousness' and Heart is 'unconsciousness'.

[3] See notes, page 126.

It is important to realize that both Mind and Heart 'know', but with different kinds of knowledge, for which there is unfortunately no corresponding distinction in modern language.[4] Adapting the terms of modern psychology, let us call the knowledge of the Mind 'conscious knowledge', and the knowledge of the Heart 'unconscious knowledge'. Then, according to Keats, the 'conscious knowledge' of the Mind works upon the 'unconscious knowledge' of the Heart. But in a peculiar and unexpected way. Not by judging and rejecting, but rather by assimilating. Above all, 'conscious knowledge' does not assume any attitude of superiority towards 'unconscious knowledge'. 'The Heart', Keats says emphatically, 'is the Mind's Bible'—the phrase is important, for Keats' mind thinks not with the logic of discourse, but with the finer instruments of analogy and metaphor, and such a phrase as this, which may easily be passed over as a mere phrase by those unfamiliar with the process of Keats' thinking, contains the equivalent of a vital definition. It means that the attitude of 'conscious knowledge' towards 'unconscious knowledge' must be one not of superiority, but of deference; not of judgement, but of reverence; not of condescension, but of loyalty. At the extreme its function is but one of interpretation, and it must be one of faithful interpretation.

It will be a temptation for those who are not prepared to struggle to grasp Keats' thought, which cost him a struggle to grasp, to diminish and degrade it into a commonplace. 'Mind works upon experience', they will say. 'Of course: it has nothing else to work on.' But Keats is saying far more than this; he is saying Mind must be utterly loyal to immediate and unintellectual experience—to the passions, to the affections, to the intuitions. These are the Bible of the Mind, not its own constructions and vaticinations.

By this loyalty, by this submission of consciousness to unconsciousness is slowly created—the Soul. Keats describes this achievement of Soul as 'the possession of a sense of identity' by the Mind or consciousness. The Mind comes to be 'personally itself', and to possess 'a bliss peculiar to its individual existence'. This condition, in which the Soul, or true Self, has now come into existence, is quite different from 'conscious knowledge'; it involves a change in the very nature of 'conscious knowledge'. 'Conscious knowledge' is somehow merged together with 'unconscious knowledge', to form this deeper knowledge of an indefeasible self-existence. This self-existence is the soul, and that which knows it is the soul. The soul knows itself, and a true and inviolable personality is achieved. And now we have reached yet a third kind of knowledge, born of the union of the two previous kinds of knowledge. This knowledge may be called 'soul-knowledge'.

[4] See notes, page 126.

This condition of 'soul-knowledge', which appears, when approached in this way, to be primarily a knowledge that the soul *is*, a knowledge of the individual's true self-existence, has strange consequences; for it results immediately in a knowledge of the harmony and necessity of that universe, whose workings upon the Heart are the primary source of 'soul-knowledge'. 'Do you not see', cries Keats, 'how necessary a world of Pains and Troubles is to school an Intelligence and make it a Soul?' The answer to that from anyone who trusts his intellect alone, and for whom his Heart is not the Bible of his Mind, will assuredly be: 'No, I do *not* see.' And there is an end. No argument is possible. But Keats did see.

In saying that the achievement of this condition of soul-knowledge results immediately in a knowledge of the harmony and necessity of the universe, I have assumed that Keats himself had at that moment himself reached the condition of 'soul-knowledge'. That may appear an unwarrantable assumption. But it is not so; it is, and it evidently must be, inherent in the nature of such knowledge as Keats here is trying to describe, that it should be a record of personal experience. Leaving aside what we have come to know of Keats' character—his own complete loyalty to experience, his instinctive refusal of all abstract speculation, his refusal to speak save from the complete being—it is obvious that knowledge of this kind *cannot* be merely speculative. Keats is trying to put into words, and thereby to make wholly conscious to himself, a process which he has actually lived through. We are reading his own account of the manner in which he achieved his soul; and more than that, we are reading an account of it written at the very moment when the process was being finally completed. For this consciousness of its own nature after which Keats is now struggling is the perfection of soul-knowledge itself. At the moment when Keats finally achieves his soul he sees immediately the necessity and harmony of the universe of which he is a part, and which, acting first upon his heart and through his heart upon his mind, has finally created the soul which knows the universe as necessary and harmonious.

Probably there are two orders of minds: one for whom such things as these are mysterious and unintelligible, and another for whom they are mysterious and simple. And it may be that a gulf is for ever fixed between them. This is the re-living in the nature of a pure poet of that strange happening which is known to mystical experience as the simultaneous knowledge of the soul and the knowledge of God. Soul-knowledge is God-knowledge, for the reality in the phrase 'to know God' is nothing other than the knowledge of the necessity and harmony of the universe which Keats declared when he cried, 'Do you not see how necessary a world of Pains and Troubles is to school an

Intelligence and make it a Soul?' No man can *explain* that mystery. It came to pass in Keats, and Keats tried to communicate to his brother the process by which it came to pass.

'Soul-knowledge is God-knowledge.' I have not dragged in the word or the thought; I know only too well that it is an offence against decorum in modern criticism, and I would never have ventured it upon my own authority. I am not expounding my own beliefs, but Keats'; and if I deviate by a hair's breadth from his own meaning, then so far as my purpose is concerned, I have failed. But Keats himself uses the word 'God' with no uncertain voice in this letter. Not only does he say that 'the atoms of intelligence', the germs of consciousness, 'know and see and are pure, in short they are God', but he concludes his account of the system of soul-creation with the emphatic words: 'Thus does God make individual beings, Souls, Identical Souls, of the sparks of His own essence.' And I should not be adding a fraction of a thought of my own to Keats' thought if I were to describe the process of soul-creation which he has apprehended, as a knowledge of life as a necessary means by which the atom of God comes to self-consciousness of its own divine nature. But, indeed, Keats may speak for himself:

> I am convinced [he goes on] that many difficulties under which Christians labour would vanish before this system—there is one which even now strikes me—the salvation of Children. In them the spark or intelligence returns to God without any identity—it having no time to learn of and be altered by the heart—or seat of the human Passions. It is pretty generally suspected that the Christian scheme [he means, of theology] has been copied from the ancient Persian and Greek philosophers. Why may they not have made this simple thing [it will be noticed that though 'he could scarcely express what he dimly perceived', the thing is, nevertheless, 'simple'] even more simple for common apprehension by introducing Mediators and Personages in the same manner as in the heathen mythology abstractions are personified? Seriously I think it probable that this system of Soul-making may have been the parent of all the more palpable and personal schemes of Redemption among the Zoroastrians, the Christians and the Hindoos. For as one part of the human species must have their carved Jupiter; so another part must have the palpable and named Mediator and Saviour, their Christ, their Oromanes and their Vishnu.

Once more Keats means what he says: that he seriously thinks that the system of soul-making he has apprehended is the fundamental and essential religious truth, of which all religions are partial and simplified statements. That I also believe this to be true is of no account save in so far that it may have made me more than others liable to the conviction that Keats means what he says, and that what he is saying is something of importance to all men. And it will be clear from what Keats now says that those would do violence to his thought who should endeavour to identify the God of whom he speaks with the God of a particular sect. Keats' God is not the God of the Christian, if that God is different from the God of the Hindoo, or the Persian, or the Greek. His God is the God whom exclusive religions can, by reason of their partiality, apprehend only in part. He is, indeed, God.

And, for that very reason, it is only here in his letters that Keats makes deliberate and considered use of the name, for the purpose of revealing the nature of his thought, or his knowledge, to his brother. What his God really is cannot be expressed directly in speech; but it can be quite simply apprehended from the terms of this letter and the 'indolent' letter of 19th March. God is that with which the human soul comes into contact and communion at the moment it knows itself for a soul; God *is* that harmony of the universe which flowers into a consciousness of its own nature through the human being who can make his Heart his Mind's Bible, and thereby achieve his soul. And because God was this for Keats at the moment that he knew Him through the knowledge of his own soul, when he came in his *Odes* to declare Him, he did not make use of the dangerous word; he declared what he knew as he knew it, he proclaimed the truth as he apprehended it and not otherwise:

> 'Beauty is truth, truth beauty,'—that is all
> Ye know on earth, and all ye need to know.

In a sense the truth which Keats expressed in those words, and in the letter in which he tried to show the means by which man could attain to the knowledge of the truth, is indeed simple, as Keats implied in his poem and asserted in his letter, because true mysteries are simple, just as true simplicities are mysterious; but they are mysteries. What is a simple act of apprehension for soul-knowledge is a complicated and impossible one for mind-knowledge. Theology can only be truly interpreted by those who have no need of it; and so with all attempts, inevitable though they are, to translate soul-knowledge into terms of mind-knowledge. In this realm of soul-knowledge, those more mysterious and terrible words do literally apply: 'To him that hath shall be given, and from him that hath not it shall be taken away, even that which he hath.' In the realm of soul-knowledge the tiniest gleam, loyally followed, flames slowly into full comprehension; but the most arduous and subtle efforts of mind-knowledge to enter that realm end only in confusion and bitterness. This tiny gleam is given to everyone who is thrilled and haunted by some strange validity in a line of pure poetry, of which he can render to himself no rational account: if he will stick faithfully to what he has felt, take it for a proven and incontrovertible fact, no matter what his mind may tell him, then by slow degrees fact will join itself to fact until there is formed within him a body of certitude concerning the nature of poetry and the nature of the reality to which it alone can give complete and palpable expression. This process is, in miniature at least, what Keats meant when he said that the Heart must be the Mind's Bible.

In this matter, we have to make a choice: on the one side, the rationalists, on the other Keats and Shakespeare, and the whole fact of religion and great art. For it is not really possible to compromise, as many would like to do, by regarding this, the strangest and most astonishing of all Keats' letters—as a mere speculation, or as the groping of 'an untrained mind' into the mysteries of metaphysics. That attitude is taken by those critics who deign to pay any real attention to the letter at all. But the Keats who wrote that letter was not an apprentice to knowledge; he was one of the most marvellous human beings of whom the world holds record. He was twenty-three; and at the moment he wrote this letter he was writing day after day the *Odes,* to Psyche, to the Nightingale, on a Grecian Urn, on Melancholy—poems comparable to nothing in English literature save the work of Shakespeare's maturity. We cannot have it both ways: we must choose. Either we choose a Keats who is homogeneous, whose poetry and thought and knowledge are one and homogeneous; or we choose a Keats who thought childish thoughts with 'an untrained mind' and by some miracle wrote poems which surpass for profundity of experience and splendour of statement anything that 'a trained mind' has ever conceived. If we can believe in this monster we may; but it is worth while to pause a moment to consider whether we are not, for the sake of allegiance to a rigidly rational prejudice concerning reality, being forced to accept a naked impossibility.

What I am now contending for is not to prove that what Keats thought is true—that cannot be *proved*, and what Keats thought or wrote must be left to make its own impression on men's minds—but that Keats was indeed homogeneous and at one within himself, that he conquered this oneness, that in his letter on 'Soul-making' he gave the most faithful account he could of the process by which he conquered it. This was the process by which Keats himself believed he attained the condition of soul in which he wrote the first poetry which was indubitably and unmistakably Keats' and Keats' alone; by which he became, in fact, a great English poet, second only to Shakespeare. It may be said that Keats was mistaken about himself. If Keats was mistaken in this, he was mistaken in everything. This letter is but the inevitable and harmonious outcome of all his thinking: it is utterly consistent with all that he thought and was. If we choose to believe that Keats was mistaken in everything, and that out of this abysm of error he sent forth the great *Odes*,—then we will believe anything.

Notes

[1] And yet it seems to be true that in the process of the supremely rational thought of metaphysics or science, a moment always comes when the mind in its effort towards an exacter comprehension of reality is compelled, apparently by the nature of things, to make an irrational movement. In metaphysics this abnegation by the rational mind of its own nature in order to reach a further stage of comprehension is, for a literary critic, not impossible to detect. In the more arduous sciences, for which the training of the specialist is necessary, this act of detection is difficult, if not impossible, for the layman: and very few scientific minds are sufficiently self-conscious to be aware of the nature of their own activity. But, though I speak with all diffidence in this matter, it does appear to me that the highest kind of scientific discovery is achieved by thought of the same order as that by which the highest poetic discovery is achieved. Suddenly, and often without the man of science being aware of it, his assumption changes: he assumes no longer that reality is rational, but that it is harmonious. By an act of intuition he sees that it is harmonious, and this harmony is for him a truth. A new assumption, and with it a new kind of thought has supervened.

By the necessities of exposition I am forced here and elsewhere to present the non-rational thought of pure poetry and the rational thought which reaches its absolute perfection in mathematics as exclusive of each other. This is not the truth. The non-rational thought of pure poetry and the rational thought of pure mathematics are set in a true opposition. That is, they are complementary to, rather than exclusive of, each other. They present the fundamental harmony under its two real aspects; and as I have tried to indicate in my text the thought of pure mathematics at its highest is also non-rational.

To discuss this question would carry me into a region of exalted metaphysic where, perhaps, my wings would melt. But I may say this: the supremely rational thought of pure mathematics is concerned with *structure*; the non-rational thought of pure poetry is concerned with *being*. In its most elementary form the rational thought of mathematics is concerned with structure at the point where it is least essential. 2 plus 2=4 is the least important of all truths about any pair of two objects. The progress of mathematical thought is governed by the attempt to approach ever more closely to the *essential structure* of the universe. At the last this essential structure must become identical with *being*. I believe that every advance of mathematical thought in this process of approximation is marked by an act of non-rational perception. The nature of these advances is frequently disguised from the mathematician himself because he works in abstract symbols. First, for example, Minus quantities enter his calculations—he does consider their implications—then what he himself calls irrationals, e.g. $\sqrt{-1}$ —he does not consider their implications—then at the modern end of the long evolution, Quanta—he does not consider their implications.

[2] Perhaps no more striking analogy to Keats' process of soul at the moment of writing the 'indolent' letter, and no more illuminating commentary on the whole mystery of Soul-making, can be found than the following brief quotation from the third sermon of Meister Eckhart (trans. C. de B. Evans, p. 17):

> What the active intellect does for the natural man that and far more does God do for the solitary soul: he turns out active intellect, and installing himself in its stead he himself assumes the duties of the active intellect.
>
> When a man is quite idle, when his intellect is at rest within him, then God takes up the work: he himself is the agent who produces himself in the passive intellect. What happens is this. The active intellect cannot give what it has not got: it cannot have two ideas together, but first one and then the other. What though light and air show multitudes of forms and colours all at once, thou canst only observe them one after the other. And so with thy active intellect, which resembles the eye. But when God acts in lieu of thy active intellect, he engenders many images together in one point. . . .

[3] Once more the appropriate commentary upon this mysterious statement is a passage from Meister Eckhart. 'The eye with which I see God is the same eye with which he sees me.' Doubtless others of the great mystics, with whom I am unfamiliar, would provide analogies equally striking.

[4] I have lately come across a remarkable, though difficult, discussion of this very point in a book called *Cosmic Anatomy,* by 'M.B. (Oxon)'. This book deals with many matters clean beyond my comprehension. It contains many of those strange 'borderline' speculations which are almost invariably dismissed as 'mystical'. I have never seen any reference to the book in print. But I think it is an important piece of work, and one which deserves to be studied carefully by those—they are not plentiful—who can approach without prejudice the efforts of a very original and serious mind towards the truth. The book is published by Mr. J. M. Watkins, Cecil Court, W.C.2.

16

KEATS AND WORDSWORTH

From Keats *(Cape, 1955). This book first appeared in 1930, with the title* Studies in Keats. *It was re-issued, with revisions and additional material, in 1939, 1949, and 1955.*

'I AM convinced', wrote Keats to Haydon on January 10th, 1818, 'that there are three things to rejoice at in this Age—The Excursion, your Pictures, and Hazlitt's depth of Taste.' He repeated his judgment in a letter to his brothers. He had changed significantly in the year and more since he wrote his sonnet, *Great spirits now on earth are sojourning* . . . Not only had Hazlitt taken the place of Hunt in the trinity of contemporary genius (and I think he was to keep it to the end) but a more general and inclusive praise of Wordsworth seems to be concentrating, not indeed on *The Excursion* alone, but upon that element in Wordsworth's genius of which *The Excursion* is typical, and of which the first two books of *The Excursion* are perhaps the noblest expression which Wordsworth achieved. That this high estimate of *The Excursion* should have coincided with a new appreciation of Hazlitt's depth of taste is peculiarly interesting, because Hazlitt himself did not adequately appreciate *The Excursion.*

There are delightful passages in *The Excursion*, both of natural description and of inspired reflection (passages of the latter kind that in the sound of the thoughts and of the swelling language resemble heavenly symphonies, mournful *requiems* over the grave of human hopes); but we must add, in justice and in sincerity, that we think it impossible that this work should ever become popular, even in the same degree as the *Lyrical Ballads*. It affects a system without having any intelligible clue to one, and instead of unfolding a principle in various and striking lights, repeats the same conclusions till they become flat and insipid. Mr. Wordsworth's mind is obtuse, except as it is the organ and the receptacle of accumulated feelings; it is not analytic but synthetic; it is reflecting rather than theoretical. *The Excursion*, we believe, fell still-born from the press.

There was something abortive, and clumsy, and ill-judged in the attempt. It was long and laboured. The personages, for the most part, were low, the fare rustic; the plan raised expectations which were not fulfilled; and the effect was like being ushered into a stately hall and invited to sit down to a splendid banquet in the company of clowns, and with nothing but successive courses of apple-dumplings served up. It was not even *toujours perdrix*!

The judgment is, no doubt, juster than any that was pronounced by a contemporary critic. Coleridge alone *might* have done better. There is undoubtedly a contrast, amounting almost to anticlimax, between the magnificent passage from *The Recluse* which Wordsworth quotes in his preface, 'as a kind of *Prospectus* of the design of the whole Poem' (i.e. *The Prelude, The Excursion* and the unwritten third part), and *The Excursion* itself. But the prospectus-passage is Wordsworth at the height of his inspiration, a great poet if one ever was; and it is impossible to imagine a poem sustained on such a level. Disappointment, of some kind, was inevitable, in any poem that followed such a preface. Hazlitt seems hardly to have realized quite how superb that invocation was.

The second point to remark is that Hazlitt is criticizing *The Excursion* for not containing an explicit system of philosophy. It was on this matter that his mind directly clashed with Wordsworth's, and Wordsworth was bewildering to Hazlitt. For Wordsworth, in his prose-preface, first declared that the poem arose out of 'a determination to compose a philosophical poem', and concluded by saying: 'It is not the author's intention formally to announce a system; it was more animating to him to proceed in a different course; and if he shall succeed in conveying to the mind clear thoughts, lively images and strong feelings, the Reader will have no difficulty in extracting the system for himself.' The evasion was unconscious; but to Hazlitt's mind it must have seemed almost deliberate. In fact, Wordsworth's difficulty was intrinsic. What he was trying to do was partly to communicate a profound spiritual experience, partly to expound a religion based upon this experience; and this religion was in process of identifying itself with Christianity. Unfortunately, the specific Christian mysticism—the experience of the eternal Christ—was not original to Wordsworth's mysticism; so that the transition from his mysticism to Christianity generally appears either elusive or arbitrary. What Hazlitt understood by a philosophical system was very different from anything Wordsworth had to offer.

This failure of Hazlitt's mind to engage with Wordsworth's is notable in itself, for it led Hazlitt to a manifest underestimate of

Wordsworth's imaginative powers, and an undue and slightly contemptuous emphasis on that part of Wordsworth's poetry which was most influenced by Wordsworth's conscious poetic theory: namely, his versification of the sentiments of simple people in realistic language. Coleridge made the classical criticism of this Wordsworthian dogma, and since the publication of the *Biographia Literaria* no one, except the late Andrew Bradley, has been tempted to explore the matter further. But there is something more to be said, or suggested. Probably it was not Wordsworth's instinctive practice that was at fault—*Margaret, We are Seven*, and dozens of others are beautiful and altogether successful poems—but some of Wordsworth's practice after it had been made self-conscious by theory. I incline to believe that Coleridge should bear the chief responsibility for this contamination. The planning of the *Lyrical Ballads*, and the definite allotment to the two poets of two separate provinces of the imagination (which was, I suspect, mainly Coleridge's doing) was a chief cause of this theoretical rigidity. If that is so, then Coleridge in tearing the theory to pieces in the *Biographia Literaria* was demolishing what was his own invention rather than Wordsworth's, and removing from Wordsworth's genius an incrustation which was largely deposited by himself.

If that is true, or partly true, it explains why Wordsworth was hurt rather than instructed by Coleridge's criticism. For long before Coleridge's criticism was written Wordsworth had found his own solution to the real problem: of which the character of the Wanderer himself in *The Excursion* was symbolic. The Wanderer was a simple pedlar, but a man of education and imagination—an improbable pedlar maybe, but an easily acceptable one; and certainly a character who enabled Wordsworth to achieve his complex purpose—to express in poetry the religion and the morality and the life-wisdom which, he was convinced, was stored in the hearts of simple folk who lived in the bonds of 'natural piety'. In the first book of *The Excursion* Wordsworth expresses what is in his mind, and explains how the character of the Wanderer was a solution of the problem of expression which had been set him by his own matured conviction concerning the nature of true wisdom.

> Oh! many are the Poets that are sown
> By Nature; men endowed with highest gifts,
> The vision and the faculty divine;
> Yet wanting the accomplishment of verse,
> (Which, in the docile season of their youth,
> It was denied them to acquire, through lack

Of culture and the inspiring aid of books,
Or haply by a temper too severe,
Or a nice backwardness afraid of shame)
Nor having e'er, as life advanced, been led
By circumstance to take unto the height
The measure of themselves, these favoured Beings
All but a scattered few, live out their time,
Husbanding that which they possess within,
And go to the grave, unthought of. Strongest minds
Are often those of whom the noisy world
Hears least; else surely this Man had not left
His graces unrevealed and unproclaimed.

There is, moreover, an affinity between Wordsworth's thought in these lines and that of the opening of *The Fall of Hyperion*.

For Poesy alone can tell her dreams—
With the fine spell of words alone can save
Imagination from the sable charm
And dumb enchantment—Who alive can say,
'Thou are no poet—may'st not tell thy dreams'?
Since every man whose soul is not a clod
Hath visions, and would speak, if he had lov'd,
And been well nurtured in his mother tongue.

Precisely that condition—'if he had lov'd'—is fulfilled by the Wanderer, though the word carries a different nuance of meaning in Wordsworth and in Keats.[1] But in the essential I believe Wordsworth and Keats were at one concerning the nature of the love which is the source of 'the vision and the faculty divine', whether it finds utterance in poetry or not. For both of them the essential character of this love was that it was 'self-destroying'. The Wanderer is portrayed as one prepared in boyhood

By his intense conceptions, to receive
Deeply the lesson deep of love which he,
Whom Nature, *by whatever means*, has taught
To feel intensely, cannot but receive.

And to the Wanderer in youth Wordsworth gives perhaps the most exquisite and magnificent of all his descriptions of his own mystical beatitude in contemplating Nature.

[1] See notes, page 145.

He looked—
Ocean and earth, the solid frame of earth
And ocean's liquid mass, in gladness lay
Beneath him:—Far and wide the clouds were touched,
And in their silent faces could he read
Unutterable love. Sound needed none,
Nor any voice of joy; his spirit drank
The spectacle: sensation, soul, and form,
All melted into him; they swallowed up
His animal being; in them did he live,
And by them did he live; they were his life.
In such access of mind, in such high hour
Of visitation from the living God,
Thought was not; in enjoyment it expired.
No thanks he breathed, he proffered no request;
Rapt into still communion that transcends
The imperfect offices of prayer and praise.
His mind was a thanksgiving to the power
That made him; it was blessedness and love!

'And in *their silent faces* could he read Unutterable love.' The expression comes again in Book II, applied to the Wanderer himself.

And in *the silence of his face I read*
His overflowing spirit.

His spirit was overflowing with love of God's creation. 'He loved them all.' I believe it was due to something more than unconscious memory that Keats used the phrase at the critical moment of Apollo's dying into life in Book III of *Hyperion:*

Mute thou remainest—Mute! yet I can read
A wondrous lesson in thy silent face:
Knowledge enormous makes a God of me.
Names, deeds, gray legends, dire events, rebellions,
Majesties, sovran voices, agonies,
Creations and destroyings, all at once
Pour into the wide hollows of my brain,
And deify me, as if some blithe wine
Or bright elixir peerless I had drunk,
And so become immortal.

I do not imply that the experience is identical in Wordsworth and Keats; but I think it has the same spiritual import, involves the same depths of being, and is reached by the same means, namely love, experienced with a self-destroying intensity. The difference is rather in the province of reality from which the imaginative intensity derives. In Wordsworth it is primarily and pre-eminently the world of physical nature, including the folk whose lives are shaped by natural piety; in Keats it is the world of history, of human destinies, including his own.

The relation between Wordsworth and Keats is peculiarly intimate; and probably impossible to unravel. Even after his hero-worship of Wordsworth had received a shock in personal encounter, when the Wordsworth family came to town in the winter of 1817–18, Keats still could not help regarding Wordsworth as the great living hero of poetry—the one contemporary poet who had faithfully explored the mystery of life. He reacted momentarily against the dogmatic simplicities of Wordsworth's verse; he urged Reynolds not 'to be rattle-snaked' into 'tender and true'; they were not 'for the sake of a few fine imaginative or domestic passages . . . to be bullied into a certain philosophy engendered in the whims of an Egotist': nevertheless he is constrained to admit 'Wordsworth's grandeur'. This was on February 3rd, 1818. A fortnight later, on February 21st, he tells his brothers that he is sorry 'that Wordsworth has left a bad impression where-ever he visited in town by his egotism, Vanity and bigotry. Yet he is a great poet if not a philosopher.' The wound made by Wordsworth's condescension to his Hymn to Pan as 'a pretty piece of Paganism' was evidently healing. No doubt it had smarted particularly, since *Endymion* was just on the point of publication. By March 14th, when he 'can't help thinking' Wordsworth 'has returned to his Shell—with his beautiful Wife and his enchanting Sister'—he can make a joke of it all; and a very good one.

It is hardly possible to sort out the different strains in Keats's momentary disillusion with Wordsworth. He had looked forward to meeting Wordsworth very ardently, because Wordsworth meant more to him than any living poet; moreover, during the weeks he spent at Oxford with Bailey in the previous September, Wordsworth had been their constant reading. Within six weeks [*sic*], September 14th to November 22nd, 1817, there are no less than three quotations from the *Immortal Ode* in Keats's letters—all different, and all appropriate to and illuminative of Keats's deepest feelings. Yet he was not lost in uncritical admiration. His defence of Wordsworth's *Gipsies* against Hazlitt's criticism, is itself a fine criticism of the poem:

If Wordsworth had not been idle, he had not been without his task—nor had the Gipseys—they in the visible world had been as picturesque an object as he in the invisible. The Smoke of their fire—their attitudes—their Voices were all in harmony with the Evenings—It is a bold thing to say and I would not say it in print—but it seems to me that if Wordsworth had thought a little deeper at that Moment he would not have written the Poem at all—I should judge it to have been written in one of the most comfortable Moods of his Life—it is a kind of sketchy intellectual Landscape—not a search after Truth—nor is it fair to attack him on such a subject—for it is with the Critic as with the poet; had Hazlitt thought a little deeper and been in a good temper he would never have spied an imaginary fault there.

In temper and penetration it is admirable. Keats is applying to one of Wordsworth's later poems the criterion of an earlier one, which was a favourite with Keats, *The Old Cumberland Beggar*. 'But deem not this Man useless,' cries Wordsworth.

> 'Tis Nature's law
> That none, the meanest of created things,
> Of forms created the most vile and brute,
> The dullest or most noxious, should exist
> Divorced from good—a spirit and pulse of good,
> A life and soul, to every mode of being
> Inseparably linked.

That was written in 1797, and *Gipsies* was written ten years later: when Wordsworth's morality was beginning to get the upper hand of his imagination. But the simple fact that Wordsworth's phrase 'a spirit and pulse of good' is one of the clues to Keats's beautiful letter to Reynolds on 'diligent indolence', on February 19th, 1818, when he was superficially most annoyed with Wordsworth; and that another phrase—'we have all of us one human heart'—from the same poem, *The Old Cumberland Beggar*, is likewise a key to the lovely passage of his letter of March 1819 ('The creature hath a purpose and his eyes are bright with it'), indicates how deeply Wordsworth had entered into Keats's being. In part Keats had, as Goethe said of himself in relation to Spinoza, 'discovered himself' in Wordsworth.

This deep response of Keats to Wordsworth—so intimate that he can use the essential Wordsworth as a touchstone for the moody one—made Keats's meeting with Wordsworth a tremendous event for him. And it must have been no small shock when, on the occasion of his first call, he was kept waiting a long while, only to be hurriedly greeted by a Wordsworth all dressed up for the real event of the day—dinner with Mr. Kingston, one of the Commissioners of Stamp Duties. Wordsworth, of course, had his family to provide for; it was imperative that a mere Collector should be on good terms with a Commissioner, and one would imagine that Wordsworth ran a considerable risk of offending Mr. Kingston at Haydon's party: when Charles Lamb, tipsy and irrepressible, took a candle across the room for the purpose of examining the gentleman's 'organ'. Keats was of an age when young genius finds it difficult to make allowances for old. Mr. Kingston in particular seems to have stuck in Keats's gizzard. He wrote to Haydon on April 8th, 1818:

I am affraid Wordsworth went rather huff'd out of Town—I am sorry for it, he cannot expect his fireside Divan to be infallible, he cannot expect but that every Man of worth is as proud as himself. O that he had not fit with a Warrener, that is din'd at Kingston's.

But Keats's admiration recovered from the set-back; and Wordsworth became the subject of his conscious meditation, in the letter to Reynolds of May 3rd, 1818, from which we can see more clearly the unique position held by Wordsworth in Keats's hierarchy. The question with which he begins is the desirability of knowledge for 'widening speculation'—that is, according to Keats's constant usage of the word, extending the scope of the contemplative imagination—and 'easing "the burden of the mystery" '. With this burden he has been struggling, and in grappling with it he has been led to consider Wordsworth's genius, and how he differs from Milton. Uppermost in Keats's mind at the moment appear to have been the prefatory lines from *The Recluse*, with their implicit but friendly challenge to Milton. Milton is the standard of reference, in Keats's inquiry, as gold is 'the meridian line of worldly wealth'.

And here I have nothing but surmises, from an uncertainty whether Milton's apparently less anxiety for Humanity proceeds from his seeing further or no than Wordsworth: And whether Wordsworth has in truth epic passion, and martyrs himself to the human heart, the main region of his song.

The reference is to Wordsworth's claim, in the preface of *The Recluse*, that he is essaying a more arduous flight than Milton. 'Urania, I shall need Thy guidance, *or a greater Muse* . . .'

For I must tread on shadowy ground, must sink
Deep—and, aloft ascending, breathe in worlds
To which the heaven of heavens is but a veil.
All strength—all terror, single or in bands,
That ever was put forth in personal form—
Jehovah—with his thunder, and the choir
Of shouting Angels, and the empyreal thrones—
I pass them unalarmed. Not Chaos, not
The darkest pit of lowest Erebus,
Nor aught of blinder vacancy, scooped out
By help of dreams—can breed such fear and awe
As fall upon us often when we look
Into our Minds, into the Mind of Man—
My haunt, and the main region of my song.

The comparison between Milton's task and Wordsworth's is almost explicit; and the implication that Wordsworth's is the greater and more daring evident enough. So that Keats's question partly misses the mark. Wordsworth is not claiming that he has 'epic passion' and that he martyrs this to the human heart; but that his poem is to be more than the equivalent of Milton's epic, and is (so to speak) to be the veritable epic of the human soul. From this point of view it is worth consideration whether, in fact, Keats, when he attempted his epic, did not find himself inevitably caught between the Miltonic objectivity and the Wordsworthian subjectivity.

In the main, Keats admits Wordsworth's claim. Milton's 'philosophy' is in Keats's firm but modest judgment not adult: 'it may be tolerably understood by one not much advanced in years'. But Wordsworth's philosophy—if it is to be called a philosophy, seeing that 'Wordsworth is a great poet, if not a philosopher'—is beyond Keats's entire comprehension. He thinks he can understand and follow Wordsworth up to *Tintern Abbey*; and his idea is that Wordsworth, when he wrote that poem, was more or less in the position in which Keats is now, when the Chamber of Maiden Thought is gradually darkened, by consciousness of the mystery of pain and evil, but at the same time 'many doors are set open—all leading to dark passages'.

It seems to me that his Genius is explorative of those dark Passages. Now if we live, and go on thinking, we too shall explore them—he is a Genius and superior to us, in so far as he can, more than we, make discoveries, and shed a light in them—Here I must think Wordsworth is deeper than Milton—though I think it has depended more upon the general and gregarious advance of intellect, than individual greatness of Mind.

Still, Milton 'did not think into the human heart, as Wordsworth has done—Yet Milton as a Philosopher, had sure as great powers as Wordsworth'.

Behind Keats's difficulty is the fact that his problem is not one of philosophy, but of religion. Wordsworth is searching for a religious solution *de novo*, seeking it in the experience of the 'intensely feeling' natural man; whereas Milton is content with the solution offered by his peculiar version of Calvinist theology. How he came to be content with this is a question which can perhaps be answered only as Keats answered it: 'It proves that a mighty providence subdues the mightiest Minds to the service of the time being, whether it be in human Knowledge or Religion.' The complete freedom of the human Reason which Milton asserted under cover of his sterile theology was the means by which such minds as Wordsworth's and Keats's had been emancipated for their re-exploration of human experience, and their rediscovery of the truth of religion—that is, of the necessity and inevitability of the religious mode of apprehension.

In *The Excursion*, which Keats set at the head of Wordsworth's poetry, Wordsworth did explore the dark passages which Keats hoped to explore; and in the lovely tale of *Margaret* set before the human imagination, without flinching but also without fever, the problem of human pain. And Wordsworth has his answer—at once profoundly religious and completely simple.

> I stood, and leaning o'er the garden wall
> Reviewed that Woman's sufferings; *and it seemed*
> *To comfort me while with a brother's love*
> *I blessed her in the impotence of grief.*

Thus 'the burden of the mystery' is not merely lightened, but changed in the experience of the imaginative man who, like the Wanderer, 'could *afford* to suffer With those whom he saw suffer'. A great depth of experience lies beneath that bare and simple sentence of Wordsworth's—an experience which seems impossible to put in other words than his own. Says the Wanderer:

> But we have known that there is often found
> In mournful thoughts, *and always might be found,*
> A power to virtue friendly; were't not so,
> I am a dreamer among men, indeed
> An idle dreamer!

I suspect that Keats's desperate question in *The Fall of Hyperion*, concerning the poet and the dreamer, had behind it ineradicable, almost organic, memories of *The Excursion*, and of Wordsworth's solution to the mystery: which is, that pain, experienced to the depths of an 'intensely feeling' nature, mysteriously creates its own consolation. As it is with the imaginative man who, by the depth of his own experience, 'can afford to suffer With those whom he sees suffer', so with the directly suffering soul itself.

> 'My Friend! enough to sorrow you have given,
> The purposes of wisdom ask no more:
> Nor more would she have craved as due to one
> Who, in her worst distress, had ofttimes felt
> The unbounded might of prayer; and learned, with soul
> Fixed on the Cross, that consolation springs,
> From sources deeper far than deepest pain
> For the meek Sufferer.'

There, too, in unforced language, is the natural and unforced transition between Wordsworth's rediscovered religion and Christianity. I think those are astray who represent that there was a gulf between

Wordsworth's religion of Nature, and Christianity; it seems to me that the passing from the one to the other was unstrained. The Cross was, indeed, the symbol of that which was revealed to Wordsworth through his imaginative experience of Nature and the destinies of men. And surely it is true that it was the Cross, and its power to temper and change and regenerate the faculties of man in successive generations, which had made Wordsworth's 'natural' sensibility what it was. Where, it seems to me, Wordsworth failed himself and us was by his effort, when the power of sustained imagination had largely left him, to represent the actual process of his self-discovery as much more orthodox from the beginning than it had been.

However that may be, there can be no doubt, I think, that for Keats —in spite of a temporary reaction—Wordsworth was eminently gifted with Negative Capability. There was no irritable reaching after fact and reason in this teacher of a wise passiveness. It is Coleridge, not Wordsworth, who 'would let go by a fine isolated versimilitude caught from the Penetralium of mystery from being capable of remaining content with half-knowledge'. Even Keats's conclusion that 'This, pursued through volumes would perhaps take us no farther than this, that with a great poet the sense of Beauty overcomes all consideration', has its parallel in Wordsworth's words in the Preface to *The Recluse:*

> Beauty—a living Presence of the earth,
> Surpassing the most fair ideal Forms
> Which craft of delicate Spirits hath composed
> From earth's materials—waits upon my steps;
> Pitches her tents before me as I move,
> An hourly neighbour. Paradise, and groves
> Elysian, Fortunate Fields—like those of old
> Sought in the Atlantic Main—why should they be
> A history only of departed things,
> Or a mere fiction of what never was?
> For the discerning intellect of Man,
> When wedded to this goodly universe
> In love and holy passion, shall find these
> A simple produce of the common day.

But there we are made conscious no less of the distinction than of the affinity between Wordsworth's genius and Keats's. Wordsworth is in pursuit, not of beauty, but of a particular beauty—the beauty of the real world. It is not that he martyrs his epic passion to the human heart; but that he is a genius with a mission and a message. God, in him, had rediscovered God in the universe; an eternal harmony between the mind of man and the world, whereby the world of experience was transfigured in the awakened soul. He would tell how the prophet-poet came to be what he was, as a necessary phase of the unfolding of the omnipresent beauty of the whole, discerned by him when his own unfolding was fulfilled. He would tell of the falling-in-love of the discerning intellect with the universe, as a necessary prelude to 'the spousal verse of the great consummation' of the marriage:

> with the thing
> Contemplated, describe the Mind and Man
> Contemplating; and who, and what he was—
> The transitory Being that beheld
> This Vision.

That, from first to last, Wordsworth was—the man who had beheld a Vision. It was in vain that Hazlitt demanded his promised 'system'. System Wordsworth had none: save the history of his own experience culminating in the reality and truth of the self-surpassing Imagination, and the power of those in whom Imagination had been awakened to endure suffering and find consolation in the very experience of suffering itself. Wordsworth had no system; but he had a gospel.

In the light of these considerations, the previous suggestion that in *Hyperion* Keats was in fact caught between a desire for Miltonic objectivity and a compulsion towards Wordsworthian subjectivity, becomes more substantial. Keats was driven along the Wordsworthian path. He had to put to himself Wordsworth's questions; they were inescapable, not merely because of the events of his own life, but because he was a man of genius who began, like Wordsworth, with an 'intensely feeling' nature emancipated from religious assumption. One says 'emancipated', without hesitation, because the forms assumed by Protestantism in England by the end of the eighteenth century were such as could not conceivably command the allegiance of the sensitive and imaginative man. The Calvinist theology which supplied the structure to Milton's epic had lost its vitality for the imaginative mind, and Milton's own epic, as Blake acutely saw, derived its most splendid vitality from the rebellion of the unconscious Milton against the fetters imposed upon him by his conscious theology. If Milton's work were to be emulated, it could be emulated only as Wordsworth had emulated it, by attempting to create an epic of the rediscovery of vital religion in the experience of a prophetic man. Wordsworth, indeed, never completed his great enterprise; but what was revealed of it to Keats in *The Excursion* aroused in him thoughts beyond the reach of his soul. When he himself attempted an epic, in *Hyperion*, he experienced, at first hand, the nature of the prophetic compulsion to which Wordsworth had had to submit.

It was no wonder that Keats, in whom these half-conscious urges were contending, should have turned towards the Shakespearian ideal as he understood it. On the technical side, it meant for him the concrete objectivity of the drama, which seemed to dispense him from the need of a declared 'philosophy'; on the experiencing side, it would enable him to be as it were merely passive and receptive towards experience. But this latter ideal was not so easy to realize. Life is act, as well as contemplation, and Keats was compelled to make decisions: he had to decide to write for a living. In consequence, he collaborated with Brown on *Otho the Great*, he wrote a narrative poem, *Lamia*, and he decided to fag (if he could find the opening) as a journalist on the Liberal side. But by then, the beginning of the end was come; and we can only dream about the solution he might have found. The pinnacle of his actual poetical achievement is the *Hyperion*, in which the conflict between the Miltonic ideal and Wordsworthian necessity is apparent; *The Eve of St. Agnes*, in which there is a momentary and perfect fusion between the objective bent of his genius and his subjective experience; and the great *Odes*, wherein his total nature finds perfect utterance. The *Lamia* is not on this high level; it is an attempt to find an honourable compromise between the necessities of his own nature and the demands of the public—to tell a tale in verse which should have deep spiritual significance for the few and popular appeal for the many. Indeed, the works on which he was engaged in the summer of 1819, when the plenary inspiration of the spring had ebbed, and he had had to choose 'between despair and energy', reveal the complexity of the life-problem with which he was struggling. *Otho the Great* was mere hackwork; *Lamia* was an attempt to reach an actual public; the revision of *Hyperion* was largely a reaction against both these activities—an effort to create in conscious independence of any possible audience. It was 'the egotistical sublime' in a different sense from that in which Keats applied the phrase to Wordsworth, and it involved him in an intense inward struggle—a desperate questioning of his own purpose and significance, which, as I have already suggested, came to him with a Wordsworthian background.

The question of Moneta, in the rejected lines (ll. 188–210)—

> Art thou not of the dreamer tribe?
> The poet and the dreamer are distinct,
> Diverse, sheer opposite, antipodes.
> The one pours out a balm upon the world,
> The other vexes it.—

arose, in the mind of a man saturated, I believe, in the questionings of Wordsworth, above all in *The Excursion*. Unless the imaginative contemplation of the pain and evil of the world does engender in the mind 'a power to virtue friendly', cries the Wanderer in Book I: unless consolation verily does spring 'from sources deeper far than deepest pain'—then he is 'a dreamer, an idle dreamer'. In Book III, Poetry and Philosophy are pitted against one another. Says the narrator:

> if smiles
> Of scornful pity be the just reward
> Of Poesy thus courteously employed
> In framing models to improve the scheme
> Of Man's existence, and recast the world,
> Why should not grave Philosophy be styled,
> Herself, a dreamer of a kindred stock,
> A dreamer yet more spiritless and dull?
> Yes, shall the fine immunities she boasts
> Establish sounder titles of esteem
> For her, who (all too timid and reserved
> For onset, for resistance too inert,
> Too weak for suffering, and for hope too tame) . . .

The underlying drift of the incessant waves of intense meditative reflection in *The Excursion* is that philosophy, unless it is religion, is vain; and that poetry at its own imaginative height is religion, or the handmaid of religion. The poet who is faithful to his experience becomes the instrument by which the verity of religion is revealed anew. After a moment of agonized hesitation (of which the rejected lines are the witness) Keats also claimed for and in himself the operation of 'a power to virtue friendly'.

It is only when Wordsworth's and Keats's poetry are equally familiar, and equally intimate, that we can appreciate the depth and subtlety of Wordsworth's influence on Keats, or understand how superficial and transient was his impatience with what he called at one moment Wordsworth's 'philosophy', at another his lack of it. That was at a time when Keats was enamoured of the idea of 'turning all his soul' to Philosophy, and of preparing himself 'to ask Hazlitt in about a year's time the best metaphysical road I can take'. The last powerfully suggests that Keats's casual verdict that Wordsworth was 'no philosopher' was derived from Hazlitt. Assuredly, at this time Keats understood by 'philosophy' he knew not what; but Hazlitt possessed it—a mysterious something that would 'ease the burden of the mystery': something very different from Wordsworth's 'philosophy' which 'was engendered in the whims of an Egotist'. In order to acquire this mysterious knowledge, Keats was (he told Taylor on April 24th, 1818) preparing to forgo his promised tour in the North. 'There is but one way for me—the road lies through application, study and thought.'

He did not forgo his tour, and it took him straightway to Wordsworth's country. How saturated his being was with Wordsworth is shown by his pride in the fact (twice mentioned) that he 'discovered without a hint "that ancient woman seated on Helm Crag" '. That discovery, and his triumph in it, were possible only to one to whom even Wordsworth's minor poems had become a second nature. The moment Brown and he arrived at Bo'ness, Keats 'enquired of the waiter for Wordsworth'.

He said he knew him, and that he had been here a few days ago, canvassing for the Lowthers. What think you of that—Wordsworth versus Brougham!! Sad—sad—sad—and yet the family has been his friend always. What can we sav? We are now about seven miles from Rydale, and expect to see him to-morrow. You shall hear all about our visit.

Unfortunately, Wordsworth was not at home and Keats had to be content with leaving a note and 'sticking it up over what I knew must be Miss Wordsworth's portrait'. He confessed his great disappointment. But I suspect that Wordsworth's spirit was at work in Keats, when he meditated over the waterfall he had seen before breakfast.

What astonishes me more than any thing is the tone, the coloring, the slate, the stone, the moss, the rock-weed; or, if I may so say, the intellect, the countenance of such places. The space, the magnitude of mountains and waterfalls are well imagined before one sees them; but this countenance or intellectual tone must surpass every imagination and defy any remembrance. I shall learn poetry here and shall henceforth write more than ever, for the abstract endeavor of being able to add a mite to that mass of beauty which is harvested from these grand materials, by the finest spirits, and put into etherial existence for the relish of one's fellows. I cannot think with Hazlitt that these scenes make man appear little. I never forgot my stature so completely—I live in the eye; and my imagination, surpassed, is at rest.

Part of the language and part of the thought come, I think, from the Preface to *The Recluse:*

> Beauty—a living Presence of the earth,
> Surpassing the most fair ideal Forms
> Which craft of delicate Spirits hath composed
> From earth's materials—waits upon my steps.

And, there is possibly a connection between this unconscious identification with Wordsworth, and his disagreement with Hazlitt. Though it is interesting to note, as a glimpse of Keats's way of 'feeling his own life'—to use Maine de Biran's phrase—that Keats really misunderstands Hazlitt, in a peculiar way. When Hazlitt said that the mountain-scenery of the Lakes made one appear small, it certainly never occurred to him to think what might be its effect on one who was very conscious of his own diminutive stature. Hazlitt, we may be sure, would have stared in surprise had Keats answered him, viva voce: 'No, I never forgot so completely that I was five foot and half an inch.' To be taken out of himself, for Keats, was to *forget* that 'he felt small'; for Hazlitt, most likely, it was to be made 'to feel small'.

We have already seen, in the case of Hazlitt's criticism of the *Gipsies*, with what fine intuition Keats, when his judgment was undisturbed, steered between uncritical admiration of Wordsworth and accepting Hazlitt's view of him, even though he revered Hazlitt's 'depth of taste' almost as much as *The Excursion*. But perhaps he would have accepted this part of Hazlitt's description of Wordsworth.

Milton is his great idol, and he sometimes dares to compare himself with him. His Sonnets, indeed, have something of the same high-raised tone and prophetic spirit . . . We do not think our author has any very cordial sympathy with Shakespeare. How should he? Shakespeare was the least of an egotist of anybody in the world.

There is indubitably an affinity between Wordsworth and Milton, and Wordsworth was conscious of it; and just as Wordsworth felt more sympathy with Milton than with Shakespeare, so Keats felt more sympathy with Shakespeare than with Milton. But Keats's feelings towards Milton and Wordsworth were very different. Milton was remote, Wordsworth was near: and this not merely in point of time. Wordsworth, we may fairly say, was almost as intimate to Keats's experience as Shakespeare himself. When Keats imitates Milton he is conscious of what he is doing; the echoes of Wordsworth are innumerable and unconscious. At least, I can hardly conceive that Keats was aware that a vital germ of the thought of the *Ode on a Grecian Urn* came from the ninth of Wordsworth's *Miscellaneous Sonnets*, on the sight of a picture painted by Sir George Beaumont:

> Praised be the Art whose subtle power could stay
> Yon cloud, and fix it in that glorious shape;
> Nor would permit the thin smoke to escape,
> Nor those bright sunbeams to forsake the day;
> Which stopped that band of travellers on their way,

Ere they were lost within the shady wood;
And showed the Bark upon the glassy flood
For ever anchored in her sheltering bay.
Soul-soothing Art! whom Morning, Noontide, Even,
Do serve with all their changeful pageantry;
Thou, with ambition modest yet sublime,
Here, for the sight of mortal man, hast given
To one brief moment caught from fleeting time
The appropriate calm of blest eternity.

I do not believe that he knew, when he composed the *Lines Written in the Highlands after a Visit to Burns's Country*, that he was echoing the thought and the cadence of Wordsworth's *Star-Gazers*. Why, asks Wordsworth, watching an eager crowd in Leicester Square taking turns to gaze through a telescope, does each man go away slackly, 'as if dissatisfied'?

Or is it that, when human Souls, a journey long have had
And are returned into themselves, they cannot but be sad?

Does, then, a deep and earnest thought the blissful mind employ
Of him who gazes, or has gazed? a grave and steady joy,
That doth reject all show of pride, admits no outward sign,
Because not of this noisy world, but silent and divine!

In Keats's poem Burns's birthplace takes the place of the remote moon, as the object of contemplation which draws the soul out of its bodily sheath.

At such a time the soul's a child, in childhood is the brain;
Forgotten is the worldly heart—alone, it beats in vain—
Ay, if a madman could have leave to pass a healthful day,
To tell his forehead's swoon and faint when first began decay,
He might make tremble many a one whose spirit had gone forth
To find a bard's low cradle-place about the silent North!
Scanty the hour and few the steps beyond the bourn of care,
Beyond the sweet and bitter world—beyond it unaware!
Scanty the hour and few the steps, because a longer stay
Would bar return, and make a man forget his mortal way.

Keats's experience is the more intense; but thought and metre alike seem to derive directly from Wordsworth.

Such reminiscences, though surely worth collecting, belong rather to the surface of an influence of Wordsworth on Keats which, as I have come more deeply to appreciate Wordsworth's greatness, has appeared to me continually more subtle and more pervasive. In such a province of inquiry it is very difficult to be positive in one's judgments; difficult above all to distinguish between the inevitable fusion of two profound poetic influences in the critic's own mind and the direct influence of the one poet upon the other. And I am inclined to be thankful that when I wrote *Keats and Shakespeare*, I did not know Wordsworth so well as I have come to know him since.

Anyhow, I am glad I was not acutely conscious of Wordsworth's influence on Keats; it might have 'cramped my style'. As things are now, I am free to speculate. I can wonder, for example, whether the real seed of Keats's 'sensation' of *Hyperion* was not sown in him by the forty lines in *The Excursion*, Book IV, describing the religion of Greece, when the

lonely herdsman, stretched
On the soft grass through half a summer's day,
With music lulled his indolent repose:
And, in some fit of weariness, if he,
When his own breath was silent, chanced to hear
A distant strain, far sweeter than the sounds
Which his poor skill could make, his fancy fetched,
Even from the blazing chariot of the sun,
A beardless Youth, who touched a golden lute,
And filled the illumined groves with ravishment.[2]

Far more, it seems to me, than in anything of Milton's, in these lines of Wordsworth's is the germ of the imaginative feeling of *Hyperion*. This is not the classicism of Milton at all, though to define the difference would need an essay; but I will say at a venture that Milton's classicism is still in the main a medieval classicism that sees through a glass darkly and not face to face. Wordsworth's classicism is that of an emancipated soul which has inherited the intellectual freedom to see things in a pagan clarity, at the very moment that it is laying anew the foundations of the Christian religion. Greek myth is a legend for Milton, for Wordsworth a vision.

[2] See notes, page 145.

Great God! I'd rather be
A Pagan suckled in a creed outworn;
So might I, standing on this pleasant lea,
Have glimpses that would make me less forlorn;
Have sight of Proteus rising from the sea;
Or hear old Triton blow his wreathèd horn.

That is the feeling-tone, the 'sensation' of the Greek world for Keats. I think it was Wordsworth who opened the gates of his senses to it.

NOTES

[1] I am now inclined to wonder whether my reading of 'if he had lov'd' is correct. De Selincourt prints the lines with a comma:

if he had lov'd,
and been well nurtured in his mother tongue.

Garrod prints them without the comma. It is many years now since I saw the Woodhouse transcript on which Garrod's text is based. If the comma is deleted, it becomes rather more probable that Keats meant: 'If he had loved his mother tongue and been well nurtured in it'. The presence or absence of the comma would not, of course, settle the question. It is perhaps enough to say that another interpretation than mine is possible, though I think the alternative interpretation imposes a rather un-Keatsian rhythm.

[2] Bailey remembered that 'Keats said this description of Apollo should have ended at the "golden lute", and have left imagination to complete the picture, how he "filled the illumined groves" '. A subtle question of taste, on which, despite my admiration of the beautiful line to be sacrificed, I feel Keats was right. The criticism shows how carefully Keats had pondered the passage.

17

KEATS AND FRIENDSHIP

From Keats.

KEATS's reply of October 27th, 1818, to Woodhouse's remonstrance with him for having said he would write no more poetry, is justly famous. It contains his definition of the poetical character—of the kind which he himself possessed, as distinct from 'the Wordsworthian, or egotistical sublime'. The peculiarity of this poetical character is that it has no fixed character, no 'unchangeable attribute', no 'identity'; it is 'continually in for and filling some other body'. Because of this, although 'it is a wretched thing to confess', nevertheless 'it is a very fact that not one word I ever utter can be taken for granted as an opinion growing out of my identical nature—how can it, when I have no nature?'

Thus he repudiates responsibility for his declaration that he would write no more poetry. And in the second part of his letter he reaffirms his determination 'to reach to as high a summit in poetry as the nerve bestowed upon me will suffer'. He says he feels assured he would go on writing poetry from 'the mere yearning and fondness he has for the beautiful' even if his 'night's labours should be burnt every morning'. Then, like a philosopher, he reflects that even in this asseveration, 'I am perhaps not speaking from myself, but from some character in whose soul I now live'. But he concludes: 'I am sure however that this next sentence is from myself. I feel your anxiety, good opinion and friendliness in the highest degree.'

So Keats has a self, after all. He has an 'unchangeable attribute', and 'identical nature'. It consists in his unvarying response to genuine friendship. That this was a true estimate of his own character his letters are a witness that cannot be gainsaid.

From the very beginnings of his conscious thinking about his own nature his awareness of the two main elements of which it was composed is visible. 'I am certain of nothing', he wrote to Bailey on November 22nd, 1817, 'but of the holiness of the Heart's affections, and the truth of Imagination—what the imagination seizes as Beauty must be truth.' These are, from the beginning, his two faiths, his two loyalties: to friendship and love, and to beauty and truth. The absorbing spiritual quest of his life was to reconcile them, or rather to make apprehensible to himself the reconciliation of which he was intuitively convinced. This was the theme of *Endymion*.

Perhaps we may put it, tentatively, that there were two kinds of beauty to which Keats felt instinctive allegiance: moral beauty and 'the principle of beauty in all things'. Poetic genius was the gift of discovering that universal beauty, which was truth. It began with the absorbed delight in the pleasant wonders of the obviously beautiful in nature and mankind which he ascribed to the Chamber of Maiden Thought, and described in such a passage as the opening of *Endymion*; it passed beyond this into a painful awareness that 'the world is full of misery and heartbreak, pain, sickness and oppression' and became dedicated to the search for 'the balance of good and evil'. This was the object of that 'philosophy' to which Keats turned. 'I have been hovering for some time', he told Taylor on April 27th 1818, 'between an exquisite sense of the luxurious and a love for philosophy—were I calculated for the former I should be glad—but as I am not I shall turn all my soul to the latter.' Philosophy, for Keats, meant the search for wisdom; and wisdom consisted in seeing the beauty of the truth. Because he had sought it with passionate devotion, and paid the price of 'dying into life', he was rescued by Moneta in *The Fall of Hyperion*.

> None can usurp this height (returned that shade)
> But those to whom the miseries of the world
> Are misery, and will not let them rest.

This is the poet's final vindication: that he seeks, and seeks to declare, the beauty of the whole truth. In the last resort it depends upon his spiritual integrity.

On the way to that final discovery or final self-judgment, Keats never left his hold of his admiration for simple moral beauty. He deliberately preferred it to genius, if there had to be a choice between them.

> So I do believe [he wrote to his brothers on January 13th, 1818]—not thus speaking with any poor vanity—that works of genius are the first things in this world. No! for that sort of probity and disinterestedness which such men as Bailey possess does hold and grasp the tiptop of any spiritual honors that can be paid to anything in this world. And moreover having this feeling at this present come over me in its full force, I sat down to write to you with a grateful heart, in that I had not a brother who did not feel and credit me for a deeper feeling and devotion for his uprightness, than for any marks of genius however splendid.

There, evidently, speaks the inmost self of Keats. And this integrity, or moral beauty, is for Keats, the condition of friendship. Friendship is the mutual response to this quality. Hence his admiration for Georgina Wylie, his brother George's wife. 'I like her better and better—she is the most disinterested woman I ever knew.' And that is why, in the extempore acrostic he wrote on her name, he declared his faith again that loyalty in friendship was as noble and indeed divine as supreme poetic achievement: they equally belonged to the order of ultimate reality.

> Imagine not that greatest mastery
> And kingdom over all the realms of verse
> Nears more to heaven in aught than when we nurse
> And surety give to love and brotherhood.

To the same effect is the conclusion of his letter to Reynolds on the Chamber of Maiden Thought. Though he has passed into the Third Chamber, whence all the passages are dark, and the burden of the mystery is full upon him, nevertheless,

> After all, there is something real in the world—Moore's present to Hazlitt is real—I like that Moore, and am glad I saw him at the theatre just before I left town. Tom has spit a leetle blood this afternoon, and that is rather a damper—but I know—the truth is there is something real in the world. *(May 3rd, 1818)*

In exactly the same terms he wrote to Bailey: 'Your tearing a spiritless and gloomy letter up to rewrite to me is what I never shall forget —it was to me a real thing.'

(January 23rd, 1818)

Friendship, based on a respect for integrity, is a reality, proof against all scepticism and moral bewilderment. Though imagination

> Lost in a sort of purgatory blind,
> Cannot refer to any standard law
> Of either earth or heaven—

still friendship and love are real. Keats knows. Therefore he can, without any pretence or amicable self-delusion, prophesy that Reynolds's 'third Chamber of Life shall be a lucky and a gentle one —stored with the wine of love—and the bread of friendship'.

Keats himself, indeed, had a genius for friendship only less remarkable than his genius for poetry. He made allowances for his friends that his friends seldom made for one another. Reynolds and Haydon had fallen out; so had Haydon and Hunt.

Considering all things [Keats wrote to his brothers on January 13th, 1818], Haydon's frequent neglect of his appointments &c, his notes were bad enough to put Reynolds on the right side of the question—but then Reynolds has no powers of sufferance; no idea of having the thing against him; so he answered Haydon in one of the most cutting letters I ever read; exposing to himself all his own weaknesses and going on to an excess, which whether it is just or no, is what I would fain have unsaid, the fact is they are both in the right, and both in the wrong.

In regard to the quarrel between Hunt and Haydon, 'all I hope is at some time to bring them together again'. He returns to the same theme in a letter to Bailey on January 23rd, 1818.

Things have happen'd lately of great Perplexity. You must have heard of them. Reynolds and Haydon retorting and recriminating—and parting for ever—the same thing has happened between Haydon and Hunt—It is unfortunate—Men should bear with each other—there lives not the man who may not be cut up, aye hashed to pieces on his weakest side. The best of Men have but a portion of good in them—a kind of spiritual yeast in their frames which creates the ferment of existence—by which a Man is propell'd to act and strive and buffet with Circumstance. The sure way, Bailey, is first to know a Man's faults, and then be passive—if after that he insensibly draws you towards him you have no Power to break the link. Before I felt interested in either Reynolds or Haydon—I was well read in their faults yet knowing them I have been cementing gradually with both. I have an affection for them both for reasons almost opposite—and to both must I of necessity cling—supported always by the hope that when a little time—a few years shall have tried me more fully in their esteem I may be able to bring them together—the time must come because they have both hearts—and they will recollect the best parts of each other when this gust is overblown.

And there were moments when he was aware that his genius for poetry and his genius for friendship were intimately connected.

They do not know me [he wrote to George in October 1818], not even my most intimate acquaintance—I give into their feelings as though I were refraining from irritating a little child—Some think me middling, others silly, others foolish—every one thinks he sees my weak side against my will, when in truth it is with my will—I am content to be thought all this because I have in my own breast so great a resource. This is one great reason why they like me so; because they can all show to advantage in a room, and eclipse from a certain tact one who is reckoned to be a good Poet—I hope I am not there playing tricks 'to make the angels weep': I think not: for I have not the least contempt for my species; and though it may sound paradoxical: my greatest elevations of Soul leave me every time more humbled.

Unlike most of his friends, Keats 'cared not to be in the right'; he did not in the least mind 'having the thing against him'. He did not identify his opinions with his self, nor believe that his own integrity was menaced if they were challenged. He strove, by instinct, and conviction, to keep his mind 'a thoroughfare for all thoughts: not a select party'. And the attitude embraced his friends. He gratefully accepted their 'light and shade', but never hesitated to criticize them when they failed in humanity. All his admiration for Hazlitt did not prevent him from regretting his reference to Southey's 'few contemptible grey hairs'; nor his affection for Reynolds from wishing unsaid his exposure of Haydon's weaknesses; nor his respect for Bailey from condemning (before he imaginatively condoned) his behaviour to Jane Reynolds. But he was infinitely tolerant towards them. Reading Keats's letters one understands better why Shakespeare's friends called him 'gentle', because it seems there is no other word for this rare quality of soul. But this 'gentleness' is consubstantial with an extraordinary strength. It was intimately allied to what Keats called his 'passiveness', which when pressed home, appears as a truly remarkable absence of egotism, in every sense of that protean quality.

Keats, indeed, seems always to be waiting and listening for the response of something in himself that is not himself, to all experience. Of these responses two are pre-eminent, in Keats's own mind, and consequently in ours who study him. One is the response of the Heart; the other the response of the Imagination. Both these faculties, or conditions, of the soul are, in his language, 'self-destroying'. The response of the Heart is human love; the response of the Imagination is—may one, in these days, say it?—divine Love. The connection between them—or one important thread of the connection—is that the divine Love supervenes through the disappointment of human love: the convincement of the nerves that 'the world is full of misery and heartbreak, pain, sickness and oppression'. The human love dies, as it were, and is reborn into an imaginative understanding that its defeat is part of the divine pattern for the regeneration of man.

Do you not see how necessary a World of Pains and troubles is to school an Intelligence and make it a Soul? A Place where the heart must feel and suffer in a thousand diverse ways. Not merely is the Heart a Hornbook, it is the Mind's Bible, it is the teat from which the Mind or Intelligence sucks its identity.

So likewise the simple response to beauty, which belongs to the same level of naïve experience as simple human love, is also required to die and to be reborn as a perception of the beauty which includes both good and evil.

The clue to which Keats clung in the labyrinth was 'the holiness of the Heart's affections'. These, he declared to Woodhouse, belonged to the 'identical self'. They, in him and others, were real: a manifestation of an ultimate reality. But this 'self', to which the promptings of the heart gave voice, was not a self in the ordinary meaning of the word; or, at any rate, it was the enemy of the egotistical self. It was the heart in each which would in time overcome the selfish pride of Reynolds and Haydon; it was the heart to which the mind must humbly listen and obey in order to become an individual soul.

Keats's fidelity to 'the holiness of the Heart's affections' did not make him a poet; but they made him a great one.

18

THE SHAKESPEARE MAN

This essay is extracted from pages 159–187 of Shakespeare *(Cape, 1936). The passage omitted is indicated by a line of dots. The title is taken from a later chapter.*

The Bastard is a cynic, and not a cynic at all. He is realist and idealist at once, yet he is not divided. He is the natural Man, in whom the gift of consciousness has served only to make nature more truly itself. He is detached from the world only to be more effectively a part of it. A new *kind* of experience, different from any that had hitherto found utterance in Shakespeare's plays, speaks in him. He is conscious, as no Shakespearian character has been conscious before. Listen to the comment of his soul on the match between Lewis and Blanch:

Mad world! mad kings! mad composition!
John, to stop Arthur's title in the whole,
Hath willingly departed with a part,
And France, whose armour conscience buckled on,
Whom zeal and charity brought to the field
As God's own soldier, rounded in the ear
With that same purpose-changer, that sly devil,
That broker, that still breaks the pate of faith,
That daily break-vow, he that wins of all,
Of kings, of beggars, old men, young men, maids,
Who having no external thing to lose
But the word 'maid', cheats the poor maid of that,
That smooth-fac'd gentleman, tickling Commodity,
Commodity, the bias of the world,
The world, who of himself is peised well,
Made to run even upon even ground,
Till this advantage, this vile-drawing bias,
This sway of motion, this Commodity,
Makes it take head from all indifferency,
From all direction, purpose, course, intent:
And this same bias, this Commodity,

This bawd, this broker, this all-changing word,
Clapp'd on the outward eye of fickle France,
Hath drawn him from his own determin'd aid,
From a resolv'd and honourable war
To a most base and vile-concluded peace.
And why rail I on this Commodity?
But for because he hath not woo'd me yet:
Not that I have the power to clutch my hand
When his fair angels would salute my palm;
But for my hand, as unattempted yet,
Like a poor beggar, raileth upon the rich.
Well, whiles I am a beggar, I will rail
And say there is no sin but to be rich;
And being rich, my virtue then shall be
To say there is no vice but beggary.
Since kings break faith upon commodity
Gain, be my lord, for I will worship thee.

(II. i. 561–98)

We are not deceived. The Bastard's cynicism about himself is simply that of a man who hates to strike an attitude in his own eyes. He can afford to be cynical about himself, because he knows he cannot do anything base. He has no need of virtue, because he has no vice to conceal.

The raw material of the Bastard is the crude character in *The Troublesome Raigne of King John*. Shakespeare simply took him and made him live. His one trait in the old play was that at the critical moment he preferred to sacrifice his lawful inheritance for the honour of being known to be the bastard of Cœur de Lion. With this one trait—no slight one—to build on, Shakespeare made him into the likeness of a King of England, by 'sovereignty of nature'. He becomes the champion of English unity, and the victorious assailant of Papal pretensions: the healthy substance of the corrupt shadow which is King John. But his political function, though glorious, is subordinate to his function of being himself. He is the first of Shakespeare's great characters, who speaks with a voice of his own, sentiments of his own. He is *the* Englishman, the 'madcap' revolutionary Englishman. His contempt for the externalities of rank is complete.

ELI. Whether hadst thou rather be a Faulconbridge
And like thy brother, to enjoy thy land,
Or the reputed son of Cœur de Lion,
Lord of thy presence and no land beside?

BAST. Madam, an if my brother had my shape,
And I had his, Sir Robert's his, like him;
And if my legs were two such riding-rods,
My arms such eel-skins stuff'd, my face so thin
That in mine ear I durst not stick a rose
Lest men should say, 'Look, where three-farthings goes!'
And, to his shape, were heir to all this land,
Would I might never stir from off this place,
I would give it every foot to have this face,
I would not be Sir Nob in any case.

(I. i. 134–47)

To quote the Bastard is dangerous: since he is one of the most splendid of Shakespeare's creations, and one of the most neglected, one is tempted to go on and on. High-spirited, brave, dare-devil, witty, humorous, penetrating, yet capable of a profound depth of feeling, he is manifestly Shakespeare's ideal of an Englishman. He has an easy contempt for the Englishman who does not rest true to himself, but apes foreign manners; he laughs at the super-subtlety of Machiavellian 'policy'. It is largely because the solid coherence of his character is not realized that misguided attempts have been made to emend his comment on his own 'wild counsel' that Lewis and John should first unite forces against obdurate Angiers, and then fight it out between themselves:

How like you this wild counsel, mighty states?
Smacks it not something of the 'policy'?

(II. i. 395–6)

Some editors would read 'true policy'; but 'the policy' is precisely 'the bare and rotten policy' denounced by the Bastard's lineal successor, Harry Percy—something unEnglish and unnatural, which the Bastard contemptuously recommends to kings whom he contemns; 'for', as he says, with his peculiar humorous cynicism,

For he is but a bastard to the time
Who doth not smack of observation.

He is the detached observer of a hypocritical and hollow world. Because he has his way to make, he cannot afford to stand aloof; because he lacks 'the inward motion'

to deliver
Sweet, sweet, sweet poison for the age's tooth

—namely, the outward courtesy and compliment which smooths the road to advancement—he must acquire the art,

Which, though I will not practise to deceive,
Yet, to avoid deceit, I mean to learn;
For it shall strew the footsteps of my rising.
(I. i. 214–6)

He cannot learn it. His is a nature on which nurture of this kind will never stick. *C'est plus fort que lui:* he cannot hold his tongue; it will dart out to lash pretentiousness of rank or fashion. He satirizes the conceited sonnetteering in which Shakespeare himself had copiously indulged:

K. PHI. What say'st thou, boy? Look in the lady's face.
LEW. I do, my lord; and in her eye I find
A wonder, or a wondrous miracle,
The shadow of myself form'd in her eye;
Which, being but the shadow of your son,
Becomes a sun, and makes your son a shadow.
I do protest I never loved myself,
Till now infixèd I beheld myself
Drawn in the flattering table of her eye.
(II. i. 494–502)

That is altogether too like Sonnet 24, to permit us to suppose that Shakespeare was not laughing at himself also, when he made the Bastard continue:

BAST. Drawn in the flattering table of her eye!
Hang'd in the frowning wrinkle of her brow!
And quarter'd in her heart! he doth espy
Himself love's traitor: this is pity now,
That, hang'd and drawn and quarter'd, there should be
In such a love so vile a lout as he.
(II. i. 503–9)

Rhetoric goes the same way as fashionable love-conceits in the Bastard's comment on the defiant hyperboles of the citizens of Angiers:

BAST. Here's a stay
That shakes the rotten carcase of old Death
Out of his rags! Here's a large mouth, indeed,
That spits forth death and mountains, rocks and seas,
Talks as familiarly of roaring lions
As maids of thirteen do of puppy-dogs!
What cannoneer begot this lusty blood?
He speaks plain cannon-fire, and smoke and bounce;
He gives the bastinado with his tongue:

Our ears are cudgell'd; not a word of his
But buffets better than a fist of France:
Zounds! I was never so bethump'd with words
Since I first call'd my brother's father dad.

(II. i. 454–67)

The last line is superb; and for the full flavour of the passage one needs to remember that *Bounce!* in Shakespeare's day rendered the sound of a cannon—perhaps not quite so impressive as the modern *Boom!*—but neither were the cannon.

On every level the Bastard is the triumphant enemy of pretension. He justifies the claim made falsely years later by Edmund in *King Lear*:

Why brand they us
With base? with baseness? bastardy? base, base?
Who, in the lusty stealth of nature, take
More composition and fierce quality
Than doth within a dull, stale, tired bed
Go to the creating a whole tribe of fops
Got 'tween asleep and wake? Well, then
Legitimate Edgar, I must have your land.

(*Lear* I. ii. 9–16)

The Bastard's behaviour is the exact opposite of Edmund's. He sacrifices his land rather than forgo the honour of being his true father's son. He is born out of convention to display the hollowness of convention. When he is knighted:

A foot of honour better than I was;
But many a many foot of land the worse.
Well, now can I make any Joan a lady.
'Good-den, Sir Richard!'—'God-a-mercy, fellow!'
And if his name be George, I'll call him Peter;
For new-made honour doth forget men's names:
'Tis too respective and too sociable
For your conversion. Now, your traveller,
He and his tooth-pick at my worship's mess;
And when my knightly stomach is sufficed,
Why then I suck my teeth, and catechize
My picked man of countries: 'My dear sir,'
Thus, leaning on my elbow, I begin,
'I shall beseech you'—that is question now;
And then comes answer like an Absey book:
'O sir,' says answer, 'at your best command;

At your employment; at your service, sir:'
'No, sir,' says question, 'I, sweet sir, at yours:'
And so, ere answer knows what question would,
Saving in dialogue of compliment,
And talking of the Alps and Apennines,
The Pyrenean and the river Po,
It draws towards supper in conclusion so.
But this is worshipful society . . .

(I. i. 182–204)

His taunt to Austria—'And hang a calf-skin on those recreant limbs'—is flashed at the Emperor so surprisingly that it is truly comic; but it is more than comic. It shows the quickness of the Bastard's natural sympathy with Constance's wrongs; and at every repetition it illuminates the cowardice and corruption of 'the mighty states'.

In Act IV, Scene iii, the Bastard reaches his pinnacle. The sight of the dead body of Arthur bewilders him. He, who knows so well what Commodity may do, nevertheless cannot believe that the King would command a murder so devilish. The three barons, Salisbury, Bigot, and Pembroke, are eloquent in horror; the Bastard is silent. Salisbury appeals to him. Still he is silent. Then he says, simply:

It is a damned and a bloody work;
The graceless action of a heavy hand,
If that it be the work of any hand.

(IV. iii. 57–9)

He is in control, rushing to no conclusions. When Hubert enters, Salisbury draws his sword upon him. Then the Bastard speaks with the authority and the accent of an Othello:

Your sword is bright, sir, put it up again!

The fierce quarrel blazes.

PEM. Cut him to pieces.
BAST. Keep the peace, I say.
SAL. Stand by, or I shall gall you, Faulconbridge.
BAST. Thou wert better gall the devil, Salisbury:
If thou but frown on me, or stir thy foot,
Or teach thy hasty spleen to do me shame,
I'll strike thee dead. Put up thy sword betime;
Or I'll so maul you and your toasting-iron
That you shall think the devil is come from hell.

(IV. iii. 93–100)

He quells them all, and they depart, leaving Hubert and himself alone. Then, immediately they are gone, hard upon the splendid line of 'the toasting-iron', comes a splendour of a different kind:

> Here's a good world! Knew you of this fair work?
> Beyond the infinite and boundless reach
> Of mercy, if thou didst this deed of death,
> Art thou damned, Hubert.
>
> (IV. iii. 116–19)

It thrills us, and fires the heart, as nothing in Shakespeare yet. It is the voice of a king by nature: moved to the depths, yet not moved in such sort that he cannot distinguish the voice of innocence in Hubert.

> Go, bear him in thy arms.
> I am amazed, methinks, and lose my way
> Among the thorns and dangers of this world.
> How easy dost thou take all England up!
> From forth this morsel of dead royalty
> The life, the right and truth of all this realm
> Is fled to heaven; and England now is left
> To tug and scramble and to part by the teeth
> The unowed interest of proud-swelling state.
> Now for the bare-pick'd bone of majesty
> Doth dogged war bristle his angry crest
> And snarleth in the gentle eyes of peace.
> Now powers from home, and discontents at home
> Meet in one line; and vast confusion waits,
> As doth a raven on a sick-fall'n beast,
> The imminent decay of wrested pomp.
> Now happy he whose cloak and cincture can
> Bear out this tempest.
>
> (IV. iii. 139–56)

The Bastard is a true hero, and he is Shakespeare's first. That Shakespeare was fascinated by his own creation is probable in itself, and, to my mind, confirmed by the fact that the name pops up, very oddly, in a play which followed soon after *King John*. The English suitor to Portia's hand in *The Merchant of Venice* is a Falconbridge. I think it is a shadow of the same man, or the same substance.

> NER. What say you, then, to Falconbridge, the young baron of England?
>
> POR. You know I say nothing to him, for he understands not me, nor I him: he hath neither Latin, French, nor Italian, and you will come to court and swear that I have a poor pennyworth in the English. He is a proper man's picture, but, alas, who can converse with a dumb-show?
>
> (*M.V.* I. ii. 71–7)

For a moment, we are tempted to regret that he did not marry Portia; he would have made her a nobler husband than Bassanio. But we cannot imagine him speaking anything but English—nor her either, for that matter.

Then we remember that we need not worry our heads with finding him a wife. Shakespeare has seen to it in *Henry V*. The Bastard's Portia is a French princess; her name (as it would be in Shakespeare) is Kate; and the manner of the wooing will be found at length at the end of the play.

> And while thou livest, dear Kate, take a fellow of plain and uncoined constancy; for he perforce must do thee right, because he hath not the gift to woo in other places: for these fellows of infinite tongue, that can rhyme themselves into ladies' favours, they do always reason themselves out again. What! a speaker is but a prater, a rhyme is but a ballad. A good leg will fall; a straight back will stoop; a black beard will turn white; a curled pate will grow bald; a fair face will wither; a full eye will wax hollow: but a good heart, Kate, is the sun and moon, or rather the sun and not the moon; for it shines bright and never changes, but keeps his course truly. If thou wilt have such a one, take me; and take me, take a soldier; take a soldier, take a king.
>
> (*H5*. v. ii. 148–65)

§

Before his final avatar as Harry the King, the Bastard was to undergo an exciting metamorphosis. He was to divide, by an imaginative fission, into Falstaff and Hotspur: into the cynical critic of honour, and its idolator. His bluntness and his bravery into Harry Percy; his wit and his humour into Jack Falstaff. But that is a mechanical way of describing the affiliation. There are no such simple equations in the world of the imagination. Hotspur is a complete man, witty enough in all conscience. It is simply that what was one character grows into two.

In consequence, the writing of histories began to be unmanageable. The imaginative world threatened to burst the historical frame. Fortunately, there was not much farther to go. Once the gap between *Richard II* and the first *Henry VI* was filled, the sequence would be complete, because the Tudors were sacrosanct. But the new afflatus made things difficult; or rather, by making things easy, made it difficult to 'join the flats' of history. Shakespeare did his best. *Richard II* had ended with Bolingbroke's perfunctory repentance, and his unconvincing resolve to go crusading. The link is picked up at the beginning of *Henry IV*, Part 1. The king is supposed to have been considering ways and means for his crusade, when the news of the fighting in Wales and the North was brought to him. The episode is unhistorical and without consequences; it is dragged in to make a connection, and is evidence of the interruption by *King John*. Historical continuity and imaginative continuity are of two houses. And nothing could make *Henry IV* imaginatively continuous with *Richard II*.

The person of Henry IV suffers for the interruption. As Bolingbroke in *Richard II* he was a clamorous nonentity, because Shakespeare was not interested in him; as a crowned king, he remains a nonentity, again because Shakespeare is not interested in him. But the causes of Shakespeare's indifference to him are different. He was not interested in Bolingbroke in *Richard II*, because he was interested for a moment not in the fact but in the problem of rebellion. The problem of the deposing of an anointed king interested him; therefore he was not interested in the mere instrument of his deposition. Now that Bolingbroke himself is an anointed king, Shakespeare is not interested in him, because he is not interested in history any more: it is become an excuse and framework for creating characters—characters with a national significance: Englishmen. This is good history: far better history indeed than would ever be written until the age of authentic history began, because it is not history at all. It is imaginative drama of contemporary England.

The Bastard had begun it. He was contemporary through and through. There was nothing remote about his 'I would not be Sir Nob in any case', his laughing contempt for the Italianate intelligentsia and the fashions in conversation, in sonnetteering and in rhetoric; on the contrary, he was own brother to Shakespeare himself, having digested his experience, and being resolved like him to make his way. We know the motto on the Bastard's coat-of-arms: it is the same as Shakespeare's—*Non sans droict*; and, I think we can guess the quality of Shakespeare's resolution; it is not very different from the Bastard's—he will learn, if he can,

from the inward motion to deliver
Sweet, sweet, sweet poison for the age's tooth:
Which, though I will not practise to deceive,
Yet, to avoid deceit, I mean to learn.

This compromise with the demands of the age—instinctive adjustment rather than compromise—was to be Shakespeare's own. The critic of sonnets wrote a hundred and fifty of them; the laugher at rhetoric was to compose still more splendid rhetoric for Hotspur and King Harry; the jiber at Italianization had in mind at this moment a series of plays in Italian settings. He wears his rue with a difference;

he does not practise to deceive. His Italians are Englishmen, with no possibility of mistake. Mercutio's divinity is, astonishingly, Queen Mab, and, for a man of his name and country, he has a singular attitude towards things Italian.

BEN. Why, what is Tybalt?
MER. More than prince of cats, I can tell you. O, he is the courageous captain of compliments. He fights you as you sing prick-song, keeps time distance and proportion; rests me his minim rest—one, two, and the third in your bosom: the very butcher of a silk button, a duellist, a duellist; a gentleman of the very first house, of the first and second cause: ah, the immortal passado! the punto reverso! the hai!
BEN. The what?
MER. The pox of such antic, lisping, affecting fantasticoes; these new tuners of accents! 'By Jesu, a very good blade! a very tall man! a very good whore!' Why, is not this a lamentable thing, grandsire, that we should be thus afflicted with these strange flies, these fashion-mongers, these perdonami's, who stand so much on the new form, that they cannot sit at ease on the old bench? O, their bones, their bones!

(*RJ*. II. iv. 18–38)

The artifice is transparent: this is no more Italian than it is Chinese. It is right English, and from the same mould as the Bastard. It has just so much of 'the smack of observation' as the Bastard recommended if he were not to be 'a bastard to the time'; just so much outward inclining to the fashion as was necessary to take contemporary attention. To suppose that in order to acquire this thin veneer of Italianization it was necessary for Shakespeare to travel in Italy is extravagant.

Shakespeare indulges the fashion and smiles at it: not, I think, in order to smile at it. He is no deliberate satirist: he is something rarer—a conscious man, who can surrender himself to this and to that, and yet know what he is doing. Falstaff and Hotspur are equally valid. They are imaginative brothers, sons of the Bastard, each with 'a wild trick of his ancestor', both essentially 'madcap'. One pursues honour; the other will have none of it. How did Shakespeare think of honour? As neither, as both. One is a master of blank verse rhetoric, the other laughs at it.

FAL. Weep not sweet queen, for trickling tears are vain.
HOST. O, the father, how he holds his countenance!
FAL. For God's sake, lords, convey my tristful queen,
For tears do stop the flood-gates of her eyes.
HOST. O Jesu, he doth it as like one of these harlotry players as ever I see.

(*H4 Pt. I*. II. iv. 431–6)

How did Shakespeare think of rhetoric? As neither, as both. Falstaff and Hotspur were the creations of a brain that was 'a thoroughfare for all thoughts, not a select party', as Keats put it. But that was an overstatement. Shakespeare's brain could not really entertain all thoughts; we can tell the difference between the thoughts which he did entertain creatively, and to which his being was responsive, and those which were merely thoughts. It is the difference between characters with which he could identify himself, and those with which he could not: and between these poles there is a whole range of characters with whom his identification was more or less complete, and we can distinguish the degree. But even when we feel that the identification is complete—as it is, at this period, with the Bastard, with Hotspur, with Falstaff, with Mercutio—we cannot say: this was Shakespeare. What we can say, however—and it is a good deal more than nothing—is that this, or this, was an imaginative form in which Shakespeare felt at home. Into this shape, or this, Shakespeare's creative spontaneity could pour itself without constraint: this was a congenial incarnation of his impersonal self.

It is the sense of this distinction which underlies Shakespeare's own remark concerning Mercutio, which Dryden recorded:

> *Shakespear* show'd the best of his skill in his *Mercutio*, and he said himself, that he was forc'd to kill him in the third Act, to prevent being kill'd by him. But for my part, I cannot find he was so dangerous a person: I see nothing in him but what was so exceeding harmless, that he might have liv'd to the end of the play, and dy'd in his bed, without offence to any man.

Dryden's judgment (which was not so good as it has been the fashion of late to represent it) was completely at fault. Mercutio is a wonderful creation. And he is precisely the *kind* of character of whom we can imagine Shakespeare saying that 'he was forced to kill him to prevent being killed by him'. He was so natural a vehicle for Shakespeare's creative spontaneity that he was like to make havoc with Shakespeare's dramatic design. In the 'tragedy' of *Romeo and Juliet,* he played the same creative-destructive part as Falstaff and Hotspur played in the 'history' of *Henry IV*. History itself killed Hotspur, Falstaff had to be killed by Shakespeare's fiat.

Falstaff, indeed, had to be killed twice over. He had to be dismissed by King Harry; and then he had to die. Those who complain of the King's treatment of Sir John show indeed that they have good hearts, which are most necessary to have, but they have not entered very deeply into the necessities imposed on the creative imagination. Falstaff had, somehow, to be brought back into the framework of 'history'; and Prince Hal's character had to be sacrificed in the process.

The commiseration of the kind hearts goes to the wrong address. It is not Falstaff who needs to be pitied, but Prince Hal. From another congenial madcap, he had to be changed for the moment into an ingrate and a hypocrite—a painful and an arbitrary transformation, but no less drastic an operation was necessary if the fragments of exploded history were to be put together again.

There is evidence that Shakespeare was embarrassed by the necessity. That he was poetically embarrassed is plain from the words with which his Prince abandons Falstaff:

FAL. My King! my Jove! I speak to thee, my heart!
KING. I know thee not, old man: fall to thy prayers;
How ill white hairs become a fool and jester!
I have long dream'd of such a kind of man,
So surfeit-swelled, so old and so profane;
But, being awak'd, I do despise my dream.
(*Pt.* 2. v. v. 50–5)

It was the best Shakespeare could do; but neither he, nor anyone else, could alter the fact that the dream was the reality, and the reality the dream. The words are, of course, preposterous on Prince Hal's lips: but their preposterousness reflects the hiatus that now yawned between the world of Shakespeare's spontaneity, or imaginative truth, and the world of theatrical necessity, or historical fact. To fill the hiatus, in appearance only, for the chasm is unbridgeable, Falstaff is cast off, and the King made a dastard. Neither deserved it, and neither suffers from it: because it happens in a different world from that in which they have their being. Their ghosts merely are entangled in this summary process of rejoining earth.

It was a job of work that had to be done, in order to bring *Henry IV* to an end. At the moment, probably, Shakespeare thought no more about it. Probably, he laid down his pen and called for a drink. Then up with his pen again, for an Epilogue.

One word more, I beseech you. If you be not too much cloyed with fat meat, our humble author will continue the story, with Sir John in it, and make you merry with fair Katharine of France: where, for anything I know, Falstaff shall die of a sweat, unless already a' be killed with your hard opinions; for Oldcastle died a martyr, and this is not the man.

At the moment of writing that, I imagine Shakespeare rather tired with his own work of creation, with scarce energy enough to consider *how* he was to 'continue the story with Sir John in it'. At one time I inclined to believe that Shakespeare really did intend to bring Falstaff on again alive in *Henry V*, but the royal command that Falstaff should 'be shown in love' intervened; with the effect that Shake speare grew sick of Falstaff, and killed him off incontinently. But I was the victim of the peculiar delusion that lays wait for the Shakespearian—the delusion that Shakespeare's great characters are creatures of flesh and blood who, once killed, could not be resurrected. It was hallucination. For what could Falstaff's death avail against a Royal command that he should live again?

The Merry Wives may have come between *Henry IV*, Part II and *Henry V*; but I doubt it. It is more likely that the Royal command (about the fact of which I have little doubt) compelled a positive exhumation. The Falstaff of *The Merry Wives* is a good figure of fun; but he is not even the ghost of the true Sir John. Even granting that the play had to be vamped up in a fortnight, and that it was produced by a hurried re-writing of some stock comedy, I think it almost certain that Shakespeare would have produced something more closely resembling the real Sir John, if he had been writing *The Merry Wives* between *Henry IV* and *Henry V*. For, in the true imaginative sense, Falstaff, though he dies in *Henry V*, lives in it; while, though he lives in *The Merry Wives*, he is dead in it.

. . . . .

We few, we happy few, we band of brothers;
For he to-day that sheds his blood with me
Shall be my brother; be he ne'er so vile,
This day shall gentle his condition.

Shakespeare was no fool. The promised 'Homes for heroes' proved to be shadowy enough at the end of a war three hundred years after he was writing. In Shakespeare's time, the maimed soldier remembered nothing 'with advantages'. 'I have led my ragamuffins where they are peppered,' says Falstaff. 'There's not three of my hundred and fifty left alive, and they are for the town's end, to beg during life.' Complete destitution was all the wounded soldier had to look forward to. Shakespeare was not forgetting what Falstaff had come to remind him of. 'Can honour set to a leg? no; nor an arm? no; or take away the grief of a wound? No.'

Shakespeare was not forgetting these realities. He was remembering them, even while he surrendered himself to the idea of what a king should be and do. That imaginative surrender to the ideal of kingship was his way of remembering the realities. Honour had to be *made* a reality. To Hotspur's honour, Falstaff's was the inexpugnable reply. Of the shadow honour that was an aristocratic luxury the maimed and begging soldier was the substance. Honour that was real was differently won. Let the pressed and unwilling man depart, says Harry the king; true honour is achieved by a band of brothers, and the king is he who knows it, and will acknowledge and fulfil the obligations of brotherhood.

It was a dream: it has never been fulfilled. Perhaps the nearest it ever came to fulfilment in this country was in Cromwell's New Model army, wherein men of no birth nor substance did 'gentle their condition', and russet-coated captains 'knew what they fought for and loved what they knew'. But that band of brothers was bent not on following an anointed king, but on deposing him. So different is the ideal from the real. Nevertheless, the ideal is the real. Only in so far as a king does incorporate the brotherhood of a nation, is kingship justified at the bar of the imagination which is reason. He personifies the nation: if unworthily, he is a mere abstract symbol of the unity of his people; if worthily, it is because his effort is to bring that unity from an outward show to an inward reality.

In Shakespeare's *Henry V* the usurpation of Bolingbroke is validated. The divine right of Richard had given way before the necessity of Order; but Order alone is not enough. Order must be organic and creative. This organic and creative order is embodied in Harry the king. It is an order which grows out of the nation and is reflected back upon it again, through the person and by the will of the king. He gives utterance to the dumb striving of the nation towards a higher order—not an order of mechanical equality, but an order in which nobility is the reward of those who of their own free-will are ready to hazard their lives and their all for the common weal.

That is Shakespeare's answer to the problem of kingship. It seems to me a very noble answer, and one almost as far in advance of the society of our day as it was in advance of the society he knew. Perhaps it may one day prove to have been prophetic of the people whose genius conceived it; and Shakespeare will be revealed as the unacknowledged legislator of his countrymen. But it was by the act of no such king, or queen, that he gentled his own condition. He acquired his rank of *armiger* by the familiar means: he paid for it. But there is a sweet and subtle poetic justice in the fact that it was through the instinctive response of the English people to Shakespeare's representation of themselves, their nature, and their goal of good, in *Henry IV* and *Henry V*, that he was enabled to acquire the substance and the quality of an English gentleman. *Non sans droict*, indeed: not without human right, not without right divine.

And that should teach us
There's a divinity that shapes our ends
Rough-hew them how we will.

With *Henry V*, Shakespeare's histories end. Factually it was impossible for him to continue. The Tudors were sacrosanct; and he had completed the sequence which led to them. But ideally, also, he had said his say. In this realm of history there was no more to be done. In imagination he had taken England to a zenith—the real England, with which he was consubstantial. He called it history and the past:

> Small time, but in that small most greatly lived
> This star of England . . .

but it was imagination and the future. Out of his experience of England, of the England outside himself and the England within, there had shaped itself the figure of an English king—the son of a usurper in historical fact, the descendant of the Bastard, and the offspring of Falstaff and Hotspur in the poetic succession, but in the imaginative order, simply Shakespeare as king. And Shakespeare as king is greater far than Harry the king; he is a king who does what Harry cannot do. Harry must kill Hotspur with his sword, and Falstaff by his faithlessness. Shakespeare makes all three immortal. In the English Elysium they become the brothers which they are, yet could not be:

> Where souls do couch on flowers, we'll hand in hand,
> And with our sprightly post make the ghosts gaze:
> Dido and her Aeneas shall want troops,
> And all the haunt be ours.

19

SHAKESPEARE'S METHOD: THE MERCHANT OF VENICE

From Shakespeare.

The Merchant of Venice probably shares with *Hamlet* the distinction of being the most popular of all Shakespeare's plays. It was not always so. After the Restoration, *The Merchant of Venice* suffered eclipse. When it was at last revived (in a drastic adaptation) at the beginning of the eighteenth century, Shylock was played as a purely comic part. Not until 1741, when Macklin played Shylock at Drury Lane, did something near to Shakespeare's text come back to the stage. The return was triumphant. 'Macklin made Shylock malevolent,' says Mr. Harold Child, 'and of a forcible and terrifying ferocity.' Macklin's Shylock, which Pope accepted as Shakespeare's, dominated the stage for nearly fifty years; and it imposed the conception described by Hazlitt:

> When we first went to see Mr. Kean in Shylock, we expected to see, what we had been used to see, a decrepit old man, bent with age and ugly with mental deformity, grinning with deadly malice, with the venom of his heart congealed in the expression of his countenance, sullen, morose, gloomy, inflexible, brooding over one idea, that of his hatred, and fixed on one unalterable purpose, that of his revenge.

With this conception of Shylock *The Merchant of Venice* became truly popular. Garrick chose it for the opening performance of Drury Lane under his management in 1747, and in it Kean made his triumphant first appearance at the same theatre in 1814. It was Kean's Shylock, as Hazlitt makes plain, which caused a revolution in the attitude of criticism towards the character. 'In proportion as Shylock has ceased to be a popular bugbear, "baited with the rabble's curse",' wrote Hazlitt, 'he becomes a half-favourite with the philosophical part of the audience, who are disposed to think that Jewish revenge is at least as good as Christian injuries.'

That is a singular and significant stage-history. For both these popular Shylocks are Shakespeare's: or rather both are to be found in Shakespeare. As the attitude to the Jew became more civilized, at the beginning of the nineteenth century, so it was discovered that the new attitude also was prophetically contained in Shakespeare's Jew.

But *The Merchant of Venice* is more than Shylock. It is, more even than *Hamlet,* more than any other of Shakespeare's plays, a matter-of-fact fairy tale: a true folk story, made drama; and it makes its secular appeal to that primitive substance of the human consciousness whence folk-tales took their origin. Or, without reaching back to these dark and dubious beginnings, we may say that it is, as nearly as possible, a pure melodrama or tragi-comedy, an almost perfect example of the art-form which being prior to art itself, most evidently and completely satisfies the primitive man in us all. If the English theatre be considered as a place of popular entertainment, strictly on a level with the football field, the prize-ring and the racecourse, then *The Merchant of Venice* is the type of entertainment the theatre should supply—villain discomfited, virtue rescued, happy marriages, clowning, thrills, and a modest satisfaction of the general appetite for naughtiness.

The Merchant of Venice happens to be Shakespeare's; but Shakespeare has not much to do with its popularity. True, *The Merchant of Venice* almost *is* Shakespeare in the popular mind. But this popular Shakespeare, who wrote *The Merchant of Venice* and *Richard III*, is scarcely a person. He is rather a name which gives to these satisfactions of our elementary appetites for melodrama the prestige of art. This impersonal 'Shakespeare' is a great stumbling-block to criticism, which is for ever engaged, consciously and unconsciously, in the effort to dissolve him out of existence. But he did most certainly exist: he is the Shakespeare who, in his own day as in ours, was veritably popular, who tickled the groundlings because his living lay that way (and surely it was a better way than being hand-fed by the aristocracy, gratification for dedication), who did what he could to season his caviare to the general appetite, and made not a virtue of his necessity —that was hardly his nature—but the best of it.

It is the more striking, therefore, that of all the plays of this period *The Merchant of Venice* is the most typical of Shakespeare—the most expressive of what Coleridge once called his 'omni-humanity'. It contains tragedy, comedy high and low, love lyricism; and, notably, it does not contain any 'Shakespearian' character. The Berowne-Mercutio-Benedick figure, witty, debonair, natural, is diffused into a group of young Venetian noblemen, all credible and substantial, but none possessing the inimitable individuality of their progenitor. Antonio, who stands apart from them, and was (if my judgment of the various verse-styles of the play is to be trusted) the last figure in it to have been elaborated, is a singular character. He supplies a background of sadness to the whole drama. He seems to be older than the friends who surround him, and detached from their thoughtless extravagance. Actually, in his final elaboration, by reason of the quality and colour given to him by Shakespeare's rewriting of Act I, Scene i, he becomes, as a character, slightly inconsistent with the contemptuous opponent of Shylock of later scenes; but it is not the function of Antonio to be primarily a dramatic 'character'. In that capacity, he is negative; he is a shadow beside Shylock and Portia, and unsubstantial even in comparison with his Venetian entourage. But as the vehicle of an atmosphere, he is one of the most important elements in the play. He provides, for the beginning of the play, what the lyrical antiphony of Lorenzo and Jessica supplies for the end of it—a kind of musical overtone which sets the spiritual proportions of the drama. He shades into the Duke of *Twelfth Night*.

The analogue between *The Merchant of Venice* and a musical composition is significant, I think, when taken in conjunction with the basic popularity of the play and the probability that its origin is to be sought in a play of many years before called 'The Jew', which Stephen Gosson exempted from abuse in 1579 because it displayed 'the greediness of worldly chusers and the bloody mind of usurers'. That is too apt a summary of the purely dramatic content of *The Merchant of Venice* to be accidental, and it fits too well with our impression of the play as the product of much re-writing to be ignored. Whether or not *The Merchant* is, as Malone suggested, the 'Venetian Comedy' mentioned by Henslowe in 1594,—a date which would suit very well for Shakespeare's first drafting of *his* play—may be left undecided. The important fact is that in *The Merchant* we have, almost certainly, Shakespeare's treatment of a dramatic plot which came to him, substantially, as a datum.

Out of this substance Shakespeare wrought a miracle. He transformed it, and yet he left the popular substance essentially the same. What he did not, could not, and, so far as we can see or guess, would not do, was to attempt to make it an intellectually coherent whole. That seems to have been no part of his purpose; he did not entertain the idea because he knew it was impossible. The coherence of *The Merchant of Venice* is not intellectual or psychological; and there has been much beating of brains in the vain effort to discover in it a kind of coherence which it was never meant to possess.

As an example of what I believe to be a radical misunderstanding of the nature of *The Merchant of Venice*, we may take the edition of the play in the *New Cambridge Shakespeare*. It will serve as a typical example of a mistaken approach to Shakespeare, for *The Merchant* in its origins, its methods of composition, and its final splendour, is typical of Shakespeare's achievement. The very stubbornness of his material compelled, I believe, a more or less complete abeyance of Shakespeare's personality. In his work upon this play he was pre-eminently the 'artist', but not in the modern and largely romantic sense of the word.

When the news of the disaster to Antonio's ventures comes to Belmont, in the very ecstasy of happiness there, Jessica adds her witness to Salerio's report of Shylock's implacability:

> When I was with him, I have heard him swear
> To Tubal and to Chus, his countrymen,
> That he would rather have Antonio's flesh
> Than twenty times the value of the sum
> That he did owe him: and I know, my lord,
> If law, authority and power deny not,
> It will go hard with poor Antonio. (III. ii. 285–91)

On this passage, the New Cambridge editors have the following note:

> We are tempted to put this speech into square brackets as one from the old play which Shakespeare inadvertently left undeleted in the manuscript. Note (1) it jars upon a nerve which Shakespeare of all writers was generally most careful to avoid: that a daughter should thus volunteer evidence against her father is hideous . . .

This fits, precisely, with the description of Jessica given in the essay of general introduction to the play:

> Jessica is bad and disloyal, unfilial, a thief; frivolous, greedy, without any more conscience than a cat, and without even a cat's redeeming love of home. Quite without heart, on worse than an animal instinct—pilfering to be carnal—she betrays her father to be a light-of-lucre carefully weighted with her father's ducats.

This is, indeed, to break a butterfly upon a wheel. But more alarming than the severity of the sentence is its irrelevance. *The Merchant of Venice* is not a realistic drama; and its characters simply cannot be judged by realistic moral standards. Jessica, taken out of the play, and exposed to the cold light of moral analysis, may be a wicked little thing; but in the play, wherein alone she has her being, she is nothing of the kind—she is charming. She runs away from her father because she is white and he is black; she is much rather a princess held captive by an ogre than the unfilial daughter of a persecuted Jew. Whether or not it is true that Shakespeare 'of all writers' was most careful to avoid representing unfilial behaviour without condemning it—and the proposition becomes doubtful when we think of *Romeo and Juliet* and *Othello*—it is almost certainly true that he did not himself conceive, or imagine that others would conceive, that Jessica's behaviour was unfilial. The relations between the wicked father and the lovely daughter are governed by laws nearly as old as the hills.

Yet even so, in rejecting Jessica's words as un-Shakespearian because morally hideous, the *New Cambridge Shakespeare* is not consistent; for the introductory essay discusses the problem how it is that Shylock is made 'sympathetic' to us, and argues that it is because he is deserted by his bad and disloyal daughter: 'he is intolerably wronged', and we feel for him accordingly. We cannot have it both ways; we cannot argue that Shakespeare deliberately made Jessica unfilial in order to gain our sympathy for the Jew, and at the same time reject a passage as un-Shakespearian because in it Jessica reveals herself unfilial. The dilemma is absolute, but it is of the modern critic's making, not Shakespeare's. It is the direct result of applying to *The Merchant of Venice* a kind of criticism which it was never meant to satisfy.

Criticism of this kind seeks for psychological motives where none were intended or given. Shylock's hatred of Antonio is, in origin, a fairy-tale hatred, of the bad for the good. And perhaps this fairy-tale hatred is more significant than a hatred which can (if any hatred can) be justified to the consciousness. At any rate Shakespeare was at all times content to accept this antagonism of the evil and the good as self-explanatory. Not to speak of Iago, or Goneril, or Edmund, in the very next play in the Folio, *As You Like It*, which was probably written at about the same time as *The Merchant of Venice*, Oliver, in plotting Orlando's death, similarly confesses his elemental hatred of his brother: 'I hope I shall see an end of him; for my soul, yet I know not why, hates nothing more than he.' Some would explain these simple assertions of a primal antagonism as compelled by the conditions of the Elizabethan theatre, which required the characters clearly to label themselves as villains or heroes; but it is quite as likely that Shakespeare accepted the sheer opposition of good and evil as an ultimate fact of the moral universe. Assuredly, if it was a necessary convention of the Elizabethan theatre, it was a convention which Shakespeare found it easy to use for his own purposes. For the hatred of his villains always lies deeper than their consciousness.

Thus Shylock at one moment declares that he hates Antonio 'for he is a Christian'; at another, because he is a trade rival: 'I will have the heart of him if he forfeit, for were he out of Venice, I can make what merchandise I will.' If we take the psychological point of view, the contradiction should not trouble us. We may say that Shylock is trying, as later Iago will try, to rationalize his hatred of Antonio: that he contradicts himself in so doing, is in accord with everyday experience. Or, on a different level, we may say that Shakespeare himself is trying to rationalize his elemental story. Unlike Oliver, who appears only at the beginning and the end of *As You Like It*, unlike the unsubstantial Don John in *Much Ado*, Shylock is the main figure of the play. What is in reality the simple fact of his hatred has to be motivated. Oliver and Don John are not required to be credible; Shylock is.

But these two kinds of explanation are not contradictory, as some critics think they are. They are two modes, two levels, of the operation of the same necessity: the 'psychologization' of a story that is a datum. In the process, Antonio's character suffers some slight damage. He spits upon Shylock's Jewish gaberdine. If we reflect in cold blood on Antonio's reported behaviour to Shylock, we are in danger of thinking that Shylock's intended revenge was not excessive. But we are not meant or allowed to reflect upon it. We are not made to *see* this behaviour. It is a sudden shifting of the values in order to make Shylock sympathetic to us at the moment he is proposing the bond. This is a dramatic device of which Shakespeare was always a master. But because Shakespeare was Shakespeare it is something more than a dramatic device.

Shylock undoubtedly is, to a certain degree, made sympathetic to us; and it is important to discover how it is done. For this, almost certainly, was a radical change wrought by Shakespeare in the crude substance of the old play. But the effect was certainly not achieved by Shakespeare's representing Shylock as the victim of Jessica's ingratitude. On the contrary, Shakespeare is most careful to prevent any such impression from taking lodgment in our minds. At the moment when we might feel a little uneasy about Jessica's treatment of her father, any nascent misgiving is stifled by Salerio's description of Shylock's outcry at the discovery:

> My daughter! O my ducats! O my daughter!
> Fled with a Christian! O my Christian ducats!
> Justice! the law! my ducats, and my daughter!
> A sealed bag, two sealed bags of ducats,
> Of double ducats, stolen from me by my daughter!
> And jewels, two stones, two rich and precious stones,
> Stolen by my daughter! Justice! find the girl;
> She hath the stones upon her, and the ducats.
>
> (II. viii. 14–22)

It is not the loss of his daughter that moves Shylock, but only the loss of his money. Shylock, at this moment, is presented as an ignoble being whom Jessica does well to escape and despoil.

Shylock is deliberately made unsympathetic when it is required to cover Jessica. He is made sympathetic when Shakespeare feels the need, or welcomes the opportunity of making a truly dramatic contrast between Shylock and Antonio. At critical moments he is given dignity and passion of speech and argument to plead his cause to us and to himself. His hatred then is represented as deep, irrational and implacable, but not as mean and mercenary. It is then a force of nature—something greater than himself:

> So can I give no reason, nor I will not,
> More than a lodged hate and a certain loathing
> I bear Antonio, that I follow thus
> A losing suit against him.
>
> (IV. i. 59–62)

'A losing suit', because he, who grieves more for his ducats than his daughter, refuses many times the value of his debt to have his bond of Antonio; and his implacability is supplied with excuses enough to more than half persuade us—Antonio's expressed contempt for him, and the magnificent speech, which may have been hardly less magnificent in the verse from which Shakespeare seems to have changed it.

> And if you wrong us, shall we not revenge?
> If we are like you in the rest, we will
> Resemble you in that. If a Jew wrong
> A Christian, what is his humility?
> Revenge! And if a Christian wrong a Jew
> What should his sufferance be?
> By Christian example, why, revenge!
> The villainy you teach me
> I will execute: and it shall go hard
> But I will better the instruction.
>
> (III. i. 71 *sq.*)

Not content with that, Shakespeare in the trial scene gives Shylock a truly tremendous argument:

> DUKE. How shalt thou hope for mercy, rendering none?
> SHY. What judgment shall I dread, doing no wrong?
> You have among you many a purchased slave,
> Which, like your asses and your dogs and mules,
> You use in abject and in slavish parts,
> Because you bought them: shall I say to you,
> Let them be free, marry them to your heirs?
> Why sweat they under burthens? let their beds
> Be made as soft as yours, and let their palates
> Be seasoned with such viands? You will answer
> 'The slaves are ours': so do I answer you:
> The pound of flesh, which I demand of him,
> Is dearly bought: 'tis mine and I will have it.
> If you deny me, fie upon your law!
> There is no force in the decrees of Venice.
> I stand for judgment: answer, shall I have it?
>
> (IV. i. 87–103)

Shall I not do as I will with mine own? It is the morality of a whole society, to which Antonio and his friends belong no less than Shylock, which Shylock challenges here, and by anticipation blunts the edge of Portia's great plea for mercy. As Hazlitt put it, in his tempestuous way, 'the appeal to the Jew's mercy, as if there were any common principle of right and wrong between them, is the rankest hypocrisy, the blindest prejudice'. The world where mercy prevails is not the world of the play. That is a world where justice is the bulwark of injustice.

This is much more than a dramatic device to gain a momentary sympathy for Shylock; yet it is less, or at least other, than a deliberate posing of a profound moral problem. *The Merchant of Venice* is not a problem play; it is a fairy story, within the framework of which Shakespeare allowed free working to the thoughts of his mind and the feelings of his heart. What an unfettered Shylock might say, this fettered Shylock does say.

In other words, Shylock is both the embodiment of an irrational hatred, and a credible human being. He is neither of these things to the exclusion of the other. And if we ask how can that be? the only answer is that it is so. This was Shakespeare's way of working. If we choose, we may say that there are in the story primitive elements which he could not wholly assimilate to his own conception; but such an explanation, in *The Merchant of Venice* as in *Hamlet*, brings us against the fact that the dramatic impression made by these plays is the impression of an artistic whole. And, indeed, it seems more probable that Shakespeare did not deal in 'conceptions' of the kind that are often attributed to him. He set himself in successive attempts to infuse a general impression of credibility into an old story, and to secure from his audience no more, and no less, than 'that willing suspension of disbelief which constitutes poetic faith'.

One cannot too often emphasize the nature of Shakespeare's dramatic 'method'. It was not chosen by him, neither was it imposed upon his reluctant genius; it was simply the condition of the work he had chosen to do. The situation was given; necessarily, therefore, the 'characters' in a certain primitive sense—much the same sense in which we can speak of 'characters' in a nursery-story like Cinderella or Robin Hood or a Punch and Judy show. They are simply the necessary agents for that situation or that story. Shakespeare proceded to endow them with poetic utterance, and with character in a quite different sense. He did what he could to make them credible human beings to himself. He gave them so far as was possible, humanly plausible motives for their acts and situations, although these were often in fact prior to humane psychology. In a word, the method of Shakespeare's drama consists, essentially, in the humanization of melodrama. And each of those terms must have real validity for the Shakespeare critic who is to avoid ascending or descending into some private universe of his own and calling it Shakespeare.

20

BECOMING A CLASSIC

From Shakespeare.

It took Shakespeare roughly one hundred and fifty years to become a classic. If might-have-beens have meaning—and their value is that they sometimes help towards description of the thing that was—we may say that Shakespeare might have become a classic much more quickly than he did. For in the eighteen years that fell between the issue of the First Folio, in 1623, and the outbreak of the Civil War, in 1641, Shakespeare stood high in the esteem of those in authority. The flights that 'took Eliza and our James', took the first Charles more deeply still.

But the two great upheavals of national sentiment which followed —the Puritan revolution, and the anti-Puritan reaction—were alike unfavourable to him. In the first case, it was not merely that his works were involved in the general proscription of the acted drama. His works are irremediably anti-Puritan in sentiment. From this it has been rashly deduced that there is substance in the story that 'he died a Papist'. To put it at the lowest, it is no more likely that Shakespeare died a Papist than that King Charles I himself died one. The people who admired him most, and most intelligently, before the Civil War began were as anti-Papist as they were anti-Puritan.

But Shakespeare's anti-Puritan sentiment was not of a kind to profit by the anti-Puritan reaction of the Restoration. He was anti-Puritan, as a whole humanity is opposed to the tyranny of a part of human nature. Therefore the opposition between Shakespeare and the taste of the Restoration was just as deep as it was between Shakespeare and the taste of the Commonwealth. If any moment in English history could be called congenial to the genius of a poet who was not of an age but for all time, it would be the halcyon time before the outbreak of the Civil War. It was, at least, more nearly Shakespearian than any subsequent moment. Before the Parliament-men had conquered, Shakespeare had the King and the wits on his side; but when, after a gap in the very history of the theatre, a new King and new wits arrived, their taste was different. It was more superficial, less English and less Royalist—in the deeper sense of the word. Shakespeare was a king's poet; but not the poet of a king like Charles II, who was too cynical to believe in his own divine right. So Shakespeare became simply what he was at the beginning: the playwright of the people and the actors themselves. It was neither the Court nor the critics—for both of whom he had become unfashionable—that carried him beyond the bank and shoal of time, but the favour of the people.

In the seventeenth century Shakespeare was not a distinct figure to the intelligence, any more than he is to-day; he was, then as now, distinct only to the affections and to the imagination. Even the solid flesh quickly melted. The direct line of descent from Shakespeare died out within sixty years of his own death. If he left any manuscripts—other than those scarce-blotted papers which were once in the hands of Heminge and Condell—they appear only to disappear among the £4 worth of 'old goods and lumber at Stratford' in the inventory of the estate of his granddaughter's husband, Sir John Bernard. Destiny, in denying him physical successors, and us all but the most shadowy visible relics of his actual presence, seems to have been bent on validating his own final surmise that 'we are such stuff as dreams are made on'.

Something of the same elusiveness seems to have mocked such efforts as were made by the seventeenth century to particularize him as a poet and a dramatist. Even in the deliverances of the critical masters of the age, Ben Jonson and Dryden, there is an instability which, when all allowances have been made, is little short of astonishing. Take Jonson's 'He was not of an age, but for all time': take Dryden's 'He was the man who, of all Modern, and perhaps Ancient poets, had the largest and most comprehensive soul'—by these large utterances the extreme demands made by later romantic appreciation of Shakespeare are fully satisfied. Yet at another moment Jonson could be petty to the point of malignancy; and Dryden could put Shakespeare and Fletcher on the same level—which was more or less critical commonplace by that time—only to dismiss them both as barbarians.

The feeling behind this strange inconsistency is easier to understand than to define. It might be described as a feeling that Shakespeare ought not to have been. And certainly the critical intelligence of the seventeenth century would have been more comfortable if Shakespeare had never existed; because he created in the minds of his successors precisely that division which is recorded in their utterances. If they submitted to him, they were overwhelmed. They resented being overwhelmed; they did not want to submit. Their recalcitrance was natural. The intelligence meant much to them: it was what they represented, the element for the recognition of which they were fighting. In the recurrent phrase of the time they stood for Art against Nature and, as a corollary of this, for the recognition of the function and dignity of the artist—the representative of the ordered and ordering intelligence. In this struggle Shakespeare lent them no aid, as it seemed to them.

Perhaps it was even worse than this. Perhaps they could only recognize Shakespeare for what he was in moments when their intelligence was off its guard; perhaps he even drove their intelligence from its guard. They could do justice to him only in moments of 'inspiration'—'not laboriously but luckily', as Dryden put it; and since trusting to luck was the enemy they were fighting, Shakespeare was perpetually tempting their bad angel to fire their good one out. After all, something of the kind had happened in those memorable words of Dryden's to which we have alluded:

> All the Images of Nature were still present to him, and he drew them not laboriously, but luckily; when he describes anything, you more than see it, you feel it too. Those who accuse him to have wanted learning, give him the greater commendation: he was naturally learned; he needed not the spectacles of books to read Nature; he looked inwards and found her there.

This was to surrender the fort with a vengeance; indeed, to make a breach in the wall so big that a great deal besides Shakespeare might enter in. This impulsive generosity—though it was the finest appreciation of Shakespeare that had been written—was dangerous. Dryden had to withdraw. To praise Shakespeare, as the spirit was moved to praise him, was to desert Jonson—that great Jonson to whose efforts was due the condition of things against which John Boys, the Dean of Canterbury, inveighed in folio some time before 1629. 'The writing of the learned are called their works, *opera Hieronymi*, the workes of *Hierome, Augustine, Gregorie*; yea, the very *plaies* of a moderne Poet are called in print his *workes*.'

For that minor revolution—and it was nothing less—Jonson and not Shakespeare was responsible. Had it been left to Shakespeare, nothing would have been done; for it seems he was perfectly content to let his plays remain plays, never to emerge from their condition of being the stock-in-trade of the King's Men. He was the playwright of the playhouse, not the study.

What he was is perhaps described best in the neglected verses of Leonard Digges, prefixed to the *Poems* of 1640:

But oh! what praise more powerful can we give
The dead, than that by him the King's men live . . .
So have I seen, when Caesar would appear,
And on the stage at half-sword parley were
Brutus and Cassius: oh, how the audience
Were ravish'd, with what wonder they went thence,
When some new day they would not brook a line
Of tedious (though well labour'd) *Catiline*:
Sejanus too was irksome, they priz'd more
Honest Iago, or the jealous Moor.
And though the *Fox* and subtle *Alchemist*,
Long intermitted, could not quite be miss'd,
Though these have shamed the ancients and might raise
Their author's merit with a crown of bays:
Yet these sometimes, even at a friend's desire
Acted, have scarce defray'd the sea-coal fire
And door-keepers: when let but Falstaff come
Hal, Poins, the rest, you scarce shall have a room,
All is so pester'd: let but Beatrice
And Benedick be seen, lo, in a trice
The cockpit, galleries, boxes, all are full
To hear Malvolio, that cross-garter'd gull.
Brief, there is nothing in his wit-fraught book,
Whose sound we would not hear, on whose worth look . . .

That is the tribute of a man who knew his Shakespeare in the playhouse, and learned to love him there.

The *Shakespeare Allusion Book* reminds us forcibly how very gradual, almost imperceptible, was the process by which his works emerged from this warm and familiar obscurity. His characters rather than himself were remembered; the words that stick were obviously heard from the stage, not read in a book. Only *Venus and Adonis* stood apart. Quite exceptionally, in the case of *Venus and Adonis*, we find almost immediately the response of a literary appreciation. Even though it takes the form of what we should now call plagiarism, but what was then indeed the sincerest form of flattery, Richard Barnfield's imitation in 1595 of the most notable image in the poem (*ll.* 815–16) shows genuine admiration. It is particular.

Look how a brightsome planet in the sky,
(Spangling the welkin with a golden spot)
Shoots suddenly from the beholder's eye,
And leaves him looking there where she is not:
  Even so amazed Phoebus to descry her
  Looks all about, but nowhere can espy her.

For an equally particular appreciation of any passage from Shakespeare's plays we have to wait twenty-five years, until the bold Master Richardson, of Magdalen College, preached at St. Mary's, Oxford, a sermon in which he quoted:

> 'Tis almost morning; I would have thee gone:
> And yet no further than a wanton's bird,
> Who lets it hop a little from her hand,
> Like a poor prisoner in his twisted gyves,
> And with a silk thread plucks it back again,
> So loving-jealous of his liberty.
>
> (*RJ*. II. ii. 177–82)

He applied it 'to God's love to his saints, either hurt with sin or adversity, never forsaking them'. The application was bold; but bolder still the actual quotation. And it is indeed remarkable that this first indubitable instance of a purely literary appreciation of an individually chosen passage from a play of Shakespeare's should have been made in a sermon at St. Mary's.

It may not have been fortuitous that this should have happened at Oxford, the home of loyalty to King Charles. For if there is one among the obscure traditions of Shakespeare's early fame that rests on a firm basis, it is that Shakespeare was the favourite poet of Charles and his immediate entourage. Milton bears witness to it; Dryden, in the same famous passage, which marks the highest point reached by sheer appreciation of Shakespeare in the century, gives fuller details:

> But he is always great, when some great occasion is presented to him: no man can say he ever had a fit subject for his wit and did not then raise himself as high above the rest of Poets
>
> *Quantum lenta solent inter viburna cupressi.*
>
> The consideration of this made Mr. Hales of Eton say that there was no subject of which any poet ever writ, but he would produce it much better done in *Shakespeare*; and however others are now generally preferred before him, yet the Age wherein he liv'd, which had contemporaries with him *Fletcher* and *Jonson*, never equall'd them to him in their esteem: And in the last King's Court, when Ben's reputation was at highest, Sir John Suckling, and with him the greater part of the courtiers set our *Shakespeare* far above him.

The 'ever-memorable' John Hales is the man who comes before my mind when I think of the ideal Shakespearian. I think he was a man after Shakespeare's own heart; and his praise of the poet, though it may sound extravagant, is not merely a sane and substantial criticism, but one that could have been made only by a man who had his Shakespeare almost by heart. It was no use Ben Jonson jibing at Shakespeare's 'small Latin and less Greek' to Hales, who was one of the finest scholars of his day, and public lecturer in Greek at Oxford. He had been a fellow of Merton, and was fellow of Eton in 1613. He was made Canon of Windsor in 1639 by Laud, to Laud's great credit. We do not speak so glibly to-day of the Laudian tyranny as we used to do; but I have never yet seen Laud given the honour due to him for making Hales his chaplain. He had disapproved of Hales' treatise on 'Schism and Schismaticks', which Hales had written to promote peace in the distracted Church. So Hales privately wrote Laud a defence of his position, and a meeting between the two men followed: in consequence of which Laud made Hales his chaplain and Canon of Windsor.

It is an episode worth dwelling on: for Hales was a Christian of a kind that we are prone to think (though mistakenly) is more frequent to-day than it was three hundred years ago. 'He would often say,' Clarendon records, 'that he would renounce the religion of the Church of England to-morrow, if it obliged him to believe that any other Christians should be damned, and that nobody would conclude another man to be damned who did not wish him so.' That is not only charitable, but psychologically penetrating; Christian in feeling, and in understanding too. Perfectly congruous with this is Aubrey's report of him that 'he was mightily taken with the doctrine of the Familists'—whose doctrine could be summed up in *ama et fac quod vis*—'and was wont to say that some time or other these doctrines would capture the world'. More than this, Aubrey reports, 'he was one of the first Socinians in England—I think the first'. In truth, I suspect Hales was neither a Familist nor a Socinian: he was not a man to be summed up in a label. The best description of him, I should say, was that he was a Shakespearian Christian: and perhaps the first of them.

Hales suffered in the Civil War. In 1642 he was deprived of his canonry; in 1649 he was deprived of his fellowship of Eton, for refusing to take the Engagement. Persecuted as a 'malignant', he lived in poverty, on the proceeds of the sale of his precious library, until 1656. In every respect Hales was in advance of his age. He, together with his friend Lord Falkland, is the fit representative of those many humane and imaginative men who were ground between the upper and the nether millstone during the Civil War, and with their extermination there perished a culture at once Christian and English

—not a culture that is the veneer of an interest, but a culture essentially beyond and above interests.

Hales was the centre of a circle of Shakespeare enthusiasts; of whom Sir John Suckling is the best remembered. There is something altogether modern in the impulse which took Suckling to inspect whether the winding of the Trent really justified Hotspur's objections—'See how this river comes me cranking in.'

> We are at length arriv'd at that river [he wrote in a letter], about the uneven running of which, my Friend Mr. *William Shakespear* makes *Henry Hotspur* quarrel so highly with his fellow Rebels; and for his Sake I have been something curious to consider the Scantlet of Ground that angry Monsieur wou'd have had in, but cannot find it cou'd deserve his Choler, nor any of the other side ours, did not the King think it did.

'My friend, Mr. William Shakespeare': 'the wish was father, Harry, to that thought'. For Suckling was only seven when Shakespeare died. None the less in Suckling's remains we find a touch of real intimacy with Shakespeare which is as unique as it is tantalizing. It is not merely that he quotes, or copies, Shakespeare with more discrimination than others:

> Farewell the plumed Troops, and the big Wars
> Which made ambition vertue . . .
>
> So pale and spiritless a wretch
> Drew *Priams* curtaine in the dead of night
> And told him half his Troy was burnt . . .

nor that, in a verse letter to John Hales inviting him to town, he makes plain where their preference lay between Shakespeare and Jonson:

> The sweat of learned *Jonson's* brain,
> And gentle *Shakespear's* easier strain,
> A hackney-coach conveys you to,
> In spite of all that rain can do:
> And for your eighteen pence you sit
> The Lord and Judge of all fresh wit . . .

but that there is some evidence that he possessed a fragment of a first version of *The Rape of Lucrece* which differed substantially from the one we know. Suckling's 'Supplement of an imperfect Copy of Verses of Mr. Wil. Shakespear's' in his *Fragmenta Aurea* is a unique document. There is no good reason to doubt that the first nine lines, ending with the marginal note: *Thus far Shakespear*, are genuine Shakespeare:

One of her hands, one of her cheeks lay under
  Cozening the pillow of a lawful kisse,
Which therefore swel'd and seem'd to part asunder,
  As angry to be robb'd of such a bliss:
    The one lookt pale, and for revenge did long
    Whilst t'other blush't, cause it had done the wrong.

Out of the bed the other fair hand was
  On a green sattin quilt, whose perfect white
Lookt like a Dazie in a field of grasse
  And shew'd like unmelt snow unto the sight,
    There lay this pretty perdue safe to keep
    The rest o' the body that lay fast asleep.

'Pretty perdue' could have been added only by a true Shakespearian. The theory that Suckling himself altered the lines from their familiar form (*Lucrece*, 386–96) has nothing for it but the solemn determination that we are never to accept any evidence of any kind about Shakespeare. For why should Suckling have indulged in so pointless a deception? And, when we take into consideration the peculiar knowledge and admiration of Shakespeare which his circle shared, the theory is surely untenable. It seems as certain as such things can be, unsupported by an affidavit from Shakespeare himself, that here we have—as Dr. Brinsley Nicolson contended—some lines from an original version of *Lucrece*, written in the same six-line stanza as the *Venus*.

It is but a small point; but it confirms the impression that Suckling's knowledge of Shakespeare was peculiarly intimate. And Dryden is our authority for Suckling's importance, in matters of literary judgment, at the Court of Charles I, and for the lead he gave in preferring Shakespeare. Nothing is more solidly attested in the whole misty history of the Shakespeare tradition than the existence of a body of enlightened Royalists in the reign of Charles I who shared and no doubt encouraged their King's native admiration of Shakespeare. To call them 'courtiers', as Dryden does, is misleading. It was only the grim pressure of events that brought Lord Falkland over to the King's party. When the final choice was forced upon him, he chose the King; but his desire was peace. 'Sitting among his friends, often, after a deep silence and frequent sighs, he would, with a shrill and sad accent ingeminate the word *Peace, Peace;* and would passionately profess "that the very agony of the war, and the view of the calamities and desolation the kingdom did and must endure, took his sleep from him and would shortly break his heart".' To men so civilized, one may guess, Jonson seemed pedantic, and perhaps even parvenu. They were not the kind of people to be impressed by his too insistent claims to learning. And, anyhow, they had John Hales of Eton to quell with authority any uncouth claims made by or on behalf of Jonson because of his knowledge of the ancients. In all respects they were well armed to defend Shakespeare, and well equipped to establish him in a position of pre-eminence. Nor can one help conjecturing that Neander's magnificent praise of Shakespeare in the *Essay of Dramatick Poesie,* which was the earliest of Dryden's considered utterances on Shakespeare, owes something of its magnificence to the persistence of this humane tradition.

That Dryden, to a large extent, abandoned this position was due to the pressure of French critical influences under the new regime. In so far as he began to prefer Jonson before Shakespeare, it was because Jonson was an English symbol of the 'classical' standards set up by contemporary French taste. It was not that the new court reversed the judgment of the old one. Probably both Shakespeare and Jonson left the new courtiers equally indifferent. The one thing that was certain was that the new standards of elegance and refinement were French: some sort of accommodation between Jonsonian classicism and French classicism seemed possible, none between French standards and Shakespeare. Under the banner of Jonson, therefore, it seemed practical to advance those claims for the seriousness of literature with which Dryden was at heart most deeply concerned. It is doubtful whether anything was really achieved; and it is probable that the status of the poet and the theatre was in fact more really degraded at the end of Charles II's reign than it was in the times of Elizabeth and James. It had ceased to be popular, and had become parasitic. Royalty had ceased to have the same taste as its subjects.

After the Restoration the familiar knowledge of Shakespeare gradually fades away. Neither from book, nor from the theatre do the playwrights seem to know their Shakespeare any more. They know Falstaff, and they know Prince Hamlet, but by name rather than substance. And yet, as Pepys' diary shows, a good deal of Shakespeare was produced, even though it was adapted and 'modernized'; and it was popular. It seems to have been still true that Shakespeare was the actor's stand-by, and that, as in outlying parts to-day, *Hamlet* would fill the house when nothing else would. If the halcyon days when the taste of the King and the Court coincided with the taste of the people were over, the people remained faithful to Shakespeare; not because of his poetry, but because he had been, as neither Jonson nor Fletcher had been, nor any of the Restoration dramatists were, the playwright of the popular playhouse. He was the man who had given Burbage his parts, and now gave them to Betterton—the Shakespeare with whom in these latter days Henry Irving had some sort of understanding, a Shakespeare with whom literary criticism has been very little concerned.

By the end of the seventeenth century the separation between the Shakespeare of the playhouse, who no doubt still pursues his independent existence, and the Shakespeare of the study was more or less accomplished. The history of what we know as Shakespeare criticism really begins. The separation which it posits was perhaps inevitable; but one cannot help looking back with regret on the courtly company of Shakespearians who surrounded Charles I. The study was not so far from the playhouse then; and if Shakespeare was extant in Folio, he was still primarily the book of the play. Shakespeare performances by now have become so much the play of the book that we can hardly make real to ourselves the vast difference. Even the notion that a King of England should have found his greatest pleasure in seeing and reading Shakespeare sounds like a fairy tale. It was a symbol of a condition of things too gracious and too precarious to last. The reign of the great middle classes was destined to begin; and whatever the open and free nature of Shakespeare was, it was not middle class. The great wedge that began to divide the nation divided Shakespeare also: for he was in fact and in sentiment the dramatist of a nation united in a real kingdom. Part of him descended into the playhouse; part of him ascended into the library: and no one has ever quite succeeded in putting him together again.

21

NEWMAN AND SIDGWICK

From Things to Come *(Cape, 1928).*

It lately chanced that, in an endeavour to investigate for myself some characteristics of the Christian mind, I read more or less simultaneously Newman's *Apologia pro Vitâ Suâ* and a little treatise by J. M. Lloyd Thomas: *A Free Catholic Church.* The comparison of these books in themselves was illuminating, for it showed the extraordinary difference of ultimate conviction in which a kindred, one might almost say, an identical, primary certitude can be manifested in the sincere Christian. I do not compare the powers of these two men; but the contrast between the movement of their minds, the ground of initial certitude once left, is astonishing. In Newman the movement becomes ever more narrow and exclusive: his immediate conviction of the existence of God instantly becomes a cause of anxiety and profound misgiving: he is tortured, his soul is pierced to the quick, by the terror lest he should be cast out from the grace of that God whom he knows to exist: and the terror does not abate until he finds refuge, where so fearful, though so noble, a soul must needs find refuge—in the Church which gathers under its wing the greater part of Christendom. It was a small shock, indeed, to realize that Newman was one who must be with the majority. But in no ignoble sense. He believed in God, but he did not trust Him: he was afraid of Him. Where but in the largest cavern should he hide him from the wrath to come?

In a Lloyd Thomas the fear does not exist. The movement is not narrow and exclusive: on the contrary, trusting in the God in whom he believes, he longs to unite in his 'Free Catholic Church' all truly religious-minded men. He is never for one moment perturbed about the possibility of his own damnation: probably the very idea of damnation never entered his head in any shape or form. He does not even demand of the members of his ideal Church that they should believe in God in any dogmatic sense: they might perfectly well be Deists or Pantheists or Agnostics. So long as they are men of good will, he is confident that the grace of God—of which he probably has no very definite idea—will be vouchsafed to them.

This incidental contrast is remarkable enough: two transparently sincere and deeply religious men march from an identical premiss to antipodal conclusions. Yet an even more striking comparison is suggested by those same two books. Among those whom Lloyd Thomas most eagerly seeks to include in the new Church are those who hold 'a not un-Christian agnosticism which is too full of faith and spirituality to tolerate so mean a thing as a theological dogma'. As a type of the attitude, he quotes the words of the Cambridge philosopher, Henry Sidgwick:

> If I am asked whether I believe in a God, I should really have to say I do not know, that is, I do not know whether I *believe* or *merely hope* that there is a moral order in the universe that we know, a supreme principle of Wisdom and Benevolence guiding all things to good ends, and to the happiness of the good. I certainly *hope* that this is so, but I do not think it capable of being *proved*. All I can say is that no opposed explanation of the origin of the cosmos . . . seems to me even plausible, and that I cannot accept life on any other terms, or construct a rational system of my own conduct except on the basis of this faith. . . . Duty is to me as real a thing as the physical world, though it is not apprehended in the same way; but all my apparent knowledge of duty falls into chaos if my belief in the moral government of the world is conceived to be withdrawn. Well, I cannot resign myself to disbelief in duty: in fact if I did, I should feel that the last barrier between me and complete philosophical scepticism, or disbelief in truth altogether, was broken down. Therefore I sometimes say to myself, 'I believe in God,' while sometimes again, I can say no more than I *hope* this belief is true, and I must and will act as if it was.

That is deeply interesting, as are all sincere statements of belief by men capable of making them; but what is peculiarly striking is a very marked resemblance between Sidgwick's profession and Newman's own in the *Apologia*:

> I am a Catholic by virtue of my believing in God; and if I am asked why I believe in a God, I answer that it is because I believe in myself, for I feel it impossible to believe in my own existence (and of that fact I am quite sure) without believing in the existence of Him who lives as a Personal, All-seeing, All-judging Being in my conscience. I dare say I have not expressed myself with philosophical correctness, because I have not given myself to the study of what others have said on the subject: but I think I have a strong, true meaning in what I say, which will bear examination.

What Newman says is this: 'I know that I exist, and by the same act of knowledge I know that my conscience exists. This conscience sees all, judges all, my acts: it is a personal God living in me.' And

Sidgwick says: 'Duty is to me as real a thing as the physical world, though it is not to be apprehended in the same way. . . . I cannot resign myself to disbelief in duty.' Is it not clear that the basic experience is the same in both men? And if we require a yet closer link of connection than the accepted bond between duty and conscience, it is supplied by Wordsworth's invocation of Duty as the 'stern daughter of the Voice of God'.

The fundamental fact on which Newman and Sidgwick build their so different edifices of faith or agnosticism is the same: it is the reality of conscience, which is for Sidgwick as real as the physical world, and for Newman as real as his own self-existence; it is the same basic and primary experience as that which was the cause of the conversion of the French poet, Paul Claudel:

> J'ai fui partout: partout j'ai retrouvé la Loi:
> Quelquechose en moi qui soit plus moi-même que moi.

The French poet in these words goes perhaps farther than Newman, in that he declares that the inward Law—Duty or Conscience—from which he cannot flee, is more truly himself that he. This reality, of whose enduring existence he has immediate knowledge, Newman declares to be God himself 'living as a Personal, All-seeing, All-judging Being' in his conscience. Claudel would agree with him: so also, manifestly, would Wordsworth have done.

At this further step, if it be indeed a further step, Sidgwick seems to hesitate. The nature of his apparent hesitation deserves to be studied. Duty is to him as real a thing as the physical world, though it is not apprehended in the same way. Concerning this knowledge of Duty, Sidgwick says: 'But all my apparent knowledge of Duty falls into chaos if my belief in the moral government of the world is conceived to be withdrawn.' Why he should now call his knowledge of Duty (which was as real as his knowledge of the physical world, though of a different kind) 'apparent' knowledge is not clear. Either he was prejudiced as a logician in favour of confining the term 'knowledge' to intellectual knowledge; or the fact that the knowledge of Duty either necessitated or depended upon a belief in 'the moral government of the world' made the burden of belief in his knowledge of Duty at times too onerous.

But in truth Sidgwick, in spite of his seeming clarity, is very difficult to follow at this all-important point. Seeing, however, that the primary and original fact is his knowledge of Duty, which is as certain as his knowledge of the physical world, it seems that the relation between this knowledge of Duty and the knowledge of 'the moral government of the world' must be the relation of cause to effect. That is to say, knowledge of Duty necessitates, not depends upon, knowledge of the moral government of the world. Yet, apparently, this knowledge of the moral government of the world can be conceived to be withdrawn; and, if it is withdrawn his knowledge of Duty also fails: it becomes merely 'apparent'. Beneath this evident vacillation lurks a real uncertainty, which is perhaps impossible to define precisely. Probably it is this. Knowledge of Duty is primary and really unintermittent. But it necessitates knowledge of the moral government of the world. This knowledge, however, is intermittent, and when it fails, it reacts on the felt certainty of the knowledge of duty. In simpler words: belief in duty, which is no effort, necessitates belief in the moral government of the world, which is an effort. Sometimes this effort is unsuccessful. When it was successful Sidgwick could say 'I believe in God'; when it was unsuccessful he could only say he hoped the belief in God was true, but that he must and would act as if it was.

That may be a tedious, perhaps an obvious, piece of analysis. But I cannot help thinking that there is but little chance of making a real advance in psychology, or rather of establishing it as a true science, unless we are prepared to dig new foundations (or excavate old ones) for it. We must use the self-recorded experiences of highly conscious men as our data. Newman describing the origins of Newman's faith, Henry Sidgwick describing the foundations of Henry Sidgwick's belief,—a faith and belief which actually did shape their lives—are surely of more real importance as data for a true (and therefore a dynamic and creative) psychology than the external observations of others by experimentalists and physicians. It is time, high time, a serious beginning was made with the work of co-ordinating the inward experiences of that great body of men in whom the human consciousness came nearest to perfection—the great priests and prophets, the great philosophers and the great artists. Perhaps the question may appear to be begged by saying that in them the human consciousness came nearest to perfection. But, in that matter, we have the consensus of centuries to approve the choice. And, again, if it be said by the 'scientific' psychologist, that the data thus used are selected, uncharacteristic, and abnormal, the conclusive reply is that it needs something approaching a great man even to attempt to tell the truth about himself. It may be objected, finally, that great men are prone to deceive themselves, that they do not, because they cannot, tell the truth about themselves. That is an easy form of scepticism. The fact is that, whether or not a great man can tell the whole of the truth about his inward experience, he knows and can tell infinitely more of it than any outside observer. Take Newman, for example: his acts and utterances disturbed, perplexed and scandalized the most part of his contemporaries, he seemed to them casuistical, shifty and treacherous. When he gave to the world the story of his own life as he himself knew it, his obvious sincerity instantly prevailed. His *Apologia* was manifestly the truth concerning a rare human soul. That Newman deceived himself, as all men do, does not diminish the truth of his record by a single scruple. It is because his record is true that we can detect the self-deception.

The sooner a systematic and concerted effort is made to co-ordinate the most intimate and fateful experiences of men whom we know to have touched the reality of themselves a little (or a great deal) more closely than the ruck of mankind, the better for us all. We might begin to economize something of that enormous waste of spiritual effort which is entailed upon those who are engaged in a perforce lonely struggle for a meaning, a purpose, and a truth; they might no longer need to begin everything, every time, all over again from zero. And this new psychology which we venture to adumbrate might indeed eventually possess that characteristic of science which is most to be envied by those who practise in more lonely provinces—its real collaboration. The scientific novice begins where the mightiest of his predecessors ended: the investigator of the human soul begins from nothing, generation after generation.[1]

Though this has the appearance of a digression, it is not: for this comparison and contrast between two men ostensibly so opposed as Newman and Sidgwick was begun solely with the purpose of showing by example how the new 'psychologist' might set to work. It would not be difficult, though it might be delicate, to show not merely how, but why these two men, starting from the same initial certainty, reach in the end positions so widely sundered; but even in this elementary stage of the inquiry it has become clear that the *sine quâ non* of such an inquiry is a new terminology if we are to avoid vagueness and waste of effort. That the one word 'knowledge' should have to be used, even by a philosopher like Sidgwick, to cover two utterly different kinds of apprehension, equally certain, and equally real, is obviously intolerable. Not only does it make advance in this realm difficult by impeding the communication of results; it also gives every scope to the wilful obscurantism of the pure rationalist.

For it is pathetically easy for the rationalist to object to any investigator in this realm that he is using the word 'knowledge' in a sense which he does not understand; and yet I do not suppose that the average rationalist is really possessed of greater sincerity or dialectical ability than either Newman or Sidgwick. Both these men were compelled to use the word 'knowledge' to cover two modes of apprehension which they recognized as generically different. The rational-

[1] In his *Holism and Evolution* General Smuts puts forward a powerful plea for a psychology of precisely the kind which I suggest here. He calls it Personology.

ist may object that one of these modes of apprehension is 'faith'. 'Faith' it may appear to those who have no experience of it; but to those who have it is not faith at all. Sidgwick declares that Duty is *as real to him as the physical world*. An element which can properly be called 'faith' enters only when Sidgwick tries to believe in the moral order of the universe.

The point is that the rationalist begs the whole question, and begs it in a rather puerile way. He is manifestly false to his own primary experience. For though it goes without saying that he has no experience of that 'knowledge' of which Newman and Sidgwick speak, he undoubtedly knows that he exists. Are we to believe that when the rationalist says: 'I know that I exist' he means simply that he concludes that he exists because other people tell him so, or behave as though he did? Or are we to understand that he never says or thinks: 'I know that I exist', but merely 'I believe that I exist'? The truth is that this elementary act of non-rational knowledge—'I know that I exist'—is made by every conscious being.

But in order to explore further this domain of non-rational knowledge, we need a new terminology. Every one who is not a professional obscurantist attaches a real meaning (though perhaps not a definable one) to the statement 'I know that I exist'; and only the professional obscurantist would say it was an illegitimate use of the word 'to know'. And there is a real objection to the rationalist's demand that the word 'knowledge' should be restricted to intellectual knowledge. He begs the question. 'Knowledge' does, in fact, include more than that. In the language of the Bible it includes even the act 'to know a woman'—and that, however fantastic it may sound to the rationalist, is a very real knowledge indeed. Knowledge cannot be restricted to the knowledge of concept and proposition. It is very important to the rationalist that it should be thus restricted, because he thereby creates odium and prejudice against non-intellectual knowledge. But we are concerned not with theories but with the truth. So that it should be our task to distinguish between kinds of knowledge, retaining the same root-word for all, but adding various prefixes to them, as for instance body-knowledge, mind-knowledge, soul-knowledge. These faculties, and the various entities which supply their prefixes, cannot indeed be defined; but by an honest co-ordination of the mass of significant data which we have we could, I believe, give to them a fairly definite and unmistakable content. We cannot expect mathematical rigour in the new psychology; but we can fairly expect to achieve a rigour as great as, if not surpassing that of the biological sciences.

With these difficulties and these possibilities in mind, let us return to the case of Newman and Sidgwick. Both start from the acceptance of the voice of conscience as a primary reality: but whereas for Newman this voice becomes immediately the voice of a personal, all-seeing and all-judging God, Sidgwick hesitates. He does not care to make the perilous leap. He might make it, however, if he could be sure 'that there is a moral order in the universe we know'. But he does not know whether 'he believes or merely hopes' that this is so. He 'certainly hopes' that it is so, but he 'does not think it capable of being *proved*'. His language suggests that in order that his 'hope' should become 'belief', it would have to be proved (in the sense of a downright logical demonstration) that there is a moral order in the universe. It is doubtful whether Sidgwick really meant that, if only because it is doubtful whether the proposition itself has any meaning; more probably he was struggling against the bias of his own vocabulary to express the fact that a moral order in the universe (if it existed) was not an unintermittent reality to him, as was the voice of conscience.

We return to Newman, who curiously enough is far clearer and more explicit than the Cambridge philosopher concerning this phase in the genesis of religious belief. Newman writes:

> Starting then with the being of a God (which, as I have said, is as certain to me as the certainty of my own existence, though when I try to put the grounds of that certainty into logical shape I find a difficulty in doing so in mood and figure to my satisfaction), I look out of myself into the world of men, and there I see a sight which fills me with unspeakable distress. The world seems simply to give the lie to that great truth of which my whole being is so full; and the effect upon me is, in consequence, as a matter of necessity, as confusing as if it denied that I am in existence myself. If I looked into a mirror, and did not see my face, I should have the sort of feeling which actually comes upon me, when I look into this living busy world and see no reflection of its Creator. This is, to me, one of the great difficulties of this absolute primary truth, to which I referred just now. Were it not for this voice, speaking so clearly in my conscience and my heart, I should be an atheist, or a pantheist, or a polytheist when I looked into the world. I am speaking for myself only; and I am far from denying the real force of the arguments in proof of a God, drawn from the general facts of human society, but these do not warm me or enlighten me; they do not take away the winter of my desolation, or make the buds unfold or the leaves grow within me, and my moral being rejoice. The sight of the world is nothing else than the prophet's scroll, full of 'lamentations, and mourning, and woe.'

There follows the famous and perhaps familiar passage: 'To consider the world in its length and breadth, its various history . . .' and Newman continues:

What shall be said to this heart-piercing, reason-bewildering fact? I can only answer, that either there is no Creator, or this living society of men is in a true sense discarded from His presence. . . . I argue about the world;—if there be a God, *since* there is a God, the human race is implicated in some terrible aboriginal calamity. It is out of joint with the purposes of its Creator. This is a fact, a fact as true as the fact of its existence; and thus the doctrine of what is theologically called original sin becomes to me almost as certain as that the world exists and as the existence of God.

That is remarkable, both for its substance and its passionate sincerity. Newman looks on the world of men and finds no vestige of moral order, no trace of the finger of God. What Sidgwick can find sometimes, Newman finds never. The difference between them emerges with greater clarity: just as, in regard to the inner world, Newman's sense of the reality of conscience is more intense than Sidgwick's, so, in regard to the outer world, his sense of the absence of any moral order, is more intense than Sidgwick's. And these two intensities seem to be interdependent. It is—to speak metaphorically—because of the whiteness of the light in the world within that the world without appears to Newman as 'irrecoverably dark, total eclipse'. For both men alike, the acceptance of the fact of conscience necessitates the existence of a moral order in the universe; but the kind of moral order necessitated varies with the intensity and the manner in which the fact of conscience is accepted. To speak metaphorically again: Newman, for whom the voice of conscience became immediately the unquestioned voice of God and the manifest evidence of His personal existence (just as the voice of a man is evidence for a normal mind of his personal existence), because of this certainty of God's existence, expects a world of pure white; and because of his expectation of pure white, the world appears pure black. His eyes are God-bedazzled, and the world is utterly dark. With Sidgwick quite otherwise: the voice of conscience does not immediately become the voice of a personal God. But it leads him also to expect, though with a less intense and exacting expectation, a moral order in the world. His eyes are not dazzled, and the world seems grey and neutral. Sometimes he can find vestiges of moral order—a gleam, as it were, whose real existence cannot be proven—and sometimes he cannot find it. When he finds it the voice of conscience is corroborated and he can say, 'I believe in God'; when he does not find it the voice of conscience receives no reinforcement, and he can say only: 'I hope that God exists.'

But whereas Sidgwick evidently finds the gleam of 'moral order', when he finds it, in the world of men that is, as it is, Newman can find it only by an intellectual sleight—if one may use the phrase for definition's sake, with no nuance of contempt for an act so fearful in its consequences. He has to reconcile intense white and deepest black; he can do it only by supposing that black is the conscious and deliberate negation of white. It cannot be merely the absence of white, it can be only the intentional withholding of white. The world of men as it is can be made to present a moral order to Newman's vision only if he supposes that it has been deliberately outcast by God.

Once that supposition became a certainty the rest of Newman's progress was inevitable. So terrible a God was terribly to be feared. What pardon would He have for courage or sanctity or goodness without the mark of election? The one narrow and scarce decipherable way of salvation which He had darkly indicated must be found. Let us hope that Newman found it, and with it, if not peace, some respite from the terror of the ultimate wrath of God—a wrath whose vehemence could be dimly conjectured from the savage fury of His punishment of generation after generation of men for an offence committed by their first parents in the dark backward and abysm of Time.

22

KEATS AND TOLSTOY

From Things to Come.

The recent re-publication of Tolstoy's *What is Art?* has been the occasion of a more serious critical discussion of that remarkable book than it has received before. Yet it has not been apparent that the more serious discussion has brought us any nearer to settling the fundamental question which it raises; the impression is rather that now, for the first time, it has been realized that the question is fundamental. Previously the correct attitude was to laugh at Tolstoy for a barbarian; now there seems to be an uneasy feeling that something more cogent is necessary. The old-fashioned appeal, still made in circles where nothing is learned and nothing forgotten, to that mysterious æsthetic sense which is the privilege of one in a hundred thousand, begins to tinkle a little wearily, like the bells on a démodé buffoon, who made his faded reputation by replying to this question of 'What is art?'—*Je ne sais quoi, mais je sais ce que tu ne sais point qu'est-ce que c'est ce je ne sais quoi*. It was a good old joke, in the good old days.

As well try to derail an express-train by putting a halfpenny on the line, as to counter Tolstoy's attack with such forlorn impertinences. That Tolstoy's attack is wrong, we all feel. But, how to repel it is another matter. To declare that art is a *je ne sais quoi* is a dangerous weapon against a giant who can reinforce his *mais, je sais, moi* by dropping *Anna Karenina* and *War and Peace* upon our diminished heads. We need less flimsy defences.

It is not easy to summarize Tolstoy's position with fidelity. He is not always consistent with himself, and his inconsistencies are not always negligible. In one place he declares that 'the function of art lies just in this: to make that understood and felt which in the form of an argument might be incomprehensible and inaccessible'; in another that 'an artist's work cannot be interpreted. Had it been possible to explain in words what he wished to convey, the artist would have expressed himself in words. He expressed it by his art, only because the feeling he experienced could not be otherwise transmitted.' The positions are obviously irreconcilable, and we must be content with assuming, from the main trend of his argument, that the latter was more truly his own position.

Indeed his fundamental proposition is that art consists in the communication of feelings, as opposed to thoughts. This absolute dichotomy underlies the whole of his argument. From it he concludes that the best art is that which communicates the best feelings. The judgment which are the best feelings depends upon the religious perception of the age; those are the best feelings which most approximate to the feelings inculcated by the common religion. Since this attitude may appear strange and almost barbarian, it may be worth recalling that it is the Greek attitude. Plato and Aristotle—as Tolstoy himself was perfectly aware—both insisted on the finality of the moral judgment in deciding the question what is good and what is bad art. Tolstoy emphatically reasserts their position. There are, he says, two acts of judgment: the first, whether a work is a work of art or not, is decided by the judgment whether the work does in fact communicate feelings; the second, whether it is good or bad art, is decided by the judgment whether the feelings communicated are good or bad. This judgment depends on the religious perception shared by society.

From this brief outline it will be obvious that to call such an æsthetic provincial is itself provincial; it is both traditional and formidable; in a word, it is classical. And this quality in it is ignored partly because it is taken at second-hand, and partly because it is forgotten that Classicism is a principle more profound than the Palladianism of the eighteenth century. The principle of the autonomy of art, in whose name the Tolstoyan æsthetic is rejected as barbarian, is a wholly romantic conception. Again, Tolstoy is perfectly aware of the situation. He says that the modern principle that artistic beauty is an end in itself, sovereign in its own right, only arose at the Renaissance, with the decay of a common religious perception. There was no longer a generally accepted tribunal to which the judgment, whether the feelings communicated by a work of art were bad or good, could be referred. The fact that feelings were communicated, irrespective of what the feelings were, alone decided the goodness or badness of a work of art.

But, in fact—and here Tolstoy makes an important and characteristic advance—the common religious perception, although ignored by the privileged classes, does still exist. The moral law of Christianity is recognized by the greater part of Western humanity. The Renaissance, which meant to the privileged few the abrogation of a common religion, meant to the many the purification of that religion from accretions and perversions. The many do know, by virtue of their active Christianity, what are good feelings and what are bad.

And their judgment, that the feelings communicated by most modern[1] art are bad, is final.

It is important to be clear as to the indictment which Tolstoy brings against modern art. He does not deny that works of art are produced, though he is scornful of the inability of the educated public to distinguish between a true work of art, which does communicate feelings, and a false one, which does not communicate anything. But he declares that the further and necessary distinction among the works of art—which are good and which are bad—is not made at all. The very necessity of making the distinction has been forgotten. A particular example of his attitude appears in his essay on Maupassant. All Maupassant's works are true works of art; they communicate feelings. But a few are very good, some a mixture of good and bad, and others wholly bad, judged by the morality of true Christianity.

It is essential (Tolstoy continues) to a true religion that its perceptions and moral feelings are capable of being shared by all. A good work of true art will therefore be universally appreciated—or at any rate appreciated by all those whose religious and moral perceptions are not atrophied. The demand for an educated taste as a preliminary condition of appreciation is unnecessary and irrelevant, for by hypothesis the work of art communicates feelings, and man's emotional nature is independent of education. 'Art is differentiated from activity of the understanding . . . by the fact that it acts on people independently of their state of development and education, that the charm of a picture, of sounds or of forms, infects any man, whatever the plane of development.' Therefore, the question what are good and what are bad works of art, resolves into the question: who in modern society have their religious perceptions still unobscured, and their capacity for absolute moral judgment uncontaminated, for they are the final court of appeal. To this Tolstoy answers unhesitatingly: the simple-minded, the peasants.

That is, I believe, a fair statement of Tolstoy's argument. There are two weak, or at least doubtful, links in the chain. Is it true, or is it wholly true, that art consists in the communication of feelings in Tolstoy's sense of the word 'feelings', a sense in which they are utterly distinct from thoughts. Secondly, is it true, or is it wholly true, that the highest religious perception which exists in modern society is the Christian perception? Some may consider that Tolstoy's contention that the judgment, whether a work of true art is good or bad, must be made, and must be a moral judgment is also wrong. I do not; moreover I regard it as indubitable that this necessary moral

[1] 'Modern' art, in Tolstoy's argument, means post-Renaissance art. I have used the epithet in the same sense.

judgment must, as Tolstoy contends, be based on a religious conception.

The problem—to take the second doubtful link first—is to determine where the religious conception is to be sought and found at the present time. Or, to translate into historical terms, was the religious significance of the Renaissance really contained, as Tolstoy asserts, in the Reformation; or was it something outside the Reformation? Tolstoy decides the question simply. At the Renaissance, he maintains, the educated classes abandoned Christianity for atheism, while the simpler folk restored and purified it. But it is not so simple. The finest minds at and after the Renaissance, once the first flush of rebellion was over, were not atheistical. They had bidden a long farewell to dogmatism and formalism: Church Christianity, as Tolstoy calls it, was no longer for them the embodiment of 'the highest life-conception' of which they were capable. They embarked on the search for a higher one. It is strange that Tolstoy, the artist, should not have recognized the nature of the effort and the achievement of the greatest post-Renaissance artists, for they fully satisfy the conditions which, he said, 'must be fulfilled to enable a man to produce a real work of art'.

> It is necessary that he should stand on the level of the highest life-conception of his time, that he should experience feeling and have the desire and capacity to transmit it, and that he should moreover have a talent for some one of the forms of art.

But Tolstoy, who was apparently insensible to the nature of Shakespeare's achievement, could not see (or would not admit) that the greatest post-Renaissance artists had stood head and shoulders above 'the level of the highest life-conception of their time'. To account for Tolstoy's blindness in this respect would take us far: we should need to search for its causes deep in his elemental nature. But a glimpse of them is given in his curious *Confession* of 1879.

> Art, poetry? . . . Under the influence of success and the praise of men I had long assured myself that this was a thing one could do though death was drawing near—death, which destroys all things, including my work and its remembrance, but soon I saw that that too was a fraud. It was plain to me that art was an adornment of life, an allurement to life. But life has lost its attraction for me; so how could I attract others? As long as I was not living my own life but was borne on the waves of some other life—as long as I believed that life had a meaning, though one I could not express—the reflection of life in poetry and art of all kinds afforded me pleasure: it was pleasant to look at life in the mirror of art. But when I began to seek the meaning of life, and felt the necessity of living my own life, that mirror became for me unnecessary, superfluous, ridiculous or painful. I could no longer soothe myself with what I now

saw in the mirror, namely, that my position was stupid and desperate. It was all very well to enjoy the sight when in the depth of my soul I believed that life had a meaning. Then the play of lights—comic, tragic, touching, beautiful and terrible—in life amused me. But when I knew life to be meaningless and terrible, the play in the mirror could no longer amuse me.

The importance of that confession is as manifest as its sincerity; it marks the climacteric in Tolstoy's spiritual evolution. But we are here concerned only with the light it incidentally throws upon Tolstoy's conception of art before what has been called his 'conversion'. Art was to him a faithful representation of life, which ceased to have meaning when life ceased to have meaning. And, in truth, after this point life never regained a meaning for Tolstoy. For some inscrutable reason the realization of the fact of death, which came late to him, was never overcome; he could not accept it. He turned to Christianity in its most paradoxical form as an escape from the inevitability of death; it was a gamble which henceforward continually allured him, but which he never really risked until that famous 'going-out' a few days before his actual death.

The immense, the overwhelming fact of death was precisely the one with which Shakespeare was pre-eminently concerned; and Shakespeare overcame it. That, I think, could be shown, though not, of course, by logical demonstration; it must suffice here to declare a conviction that the author of *Lear*, of *Antony and Cleopatra*, and *The Tempest* had achieved by successive stages a victory over death, in the sense that he had reasserted, rediscovered in the depths of his own being, without recourse to any revealed religion, the meaning of life which had been destroyed for him momentarily, as for Tolstoy permanently, by the realization of death. The great difference between these great men is that Shakespeare fought out the desperate battle in his art. To his growing despairs and his painfully won triumphs he compelled his art to be adequate, and thereby he expanded the very fabric of art. Tolstoy, on the other hand, definitely and finally abandoned art at the clutch of despair. He was like a Shakespeare who should have written *Hamlet* and thrown in his hand. It was not surprising that his most flagrant critical injustice should have been done towards Shakespeare; nor can one help suspecting that behind the insensibility to Shakespeare, which he so freely displayed, lay concealed something more radical—a profound and perhaps unconscious resentment against one who had achieved a victory where he himself had confessed and even proclaimed defeat.

Tolstoy denied that the artist, who should elect to remain an artist, could achieve a higher life-conception than that contained in

Christianity. There are many life-conceptions contained in Christianity, and I believe it would be true to say that one of them—the most essential, the one held by the founder of the Christian religion—cannot be and has not been surpassed. But, in the first place, that life-conception was not the life-conception of Tolstoy's own version of Christianity: his Christianity was shaped according to the pattern of his own secret despair—a religion of asceticism and abnegation. And, secondly, the revelation of the great artist is not of the same kind as the revelation of the great prophet. It may be akin and complementary to it, but it is not the same. The artist and the prophet, in their highest forms, do share that 'belief in an integral unity' which Baudelaire declared to be the necessary condition of a sound art; but the artist does not assert it, he reveals it in his representation of particulars.

The claim that post-Renaissance art should be judged good or bad by reference to the life-conception inculcated by Christianity is invalidated if it can be met by the counterclaim that not Christianity (Church or Tolstoyan) but post-Renaissance art itself contains and communicates the highest life-conception of which Western humanity has so far proved itself capable. And that is precisely the claim which, I believe, can be made for the highest achievements of post-Renaissance art. In these man faces, without the adventitious aid of revealed religion, the 'burden of the mystery'; and the feelings which they communicate are not, as Tolstoy asserts, mere feelings of pleasure at beauty (the 'æsthetic emotions' of modern theory), but feelings of a different and higher order. It would be a derogation, or at least a falsification, of these feelings to call them specifically 'religious'; but it would be worse to deny the truth that they are allied to the 'religious' emotion. These feelings are hard, if not impossible, to define; but certainly they have never been better *described* than by Keats in the famous definition which he deduced from the effect produced upon him by *Lear*. 'The excellence of every art is its intensity, capable of making all disagreeables evaporate from their being in close relationship with Beauty and Truth. Examine *King Lear* and you will find this exemplified throughout.' This mysterious identity of Beauty and Truth in the representation of life, and the equally mysterious power of seeing and then revealing that they are identical, are the real basis of the principle of the autonomy of art; by virtue of attaining this power the artist moves beyond the province of the moral and religious judgment—*if* he can attain it. For then he has fulfilled his final purpose, of revealing what the most exalted religion can only assert—that there is a 'meaning' in life. And we, to whom he communicates his knowledge and his revelation, are no mere blind accepters of an oracle: we

> take upon us the mystery of things
> As if we were God's spies.

Thus Tolstoy's claim that the feelings communicated by modern art must be judged good or bad by reference to the feelings inculcated by Christianity, because Christianity contains the highest life-conception of which man is capable, falls to the ground because modern art, in its highest forms, itself contains the highest life-conception of which man is at present capable. If criticism would resolutely insist on a hierarchy of artistic achievement, and show reason for the order it established, it would quickly be evident that art is indeed autonomous, furnished with both the right and the power to judge its own unworthy members, and able to protect by a sort of benefit of clergy its less exalted forms against the presumptions of the moral judgment. For it could fairly be claimed for the art of literature at least, that in its elementary acts of perception—the seizing of a true and revealing metaphor, for example—it is, however unconsciously, prophetic of a belief in that 'integral unity' which at its highest it consciously perceives and deliberately reveals. 'Every true metaphor,' said Baudelaire, 'is drawn from the inexhaustible riches of the analogy of the universe.'

But it is evident that these feelings—above all the supreme feelings of the identity of Beauty and Truth in the particularity of the world—which modern art does at its highest communicate, are not feelings which 'infect' every man 'independently of his state of development or education'. Never to have felt 'the burden of the mystery' at least is to be, as it were, disqualified from responding to such feelings, or recognizing that they have been expressed. And from this we see the falsity of Tolstoy's main dilemma.

> If art is an important matter, a spiritual blessing essential for all men, then it should be accessible to every one; if, as in our day, it is not accessible to all men, then one of two things: either art is not the vital matter it is represented to be, or that art which we call art is not the real thing.

Art *is* accessible to all men. That all men do not accede to it does not affect the fact of its universal accessibility. Certainly, if the feelings communicated by art were mere feelings, as Tolstoy believed or desired to believe, we should expect all men, irrespective of their development, to be affected by them. But they are not thus affected, and the conclusion is not 'that the art which we call art is not the real thing', but that the feelings communicated by art are not simply feelings. And indeed they manifestly are more than feelings. They partake of the nature of feelings, they partake of the nature of thoughts; yet they are neither the one nor the other. What are they?

About this vital point Tolstoy gropes. 'The function of art,' he says, 'lies just in this: to make that understood and felt which in the form of an argument would be incomprehensible and inaccessible. Usually it seems to the recipient of a truly artistic impression that he knew the thing before but had been unable to express it.' The second sentence is a true description of the 'artistic impression', the first a manifestly false conclusion from it. Take a simple example:

Men must endure
Their going hence, even as their coming hither:
Ripeness is all.

These limpid lines achieve and reveal an identity of truth and beauty. Try to express what they say in the language of discourse; with your utmost efforts you will not avoid translating them into a declaration of Stoic indifferentism. What they actually convey is something totally different—a sense of acceptance of human destiny. They may be said to contain a thought; but not what they contain, but what they are, is of importance. They are of another nature than any *thought*.

Yet it would be true to say that it seems to the reader of those lines 'that he knew the thing before, but had been unable to express it'. This is indeed a mark of 'the truly artistic impression'. And Tolstoy is in this description remarkably at one with Keats in the first of his famous axioms on poetry.

> First. I think poetry should surprise by a fine excess and not by singularity; it should strike the reader as a wording of his own highest thoughts, and appear almost a remembrance.

From this singular characteristic of the true artistic impression Tolstoy makes two chief deductions. Both are false. One, that art supplies a comprehensible equivalent of what would be incomprehensible as an argument, he himself, as we have seen, elsewhere disowns. The other, that art should be comprehensible to any man whatever his level of development, depends on the assumption that art is an affair of mere emotion. That is manifestly wrong. The lines from *Lear,* which have been used as an example, do not communicate a mere feeling, any more than they convey a mere thought. What they communicate is something of a third kind, in which feeling and thought are inextricably blended.

By thus falsifying the peculiar and unique nature of the true artistic impression, and simplifying it to a mere emotion, Tolstoy was enabled to deduce what he desired to deduce in order to justify his own despair of art: namely, that art was comprehensible to, and amenable to judgment by, 'the natural man'. Here the contrast between Tolstoy and Keats is in the highest degree illuminating: for

Keats, who, as we have seen, agreed with Tolstoy in his description of 'the true artistic impression', was also preoccupied with this question of the 'naturalness' of art. Witness his second and third axioms:

> Second. The touches of beauty should never be half-way, thereby making the reader breathless instead of content. The rise, the progress, the setting of Imagery should, like the sun, come natural to him, shine over him, and set soberly, although in magnificence, leaving him in the luxury of twilight. But it is easier to think what poetry should be than to write it. And this leads me to
>
> Another axiom—That if poetry comes not as naturally as the leaves to a tree, it had better not come at all.

Underlying all these *aperçus* of Keats is some conception or intuition of the 'naturalness' of poetry. Poetry comes naturally to the reader, its own internal progress is natural, and it comes from the poet himself as naturally as the leaves to a tree. But, unlike Tolstoy, Keats insists that what comes naturally to the reader is not what comes easy to him; it is 'his own highest thoughts'. Moreover, what comes naturally from the poet is not what comes easy from him. 'It is easier to think what poetry should be than to write it.'

Visibly Keats and Tolstoy have parted company. Whereas Tolstoy has persuaded himself that art, which is natural to man, is also easy to him—'it infects any man, whatever his plane of development'—Keats is instinctively proof against the false suggestion both as regards the reader and the writer. And Keats had to contend with the Tolstoyan æsthetic in his own time. The two contemporaries who for a time most influenced him, Leigh Hunt and Wordsworth, had both fallen into the ditch: they had both convinced themselves that poetry should employ 'the real language of real people'. Moreover, only a month before the enunciation of his axioms, Keats had had to counter Leigh Hunt's criticism that the first book of *Endymion* was 'unnatural'. 'He must first prove,' said Keats to his brother, 'that Caliban's poetry is unnatural. This with me completely overturns his objections.' One can hardly conceive a briefer or a better answer.

At this point the æsthetic question: 'What is the universality of art?' has manifestly resolved into the ethical question: 'What is natural to man?' And Tolstoy and Keats are making widely different answers. Tolstoy's is the simpler; it is Rousseau's answer. What is natural to man is what he approves 'independently of his state of development and education'. Keats' answer makes no such simple text for revolutionaries or *surréalistes*. What is natural to man is 'his own *highest* thoughts'.

One would not contend that Keats' answer, in these terms, is conclusive or even satisfactory. It would be easy to turn its point by pressing for an answer to the question: 'What are these high thoughts?' But we are already on ground where dialectic will not greatly avail to advance or discredit Keats' intuition. What is natural, for man and poet, according to Keats, is what is natural to them in a condition which both may achieve: of this condition poetry is to the reader as it were premonitory. He makes contact through it with his own highest thoughts, and it appears to him almost a remembrance.

The difference between this and the Rousseau-Tolstoy conception is vast. For Rousseau and for Tolstoy man becomes natural by becoming a barbarian. For Keats he becomes natural by advancing in some simple and mysterious way. What is this way of progress?

Keats' fundamental positions may be called intuitive, but they have commanded the assent of subsequent generations. Pure poetry comes naturally from the poet; and comes naturally to the reader. What does he mean by *naturally*? Most probably, at the moment of enouncing his 'axioms' he did not know. Does *naturally* mean the same in both cases? Obviously the poet differs from the man, in that he is a poet. He *naturally* gives expression to something, and the something expressed comes *naturally* to his reader. This something is the reader's own 'highest thoughts'. The problem of poetic expression as such does not greatly concern Keats. For him, when true poetic expression comes, it comes naturally. But the essential poetic achievement is, in some sort, independent of the gift of poetic expression. This may seem a curious position for a poet and particularly for a poet like Keats to have taken; but that he did take it is incontrovertible. In the second *Hyperion*, the last of his long poems, in which he concentrated all his agonized speculations on the worth and destiny of the poet, he asserted the position unequivocally.

> Who alive can say
> 'Thou art no poet, mayst not tell thy dreams'?
> Since every man whose soul is not a clod
> Hath visions and would speak, if he had loved
> And been well-nurtured in his mother tongue. . . .

It remained from first to last central to all Keats' thinking on the poetic faculty (which is the deepest of any known to me) that the poetic condition is attainable by all men—at a price. The price is that which he hints at in the strange lines above, which can only be interpreted in terms of his own biography. The soul of the man who would attain to the poetic condition must not be a clod; and he must have loved.

What Keats meant by love will be known to those familiar with his letters to Fanny Brawne: it was a complete self-surrender. What he meant by the soul, he had tried to explain some months before, at the moment when the agony of his love took hold of him, in a letter to his brother (April 1819). His conception of the soul, as might be expected, is exceedingly pertinent to his conception of the poetic condition as one attainable by all men. The soul is for Keats something which exists only potentially in man. In the natural man the division is twofold—into Heart, which he defines as 'the seat of the Human passions', and Mind. All direct sensational contact with the world of experience is made by the Heart; the true function of the Mind is to make this directly apprehended experience conscious. A man becomes natural by refusing to allow his Mind to become dominant and self-sufficient. If he can keep his Mind loyal to the experience of his Heart, then somehow the Soul is created. For a man to possess his Soul is to possess his Self, in the deepest sense of the word, and, mysteriously, at the moment of this Soul-possession, he sees the necessity and the beauty of the process by which he has come to achieve it. 'Do you not see,' cries Keats to his brother in the middle of this letter on the world as a Vale of Soul-making, 'how necessary a world of pains and troubles is to school an Intelligence and make it a Soul?'

Much could be written, and much in vain, on this strange letter of Keats. No mere analytical acumen will extract sustenance, or perhaps even a meaning, from it. It is obviously the record of a profound personal experience, an attempted statement of a process of self-creation which Keats had undergone. Therefore an intellectual criticism of it is condemned to futility. But its relevance to his conception of the poetic condition as *natural* to man is striking. It is, in Keats' belief, natural to man that he should come to possess his soul; but this natural process is the very reverse of easy: it is, on the contrary, the hardest thing in the world, for it depends on the maintenance of the heroic effort to keep the consciousness loyal to the unconsciousness. Out of this condition, if he can achieve it, the poet speaks, and the reader responds to his utterance as to a wording of his own highest thoughts, because he feels that the condition which underlies the poet's utterance is premonitory of a condition to which he himself may attain. This condition is at once a condition of being and a condition of knowing. Only by having achieved his soul can the poet see the necessity and the beauty of the process by which he attained it. Keats' letter is indeed a fuller enunciation of Baudelaire's disconcerting (and therefore neglected) proposition: 'La première condition pour faire un art sain est la croyance à l'unité intégrale.'

The relevance of Keats' transcendental conception of the self-created soul (which, it must be emphasized, is not a speculation, but an attempted statement of an actual experience) to the problem what are the strange 'thought-feelings' communicated by a supreme work of literary art, is not far to seek. Here is a condition of being, natural to man in the sense that its attainment is the final end of a natural effort to harmonize the discrepant elements of heart and mind—a condition of being in which thought and feeling are united to form a third and distinct faculty of perception. And what is perceived by this self-created faculty is that 'integral unity', of which Baudelaire spoke. 'Do you not see how necessary a world of pains and troubles is to school an intelligence and make it a soul?' That is one, and perhaps the highest object of the new faculty. Not 'Do you not understand?' not 'Do you not feel?' but 'Do you not *see*?' But the true expression of this condition is not argument but art. Keats moved a great step nearer to it in the sonnet which he wrote immediately after his letter:

> How fevered is the man who cannot look
> Upon his mortal days with temperate blood!
> Who vexes all the leaves of his life's book
> And robs his fair name of its maidenhood. . . .

And he advanced another and a still greater stride, in the days immediately following, when he found in the Grecian urn the perfect symbol of that identity of Beauty and Truth he had struggled to discern, and by the searching sincerity of his effort, created the faculty to discern it.

> Thou still unravished bride of quietness,
> Thou foster-child of silence and slow time. . . .

23

REPLY TO I. A. RICHARDS

From Things to Come. *This essay was written in 1926. Editor's title.*

TOWARDS the end of his stimulating book, *Principles of Literary Criticism*, Mr. I. A. Richards discusses what he calls the 'revelation' theory of poetry; that is to say the theory that poetry, in its highest forms, does actually reveal somewhat of the else hidden nature of reality. The theory was first maintained in this country by the 'romantic' poets of the early nineteenth century. It is to be found also in Goethe. Centuries before that we find palpable hints of it in Plotinus; and the enthusiastic sometimes discover it adumbrated in Aristotle's famous dictum that 'Poetry is more highly serious and more philosophic than history'.

Mr. Richards is distinctly scornful of the suggestion.

> The joy (he writes) which is so strangely the heart of the experience [of high tragedy] is not an indication that 'all's right with the world', or that 'somewhere, somehow there is justice'; it is an indication that all is right here and now with the nervous system.

He is ruthless, you see, with our little illusions. When we respond to *King Lear* or *The Cherry Orchard*, and leave them with the sweet solemnity of a *Nunc dimittis* sounding within our souls, a conviction that our eyes have seen our salvation, we are the victims of romantic delusion, pardonable perhaps in such foolish children of earth as we, but to be regarded by the cool-headed expert in knowledge with a blend of amusement and pity.

And yet, I wonder . . . 'All is right here and now with the nervous system.' It is downright enough. Mr. Richards is obviously quite certain that he knows. Yet Goethe, Coleridge, Keats . . . were no fools either. We had better take another look at the new theory before we bid a long farewell to the old one.

'All is right with the nervous system.' Queer that we should read *King Lear* only to find that out. The last thing that entered Keats's head, when he sat down once more to read the play:

O golden-tongued romance with serene lute!
  Fair-plumèd Syren! Queen of far away!
  Leave melodizing on this wintry day,
Shut up thine olden volume, and be mute.
Adieu! for once again the fierce dispute
  Betwixt damnation and impassion'd clay
  Must I burn through . . .

He misunderstood himself. What he was really after was to determine whether he could stick it. He ought to have known that Monk Lewis was a better test of nerves.

Probably we misunderstood Mr. Richards. The 'nervous system' sounds a very businesslike affair. No humbug about that, so to speak. And yet, I fancy, it is as vague and nebulous a conception as the 'soul'. In spite of his appearance of scientific rigour, Mr. Richards is saying no more than that the strange and profound satisfaction that comes to us through great tragedy is purely emotional and subjective. We feel it, and that is all. If that is what he means, he might have chosen a less ambiguous way of saying it. Simple things are best said simply.

But, in actual fact, he says more than this. He says that the profound satisfaction we derive from tragedy is an indication that *all is right* with the nervous system. Whether he meant this, we cannot tell. Perhaps his audacious pen ran away with him. For we must ask why the tragic satisfaction indicates that *all is right* with the nervous system? Is it because that strange satisfaction is the correct response to tragedy? But who is to determine what is the correct response? From the fact, on which Mr. Richards is so anxious to insist, that all we can say of great tragedy is that it calls forth a certain emotional condition in certain people, it is quite impossible to conclude that the presence of that condition is evidence that nothing is wrong with their nervous systems, or their souls, or their bank-accounts, or their drains.

Mr. Richards cannot have it both ways. He has chosen a complete subjectivism; then he must stick to it. He declares that the fact in question is that certain people, after reading or seeing *King Lear,* experience a strange satisfaction. Very good. But if we are to accept it as a statement of the fact, he must not go beyond it. The moment he attempts to make deductions from the fact, new and unwarrantable assumptions enter in. Mr. Richards's assumption is that to the people to whom this strange satisfaction comes it comes because their nervous systems are in order. First, it is an unwarrantable assumption; and it is a very doubtful one. It would be laughed at by nine neurologists out of ten, for the chances are that the soundest nervous systems belong to eupeptic Philistines, who would be bored to extinction if they were compelled to read, or even to see, *King Lear*.

Mr. Richards may reply that in his view the nervous systems of our friends the Philistines are not in order. But in that case he means by the nervous system something quite peculiar—never before described by that name. He means the very delicately refined sensibility which, he believes, is required in order to respond fully to *King Lear*. I do not doubt that it is required. But the only reason for believing that a refined sensibility is necessary to respond to *King Lear*, is that *King Lear* is a very delicate and subtle object. Our response to *King Lear* can prove that we have a refined sensibility on one condition only, that it is, *in itself*, something which requires a refined sensibility to respond to it. Except we know the nature of the object, nothing can be deduced as to the nature of the subject.

Mr. Richards has attempted an illegitimate simplification of the problem of poetry. Two things are given in the poetic experience—the poem, and the reader. It is only possible to say a clever thing, such as that the joy of the tragic experience is an indication that all is right with the nervous system, by unconsciously doing a stupid one—namely, to leave the tragedy out of the reckoning. The truth is that the strange joy that comes to the reader of high tragedy is the outcome of the meeting of two elements: some quality in the tragedy itself, and a delicate sensibility in the reader. If the experiencing of that joy indicates that the reader possesses a delicate sensibility, it indicates equally, and by precisely the same logical compulsion, that there is in the tragedy itself as object some quality which causes the delicate sensibility to function in a way so strange.

It is tedious, no doubt, to be compelled thus painfully to indicate that an egg is an egg and not a taste; but subtle logicians like Mr. Richards have to be tediously countered. At any rate, we are now in a position to rewrite his bold sentence to accord more closely with the facts:

> The joy which is so strangely the heart of the experience [of tragedy] is an indication that our sensibilities are delicate and responsive: whether it is an indication that 'all's right with the world' can only be decided by an inquiry into the nature of those qualities possessed by the tragedy, and responded to by our sensibilities—an inquiry into which I have not the patience to enter.

So far from having demolished the 'revelation' theory of poetry, Mr. Richards has touched it not at all. Like most writers on literature who are æsthetic philosophers rather than literary critics, he has bemused himself with a phrase. Mr. Richards's talisman—'the nervous system'—has failed him.

I am not anxious to embark upon the inquiry which Mr. Richards has thus avoided. To attempt it in the few pages of this brief essay would be fantastic. For it would involve a long and minute investigation into the creative process of the poet, which has never yet been attempted by any critic. Coleridge intended to undertake it, and left behind him valuable hints for the work—but they are hints, and no more. I confess that I have only glimpses of the way the work should be done; it is something which I hope, not indeed to do, but to have helped in the doing, before I die.

But the present point is that the 'revelation' theory of poetry and art emerges completely unscathed from Mr. Richards's demolition. He has delivered his blow on the empty air. That is not to say that the 'revelation' theory is right, but that we may with a good conscience retain the theory held by Goethe, Coleridge, and Keats, and still believe that the chances are that they, being at once great poets and subtle thinkers, were not wholly deluded.

Nevertheless, though it would be idle to undertake a systematic defence of the 'revelation' theory without a careful and minute investigation of the creative process, it may be worth while to point out that the real objection to the theory springs generally not from a consideration of the facts, but from an *a priori* repugnance to the implication of the theory. The philosopher cannot admit the poet's implicit claim to 'know' reality, or the reader's claim to attain through the poet's work a 'knowledge' of reality. 'Knowledge' is the privilege of the philosopher, and he very strongly resents the attempt of the poet to claim it. Therefore, he feels himself compelled, by hook or by crook, to prove that the poet's conviction of knowledge is merely subjective: it is an emotional condition. By some mysterious means (into which the philosopher never really inquires) the poet with this sense of 'knowledge' creates something which arouses in the sensitive reader the same sense of 'knowledge'. This also must be merely subjective: an emotional condition. The decision is *a priori*. For if the strange condition of soul, experienced by the poet, and called by him 'knowledge', which is communicated to us, and called by us 'knowledge', be not relegated to pure subjectivity, then the philosopher's monopoly of 'knowledge' is threatened. But, unfortunately for the philosopher, his effort to relegate this queer poetic experience to the realm of subjectivity fails, as we have seen it fail in the case of Mr. Richards.

Of course, those who uphold or incline to the 'revelation' theory of poetry do not claim that the poet's 'knowledge' is of the same kind as the philosopher's or the scientist's—it may be remarked in passing that the scientist is just as scornful of the philosopher's claim to knowledge as the philosopher is scornful of the poet's. Roughly, the 'revelation' theory holds that there is a reality outside the perceiving mind and that man has evolved several ways of seeking to know it. Of these several ways the poetic, or æsthetic alone is concerned with the real in its particularity: it does not seek to subsume particulars under universal concepts, nor does it confine itself to the measurable aspects of the world. It is primarily concerned with the world of ordinary human experience; and the materials with which the poet sets about his work are unusually vivid perceptions of real and particular objects. Like Antony in the streets of Alexandria he 'notes the qualities of people', and of things: not for any practical purposes, as an employer may note the qualities of men for a particular job, or a mason the qualities of stones for a particular building, but simply and solely for his own delight in observation. Towards the world of particulars he is passive and receptive, that not one of its qualities may be lost. It is perhaps peculiar that he should take delight in this: it is because the pursuit gives him delight. He has 'more than ordinary organic sensibility'. In fact he alone is able to *see* the world of particulars, where ordinary men, as it were, see only the headlines, and take note only of those salient features of the world which are useful for their practical ends.

This rare faculty of vividly perceiving particulars is the primary poetic gift: no one can ever be a great creative writer without it, though not all who have it become great creative writers. What further gifts are necessary, what further operations are carried on in the mind of the great poet beside this incessant intuition of particulars, cannot be discussed now: it is a fascinating and difficult inquiry. But even this brief consideration of the primary poetic perception is sufficient to show that when the poet claims to reveal reality he is not talking idle nonsense. By his most elementary act of perception and description, he does reveal, and he reveals the real.

We may surmise that the poet's activity, when he is a Shakespeare and writing *King Lear*, though infinitely more complex, is of the same kind. Just as a life-time of observation of particular things has given him the power of making us see them when he describes them, so a life-time of observation of the behaviour of men and women (above all, perhaps, of himself) has given him the power of making us understand them when he represents them. We see that they *must* act as he makes them act, speak as he makes them speak. True, they use a language which in real life they would not use. The characters of a high Shakespearean tragedy speak as poets. It is necessary that they should so speak. The poet alone can utter himself; and the characters of a great tragedy must utter themselves. And that strange peculiarity of high tragedy that its heroes speak rhythmical and recondite poems has its simple explanation in the fact that poetic utterance alone is completely expressive of the living man.

Thus the characters of high tragedy are the more real, because they are not realistic. They are presented complete, as it were in the round, to our consciousness; and as they move to their destinies we have an immediacy of contact with them which is unattainable through any other literary form. When Cleopatra cries:

O, see, my women,
The crown o' the earth doth melt. My lord!
O wither'd is the garland of the war,
The soldier's pole is fall'n: young boys and girls
Are level now with men; the odds is gone
And there is nothing left remarkable
Beneath the visiting moon.

she is uttering an emotion which in real life is never expressed—not because it is not felt, but simply because men and women have not the power to express it. High tragedy brings us into contact with creatures who experience the most grievous human vicissitude, feel the deepest human emotions, and express themselves. Therefore, in one sense they are not human. Not Shakespeare himself could have expressed his emotion at the moment that he felt it. When his dark lady betrayed him, he laughed wanly and said, 'That's a blow!' just as feebly as the rest of us. But the shudder of loathing of himself and her remained with him: he could recall it. One day he did recall it, and wrote:

The expense of spirit in a waste of shame
Is lust in action ...

This added faculty of utterance, that can be given to the creatures of a poet's imagination alone, makes them more real than men actually are, precisely as the poet's description of an object makes it more real than it actually is to the ordinary perceptions of men.

But, it may be said, when the poet describes a primrose, there *is* (or there was) a primrose which he sees and describes; when Shakespeare gives utterance to Cleopatra, there is no Cleopatra. How can he then be revealing the reality, when there is no reality to reveal? The answer is simple. He is revealing his own experience of the real, of which his Cleopatra is but one of a thousand incarnations. Thereby you admit (comes the reply) that the only reality with which we make contact in a Shakespearean tragedy is Shakespeare's experience. True, so far as it goes. But Shakespeare's experience—his emotions, his thoughts, his habits of emotion and thought—is experience of the real. His 'more than ordinary organic sensibility' was exposed, day in day out, to contact with the real world; by it he was shaped to what he was. When he utters himself through the immense complexity of a tragedy it is his experience of the real world that he utters. One man's experience of it, if you insist. But such another man you will not find in the world's history. What he brought to the equal marriage with reality was what the high gods gave him, 'an experiencing nature' the like of which they gave to no other man.

Through that experiencing nature we little men are privileged to make our nearest contact with the real, one far closer, far more comprehensive than the most sensitive among us could make—a contact that seemed prodigious and miraculous to poets of genius—to Goethe, to Coleridge, to Keats. This real is not the real of science, nor of philosophy; it is not the reality of the specialist of any sort, but it is the reality with which we ordinary humans are all our lives concerned, the world in which we suffer and delight, are defeated and conquer. To know that reality as it is may not be 'knowledge' for the philosopher, or for the scientist; it is 'knowledge' to us, and it is the only knowledge we greatly care about. We go to Shakespeare to learn it, and to learn how to learn more, to have our own small experiencing natures enlarged. We do not go to him in order to learn whether our nervous systems are in order; nor do we get any answer to that doubtless important question through him. The joy that comes to us after a tragedy of his is not indeed a sign that we know the secret of the universe, however much we may feel that we do; but it is a sign that the truer and more complete experience of reality we gain through Shakespeare does bring us, what we sometimes dream all true experience of reality would bring us were we but capable of it, joy and serenity. Once break this contact with the real, once persuade men that high tragedy has not its roots in outward life, there would be no joy and acceptance in the tragic experience any more. But in attempting to break that contact with the real, you are attempting the impossible. Every man capable of experiencing a Shakespearean tragedy at all knows, with the same certainty he has of his own existence, that he is making contact with the real. He is making contact with art also. That he sometimes forgets. But by forgetting it, he gets to the root of the matter, which far cleverer men miss by remembering it, namely, that art is but a means—the most potent of all means—of bringing reality nearer to us than we have power to bring it to ourselves.

24

CHAUCER: THE CHURCH AND THE PEASANT

From Heaven and Earth *(Cape, 1938), pages 42–52.*

G. K. Chesterton, with characteristic insight, fastened on a phrase used, in condign praise of him, by a French contemporary:

O grant translateur! Geoffroy Chaucier!

It sounds to a modern ear, said Chesterton, much as though one were to praise a man by calling him 'a great scrivener' or 'a great stenographer'; but in Chaucer's world and to Chaucer's mind it was praise indeed. There was a common fund of wisdom and achievement: and men were conscious rather of what they drew from it than of what they added to it. Yet add they did; and Chaucer added royally, but as it were impersonally. His 'translations' were free, because the substance was not his own. He was spared the burden of individualized achievement, therefore he was free in a way we can but dimly understand, with the freedom of a natural humility.

This basic communality of which Chaucer's work is the flowering in the realm of language, was the reflection of a communal substance in the elemental life of men. The common-field was the ground in which this great harvest grew. Men depended on earth and on one another; they were knit to earth and to one another; one common gesture united them all. The individual, in our sense, scarcely existed. Not even in name. If I, for example, had been one sort of man—a tiny tot of a feudal underlord, able to furnish myself with a horse and armour and one retainer with a sword, I should have been John de Larling; if I had been another sort of man, I should have been John Scrivener. But, of course, if I could be conceived as existing at all in 1350 or thereabouts, I should certainly have been in the Church—a subordinate monk or friar, or a poor parson. But in any case I should have had only my Christian name. And if, as one may suppose, I had wanted to think the kind of thoughts I am most inclined to think, it would have been hardly necessary for me to write and publish them. Those activities of mine would have been expressed probably in a long and patient copying of Boethius, uplifted by a more or less continuous meditation on the life and death and resurrection of Christ. The impulse to break through the benign atmosphere of anonymity would have been very feeble. Why should I?

This natural submergence of the individuality, this undisturbed latency of the conscious personality, which now appears so calm and comely, was not peculiar to the Church, or to the 'makers' in words or stone, but was diffused throughout society. The individuality was there, but it was not conscious. For the vast mass of people, whatever their vocation, existence was primarily communal. This living, natural and universal community is indeed singularly hard for us to imagine. We think of communal existence at a boarding-school, or in a regiment, or quite exceptionally, of life in a voluntary community. But such community is artificial. Life in a voluntary community is perhaps the nearest we can get to the medieval reality: and that brings us near (not very near) to one form only of the medieval communal society, the monastic: a very widespread form, indeed, but still the medieval community at the point where it was most conscious, and most separated from natural ties—of common toil and local habitation. The monastic community in regard to the village-community was a feudal overlord—the lord of many manors.

I believe that the village-community could have expanded naturally into a flowering of its own. I do not believe that it was necessary and inevitable that it should have been disrupted as it was, or that its complex and organic harmony should have precipitated, into unrestricted ownership on the one side, and insecure tenantry on the other. Neither do I believe that the choice lay between a victory of the lords and a victory of the peasants. The peasants did not want victory; they wanted justice—but real justice, not the formalistic parody of it which the lawyers offered them, by which, in essence, they were compelled to change their anomalous and impersonal security, for 'freedom' to be rack-rented and dispossessed.

The only kind of justice which could have served the peasants was imaginative justice. Essentially, the village-community was inarticulate, rooted in custom, not in law: and the law, even when honestly applied to it (which was seldom), was incommensurable with the reality. Bond or free? asked the Law. The answer was Neither. It was the answer of the community to the Law which recognized only 'persons'; the Law could not hear it. Because of this it was impossible that the Law could do justice to the peasant, because, in fact, the service which the peasants owed the lord could only be understood and estimated if the community were regarded not as a collection of separate persons but as a living whole.

There was one person in the village—the person *par excellence*—

the parson. He was the man marked out to represent the community. He belonged to it, in a way the lord did not. In perhaps most manors the lord was perforce an absentee—a cathedral chapter, or a monastery, or a great soldier fighting for the King in France, or a courtier. The parson belonged to the village: he lived in it, and as like as not farmed in it as well. But on a higher plane than this he represented precisely what we may distinguish as the community of the village-community—its simple and mysterious organic wholeness. As a person, he was supported by the tithe of the community as a whole; because he represented an authority as superior to the lord as it was to the villeins. The villeins owed their services to the lord; but both owned their tithe to the humble vicar of God.

One may freely grant that it was necessary that not all the tithe in every parish should have gone to the vicar alone; but it was utterly wrong that so much of it should have diverted to the upkeep of a parasitic Church establishment. The Church was rich enough in all conscience, from the innumerable manors with which the pious munificence of kings and lords and humbler men had endowed it. Its lordships should have sufficed it. The tithe should have remained to enrich and bless the country-side. It would have been simple enough, if the will had been there, to take some of the tithe of the rich and fertile parish to add to the parson's living in the poor one. What at any rate should have been manifest to the Christian conscience of the Church was that its many lordships were the true and sufficient source of the revenue to support it as a magnificent and splendid institution over and beyond the parish church and the parish priest. When it diverted tithe from the village-community to increase its institutional opulence, it was bleeding the village-community to death.

Let us look again at the picture of society in Chaucer's Prologue—remembering that it may have been exaggerated by the artist in Chaucer, and that it was probably socially exaggerated, because pilgrims are in the main likely to be relatively well-to-do. That is so even to-day: it is not the working-man who makes the trip to Soviet Russia. Nevertheless, even when full allowance is made for such exaggeration, it is very remarkable how preponderant in the picture are those whom one must describe as ecclesiastical parasites on society.

In these I do not include the Prioress, not merely because she is elegant and charming—a sort of English Marie Antoinette—but because economically she is no worse than the equivalent of the lord of many manors. She belongs with the Knight. Economically, both might be called parasitic; but surely, not morally. Economically, even the 'povre person of a toun' is parasitic; but he is a spiritual *necessity* —a necessity for more abundant life: and those who can see in such a man merely an economic parasite are blind and far astray. To have no formulable religion is one thing: to have no imagination, quite another. If men allow their incapacity for formulated religion to become incapacity for imagination, they will forget a truth profounder than any economic truth: a truth which, if it is disregarded, will assuredly turn even the recognition of economic truth into a diabolical force making not for the salvation but the devastation of mankind. The truth is simple: 'Man shall not live by bread alone.' This truth the poor parson represents in Chaucer's great picture of medieval English life. He gives to a meaningful life a consciousness of its meaning.

When I say that the Knight and Prioress are not morally parasitic, I do not mean that they fulfil a necessary function in the same simple and sublime sense that the parson does; but that they have a secure place in the upper ranks of the hierarchy without which medieval society could not conceive itself as existing at all. They are the aristocrats; and they are not unworthy of their privilege. And with his unfailing instinct Chaucer makes us aware of his feeling that they are sound. So, at a different point in the hierarchy, it is with the poor clerk of Oxenford. He also is a worthy member of what Coleridge called 'the clerisy'. But then comes a procession of real parasites: the hunting and hard-riding Monk:

What should he studie, and make himselven wood
Upon a book in cloistre alway to poure,
Or swinken with his handes, and laboure,
As Austin bit? How shall the world be served?
Let Austin have his swink to him reserved.

The Friar, whose one purpose it is to make money out of the simple and gullible—above all, from women; who devours widows' houses:

For though a widwe hadde nought a sho,
So pleasaunt was his 'In principio',
Yet wolde he have a ferthing ere he went.

The Somnour—that is, the server of summonses to appear before the Archdeacon's court:

And if he fond o-wher a good felawe
He wolde techen him to have non awe
In swich cas, of the erchedeknes curs,
But if a mannes soul were in his purs,
For in his purs he sholde y-punisshed be.
'Purs is the erchedeknes helle', seyde he.

The Pardoner—the man licensed to sell Papal indulgences, and pig's bones, and a gobbet of St. Peter's sail when he met our Lord walking upon the water, and a pillow-case which he said was our Lady's veil. It is very funny; but old Chaucer knew the reality behind it.

> But with these relikes, whan that he fond
> A povre person dwelling upon lond,
> Upon a day he gat him more moneye
> Than that the person gat in monthes tweye.

Maybe our own 'povre person', who, thinking no guile, trusted a man with the Pope's own licence. It was the doings of the Pardoners and of the Popes in this matter, when the business had assumed truly modern proportions, and was conducted in the truly modern manner —so many hundred thousand indulgences to be sold in Germany on a fifty-fifty basis by the great banking-house of Fugger for their loan of half-a-million to the Papal Curia—that set ablaze the reformation of Luther.

Put together the Shipman and the Merchant, whose one concern was that the sea between the Low Countries and the Orwell be kept open; add to them the Wife of Bath who, with her five husbands, seems to have been something of a female pioneer among the west-country clothiers, who were beginning to enter on a big way of business in those days: then the fraternity of Haberdasher, Carpenter, Weaver, Dyer and Carpetmaker, whom Chaucer significantly describes not individually, but corporately—all made 'to sitten in a yeldhalle on a deys', all with ambitious wives eager to have their husbands made aldermen, and themselves be called 'Ma-dame'—and you have the rising bourgeoisie in so far as it fulfilled a positive economic function. Perhaps we should add the Franklin to them—the country squire and M.P.

> At sessiouns there was he lord and sire
> Full ofte time he was knight of the shire.

He was the direct ancestor of the men who began the Parliamentary revolution but could not, or would not, finish it. The Franklin is emphatically the freeholder. He is outside the village-community. His labourers are all wage-labourers; and there are few wage-labourers in the village-community. But he is not the lord of many manors, or even of a few. In respect to the aristocracy of the manorial system he is a bourgeois; so is he in respect to its economy. He produces primarily for the market and the town.

Of the manorial economy only the Parson, the Plowman, his brother, and the Reeve are representative. Notably, the Parson and the Plowman are ideals of Christian neighbourliness. And the Reeve is not too bad. He is the steward who manages the manors for the absent lord; and very well he did out of it, as agents to this day have a way of doing.

> His woning was full fair upon an heeth
> With grene trees shadwed was his place.
> He coude bettre than his lord purchase.
> Full riche he was astored prively.

Parasitic? Hardly. We may allow him as one who fulfilled, though at an exorbitant price, a necessary function of co-ordination and management.

Now we have passed them all in brief review except four: the Doctor, in league with the Apothecary for their mutual advantage, who 'kepte what he wan in pestilence'. None the less, the germs of the man of science and the dietician are in him: and notably, 'his studie was but litel on the bible'. The Manciple—the domestic steward or man-matron of one of the Inns of Temple [*sic*]; and one of his masters—the Sergeant of the Law, a master of the intricate and wordy art of conveyancing. It is significant that Chaucer's emphasis is on this. Land is beginning to change hands freely. And finally, the Miller, who, though Chaucer does not say so, appears to have been the freeholder of his mill. He is at the bottom of the particular class within a class of which the Franklin is at the top.

The Knight has one yeoman to attend him, besides his son the squire; the Prioress has a nun and three priests; the band of budding aldermen, their cook or rather their chef. Even by aristocratic standards we must put down two of the Prioress's retinue as superfluous. They were not rogues perhaps, but they were parasites. So, out of a company of twenty-nine all told, there were no less than two superfluous priests, one parasitic hunting monk, and three downright ecclesiastical rogues. The proportion is tremendous. Mark well, we have allowed, as Chaucer would have allowed, that an aristocracy of religion was necessary. It is only after that has been supplied, as well as the poor parson and the Oxford clerk, that I talk of ecclesiastical parasites; yet the pure ecclesiastical parasites compose nearly one-fourth of the company. People like statistics nowadays. Then let us say that the percentage of those in Chaucer's cross-section of society who derived their living from the Church is 38 per cent; while the ecclesiastical parasites make 21 per cent. We have thus allowed as a legitimate percentage no less than 17 per cent.

In that parasitism of the medieval Church, I find the cause why the village-community was disrupted instead of advancing into a fuller flowering. Had the village parson not been starved, he might have become a man of independent authority, with the capacity to understand the subtlety of the village-community, and with the resolution to defend the rights of the inarticulate peasantry against the exactions of the lord and the irrelevant intellectualism of the lawyers. The village-church might have fulfilled the function that so manifestly belongs to it, of gathering her children under her wing, as a hen her chickens. Instead of that the village-priests were starved and degraded and stupefied. Innumerable are the protests of medieval prelates against the ignorance of the parish clergy. But it was the fault of the Church, not of the priests, that they were ignorant. It suffered the village-priest to be degraded in status beside the extra-parochial priest or the ecclesiastical official; it impoverished him and thrust him down to the level of peasant illiteracy, until for the most part, even had the will been there, he was in plain fact incapable of giving the simplest spiritual instruction to his flock.

The Church, by its economic and spiritual exhaustion of the parson, had made it impossible for him to be more than a peasant, and for his religion to be more than a superstition. Had it tended and cared for him, he would have been led to care for his people. Had he been taught his own spiritual dignity, he would have been the spokesman of the dignity of the community whose consciousness and conscience he was called to be. That this is not an idle dream, Chaucer's picture of the Parson and his brother the Plowman is witness. The possibility was there.

It was a possibility at once economic and spiritual, as was the reality of the village-community itself; and the rejection of the possibility was a spiritual and an economic process, too. By that rejection it was decided that irresponsible ownership and not responsible ownership should be the pathway by which men travelled into awareness of themselves as individuals; that the not merely un-Christian but definitely anti-Christian doctrine should be established that personality was a function of possession; that the conception of individuality should emerge only as contaminated and debased by individualism. What might have been saved from the village-community, saved, expanded and universalized, was the instinctive sense that obligation was inherent in all possession, and that ownership was essentially trusteeship. That was to become the pious sentiment of the *élite* of an individualistic and acquisitive society, as it became uneasily conscious of its spiritual emptiness. But the gospel of 'service'—before and after sales—is only pious cant. It is not, and never can be, a reality in an irreligious and capitalistic society. It might have been in a different society; but the compulsive power which could have made it a reality, and could have shaped the society in which alone it could be a reality, vanished long ago.

That compulsive power was possessed by the medieval Church; and it frittered it away by its own unworthiness. The opportunity that was lost was very great: how great we are dimly beginning to realize to-day when mankind's need of a universal spiritual authority invested with compulsive power is desperate, and the difficulty of creating such an authority is superhuman. We begin to glimpse how unique and irrevocable was the destiny which for a period established a spiritual authority as king of kings, lord of lords, and the only ruler of princes. Of that period, for the English race, Chaucer is the only voice. It is no accident that he, the first of our great poets, should be the sanest and the wisest of them all. He is, before all else, untroubled. That 'order' which was to become for Shakespeare mainly a secular and desperate necessity, has in Chaucer's world a divine organ. Its source is an eternal reality; it is not precarious. There is security. The older Chaucer grew, the more secure and solid he was, although his worldly fortunes suffered a precipitous decline. But Shakespeare though he progressed from poverty to estate, passed also from happy security into a tempest of doubt and despair, and if he emerged from it, as I believe, to a final serenity, it was a serenity too deeply disturbed by a doubt of its own validity to bear the name. It was no accident that Chaucer ended where Shakespeare began—with creative innocence. *The Tempest* is lovely; but with the loveliness of a dream. The beauty of *The Canterbury Tales* is the beauty of reality.

Part of the modest fortune of which Shakespeare died possessed consisted in a portion of the impropriated great tithes of Stratford. Most things occurred to Shakespeare; and no doubt it occurred to him to ask himself what the great tithe of Stratford was doing in his hands. I would give much to know his answer.

25

ROUSSEAU

This essay forms three chapters of Heaven and Earth.

A story is told of the late Jules Lemaître's undertaking to give a course of lectures on Rousseau to some Royalist society in Paris without having read his works; yet even so, with all the large licence of abuse that his ignorance allowed him, he did not satisfy a lady in his audience. She seriously complained: 'Monsieur, vous n'avez pas été assez injuste!' To be sufficiently unjust to Rousseau is, perhaps, an ideal impossible of attainment by the Right in France where the Left has made him the patron saint not merely of the French Revolution, which has some justification, but of 'La République des Comités', which has none at all. But it is attainable in countries where Rousseau is neither the Messiah nor the Devil of active politics; and in recent years it has seemed to be attained in the works of the late Mr. Irving Babbitt and his 'Humanist' disciples. For the disciples, at least, Rousseau has become the prime author of all the maladies from which civilized society suffers to-day.

This is not criticism, but credulity; and in a healthy reaction America itself has lately produced some of the sanest and solidest attempts to stem this tide of superstition and sciolism. Mr. Wright's *The Meaning of Rousseau* was memorable: Mr. Josephson's biography was at least serious; and Mr. Hendel's *Jean-Jacques Rousseau: Moralist* was a beautifully patient exposition of the gradual development of Rousseau's thought. He followed its growth as the true naturalist follows the growth of a living thing; and he traced the subtle influences upon Rousseau's thinking of his chequered and embittering life-experience. It is the best evidence of Rousseau's genius that he does continually arouse this kind of critical loyalty. It is not possible, as he himself foresaw, to be deeply moved by his work—perhaps one should say to be moved by his work at all—without recognizing his passionate sincerity. Of that sincerity his very contradictions are the evidence; for apparent contradictions are necessary in thinking of the kind towards which Rousseau incessantly strove—the thinking which seeks to be faithful to the total verity of human experience. Rousseau's mind was central; it never wandered far from the simple, profound and permanent problems of humanity. These problems were to him never abstract speculations of the intellect as they so often were to his colleagues, the *philosophes*; they presented themselves to him as immediate experience, in the form of urgent moral issues. The acquisition of that equivocal faculty (for it involved a miserable and harassed life for him as a man) was the real content of his 'illumination' on the road to Vincennes. Suddenly he stepped out of contemporary society; he looked upon it with genuine detachment—and he was dismayed. Ever afterwards his dominant concern was to imagine, in the creative sense of the word, a society in which a good man could live without being stultified by his environment. Since that is indeed the most permanent concern of human kind, and since Rousseau concentrated all his singular powers upon it, it is scarcely surprising that his spirit is mighty yet.

It belongs to the essence of Rousseau's insight—and no doubt also to the enduring influence of his youthful study of Plato—that there should be a manifest analogy between society and the individual man. The three ages, or phases, of the development of the individual into full awareness—the phases which William Blake distinguished as Innocence, Experience and Imagination—have their counterpart, according to Rousseau, in the history of society. The age of Innocence is the state of Nature; the age of Experience the condition of actual society; the age of Imagination is the condition of a society based on a true Social Contract, wherein society as a whole is animated by the moral purpose which the individual, in so far as he has reached the status of true manhood, knows to be that without which he cannot be truly human. The society of the true social contract is, in fact, a society in which, on entering, each individual covenants to love his neighbour as himself. In a society where such a compact was real, the individual would surrender himself in order to gain possession of his humanity. Those who have attacked Rousseau's doctrine as the charter of mob-democracy and frenzied nationalism are entirely ignorant of what he was trying to convey.

It might fairly be said that Rousseau's doctrine is vision and not politics. He would have been the first to agree; only he would have added that without vision politics is a process of inevitable degeneration. And by vision he would have meant a constant and undimmed insight into the moral purpose of society, and the will to be loyal to that purpose to the end. Nothing could be a more fantastic parody of Rousseau's doctrines than that which proceeds from those who persuade themselves that in emphasizing the necessity of an 'ethical will' in the individual and in society they are opposing Rousseau. Not since

Plato himself has there been a political philosopher who so emphasized the truth that unless the ethical will is dominant within it a human society is merely a negation of its own idea. His starting-point was the fundamental Greek principle (of which the enduring monument is Plato's *Republic*) that in order to become a completely ethical being a man must become a conscious political being also; that the good life is possible only in society, but only in a society which is created and maintained by the deliberate purpose of making the good life possible.

This, for Rousseau, was the justification of society: that society was necessary to the fulfilment of the moral being of man. 'The happy age of gold was ever a state alien to the human race, which failed to apprehend it when it was to be enjoyed, or else lost it when it was to be known.' In other words, the social state and human self-awareness arrive together, the one is the condition of the other. This self-awareness, which eventually enables man to discern how profound and ineradicable are his moral impulses—and this is what Rousseau meant by the 'natural goodness' of man—imposes upon him the new duty of making society the vehicle and instrument of those moral impulses. The society he discovers surrounding him is one which frustrates those impulses and makes their fulfilment impossible. It is an 'unnatural' society.

This conception of Rousseau's that contemporary society was 'unnatural' is based on his affirmation that men are 'naturally good'. That assertion infuriates a certain kind of orthodox Christians, and also the ultra-modern tribe who are orthodox without even being Christian by profession. The reason why it infuriates them is obvious: for the Catholic dogma is that man is 'naturally bad' and labours under the burden of Original Sin. If these two affirmations are simply set opposite one another, they bristle; and it is a cat-and-dog fight between them. That is what generally happens. Astonishingly few people understand what Blake meant when he said: 'There is a Negation, and there is a Contrary. We must destroy the Negation to redeem the Contrary.'

The dogma of Rousseau that men are 'naturally' good, and the Catholic dogma that men are 'naturally' bad, are 'contraries' not 'negations'; they simply cannot conflict with one another, because they do not touch one another—if you look upon them both from Rousseau's point of view. For Rousseau was not saying, what he is generally represented as saying, namely, that men *are* good; but that there is a deep, natural desire in men's hearts to be good.

Emile [Rousseau wrote in 1764] is a quite philosophical work on the principle advanced by the author in other writings that *man is naturally good*. To reconcile this principle with the other truth, no less certain, that men are bad, it would be necessary to show, in the history of the human heart, the origin, of all the vices. This is what I have done in that book.

His simple proof of the natural goodness of man shows plainly what he meant by it. It was proved, he said, because man, when he is not good, is always miserable. If there is not a bent towards goodness in man's nature, what on earth should make him miserable when he is not good? Nothing on *earth*, says the Catholic—but something in Heaven. Rousseau would never have dreamed of denying this; but its significance depended on what was meant by Heaven.

Well, said Rousseau, since there is this bent towards goodness in man's nature, and since there is no denying that on the whole man behaves pretty badly, what is the matter with him? There must have been a Fall, somewhere, somehow. The Catholic agreed about this. The question is: What was the nature of the Fall? The Catholic said that man fell by being born. The entry into corporeal existence was the Fall. (Blake and Shelley both inclined to agree with Catholicism on this point.) Rousseau said: No, the entry into society was the Fall. Neither the Catholic nor Rousseau, remember, was talking history. People are rather dense in these matters, these 'scientific' days; they tend to assume that a man must be talking either 'fact', or nonsense. But the question here belongs to a quite different order—whether we call it the order of Imagination and Truth, or the order of Myth and Dogma. The real issue was whether human existence was good enough for man. Was it, *intrinsically*, sufficient or insufficient for his needs?

We must not run away with the idea that this is a stupid question. Rousseau and the Catholic were both agreed that things were, in fact, pretty bad. The difference was that whereas the Catholic believed that it was impossible that things should become, essentially, any better, and that therefore the only chance of a radical improvement was to be sought in a different order of existence altogether, Rousseau held that there was a possibility of an essential improvement in temporal existence—of an improvement sufficient, in the main, to relieve men of the need or the necessity of looking exclusively to another order of existence to have their heart's desire fulfilled.

Again—since I hate to be unjust to Catholicism, and being a Rousseauist in this matter, I may be—I must point out that the Catholic belief, which seems so pessimistic, is not so really. For, even if the Rousseauist view is the true one, what of the people like himself, like you and me, and a few thousand million others, who are destined to die before temporal existence becomes relatively satisfactory? It seems that, on any showing, they get a dirty deal. Justice appears to demand that they should not be deprived of a stake in the millennium. The Catholic scheme provides as it were a long-term justice in the universal economy. But Rousseau did not bother about this. He said to himself, as a greater than he had said to himself before—that it was hardly in accord with the idea of a different and better *kind* of existence, if people in it were still to be bothered about justice. If the case for Heaven was that justice demanded it, he knew of something better himself. In his own best moments, he passed *beyond* justice, and entered into a condition 'where everything is forgiven and it would be strange not to forgive'. That would do for and probably was, Heaven; and man's instinct for justice had better get busy on things more relevant to itself. Justice for temporal existence; and forgiveness for Heaven, and man's heavenly moments.

But it is odd what different things Justice means to different men. For Rousseau the notion of Justice was blindingly simple. First, it was obviously an affair of society. For suppose men did not live in society, but in isolated independence—Rousseau did not say that men actually had lived like that, as his crasser critics assert—there would be no need of and no desire for justice. Justice is a social necessity.

Now by saying that Justice was a social necessity—necessity that arose from the congregation of men into civil society, Rousseau was not saying that, as historical fact, men congregated into society for the purpose of obtaining Justice—how could they when in 'the state of nature' they had no need and therefore no conception of Justice? —but that, once they were so congregated, a new need developed in man's nature—the need of social justice: which was negatively expressed as a condition in which society did not actually impede the natural goodness of man, and positively as one in which that natural goodness was fostered and cherished. Unless this need was satisfied, man was not better off in society than he was in the 'state of nature', but worse off. In other words, only if society became the means by which man could live in the bond of equal justice with his fellows, did life in society represent a moral advance upon life in 'the state of nature'. Unless society were a society of equal justice, or at least were consciously striving to become such a society, life in society was bound to be an insidious process of moral degeneration.

This came to Rousseau with all the force of a religious illumination in October 1748—precisely a hundred years before the *Communist Manifesto*—while he was walking from Paris to Vincennes to visit Diderot in prison. It completely overwhelmed him; his eyes streamed with tears, and when he had done weeping, he sat down under a tree to make hurried notes of all that he had so suddenly and strangely understood. It was an authentic and momentous case of conversion. The scales had fallen from his eyes; and the famous *Discourse on Inequality* was the first result.

It is curious that the historians and the critics of Rousseau should be bothered, as they are, by this experience of Rousseau. Generally speaking, they can make nothing of it. What was it (they wonder) that Rousseau then saw and understood? And they incline to the belief that it was a sort of sentimental brainstorm, although they cannot help suspecting—for indeed it is obvious, and Rousseau categorically affirms it—that all Rousseau's subsequent life and activity, which was (they allow) in some way epoch-making, grew directly out of his sudden certainty.

What was the great idea? as the Americans say. We can put the answer in American, also. Rousseau suddenly saw that the Idea of Progress was 'all bunk'. And that was, I submit, a tremendous realization—so tremendous that very few people can really get hold of it even to-day. So we must try once more to get hold of it: for it is even more important to-day than it was in 1748. Some people imagine that Rousseau's realization was superseded by Marx's realization one hundred years later. They are quite mistaken, as I will try to show in another chapter. No one (I hope) will accuse me of depreciating the significance of the *Communist Manifesto*; but I am convinced that it cannot be really understood, either in its advances or its retrogressions, except by those who equally understand the great previous charter of social revolution—namely, *Du Contrat Social*. That was the charter, and Rousseau the 'prophet', of the first great modern European revolution—the French Revolution; the *Communist Manifesto* was the charter, and Marx the 'prophet', of the second great European revolution—the Russian Revolution. (Speaking as an Englishman, I should call them the second and third, and make the first the Revolution of 1649.)

Others will say that Christianity has always insisted that Progress is 'all bunk', and that Rousseau's insight was nothing new. That may be true enough in theory; but in fact Christianity had capitulated, just as completely as secular society, to the idea of Progress. The visible Christian Church had become an apparatus for endorsing secular and nationalist society. It may have used the old phrases concerning human corruption, but it did not believe in them. The *abbés* were *philosophes*. It will be true to say that Rousseau was reaffirming the fundamental insights of Christianity, only if we simultaneously admit that the visible Church had forgotten all about them, and that Rousseau himself was the true defender of the faith, the solitary and disregarded prophet of the invisible Church against the secularism of the visible one. This was to be proved by the event. Rousseau was the main source of the revivification of Catholic Christianity in France.

However, the important fact is that Rousseau in October, 1748, suddenly saw that the idea of Progress was 'all bunk'. What was this Idea of Progress? First, it was not so much an Idea as an unconscious, instinctive faith. It was part of the intellectual and moral climate of the few in Rousseau's early days; but it was to become part of the intellectual and moral climate of Europe for two centuries—a rosy haze which only now is beginning to be dissipated. And even to-day, a prodigious number of intelligent people simply cannot accept as *reality* any social or political phenomenon that does not fit in with the Idea of Progress. They, somehow, raze from the book of memory the Great War, the Russian Revolution, and the advent of Fascism and Hitlerism. These things, for them, have not really been: and the simple reason for this startling non-existence of the real is that to allow existence to these realities would mean to uproot their unconscious faith in the Idea of Progress. It is, for the vast majority of intelligent men to-day, whether they call themselves Christians or Rationalists, Liberals or Marxists, the only *faith* they have.

There is a story of a little boy who, when taken to see the great Emperor in procession, called out that he had no clothes on. Rousseau was like that little boy; he, alone of his age, had seen through the garment of Civilization to the sorry skeleton beneath. The idea of automatic moral progress was a mirage. It was essential to the Idea of Progress that moral progress was automatic, since the Idea of Progress was none other than the idea that every advance in mechanical and material Civilization was self-evidently an advance for humanity. Since this was the common assumption of the *élite* of Rousseau's day and of the whole civilized consciousness of the epoch which followed him, and an assumption so unquestioned that it took nothing less than a European war to knock it out of me one hundred and seventy-five years after Rousseau—I have never had much difficulty in understanding, first, that it must have come as an overwhelming illumination to Rousseau, in a time of peace and prosperity and general intellectual enthusiasm, and, second, that once the conviction that the Idea of Progress was a mirage had become basic to all his thinking, the foundation of all his works, it was inevitable that those works should be revolutionary in effect—in so far as they had any—and that he himself, who tried hard to live by his new conviction, should be accounted mad. It is glibly said that he succumbed to persecution-mania towards the end of his life. In a sense, it is true. He was faced with the awful question which always does face these solitary pioneers of the human consciousness—the question that surely faced Jesus of Nazareth at the crucial moment of his earthly career: 'Am I mad? Or is the whole world mad? It must be one, or the other.' I do not believe it is possible for a man who has been faced squarely by that question to keep his sanity, in the common or garden sense. He is bound to go a little queer, or very queer. But he may be able to keep it to himself. Rousseau kept it to himself; he never became 'mad'. If you would like to know exactly what he was, read the *Rêveries d'un Promeneur Solitaire*; they are 'queer', and they are magnificent.

Now what was the consequence of having seen 'in a vision' that the Idea of Progress was a mirage? Or, to put it rather differently, that progress in the externals of Civilization—in inventions and amenities—meant absolutely nothing for the moral progress of Humanity? The first consequence was that Rousseau straightway became an exile from Civilization. By this discovery he had put himself outside society. He became, morally speaking, an outlaw. He was abruptly severed from the whole unconscious êthos of his age. At first, as one can understand if one understands his 'illumination' at all, he was bewildered by the fact of his own sudden isolation. He did things which seemed clumsy and bizarre and outrageous to his contemporaries and even to his friends, but which appear (I hope) merely simple and honest to us who owe him at least some measure of the understanding he never got in his own lifetime. He tried to put himself outside that Civilization of which he had seen the deception. He wore the simplest clothes, abandoned all the prestige and emolument that would have accrued to the literary equal of Voltaire, and took to earning his living by the only manual talent he had—that of copying music. He had a fortune in his grasp; he simply and deliberately let it drop. As far as it was possible he was determined to sever his connection with a sham civilization. He stuck to his determination to the end.

So much—and a bare allowance—for the personal consequences of Rousseau's realization. Now for the impersonal, ideal, or ideological ones. He had seen the absolute distinction between external and material civilization, and inward and moral civilization. The next step was inevitable. If, as was obvious to him, external Progress was completely independent of moral advance, then it followed that mechanical progress necessarily tended towards a large-scale moral degeneration. To take an obvious example: if a savage is armed only with a bow and arrow, there are obvious limits to the harm he can do; but put a modern incendiary bomb into his hands, and give him the modicum of instruction (of which a chimpanzee is susceptible) necessary for dropping it, and he becomes ten thousand times more potent for evil. Strictly speaking, this multiplication of the savage's potency for evil is not a moral degeneration of himself; but unless it is totally suppressed, it involves a fearful degradation of the moral condition of mankind as a whole.

More subtly, the great economic invention characteristic of Rousseau's day—the 'division of labour'—over which the economic optimists waxed eloquent, the elementary form of what we now call 'mass-production', whereby each individual workman repetitively performs some fractional part of a total productive operation, was to Rousseau, now he had seen the light, little short of diabolical. It turned a human being into a machine, and totally deprived him of his 'natural' birthright—creative joy in his work. Moreover, it took him from his 'natural' occupation (which was 'to cultivate the earth and live by its fruits'), and drained the countryside of its sturdy peasantry to heap them in the foul slums of great cities. The progress of the 'arts and sciences' of external Civilization was, to his awakened vision, merely a progress of moral decadence. It is plainer to some people now; but still only to few, although the really formidable advances of material civilization were only beginning in Rousseau's day. Put in a single phrase, he warned men against the fatal moral consequences, the fatal human consequences, of that industrial era into which they were so confidently plunging. Naturally, they did not listen to him; they did not even understand him. He was to them simply a barbarian, with a genius for paradox, who wrote divinely.

§

Rousseau foresaw the danger; he tried to turn Europe back from its blind onward drive into the industrial era, into capitalist society. But he did not merely warn men; he showed them the remedy. The remedy, or what Rousseau believed to be the remedy, is in *Du Contrat Social*: than which few books have been more fantastically misunderstood. I cannot here expound that book as it should be expounded. I will merely underline the real gist of it. It is quite simple. Such works of genius are simple if you have the clue to them—if you have in some sort *experienced* their central and germinal 'idea'—but if not, then they inevitably shatter into a mass of contradictions and logical absurdities. At Oxford I had to listen to lectures on Rousseau's *Social Contract*; it seemed to me one of the dullest of dull books. But the time came when I understood it, and I knew it was one of the most exciting.

For its fundamental idea is this: that, under an advancing material civilization, unless society becomes a moral entity, it becomes a madhouse. It must be one or the other. That recalls the former dilemma of Rousseau: 'Am I mad, or is the world mad?' *The Social Contract* is, as it were, the explication, or the magnification, of that same dilemma: or a posing of the same central problem from another angle. Many lines of real creative thinking—the thinking, not of the mere intelligence, but of the total being, which is the prerogative of creative and prophetic genius—converged to bring *The Social Contract* to birth. But one was central. It proceeded directly from Rousseau's realization. Thus. Must he go on being an outlaw from society? Obviously he must, so long as the morality of society was totally different from his own. Society, so long as it was what it was, and he remained part of it, compelled him to acts which filled him as a moral being with abhorrence. One act in particular smote his conscience terribly, as well it might, the act by which he had handed over his new-born children to the Foundling Hospital. There had been nothing else, it seemed, for him to do. He was extremely poor at the time; and he had not done it with a light heart. But it had seemed to him then that the existence they would have in the Foundling Hospital was better than any that he could secure them. Was he, Jean-Jacques, responsible for that act? He looked into his heart as honestly as he could and declared that he was not. I do not propose to discuss the question whether his answer was true, that society was really responsible. Since it was an act which he afterwards bitterly repented, it is plain that he did *not* altogether convince himself. But, indubitably, there was a solid amount of truth in his answer. He was a man with a mission: he was faced with a choice. His children or his mission. And he chose his mission. Certainly, he would have chosen differently had he been a little more certain of the nature of his mission at the time. But the fact was that, if the society in which he was entangled had been based on any sort of social justice, there would have been less need for his mission and still less compulsion to sacrifice his children.

Theoretically, there were two remedies for this internecine and crippling conflict between 'moral man and immoral society'. One was to cut oneself off from society altogether. This is the one his contemporaries, and a great portion of posterity, have accused him of advocating. Clever young men and middle-aged men will be found writing big books to-day on this assumption: that Rousseau advocated a return to the splendid savage. He did nothing of the kind. He was, by far, the profoundest political thinker of his age, and he was a man who experienced life for himself. Such men sometimes appear to take a long while to reach conclusions which are taken for granted by commonplace intelligences; and it took Rousseau some time to reach the conclusion, first, that it was impossible to cut himself off from society. If he did by some desperate expedient succeed, he would cease to be a man. The second conclusion was that it was impossible for society as a whole to return to the state of nature. But when Rousseau had reached these conclusions, they were real conclusions: not notions, but experiences. He had found that he could not cut himself from society without inflicting a mortal wound on his own nature; and that the true meaning of his first excited notions that society must return to the state of nature was that society should 'advance to nature'—in other words, that society should become 'natural'.

This was Rousseau's one remedy for the conflict between moral man and immoral society. What did it mean—that society should become 'natural'? It meant that society must correspond to the better nature of man. For the nature of man was that part of him wanted to be good, decent, just. Society, instead of exerting, as it now did, a steady pressure on man to be worse than he is, must exert an equally steady pressure on man to be better than he is. There was no point of indifference, as was assumed by the dupes of the Idea of Progress, where man in society could remain simply what he was, plus the accumulating advantages of an advancing mechanical Civilization. That was a fatal fallacy. The truth was that entry into society faced man with an inescapable dilemma: in society, he must either degenerate, or be regenerated. There was no standing still. And only if society became an instrument of man's regeneration was it a 'natural' society.

The thought was subtle and simple. And Rousseau, in a flash of genius, expounded it in *The Social Contract* with all the amazing lucidity of a pure idea. Man was a creature of a mingled yarn; there was perhaps more good than bad in him, but far more than either good or bad was the enormous amount of sheer inertia. It was this inertia which was the devil in the new social condition. The inertia did not greatly matter in the hypothetical condition of the state of nature, or in more rudimentary societies; but in the condition of highly organized society it became positive evil—for inertia had direct consequences for all the other members of society. Thus for me as an isolated individual it did not greatly matter whether I kept my drains in order; if I caught typhoid by my slackness, it was my funeral. But in society such a sin of omission brought pestilence upon my neighbours. What was mere inertia in isolation, becomes positive evil in society. There is a radical change in the moral nature of man-in-society, which is well expressed in the language of Christian morality; sins of omission become in society sins of commission.

That was a fact, patent to observation, if only men had sufficient love of the truth to observe it. Thus—and here comes a crucial point—in demanding that society should become the instrument of man's regeneration, by exerting a steady compulsion upon him to transform his inertia into a positive force for good, instead of allowing it to become a positive force for evil, Rousseau was not making some extravagant and idealistic demand upon man-in-society. On the contrary, this demand was inherent in the very idea of society. Unless society were inspired by this conscious moral purpose, it became irrational to the imaginative Reason; irrational in the sense in which a stunted, cankered plant is irrational—not because there are not sufficient causes for its condition, but because its condition is alien to its intrinsic nature, and it is become incapable of fulfilling its own inherent purpose. The trouble with society was that there was no authority outside except rare freaks like Rousseau, or his great master Plato, able to pass judgment on it in the name of the Imaginative Reason, as a gardener on his tree. The Christian Church, whose sublime function was precisely this, had capitulated to the existing order. Now a renewed consciousness of the whole, without which society was irrational, could arise only from within.

The Social Contract may be described as being, after Plato's *Republic*, the greatest attempt of the European mind to create a consciousness of the social whole—and so to bring the social whole into being. It is the effort of society itself, working through the sensitiveness, the imagination, and the reason of a single man to achieve self-awareness: it represents, and itself is, the creative struggle of society to pass from unconsciousness into consciousness. Therefore, because it is real, not an intellectual day-dream but a prophetic achievement, it necessarily takes the form of a demonstration that the elements, the germs, of the consciousness of the social whole are already present in society. There is, so to speak, an instinctive and unconscious striving towards wholeness in society, which only needs to be purified and gathered together by the consciousness to become decisive. This is the meaning of Rousseau's great and epoch-making demonstration that sovereignty resides in 'the general will' alone and is inalienable from it; and of his crucial distinction between 'the general will' and 'the will of all'. First and foremost, this was a demonstration of the essential autonomy of society. It is very hard for us to appreciate the colossal innovation which was made by Rousseau's imaginative insight at this point. For it seems to us almost a commonplace to insist that sovereignty resides in 'the general will'—that society is its own sovereign, its own ultimate authority. Having degraded Rousseau's doctrine to a democratic commonplace, we cannot understand it; neither can we be surprised by its newness, which is not ephemeral, but eternal. Indeed, we have only to watch the vain struggles of Rousseau's predecessors in the theory of society to reach this idea to realize how inordinately difficult it was to compass it. Yet they were not fools; they were at least as clever as we are. It suggests that there is more in Rousseau's doctrine than we dream.

The 'social contract' was an accepted term of previous political theory; and always the theorists had to conceive two contracts: first, the contract by which men formed a society, and then a further contract by which they corporately assigned sovereignty over themselves to a monarch or a government. They were trying, in vain, to rationalize the religious theory of 'right divine'. Rousseau brushed the legal rigmarole aside, and reasserted a religious doctrine of society. Sovereignty resided always in 'the general will' of the members of any true society. There were only two possible theories of state-authority: one was that it derived from a supernatural source—'the divine right of kings', whereunder the relation between the sovereign and the people (however it might be glossed over by benevolence or responsibility) was the relation between master and slave; the other that all authority derived from the people itself. If you abandoned the former, you must accept the latter. There was no legal and contractual halfway house between. Whether the people was conscious of its own authority was another matter. But until it became conscious of its own authority and capable of exercising it responsibly, society would be conscious and rational in 'idea' only, unconscious and irrational in fact.

But that was only the first step. This step corresponded to the period of adolescence in the individual, when he emancipated himself from paternal authority and knew and claimed and exercised his own independence. The further and far more serious lesson had to be learned, that freedom did not consist in following appetite, but in being obedient to those alone of one's impulses that could be universalized. (From this Kant derived his theory of morality.) This was the meaning of the vital distinction between 'the will of all' and 'the general will'. To use our former phrasing, 'the will of all' might perfectly well be the expression of the inertia of the people; the 'general will' is the expression of its desire for good. To secure that 'the general will' should be really expressed and truly obeyed—this and this alone was the true problem of politics. Until it was solved society would remain unnatural and irrational.

Rousseau was not optimistic about the solution. To him the mere outward form of democracy meant little; because the spirit of democracy meant everything. A democracy which merely expressed 'the will of all' was no better than a tyranny. Further, a democracy whose members did not rise to the conception that a very great measure of economic equality must be imposed by the 'general will' in order to safeguard the sacred reality of political equality, would quickly cease to be a democracy. And, in practice, looking at the world of his own day, it appeared to him that the most probable chance of achieving a natural society lay in a small, predominantly agricultural community. What Rousseau was absolutely clear about was that the achievement of a true society depended on an unremitting moral effort on the part of its members, on their being permeated by the understanding that the health of the whole depended on the health of every individual part. A true society was a society determined to overcome all inertia, and the symbol of this determination was the new and sacramental understanding of 'the social contract'—the new contract, whereby the individual surrendered himself absolutely to society, to receive a new self back again; he made a complete sacrifice of his independence to achieve his freedom. For true freedom consisted in obedience to the moral law within us; and in a true society our evanescent impulses towards the good would be consolidated and made permanent in the universal laws that were the expression of the 'general will'; they would be removed from the contagion of individual inertia.

Here is a paradox against which the most violent criticism has been directed for two centuries; it rages still. Rousseau is accused of being the prophet of the omnipotent State, the demonic enemy of individualism and Liberalism. And, if individualism and Liberalism mean *laisser-faire*—and that is what they generally do mean—why, there is no denying that Rousseau is its bitterest enemy. There is no possibility of reconciliation between them. *Laisser-faire* is simply the Idea of automatic Progress in its most sordid form. We need not worry about it: it is dying, if it is not dead. But to the germ of moral value that lurks in the core of Liberalism there is something terrifying in Rousseau's apparent demand that the individual should surrender all his 'rights' to society, and something too specious to be trusted in his assurance that by giving up his independence, the individual gains his freedom. We must examine the nature of this moral resistance of Liberalism.

Now, what is the germ of moral value which, I have admitted, lurks within the core of Liberalism? It is the conviction that the conscience of the individual is finer and more sensitive than the moral conscience of any known, or any conceivable society, and that if the individual is required to surrender to society the right of acting and speaking according to his conscience, the most potent of all the influences that work towards the moralization of society is made null.

One thing is quite certain: that Rousseau never dreamed that the effect of entering into a true social contract could be the stifling of the voice of conscience within the individual. If 'the general will' was truly general, it was inconceivable that it should enact a law so patently contrary to the interest of the whole. But that is superficial. Rousseau saw deep and clear; and he would, in reply to this objection, simply have asked: *How* can any right of the individual to speak and act according to his conscience possibly be secured to him except by society as a whole? If such a right exists, it exists simply because society allows it. To think and argue as though the individual had, or could have, a prescriptive and indefeasible right *against* society, is to be guilty of an elementary confusion between what is a 'moral' right, which may be conceived to exist, though it is not allowed or effective, and an actual right, whose reality must depend on its being allowed and effective. The real and effective right to freedom of speech obviously depends upon the state-authority in any society; and in a rational society that state-authority depends upon the 'general will'. The only right that does not depend on the authority of the State is the right to die for one's convictions. In fact, under the Rousseauist 'social contract' the Liberal is asked to surrender nothing that he had not surrendered already. His inalienable 'right' to freedom of speech is a mere illusion. He enjoys it, where and in so far as he does enjoy it, precisely because it is granted to him by society. What Rousseau is really asking is that he should recognize this fact, and not live in a dream world, and prate about illusory individual 'rights' when they are, in reality, dependent on the permission of society.

This is a hard doctrine; and people fail to understand it because they conceive the State as something alien to themselves—something hostile and inimical which, even in the Marxian millennium, has to 'wither away'. Rousseau is therefore accused of divinizing the secular, and anticipating the totalitarian, state. His doctrine is in fact the absolute antithesis of this. For him the State—in either the ordinary, or the Marxist, sense—is withered away at every moment that an individual enters into a true social contract, and only in such a moment. Socrates may serve as an example of the relation that Rousseau teaches. Socrates entered into a true social contract with the city of Athens—not the perishable, but the eternal city of Athens. He refused to be silent, and he submitted to the punishment ordained by the law. The simple paradox of that famous historical happening lays the ghost so eagerly conjured up by a false Liberalism—the ghost demanding in Rousseau's name a surrender of the individual conscience to the State. Such a surrender is humanly impossible, for the man who has the courage of his conscience. The Rousseauist obeys his conscience, and accepts the punishment of the Law. There are, for him, two sanctities: his conscience and the Law, provided it is veritably a Law, and not an arbitrary edict. Thus the necessary condition of any actual state containing a potentiality of the eternal one is the reign of universal Law. The Laws may be unwise but provided they are universal, and there is no privilege before the Law, the possibility of eternizing the temporal society is given. The totalitarian states of to-day, which deliberately reject the universality of Law, are, from Rousseau's point of view, so many reversions to political barbarism.

The only practical safeguard (and that a terribly flimsy one) of the universality of Law is the establishment, as a fundamental and unchangeable law of the constitution, of equal political rights for all men. If that could be made sacrosanct—and Rousseau came to the conclusion that there was no way of ensuring the sanctity of universal Law, short of individual regeneration—but if it were possible, then the hard task of educating men into the knowledge of what that principle really means could at least begin. As men achieve this, individual by individual, so will the eternal city take substance in the regenerated fabric of the temporal city, and the Laws will gradually be improved until they come to be the expression of the deepest human will for good in society. The totalitarian states, Fascist or Communist, are an absolute negation of Rousseau's principles: but even the democratic-liberal states are passing into the same condition. All particular legislation by edict of the executive is anathema to Rousseau.

The instinctive Liberal objection to Rousseau's 'Social Contract' thus proceeds from a complete failure to understand what that doctrine really is. It may, at first sight, seem strange that whole generations of political thinkers have completely misunderstood Rousseau, and perhaps presumptuous of me to declare that they have. But, in saying this, I am merely echoing Rousseau's own words concerning his hostile critics:

> It is possible [he wrote] that they have replied to what I have said, but they certainly have not replied *to what I meant to say*. If, therefore, someone would take the trouble to search for my real convictions among my unsatisfactory expression of them, he might find that I am wrong, but he will certainly not find that I am wrong for the reasons my adversaries give, for these reasons are totally ineffective against me.

It seems, perhaps, queerer still that the author of a book so lucid, so logically rigorous, so famous as *The Social Contract,* should make a remark like that long after it was published. But it is a case of the secular conflict between the Imagination and the Intellect, the everlasting incomprehensibility of the Reason by the Understanding, the incessant effort to compel the Idea into the Concept. Rousseau was a man of Imagination, Reason and Idea; his hostile critics have always been men of the Intellect, the Understanding and the Concept. And by some compulsion of their nature they have always been forced, so to speak, to visualize Rousseau's 'social contract' as an actual agreement made by the kind of men they think they are. Inevitably, they see Rousseau as a kind of State-Moloch, grimly demanding: 'Give me everything', and since they imagine that they possess, absolutely possess, all kinds of rights and properties, they are simply horrified. Just as ordinary people, who call themselves Christians, are always horrified by the notion that they should be compelled to take seriously the demand of Jesus—that they should lose their lives to save them. Rousseau's social demand and the religious demand of Jesus are counterparts of one another.

Rousseau's demand was simple. It was that men should understand that in society their rights were not really theirs as atomistic individuals. They had to see, with the eye of imagination, that all the 'rights' they believed they had were in fact so many permissions from society, which, so soon as society became conscious of its sovereignty and capable of exercising it, might be revoked, changed, re-changed, in order to make a better and more human order. Further, that in the degree to which men came to this imaginative understanding of their complete consubstantiality with society, so society would advance towards the condition of being conscious of its sovereignty and capable of exercising it. For, since society was a whole, the attainment by any individual of the consciousness that it was a whole and that he was no more than a part of it, meant one more atom of self-awareness achieved by society, one step of advance to the formation of a true 'general will'. And only by that means could society pass out of the condition of adolescence into the condition of manhood. In other words the formation of a true 'social contract' was, actually, an epoch-making and revolutionary event in the life of the individual man. Rousseau knew precisely what he was about when he made his theory of the social contract the culmination of his great treatise on education—the *Émile*. There it is Émile's final initiation into the wisdom of a good man. It was the product of what we may call Rousseau's second 'illumination'.

By the first he had seen the illusoriness of Progress and in consequence declared himself independent of a society which was automatically doomed to degeneration; by the second, he reintegrated himself into society, and with the same imaginative completeness with which he had formerly severed himself from society he now delivered himself up to society again—not indeed to existing society, but to the society of the future. Of that society of the future he became one of the chief architects: he discovered the moral and imaginative law upon which it must be builded, and he expounded it to those who could understand.

§

Rousseau's great effort was to make men understand society and themselves. This was the purpose of *Émile* and the *Contrat Social*: the understanding of the true social contract is the culmination of an education not into the acceptance of social conventions but into an understanding of social reality. If this were understood, one would hear less of the objection that it is too abstract, too logical. It could not be otherwise, for its sole theme is the 'idea' of society. To interpret it as recommending certain political institutions (and in particular those of the totalitarian state) is simple misinterpretation: what it recommends, as M. Gustave Lanson has said, is 'a certain way of understanding and estimating political institutions, whatever they may be'. Rousseau claimed that only when society was thus understood could it commend itself to the imaginative Reason and become the object of the highest endeavour of conscious man. That means—and Rousseau made no bones about saying it—that, once they understood society in this way, men must put into politics what they put into religion. And, as might be expected, the Church was up in arms, as it generally is at any suggestion that religion should be put anywhere but into the Church. Precisely for that reason, Rousseau contended, society is so profoundly irreligious. There was in all Europe in his day a bastard alliance between Church and State, which was legitimate enough when the theory and practice of the State was based on the divine right of kings; but became a source of evil when the divine right of kings was being challenged in theory and completely undermined in practice by the bourgeoisie. Then it became imperative that the earthly city should be the object of man's highest endeavour, and community become the reality of communion.

The existing Church, in Rousseau's view, served merely to distract the human mind from criticism of society. In fact, it had become an organ of the irreligious state. It affected independence of it, but was really subordinate to it; and its sublime function had been degraded into diverting the moral impulse of man from attempting to correct the monstrous deficiencies of the earthly city. Again, the real point of Rousseau's criticism has been entirely missed. He is represented as the advocate of a purely secular 'religion of the State', by people who have never troubled to discover what he meant by the state—namely, a 'natural' society—the *civitas Dei*. He was simply saying what Blake said: 'Religion is Politics, and Politics is Brotherhood': that religion could not be real unless it had a natural and organic connection with the social order. The kind of thing of which he was the absolute opponent was the alliance between a corrupt Church and a corrupt State which was to be so zealously defended against him by Coleridge and Wordsworth. In respect to such accommodation his attitude was entirely revolutionary. The obvious function of the Christian religion was not to sanctify the rights of property, but to insist on their subordination to the rights of persons; and the rights of persons could be established only in a society whose purpose was recognized to be the good life for all. But this was not to be achieved by abolishing the right to possess property, but by controlling it with the aim of preventing wealth from disturbing the equality of political rights on which a rational society must self-evidently be based.

In reality, Rousseau posited and defended as the ideal society the natural community which Wordsworth was to glimpse and then abandon in terror for the defence of Property, the Constitution and the Establishment. What Wordsworth theoretically deplored—the decay of the personal relation in society—Rousseau set out to remedy before Wordsworth was born. The notion which Burke and Wordsworth and Coleridge came to defend, that 'property' was the basis of a rational society, would have seemed to Rousseau a diabolical equivocation—a merely specious attempt to conceal the 'unnatural' social relations of an industrial civilization under the once natural sanctity of a paternal feudal system. The real opposition was not that falsely put forward, between property and no property, but between kinds of property—above all, between the property that was a means to the natural development of the personality, and was the basis of a reciprocal creative and personal relation between it and its owner; and the property that was mere accumulation, carrying with it no human obligation whatever. Rousseau believed it was natural for man to possess property towards which he stood in such a creative personal relation; to possess the other kind was unnatural; and he believed it was the function of the Christian religion to defend the former and condemn the latter. A healthy and a Christian social order, he believed, could be firmly built on an economically independent and morally vigorous peasantry, flourishing in a small society, not too big for every man to have an immediate consciousness of his personal responsibility for the commonweal.

Economic forces, working on moral inertia, have swept Rousseau's ideal into seeming oblivion; but that is no argument against the ideal, least of all in the case of Rousseau, whose contention from the beginning was that unless men were prepared to make a moral effort to withstand the advance of a false 'civilization', they must face a future of continuous degeneration. This was treated as a delightful paradox by his contemporaries. But there is nothing at all delightful in the paradox by which those who have belatedly become sensitive to some of the disastrous shortcomings of a condition of 'civilization' against which Rousseau was warning men nearly two hundred years ago, should denounce him as the author of their woes. He stands clean outside the dispensation under which they suffer. On him, least of all men, can be justly fastened any responsibility for the diseases of modern civilization, moral or political.

Thus it is that, in the most important sense, Rousseau has been irrelevant to the social and political history of the epoch that followed him. The main determinants of that history have been precisely those which he said would be disastrous, if men submitted to them. His position, consciously and bravely taken, was that, if these were to be the determinants, history could not be a moral process; and he, for his part, would have nothing to do with it on such terms. Therefore, to charge him with having no practical guidance to give in the problems of practical government in the nineteenth century, as John Morley did, is merely to confirm his own prescience. He was not, nor could be, concerned with showing men the way out of the bog into the morass. His mission had been to show them how to keep out of the treacherous country altogether; to require of him that he should be the guide on the path to perdition was unreasonable. He would, moreover, have retorted that the effort to get out of the slough was precisely the same kind of effort that was necessary to avoid it altogether; and that to postpone it would not alter the nature of the effort required, though it would increase the magnitude of the obstacles. But as at the first, so at the last, the creation of a social order which should encourage instead of frustrating the best in man would in the nature of things depend on the capacity of the members of a society to conceive it as a moral entity.

As we have shown, Rousseau was the solitary opponent of the Idea of Progress in his age. It is a grim evidence of the prejudice or pettiness of modern estimates of Rousseau that it is precisely this idea of automatic moral progress which, in some of its protean forms, the hostile critics of Rousseau—with the conspicuous exception of Morley—seek to father on him. That is because the Idea of Progress is still the main element in the intellectual climate of the modern age. Because we cannot think ourselves free of the Idea of Progress, whether we are for or against Rousseau personally, we unconsciously insist on dragging him into this alien circle of ideas and making him speak the language. It can be done only by violence. For, we repeat, the most crucial fact concerning Rousseau is that his career as a mature thinker began with his complete repudiation of the Idea of Progress. To him the idea of automatic progress is a moral insanity, a fearful corporate illusion, which could only be entertained by men who had forgotten the true nature of man, and had never had the courage 'to examine the human heart', as he would say. For only by such oblivion could be explained the delusion that by increasing the inertia of man, by multiplying his wants in proportion as his own individual ability to supply his needs is diminished, he became a better man, or more truly fulfilled the 'idea' of himself which he was compelled by nature to conceive.

This violent repudiation of the Idea of Progress, this sudden and final rejection of the instinctive, unquestioned faith of his century and the century to follow, sets Rousseau clean apart not merely from his contemporaries, the *philosophes*, but from the main currents of subsequent political thought. If he appears to contribute to these, it is in appearance and not in reality: and the appearance is made specious only by the arbitrary isolation of strands in a texture of creative ideas which is, as he knew and declared, singularly homogeneous. One may say categorically that where the Idea of Progress is assumed, as it is not only by Benthamism and *laisser-faire* Liberalism, but by the antithesis of those creeds, Marxian Socialism, there Rousseauism is not.

By a crowning irony Rousseau is now invoked or denounced as the prophet of the totalitarian state. *Du Contrat Social* is held to be its charter. And, characteristically in the case of Rousseau, it is not easy to *demonstrate* that the modern Fascist state is the sheer antipodes (as it certainly is) of all that Rousseau meant by a true and 'natural' society. Did not Rousseau profoundly mistrust representative democracy? Has not the totalitarian state succeeded in ousting the democratic *volonté de tous* for the mystical *volonté générale*? Does it not demand precisely that complete surrender of the individual to the social whole which Rousseau demanded? And has it not engendered precisely that 'civil religion' which he thought necessary to the maintenance of society? And to reply simply that Rousseau meant all these things quite differently seems as ineffective as to murmur 'il n'agit jamais qu'au niveau de sa source'. None the less, the apparent resemblance between a society in which Rousseau's Social Contract was an actual instead of a potential moral reality and the modern totalitarian state conceals an absolute abyss which separates them. The notion that the 'general will' should be embodied in an individual 'Leader' would have been to Rousseau a blasphemy. There was indeed a moment when, in Rousseau's theory, or mythology, the 'general will' could be represented by a single man. It was when the acknowledged Legislator—like Lycurgus or Solon—appeared. He framed the Laws, and withdrew. And the essential characteristic of the Laws he framed was that they were 'general'—universal in scope, touching no man in his particular. A Law that was not general was not a Law. Only by the fact that he enunciated general Laws which had their sanction in the 'general will', could the Legislator be recognized as the vehicle by which the 'general will' found utterance. Therefore, when Adolf Hitler, in his apology for the 'clean-up' of June 30th, 1934, declared that on that grim night he in his own person represented the Laws of Germany, and 'solemnly protested against the suggestion that there should have been a legal trial and exact weighings of guilt and blame', he was revealed, so to speak, as the Antichrist of the dispensation of which Rousseau was the prophet. For all his pessimism, we doubt whether Rousseau in his most sombre forebodings could have imagined such an absolute and explicit negation of his 'idea'.

The society to which Rousseau demanded that men should surrender their independence to receive back their freedom is the antithesis of the totalitarian state of to-day. When Rousseau said that 'it is necessary to oblige the individuals to conform to their reason; it is necessary to teach the public to know what it wants', he little dreamed what meaning that second phrase would come to convey to men born to a civilization of mass-suggestion and salesmanship, of radio and circulation and publicity. He meant real education of the public to its real needs; and those real needs he believed to be at once simple and profound. He summed them up in the tantalizing phrase—Nature. It had many meanings for him; but he was surely not mistaken in believing that these various meanings were intimately connected with one another, from the simplest—'la condition naturelle de l'homme est de cultiver la terre et de vivre de ses fruits'—to the most apparently recondite—to live in a society where equal justice is established and safeguarded by sacrosanct Laws which embody the finer conscience of all its members. When society becomes the instrument by which the highest impulses and desires of the individual are removed from the flux of individual mutability and made permanent in Laws: when the 'constitution' becomes the repository and the living record of the 'happiest moments' of the citizens who in obeying it obey their true selves, then the miracle has been achieved. Society has been made 'natural', in the deepest Rousseauist meaning, because it reflects, consolidates and encourages that goodness in man which he knows to be natural to him, yet cannot achieve unaided. The hostile critic may remark sardonically that it all ends in this: that society is to the Rousseauist what the Kingdom of God is to the Christian. Rousseau would have welcomed the criticism, and retorted that he also was a Christian, and knew by experience that a Christian could never rest content, and never be at home in the world, until the Laws spoke with the veritable voice of God.

And since, by the same experience, he found that man was naturally Christian, he believed that this was what men really wanted, and that they would find it to be so, if ever they had the courage to know themselves, to 'interrogate their hearts' as he had done. His business was to try to teach them how to do it. In order to understand society men must understand themselves; in order to transform society they must transform themselves. Hence the one authentic path from the false society to the true was education; and *The Social Contract*, in its original form, is the culmination of the *Émile*. Émile, by his understanding of the true social contract, becomes a conscious 'citizen'—the one title which Rousseau claimed for himself, and which we seek to vindicate for him here. Behind this culmination of the *Émile* lay no doubt an idealization of his own native republic; and his subsequent persecution, exile and excommunication by Geneva for the crime of having exhibited to it the moral beauty of its own hidden idea was certainly the bitterest blow that Rousseau ever received. But to us it has something of the inevitability of the condemnation of Socrates.

After that unkindest cut of all, Rousseau became perforce a solitary. He had done his work, and persevered with it to the end. If he had, as he believed, many things with which to reproach himself, failure to fulfil his mission as a conscious 'citizen' was not among them. The world had been at his feet, all that men understood then and now by success had been his for the taking. He had had the courage not to compromise with a society which he believed to be fundamentally rotten; yet he had not withdrawn, or given himself over to despair and hatred. He had toiled patiently on, living with the utmost simplicity, weaving his pattern of a society to be, in the sure knowledge that until at least the rough foundations of such a society were laid, so long would the conflict between 'moral man and immoral society' continue to gnaw at the heart of the world, and men, whether or not they knew it, be divided fatally against themselves, struggling blindly—as children tossing in a feverish sleep—against their bondage to a society that had grown, in the main, from their own moral inertia, and in its institutions reflected, at best, the negative desire to avoid death, and not the positive will to achieve life. The death of society cannot be avoided merely by eluding it; it only becomes the more insidious and fearful. It can be overcome only by the constant will to make society embody the highest morality of the individual. That was Rousseau's message. It has gained, not lost, in urgency.

26

GŒTHE

This essay forms two chapters of Heaven and Earth. *The last ten pages have been omitted.*

THE vicissitudes of Gœthe's reputation abroad—in England anyhow—have been prodigious. They have also been amusing. De Quincey was kicking hard against the pricks in 1824. 'Not baseness of Egyptian superstition, not Titania under enchantment, not Caliban in drunkenness, ever shaped to themselves an idol more weak and hollow than modern Germany has set up for its worship in the person of Gœthe.' In 1859 he suppressed that essay, realizing that he had been on the losing side; and the fury of his extravagance, which even in a calmer moment dismissed Gœthe's lyrics on the one hand and *Faust* on the other as completely unworthy of notice, is now a literary curiosity. But probably there was some substance to De Quincey's jubilant assertion that Gœthe was not read in England. 'Enough that it [*Wilhelm Meister*] has not gained and will not gain any attention in this country.' It is well worth remembering, however, that the two great charges which De Quincey brings against his *bête noire*—for Gœthe was hardly less to him—are first, immorality, and second, impiety.

Of far more real consequence are Carlyle's own misgivings while he was struggling with the task of making the translation of *Wilhelm Meister* to which De Quincey gave the monstrous slating.

I am busily engaged every night in translating Gœthe's *Wilhelm Meister*: a book which I love not, which I am sure will never sell, but which I am determined to print and finish . . . There is poetry in the book, and prose, prose for ever. When I read of players and libidinous actresses and their sorry pasteboard apparatus for beautifying and enlivening the 'Moral world', I render it into grammatical English—with a feeling mild and charitable as that of a starving hyæna. The book is to be printed in Winter or Spring. No mortal will ever buy a copy of it. 'N'importe'. I have engaged with it to keep the fiend from preying on my vitals, and with that sole view I go along with it. Gœthe is the greatest genius that has lived for a century, and the greatest ass that has lived for three. I could sometimes fall down and worship him; at other times I could kick him out of the room.

Probably there is no genuine reader of Gœthe who has not some first-hand experience of Carlyle's feeling. It is an authentic and perhaps inevitable phase of any real reaction to Gœthe. De Quincey's is not an authentic reaction at all. It is *a priori* prejudice, human enough —we all have moments when we are sick to death of hearing Aristides called the just—but it is not criticism but petulance. Carlyle's irritation is criticism; and it is more impressive in that it comes from the man who, more than any other, made Gœthe's real reputation in the English-speaking world.

Gœthe's reputation waned with Carlyle's own, and quite as unjustly. Not that we need to associate the men beyond remarking that there was an element of true greatness in Carlyle which responded to the greatness in Gœthe. It was noble in Carlyle, who needed to overcome a real reluctance in himself—the natural envy felt by the battered warrior of literature (envy which Schiller also found it hard to overcome) towards the darling of fortune—to bow himself before the genius of Gœthe. He was, it is true, a hero-worshipper. But hero-worship, when it is genuine, is an intimate and private thing. Reverence, 'that angel of the world', comes as angels do on soft and silent wings; and, seeing that she visits the human mind only in its most serene and lucid moments, she dwells in benign peace together with a most impartial acknowledgment of imperfections in the object of her worship. And that, for the public, will hardly do. Adulation it knows; but reverence is a bird of a stranger breed. So Carlyle, perhaps with too much of the wisdom of this generation, pocketed up most of his reservations with regard to Gœthe and presented him for adulation. Gœthe became one of the Victorian idols; and he has disappeared with them.

Almost it seems that a new beginning has to be made with the task of establishing Gœthe's reputation outside Germany. For the conventional picture of Gœthe, now that the nineteenth century valuation of him is discarded, is romantic in the most naive sense of the term: it presents a spectacular combination of the inspired lyric poet and the indefatigable amorist. A sigh is heard as soon as Gœthe gets to Weimar, and from that point onward we are invited to be sympathetic assistants at the funeral of a great genius—a funeral that lasts for fifty years.

Behind all this are two unconscious assumptions: first, that a genius has to behave like one, and, second, that we know precisely how a genius does behave—like Byron, in fact. The consequence of this naivety is that when, as so notably in Gœthe's case, fortune has enriched us with detailed knowledge of a great man's life and thought, the gift is not accepted gladly as a precious documentation on the nature of genius, but rather eyed askance and hurried out of sight, with the almost audible implication that it would be better for everybody if geniuses stuck to the rules of the game and died young.

Gœthe did not die young; and criticism has found it hard to forgive him. It has no real use for his science or his wisdom. Yet this limited conception of Gœthe, as a man who wrote some remarkable lyric poetry, and then pottered gently into hobbies and optimism and respectability, is in striking contradiction to the attitude of his own countrymen towards him. Indeed, of all the influences active in contemporary German thought, up to the advent of Hitler anyhow, Gœthe's is by far the most powerful and distinctive. We can mark its traces, without much difficulty, in paths ostensibly so remote from one another as Husserl's 'Phenomenology', Otto's religious psychology, Spengler's 'historical morphology', and Tillich's religious philosophy of history.

That is, at any rate, an indication which element in Gœthe satisfies his own criterion of the true work of genius—that 'it lives and works on'. Yet if we were to say, abruptly, that it is Gœthe the philosopher and not Gœthe the poet who is thus creative to-day we should beg an important question by the separation. We can make the distinction satisfactorily only if we provisionally accept the emphasis laid by Gœthe himself in his later life on the immediate occasion as the true source of poetry. 'Beware,' he said to Eckermann, 'of attempting a large work.'

> *That* is what injures our best minds, even those finest in talent and most earnest in effort. I have suffered from this cause and know how much it has injured me. What have I not let fall into the well! If I had written all that I well might, a hundred volumes would not contain it. (*Sept.* 18, 1823)

Gœthe, of course, was not condemning large works of poetry. Masterpieces had been written, and he revered them. '*Alles grosse bildet.*' But he believed that the time for premeditated, sustained, constructed poetry, in 'the grand style', was past. Now, if a poet was to be productive, he must be content to seize his moments of vision. Behind this sincere and sound advice to Eckermann was Gœthe's sense that, so soon as the poet left the narrow realm of the immediate and the occasioned, he must perforce become a philosopher. He must seek an answer to the riddle of existence, and the search and the answer must be his own. The old synthesis had broken down. The datum of accepted belief which is essential to sustained poetry of the highest order was no longer forthcoming.

There seem to be, or to have been, two principal conditions under which poetry in the grand style has been written in the Christian era —conditions represented by Dante and Shakespeare respectively. One is the universal prevalence of a systematized religious faith offering comprehensive symbols which express the mystery of human life, so that poetry can, without any sense of derogation or limitation, make itself ancillary to religion and 'justify the ways of God to man'. The other is the occurrence of a moment naturally associated with the decline of a universal religious faith, when the individualistic view of life prevails, and the mystery of life finds expression in tragedy. These moments are not simply opposed to one another. Their relation is 'dialectical'; they are phases in an historical movement. While Christianity was the universal faith, tragedy was impossible; since Christianity, obviously, does not permit the tragic view of life. As Christianity weakens, tragedy emerges. But manifestly the tragic view of life has itself no finality. As an individual and prophetic man, Shakespeare passed beyond tragedy. It would be forcing things to urge, as is sometimes urged, that he returned to Christianity; he seems rather to have passed from a sort of natural paganism with Christian overtones, through tragedy, to a reconciliation of a kind which, no doubt, was naturally found in former days by chosen spirits in Christian orthodoxy, but could no longer be confined within it. The growing compromise between the Christian Church and nationalism made necessary a prophetic enlargement of Christianity. Of all this movement in Shakespeare, Gœthe, the first philosophical student of Shakespeare, was conscious. His recognition of it found definite expression in his deliberate use of Christian imagery and symbolism at the end of the second part of *Faust*.

> You will agree [he said to Eckermann] that the conclusion where the soul soars upwards was very difficult, and that I might easily have failed in dealing with such elusive and super-sensuous things if I had not used the clearly circumscribed forms of the Christian Church to give my poetic intentions the firmness of outline they needed.

'It would be difficult,' says Professor Fairley, 'to overstate the degree of sophistication which these words imply.' Sophistication is, we think, an improper word; but its intention is correct. Gœthe was using the Christian forms deliberately as imaginative symbols, only. It was a bold expedient, and created some misunderstanding among those capable of reading the letter only; yet it is difficult to imagine what other he could have employed.

The significance of *Faust* as a whole is that it is a great poem which in itself marks a conscious end of great poetry. Gœthe's inability to make progress with it, its lingering on over the space of fifty years and more was not due to any flagging of the creative spirit in himself. He was at the end of an epoch, or rather an epoch was living itself through to an end in him. A reconciliation was being accomplished; and this was no longer a reconciliation of the individual man with his destiny, but a reconciliation of Man as a whole with Nature. The two decisive influences on Gœthe were Shakespeare and Spinoza; and the influences of these two great spirits converge in him to create a new attitude whose emergence is waveringly depicted in *Faust*, and which can only be definitely apprehended by the contemplation of his work as a whole. There is a perceptible progress towards a new synthesis.

This progress is extraordinarily difficult to describe. It corresponds to the progress which we can observe historically in the Christian epoch, from religion, through art, to science. But, we hasten to add, the science towards which Gœthe was feeling his way was profoundly different from the 'science' which generally claims sovereignty to-day. It was a science which always returned with awe and a sense of finality to what Gœthe called 'the pure phenomenon'—the thing given in all its simple and sacramental immediacy. It was a science which was preparatory to a renewal of the religious consciousness: not a science which foolishly plumed itself on having abolished religion. And above all, it was genetic and dynamic both in its investigation of Nature, and in its effect upon the man who practised it. With the growth in himself of true scientific knowledge, in Gœthe's sense, the knowing man must himself inevitably grow as a whole; he becomes a more perfect because more conscious and obedient, servant of the living process of Nature. By the delicacy of his response to the total conditions of his own day-to-day self-creation, by the completeness of his dedication to becoming—to the service of that 'divine power which is manifest in the living and not in the dead'—he conquered his own eternality. Hence, the fundamental impossibility of Faust's losing the wager; because for the truly growing man there never can be a moment to which, from the bottom of his heart, he can say: 'Stay with me!'—*'Verweile doch, du bist so schön'*. The divine power forbids that his consciousness should thus negate the life of which he is the instrument.

This, as Gœthe was well aware, was not a doctrine for everybody in his day; and it is not a doctrine for everybody to-day. But certainly it must be appreciated if we are to deal with Gœthe at all in a comprehensive and critical spirit. It is against the background of this doctrine, which was an experience and not an idea, that his poetry must be set, and the true meaning of his insistence on its 'occasional' nature sought. Professor Fairley puts it well:

> Instead of turning into an accomplishment, a vocation, a faculty separate and circumscribed, as poetry usually does, Gœthe's poetry retains from first to last its crucial importance—functional more than cathartic—for his mental and bodily health. It is as deeply rooted in him as the instinct for food and the instinct for sleep; it is equally necessary to him; and it operates with the same infallibility.

Infallibility is somewhat excessive; but the essential estimate is true. And it is of importance. For it is to this 'functional' character of Gœthe's poetic impulse that *Faust* owes its curious unity. Whatever may be said of the chief characters, however severe may be the judgment on its dramatic insufficiency, however radically mistaken the efforts to vindicate its construction, it cannot be denied that the poem grows. In spite of appearance it has life more abundantly at the end than at the beginning. We may admit that it is a different kind of life: a life more and more suffused or even diffused by consciousness; but it is real. Perhaps the simplest clue to it all is to be found in *Advice to Young Poets: Ein Wort für junge Dichter*, where Gœthe claims that he has been a liberator.

> Through me they realized that, just as men live from within outwards, so the artist must work from within outwards, since he, no matter what disguise he wears, can bring only his individuality to light . . . The root of the matter can be briefly put. Let the young poet utter what lives and is active in himself, no matter what form it takes; let him put strenuously aside all spirit of contradiction, all ill-will, all carping, and all that ends in negation: for nothing comes of it.

Like so many of Gœthe's most pregnant utterances, this has a deceptive simplicity, almost an obviousness. It will recall to some Wordsworth's teaching concerning 'emotion recollected in tranquillity' and may at the first glance seem inferior to that phrase in suggestiveness. But on longer acquaintance Gœthe's 'word of advice' makes an indelible impression. It is altogether singular in that it is at the same time advice on how to write poetry, and how to live. It is not a combination of these two elements; they are one and the same thing.

> You make no headway when you incessantly lament a beloved lost by separation, unfaithfulness or death. That is worth nothing, however much cleverness and talent you put into it. Hold fast to life as it strides on, and test yourself when the impulse comes, for then it is revealed at the moment whether we are alive, and, when we look back on it later, whether we were alive.

Poetry is, thus, an exploration of life, indeed a way of life.

Whether we finally accept Gœthe's view or not, we must allow that it is original. It is also completely unprofessional. We may, if we are niggardly, ascribe this to his own peculiar and fortunate circumstances. But in reality it belongs to the essence of the man. Moreover, if we consider it as prophecy, it has been fairly well justified by events. Professional and deliberate poetry, the dedication of a lifetime to poetry as an art, has become more and more an anachronism since Gœthe wrote. It really seems as though the destiny for which Gœthe was prepared, and which he himself experienced, was being accomplished in the world of European culture at large. For such a theory of poetry, or rather of poetic originality, may obviously lead to the cessation of the poetic activity as such. It might perfectly well be that the vital and creative experiences—*'was lebt und fortwirkt'*—would be less and less capable of specific poetic expression. It was so with Gœthe. But he certainly would have repudiated the notion that in turning more and more constantly to the scrutiny of Nature (in the widest sense) he was engaged in something essentially different from the writing of poetry. The distinction made by his romantic critics between 'scientific discovery', for which many minds are qualified, and 'the more precious discoveries in the realm of spirit and the imagination', which are the privilege of peculiar and poetic genius, was, for Gœthe, an improper and meaningless distinction. And this was not a late-found theory with him; there is no justification for regarding it as a kind of excuse for the diversion of flagging poetic powers. (There is no evidence that Gœthe's specifically poetic power did flag: the *Marienbader Elegie* is among his supreme felicities.) On the contrary, the conviction was fully formed in 1783, when Gœthe was at the climacteric age of thirty-four. In *Der Granit,* he wrote:

> I am not afraid of the criticism that it must be a spirit of contradiction which has led me from contemplation and portrayal of the human heart, the youngest, most intricate, most disturbed, most variable, most fragile piece of creation to the contemplation of the oldest, firmest, deepest, and most unshakable of the sons of Nature. For it will be granted me readily that all the things of Nature are exactly related to one another, and that the inquiring spirit will not willingly suffer itself to be excluded from anything it can attain.

It is significant that 'the spirit of contradiction' which he here justly disclaims is precisely the spirit against which he gives warning in his *Advice to Young Poets*. And, in a quite obvious sense, *Granite* is as much a nature-poem as *Über allen Gipfeln*. It also marks the beginning of Gœthe's *Welt-und-Naturforschung*, his investigation of

Nature and History. Its intrinsic merits may not be great, but its significance certainly is. It is a crucial poem, written at a crucial moment: the more crucial in that it is not, and is not meant to be, a poem at all.

It cannot be denied: there is henceforward in Gœthe a growing tendency towards what French intellectual purism calls 'confusion of kinds'. The question is whether this is a strength or a weakness in him. To that question there must be a definite answer, if there is to be any definite judgment of Gœthe. To use the term 'confusion of kinds' is, in itself, to have begged the question. Gœthe would have denied absolutely that he did 'confuse kinds'; he would have claimed that he had transcended specialism. For our part we admit his claim; and on the justice of this claim, we believe, Gœthe's title to present and future greatness will necessarily be based.

At this point we have to grapple directly with the problem of Gœthe's many-sidedness. And it is important to admit, without reserve, that the vast mass of his production is not of the first order. In poetry, he was not merely not a Shakespeare, but nothing like one; in science, he was not a Darwin; as a critic of art, he was definitely inferior; as a technical dramatist, in spite of the fact that he had a theatre at his command, he was no more than second-rate; his prose-style is laboured and heavy, it cannot be compared with the prose of a Heine or a Nietzsche. In only one recognized province was he the genuine master: the province of the *Gelegenheitsgedicht*—the 'occasioned poem'. To judge him by his positive achievement, it seems that we must conclude that he was jack of all trades and master of none. Yet such a judgment would be fantastically mistaken; and it would be mistaken in the same way as the judgment (against which De Quincey was really kicking) that he was an all-round master. The fact is that perfection, which is the standard by which Gœthe is measured in both these estimates, is really irrelevant to his particular achievement. Yet he was no amateur. It misses the point entirely to regard him as the last of the great dilettanti, a figure possible only at the very dawn of the epoch of modern science. Nor will it do to look upon him as a master of 'the art of living', whatever that may mean. He was fortunate, and he lived long. Those were his circumstances, not his achievement.

Yet he was, as much as any man in these latter days, a master of life. He was conscious, as perhaps no other man has been, of the new responsibilities which were coming to men—responsibilities to which humanity in the hundred years since his death has been so markedly indifferent. Of these responsibilities the chief, and the one to which Gœthe was marvellously responsive, was the responsibility of consciousness itself. Those moderns who owe him much, who may say of him, as he himself said of Spinoza, that they 'discovered themselves (or part of themselves) in him', know well the strange and salutary experience of being overwhelmed by the miracle of his 'awareness'. At such moments, it seems to them that there is only one judgment to be pronounced on Gœthe: that he was the first man who was really aware of man's true place in the realm of Nature. Seen in that perspective, his cumbrousness, his failures, even his magical felicities—all are irrelevant. They are merely the skins sloughed by his growing consciousness. It is the growing consciousness itself that holds us enthralled. In him, humanity becomes abidingly aware of its own past. His historical consciousness is a new event in human history. No doubt it was, in detail, imperfect, and sometimes even mistaken. Hegel, Darwin, Strauss, Marx, Frazer—a whole galaxy of explorers—were to map out the provinces which he glimpsed from his mountain-top. But all the germs of their knowledge were in him, and he was not overwhelmed by it. Perhaps it was a happy accident that he lived just at the moment when it was impossible for him to be engulfed by separate research; but it is difficult even to imagine such a fate befalling him. Again, he was too conscious. He was too well aware of his responsibility to himself, to 'the subject', as he would have put it in his detached way. His reverence for Nature was entire; so entire that it admitted, with the utmost simplicity and directness, that he himself was Nature, too, demanding the same reverence from him as Nature herself. In himself was the growing tip of the great historical creative process he discerned in Nature. The more complete was his consciousness of that process in the world without, the more positive was the growth of the process within him.

This is the substance of his doctrine of 'gradual ascent' (*Steigerung*) and 'polarity', which some think mysterious. There is nothing mysterious about it, except that it is generally neglected. Or it is misinterpreted into the admission of some internecine conflict in Gœthe himself which prevented him from being what his critics desire that he should have been. There was conflict in Gœthe, but it was the inward conflict of a man who knew that inward conflict was necessary, that in and through conflict was manifest the forward urge of life itself both in the individual man, and in the outward Nature of which he was a part. 'Without Contraries there is no progression,' as Blake put it pregnantly. Conflict, thus recognized and ratified by consciousness, and acknowledged to be the indispensable condition of growth, is different by a whole order of experience, from the debilitating conflict of the unconscious man. It is not merely a condition of inward growth, it is a discovered principle of harmony between man and the universe about him: the law which both alike obey.

Thus it is that what some have condemned as Gœthe's conflict, others have praised as his balance. It is the same element or quality in him which is being appraised; yet, as the words themselves suggest, it is being only obliquely recognized. The impact of the new thing which Gœthe represented is glanced aside. He was, in reality, neither a divided nor a balanced man; he was merely a consciously living man. To that essence we have to penetrate if we are to comprehend him in his unity. Then his baffling and contradictory manifestations trouble us no longer. We become aware of the subtle simplicity of the phenomenon he presents to us, and grateful for his lifelong refusal to allow himself to be committed to anything more definite than the unutterable. The place that Eckermann's *Conversations with Gœthe* have come to take in the corpus of Gœthe's works is significant. Nietzsche's verdict has been fully endorsed by after-generations: the book seems to be infinitely more actual and alive to-day than it was when it was published. Then, it had barely more than a 'succès d'estime'. To-day Eckermann himself seems to deserve a centenary. For by the magic of reverence he captured the exquisite evasiveness of Gœthe's incomparable mind. In his pages we hold the quicksilver in our fingers. The enchantment is indescribable. But, if we insist on analysing it, it comes back always to the sacramental quality, the simultaneous duality, of Gœthe's thought. He is at once aware of the thing that is, and of that which is behind the thing; of the 'idea' and the manifestation, of the process of becoming and the thing become. He makes the separation only by an act of thought which is immediately surpassed. The intelligence is become an instrument, and is conscious of itself as an instrument. One might collect a whole bookful of phrases in which Gœthe feels after an expression of this simple mystery; one might indeed write a whole bookful of phrases oneself in the attempt to describe this native process of Gœthe's thought. 'The supreme thing,' as he said, 'would be to comprehend that everything actual is in itself theoretical . . . We must not try to get behind phenomena—they themselves are the lesson.' This thought, which is in one form or another recurrent in Gœthe, seems outwardly to conflict with another which is an equally persistent thread in his thinking.

> No organism corresponds completely to the Idea that lies at its root; behind every one the higher idea is hidden. That is my God, that is the God we all seek after and hope to find, but we can only feel him, we cannot see him.

The conflict is superficial only. God is apprehensible, not comprehensible. The creativeness of Nature is not exhausted in the specific creation; the living object looks, as it were, beyond itself. The intuition is in part biological, in part metaphysical and religious. Thus, 'in the true symbolism, the particular represents the universal not as a dream or shadow, but as a living, momentary revelation of the unfathomable'. *Omnia abeunt in mysterium.*

Here, in the philosophic and conscious language in which Gœthe loved to express himself, is the realization which Blake uttered in his *Auguries of Innocence.* 'To see a world in a grain of sand' is precisely that 'supreme thing' which would be 'to comprehend that everything actual is in itself theoretical'. It is significant that only Christian thought has an adequate expression for Gœthe's belief: which is, simply that *everything* is 'sacramental', and that the 'supreme thing' would be to be permanently conscious of this. The object of immediate apprehension is ultimate, satisfying, awe-inspiring—other. In the terms of Schiller's famous essay, *Über naïve und sentimentalische Dichtung*, which gave Gœthe potent aid in his progress towards the awareness of his own nature, this sense of the finality and mystery of the object of immediate apprehension is a reconquest of poetic and religious naivety—an achievement beautifully expressed by Blake in the very phrase: *Auguries of Innocence.* Gœthe would have agreed with Blake that poetry, in this sense in which the reconquest of imaginative naivety was its final purpose, was not a particular art of literature, but rather a type of the pure creative and religious activity of man. This activity was not self-originated; it was the creative consequence of a new and immediate contact with the real and objective world. To break down the conventions of thought, which interposed a veil between the subject and the object, and so prevented the life-giving interchange between the parts of Nature by which alone real growth was possible—this was Gœthe's ideal. Hence the meaning of his mistrust of the 'word', that speaks in the opening line of *Faust,* and again in Mephisto's ironic advice:

Vor allem haltet euch am Worte.
Dann geht ihr durch die sichre Pforte
Zum Tempel der Gewissheit ein;
Denn eben, wo Begriffe fehlen
Da stellt ein Wort zur rechten Zeit sich ein.

Above all, cling to the word. Then you enter the temple of Science by the infallible door: for when ideas fail you, a word fills the gap.

It was not, of course, that Gœthe despised the 'word'; still less, as has often been hinted, that his inward dissatisfaction with his security at Weimar issued in a romantic hankering after the life of the man of action. Just as for him, there was a difference between the truly creative action and a mere doing, so there was a difference between the living word and the dead one. And the creative action and the living word were of one kind and nature; they were, so to speak, blood-brothers, while their relation to mere doing and the dead word was purely formal.

But what was, finally, the test of the creativeness of the act or the word? It was its continued power to operate. In the process of history the evidence of creativeness was visible: the deed or word emerged, and the necessity of its emergence was manifest by the permanence of its effects. This was the manifestation of the 'divine'. This power was, said Gœthe to Eckermann, 'more or less inherent in mankind generally, but to a high degree in a few eminently gifted minds'.

> These have, by great deeds or doctrines, manifested their divine nature; which then, by the beauty of its appearance, won the love of men, and powerfully attracted them to love and emulation.

There Gœthe was speaking specifically of spiritual achievement; but his conception of the 'divine' as the *fortwirkende*, the continually operative, was by no means thus restricted. It was also something 'beyond good and evil', for which he often used the name of 'the dæmonic', or simply 'the great'.

Gœthe's test of the creative, in history, might thus be called pragmatical, though the epithet seems far too meagre for the imaginative penetration it pre-supposes; and the test of his own creativeness, for the individual living man, was to be applied by regarding himself also as a historical process. This attitude lies behind the *Advice to Young Poets*. The poet is to discover, in the process of life in himself, 'was lebt und fortwirkt', and cling to that; he is to discover whether he is, or whether he was, 'alive', that is whether the same creative process which manifests itself on a vast scale in history is manifest also in the individual man. He himself alone can be the judge. Life is the final criterion of life.

> Das Leben ist des Lebens Pfand, es ruht
> Nur auf sich selbst und muss sich selbst verburgen.

> Life is the pledge of life; it rests on itself alone, and must supply its own security.

Thus the doctrine of Gœthe seems to resolve into the simplicity of a truism. Indeed, it is very simple; but behind it lies a lifelong submission to experience, a continuous effort towards an ever-increasing objectivity, a gradual subordination of the subjective, a new kind of humility. This was at first instinctive rather than deliberate, and hardly to be distinguished from that peculiarly 'romantic' seeking of solace and self-abeyance in Nature, which is often regarded as the 'note' of romanticism. Gœthe's attitude to Nature was, or came to be, entirely different from this. It was a conscious submission to Nature in its unique particularity, a process of increasing differentiation in the objective reality and in the subject responsive to it. It was, in fact, the precise opposite of that undifferentiated identification of Nature and the Self which is supposed to be characteristic of romanticism.

This gradual turning of himself from the subjectively to the objectively romantic (for certainly the term 'classical' is irrelevant to Gœthe's achievement) he rightly regarded as his great achievement; and one can find in his later works many traces of his belief that in this progress he was prophetic. He felt that he was battling, more or less single-handed, against the tendency of the age.

> All eras in a state of decline and dissolution are subjective; on the other hand, all progressive eras have an objective tendency. Our present time is retrograde, for it is subjective: we see this not merely in poetry, but also in painting, and in much besides. Every healthy effort, on the contrary, is directed from the inward to the outward world; as you see in great eras, which were really in a state of progression and all of an objective nature.

As a poet Gœthe did not accomplish this progress from the subjective to the objective. He made more than one attempt to do so; but it cannot be seriously maintained that the *Iphigenie* or *Hermann und Dorothea* are works of the highest intrinsic significance. Gœthe's deliberate poetical classicism is to be regarded simply as an experiment. The experiment was necessary, and we should be deprived of invaluable evidence for the nature of Gœthe's progress if the experiment had not been made. But the significance of Gœthe lies, fundamentally, in the emergence of an attitude, a *Weltanschauung*, and the self-creation of a great man. It is not in the least to be deplored that his poetical genius became diffused over investigations that were not poetical; it is not even to be regarded as an aberration that he considered his *Farbenlehre* of more importance than any other of his works. He was not quite so deluded as he is supposed to have been. He was asserting a truth in his rejection of the Newtonian theory of light—the truth of the incommensurability of the immediately apprehended phenomenon—which science has been ever since in danger of neglecting.

This attitude of Gœthe's is so far from being outmoded that it belongs still to the future. So far from having to lament that he did not write more poetry, we have to congratulate ourselves that Gœthe consciously outgrew the limitations of poetry. He knew, as few of his critics have known, that poetic genius of the highest order is manifest rather in a total flexibility and responsiveness of the being to the created world than in the continuous production of poetry; that there had been times when this rare capacity could be satisfied with a poetic career; that such times were past; and that it was his privilege to be conscious of their passing. Curiously enough, of our English romantics it was the one whose life was most nearly contemporaneous with Gœthe's own whose realization was most closely akin to his. Keats and Shelley died too young for serious comparison, but while Wordsworth and Coleridge fell wearily back on the Constitution and the Establishment, Blake alone made no retreat, but battled on to inward security. And it is no accident that Blake also is accused of having deserted poetry, of having allowed the waters of inspiration to be lost in the barren sands of 'prophecy'. It would be absurd directly to compare the *Farbenlehre* with the *Prophetic Books*; they are as different as the lives of the men who wrote them; yet their significance for their authors was of the same kind. Both were protests against the enslavement of the human mind by scientific rationalism; both were disregarded warnings against the spirit which was to be triumphant in the nineteenth century. The contrast between Gœthe's Olympian authority at Weimar and Blake's complete obscurity in London is as extreme as such a contrast could be; yet one might well hesitate to pronounce which was the happier, or which the lonelier man. But just as Gœthe would have understood at a word Blake's fundamental doctrine that the 'Poetic Genius is the True Man', so it is to Blake that we must go for a decisive statement of one of Gœthe's own most unshakable beliefs:

> The worship of God is: Honouring his gifts in other men, each according to his genius, and loving the greatest men best: those who envy and calumniate great men hate God; for there is no other God.

Gœthe would have been proud to have said that so well. But, though the resemblances between the two men are essential, in spite of their superficial contrast, there was in each something that was not in the other. Blake was a great artist, where Gœthe would have liked to be one: Gœthe had a profound historical sense, of which Blake was completely innocent. Gœthe combined with his reverence for individual greatness, a splendid awareness of the world-process. On the other hand, Blake knew more fully than he, the inward struggle of the spiritual hero, and was, of the two, the modern master of the spiritual life. Moreover, Blake's experience of the modern world was more actual and intimate than Gœthe's. Weimar was an oasis of benevolent feudalism; the England in which Blake lived belonged to the new world of industrialism. The despairs with which Blake had to contend were deeper than any Gœthe could know.

§

The two great intellectual or spiritual influences in Gœthe's life were Shakespeare and Spinoza. One may say, without much exaggeration, that Spinoza was for Gœthe the philosophic consciousness of the spirit which he found at work in the creations of Shakespeare's art. And indubitably the clue to Gœthe's 'philosophy' is to be sought in Spinoza. But that must not blind us to the fact that Gœthe is a 'philosopher' only in the noble but now rather old-fashioned sense of the seeker after life-wisdom. Spinoza, also, was primarily that, though he is generally (though frigidly) admitted to the histories of Philosophy, understood with the lamentable modern bias—as the science of epistemology: the somewhat sterile investigation into how we know.

Epistemology had no charms, neither had it any terrors, for the man who cheerfully and comfortably sang:

> Mein Kind! ich hab' es klug gemacht
> Ich habe nie über das Denken gedacht
>
> My child, I did what I didn't ought:
> On Thinking I never wasted a thought.

That is, for philosophy in the modern sense, a shameless evasion of responsibility. No epistemology, no philosophy. Gœthe laughed at the notion. Therein lies the advantage of being a poet-philosopher, 'pour qui le monde visible existe'. It is, we believe, also a decided philosophical superiority. For the diversion of philosophy into epistemology has had one lamentable consequence: it has ended by making philosophy irrelevant to ordinary human experience.

Against this growing tendency, which Gœthe immediately detected when, on his return from Italy, he came into contact with the Kantians, he was bound to react; his reaction was philosophically instructed as well. He had long since been under the influence of a greater philosopher than Kant, namely Spinoza. And it is in terms of the conflict between Kant and Spinoza for the decisive influence on Gœthe's thinking, that his own philosophic originality can most clearly be distinguished. Nevertheless, to speak of a conflict between Kant and Spinoza in Gœthe's soul is an exaggeration: the conclusion of such struggle as there was, was foregone. And this was natural, because the specific problem of philosophy for Kant—the problem of knowledge—does not exist for Spinoza, who denies to the subject-object distinction all ultimate validity. That is, perhaps, a misleading description, since it could be asserted also of the post-Kantian German idealists. But the difficulty of describing Spinoza is not due to the difficulty of his distinctive views, but rather to his unique simplicity. To understand Spinoza, we need to undergo a sort of spiritual metamorphosis. The mere intelligence does not suffice. For the crucial step in Spinozism is to recognize the intelligence itself as merely an animal faculty, and for the human being to see himself in his own totality as object. To this object there is, and can be in the ordinary philosophic sense no subject. The philosophic subject itself is become object. This notion of an object without a subject is a kind of nonsense to the non-religious philosophic intelligence, largely because it is not strictly a notion at all, but a spiritual experience.

On this essential of Spinozism, Gœthe seized eagerly; and by the simplicity and directness with which he grasped it he became a truer Spinozist than many who were better able than he to explore Spinoza's subtle distinctions between substance and mode. The most famous acknowledgment of Gœthe's debt to Spinoza is that which he made in *Dichtung und Wahrheit*; but the real nature of Spinoza's decisive influence is declared most clearly in Eckermann's record:

> Jesus conceived of one only god to whom he attributed all the qualities which he perceived as perfections in himself. God became the essence of Jesus's own inner beauty, full of goodness and love like him, and such that good men might surrender themselves to him with perfect confidence, and embrace this idea of him as the most precious point of contact with things above.
>
> Since, however, the great being we call the godhead not only manifests itself in mankind, but in a rich and vast world, and in the mighty processes of history, a conception of him founded on human attributes is naturally insufficient, and the close observer will soon run up against inconsistencies, shortcomings and contradictions, which will lead to doubt, possibly even to despair, unless he is small enough to be comforted by artificial explanations, or big enough to lift himself up on to a higher plane of thought.
>
> Gœthe, in his early years, found such a lofty standpoint in Spinoza, and acknowledges with joy how fully the needs of his youth were satisfied by the views of this great thinker. *He discovered himself in him*, and consequently could consolidate himself in Spinoza in the most natural way.
>
> Since further such views were not of a subjective kind, but had their foundation in the works and expression of God throughout the world, they were not merely a skin which had to be sloughed later as useless in his own thorough investigation into the world and nature, but were the

original seed and root of a plant which developed through the years in the same healthy way, and flowered at length into a rich knowledge.

(*Feb.* 28, 1831)

Gœthe regarded Spinoza as one who, being the true lineal successor of Jesus, had expanded and given comprehensive substance to Jesus's conception of God; he had disentangled it from its apparent anthropomorphism, and reaffirmed it. This pregnant interpretation of Spinoza and his doctrine, which Gœthe expressed to Eckermann at the very end of his life, had been reached in his early maturity. No less than fifty-seven years before, Lavater had noted in his diary (June 28, 1774): 'Gœthe told me a great deal about Spinoza and his writings. He thinks that no-one has spoken concerning the Godhead so like the Saviour as Spinoza.' Eleven years later, writing to Jacobi, Gœthe says of Spinoza: 'He does not demonstrate the existence of God, but that existence is God. And, for this, if others denounce him as an Atheist, I call him *theissimum*, yea *Christianissimum*.' His homage was to have received poetic expression in a poem of the Wandering Jew, of which the supreme moment was to have been the hero's encounter with Spinoza. The man condemned by the theologians as a heretic was to have been revealed as the one true disciple of Jesus.

In the diary of the Italian journey, Gœthe records how Herder—himself a great Spinozist—used to laugh at him for reading but one Latin book: Spinoza's *Ethics*. Gœthe explains there that he was afraid to read any other, for fear of the longing for Italy that it would arouse in him. Even in this regard Spinoza would not have failed him: for the message of Spinoza, as Gœthe understood, was not simply, or mainly, a doctrine of Pantheism, but a doctrine of renunciation. The metaphysical doctrine *Omnis existentia est perfectio*, has for its moral corollary that any mode of human existence, however limited, is completely satisfying to the man who can achieve sufficient detachment to contemplate it *sub specie aeternitatis*. It is an authentic fragment of Eternity. But renunciation of this kind, as Gœthe again understood, does not imply asceticism. A full existence is as welcome to the Spinozist as a narrow one; more welcome indeed, for the spiritual detachment from the fortunes of the animal body which is essential to Spinozism involves a recognition that the preferences of the animal body are not only real, but valid. But it is important to understand that this animal body is not quite the same as the flesh, as opposed to the spirit by the traditional dualism of Christian orthodoxy. On the contrary, to this animal body not only the flesh but much of the spirit, in the orthodox sense, equally belong; as perhaps it also did in St. Paul's conception of the *sarx*. The hunger of the soul for a personal God in the simple sense is, for Spinoza, simply an appetite of the creature. Appetites of soul, appetites of body—these are alike 'passions', from whose domination, but not from whose incidence, we are liberated when we recognize that they are 'passions' and understand them as such. That fine point of understanding is the truly active, and manifestly impersonal, Reason: which is the spirit, indeed.

From this fundamental Monism of Spinoza, in whom he 'found himself', Gœthe never departed; for the good reason that, once it has been apprehended, it is impossible to depart from it. No genuine Spinozist has ever completely abjured his faith. What Hegel called 'the bath of Spinoza' is an irremediable happening to whom it comes; and the mere fact that Hegel was aware of this, implies that unusual circumspection is necessary in interpreting *his* philosophy. All that Gœthe did, or conceived himself to have done, was to examine the ways of existence, which were the ways of the infinite substance which was God. This 'divine' substance was equally present in himself and in the objective world. The separation between these two was unreal; the only moment of real separation in the One was that non-temporal moment when the individual subject became a complete object to itself—the distinctive human moment when in and through man Nature achieves self-consciousness, or, in Spinoza's language, God knows and loves himself. As Gœthe expressed it, 'Man is the first speech that Nature holds with God.'

Between such an attitude and the Kantian there was a gulf. What he learned from Kant, Gœthe said, was merely an increased knowledge of the subject as object; it fell into place as a kind of natural science of the subject, on a level with, but more restricted than, the natural science of the objective world to which the subject also belonged. The inherent tendency to subjectivism which was in Kant he decisively rejected. Spinoza had made him proof against the epistemological illusion; so that he could speak in *Glückliches Ereignis* with clarity and concision of 'the Kantian philosophy, which so exalts the subject, while apparently confining it'. And in a letter of 1831—during that last year of his life in which his awareness of his own past attained a maximum of lucidity—he wrote:

> I am grateful to the critical and idealist Philosophy for having made me aware of myself, for that is an immense gain; but it never gets to the object: this object we must accept, as does the reason of the ordinary man, in order that, in a stable relationship towards it we may find the joy of life.

'But it never gets to the object.' The objection was, and is, fatal. But, naturally, Gœthe did not make it in the spirit of a narrow 'materialism'. He, like Spinoza, would have had no patience with the meagre modern sophistry which passes under that name. The subject and the object both had to be given their full rights in a true wisdom. The attempt to reach the subject from the side of the object was as unsatisfying as the attempt to reach the object from the side of the subject. As he wrote to Schiller:

> It always seems to me that, if the one school of thought can never reach the spirit working from without inwards, the other, working from within outwards, will only with great difficulty, attain to the body, so that one always does best to remain in a philosophic state of nature, and make the best use of one's undivided being until such time as the philosophers agree how they can unite that which for the moment they have separated. (*June* 1, 1798)

For that moment we are still waiting. Meanwhile, those who follow Gœthe's advice and remain in 'a philosophic state of nature' have the best of it. But Gœthe believed that the 'state of nature' is itself the highest achievement of philosophy. It is the sacramental reverence for the 'pure phenomenon' which, according to Gœthe himself, was the highest that man could attain. It is not the innocence of the child, but the second innocence of the grown man; and it differs from the innocence of the child most palpably in this, that its light is turned by the man upon his own nature also. It is an immensely subtle naivety, and as such incapable of direct description. As Schiller put it, in the essay: *Uber naïve und sentimentalische Dichtung,* 'They [children] are what we once were. We were once Nature, and our culture must bring us back, by the path of Reason and Freedom, to Nature once again.' The reminiscence of Jesus's teaching concerning the condition of entry into the Kingdom of God is not accidental. But such an expression, necessarily metaphorical, is only to be understood in virtue of analogous experience; it will not abide a purely intellectual analysis. Yet intellectual analysis is necessary, and may help to bring us nearer to the crucial point of Gœthe's philosophy. For, if we accept Schiller's simple formulation: that we were once Nature, and must return to it, we are bound to remark that in the period of separation from Nature we have not ceased to belong wholly to it. This is the burden of the famous *Fragment on Nature* inspired or written by Gœthe, which T. H. Huxley translated and accepted as his own creed. What distinguishes this period, and makes it possible for us to call it a period of separation, is that man is unconscious that he does belong wholly to Nature; and often (or even generally) he is not merely unconscious of his complete penetration by the natural, but actively resentful of the imputation. He persists in believing himself to be, according to Spinoza's words, *imperium in imperio*: 'a kingdom within a kingdom'. And this is the source of the particular kind of transcendentalism and supernaturalism which Spinoza and Gœthe so persistently rejected. But their rejection carried with it no refusal to recognize the specific humanity of man. Man was, indeed, an animal, but he was a human animal. The difference was essential. 'In the subject there is everything that there is in Nature, and something more.' There was no trace in this doctrine of the false simplification, which so completely vitiates vulgar materialism—the reduction of man to an order below the human. On the contrary, it demanded a lucid recognition of human nature: of Nature in its specifically human form. Thus it purified human nature in man of the dualistic impediment, and liberated him from the cramping tyranny of a merely external and authoritative morality. Man must learn to know and to accept himself.

This attitude to experience is not easy to describe; or rather it can be described from different angles. It is the pursuit of wisdom by knowing Nature, and by knowing Nature in oneself. This twofold pursuit, giving full rights to both the object and the subject, but with the primary and ultimate emphasis on the object so that the final knowledge of the subject is a detached awareness of itself as object, is dynamic and creative. It is a true process of evolution: of subjective growth through objective experience. *Jeder neue Gegenstand, wohl beschaut, schliesst ein neues Organ in uns auf*: 'Every new object, steadily contemplated, creates a new organ in us.' There it is expressed in terms of an almost purely 'scientific' knowledge of that *Welt-und-Naturforschung,* that genetic inquiry into the total history of the world, the pursuit of which was, in Gœthe's view, the true prophylactic against 'spiritual sickness'. But it expands immediately, beyond these limits. The *Gegenstand*—invaluable word—that which stands over against us, is not merely the scientific object, but the subject as object also; and the subject not merely as developed by its contemplation of the scientific object, but by its own most intimate life-experience. The continually growing subject, continually becoming object for itself, continually relegated back to the Nature which it is and to which it belongs—such was the 'dialectical' process of human growth as Gœthe experienced and conceived it.

This process of growth, because it was indeed a process of growth, cannot be analysed beyond a certain point. As Gœthe put it in *Glückliches Ereignis*:

Those who view the snug certainty of human reason from a loftier standpoint (the innate reason, that is, of a healthy human being, which doubts neither objects and their relationship, nor its own capacity to know, understand, judge, value and use them), such men will certainly gladly admit that it would be almost to attempt the impossible were one to try to describe the innumerable paths to a purified, freer, self-conscious condition. It cannot be a question of degrees of culture, rather of wrong turnings, creeping and slidings, and after that an unpremeditated and joyous leap towards a higher level of understanding.

The ways of this growth were indeed labyrinthine. None the less the main and recurrent pattern is clear enough. On the one side, a continuous opening of the whole receptivity of the subject to all experience, a constant submission of the self to the 'pure phenomenon'; and on the other side, an equally constant relegation of the self enlarged by experience to the status of the 'pure phenomenon'. It was an incessant systole and diastole. Inevitably, there always remained on the side of the subject *something* that there was not in Nature, even when the subject was wholly reintegrated into the matrix. That unattainable x had its analogue in another unattainable y at the heart of objective nature. Such an x, such a y, there must always be; nevertheless, this was not a fixed and adamantine 'unknowable': it was a continually shifting 'unknown'. Here the distinction becomes as tenuous as it is vital. It is the whole distinction between a dynamic and a static humility of mind.

27

MARXISM

From The Price of Leadership *(Student Christian Movement Press, 1939), pages 150–156. Editor's title.*

We have reached a moment of authentic religious reformation, when 'the religious life is started upon a fresh period in company with radically new ideas'. And, as is surely self-evident, this new unity will not be accomplished by taking the religious life, on the one hand, as a thing fixed, and the new ideas on the other hand, as another fixed thing, and by rearrangement here and mitigation there effecting some sort of compromise between them. For one thing, this is not how a new unity of thought and religion is ever accomplished; for another, the religious life of Christianity, in so far as it is a fixed and accepted thing, is revealing itself as inadequate even faintly to influence the conduct of nations to-day. What must happen, I believe, is a direct revivification of the religious life in the act of thinking the new thoughts and taking into one's soul the new ideas which are necessary to the thinking of reality to-day.

Chief among the new ideas which are necessary to such a thinking of contemporary reality are the ideas which are roughly comprehended under the term, Marxism. They are drastic, purgative and revolutionary ideas. The fact that they are generally presented to us as a self-sufficient philosophical and religious system, and that this pretension is absurd, does not in the least absolve us from the plain duty of submitting our minds to them in the spirit which is prepared to 'try all things and to hold fast to that which is good'. The critical idea of Marxism is good, because it is true, and because it is a truth without which the modern world cannot be understood. This critical idea is that, in an industrialized society which is built upon an economy of machine-production, the real relations between individual members of the society are in fact outside their ordinary field of consciousness altogether. Between what they really do, and what they imagine they do, between what they really are and what they imagine they are, there is a great gulf. The relations between members of an industrialized society are really determined by a process which, because it is outside the ordinary field of consciousness, escapes all conscious control, and are therefore determined by what the Marxist calls 'necessity'.

The ordinary Christian reply to this searching criticism of the life of man under the autonomy of capitalism is quite futile. The conventional Christian mind affects to be horrified at this idea that the social process in contemporary society is governed by 'necessity', for is it not essential to the faith of Christianity that the individual is free to do good or evil? That defence against the truth of Marxism is entirely irrelevant. If I am tied hand and foot, and somebody tells me that I am bound so that I cannot act, it is foolish, it is impious, to reply that 'Christianity tells me that I am free'. In such a case Christianity is degraded into pious nonsense, which deserves all the contemptuous criticism which Marxism directs against it. The truth is that in the existing economic system the individual is not free to do good or evil as he will, except on one condition, namely, that his will to 'depart from iniquity' comprehends a determination to *discover* whether he is actually free to 'depart from iniquity' or not.

What Marxism has to tell the individual member of a modern industrial society is that the ordinary man's conception of himself as a responsible, freely deciding person is almost entirely illusory. It tells him that nine-tenths, or even ninety-nine hundredths of him, is the passive and unconscious slave of an economic system which he does not understand, and which he makes no attempt to control. To talk as though Christian conduct in such a society were simply a matter of following the Ten Commandments, or accepting the current social morality and going to church besides, is contemptible. It is inevitable that such irrelevant religion should be discredited. Unless Christianity is prepared to think to the bottom of its conventional conception of Man, it is bound to become more and more a narcotic.

But a Christianity which regards it as its peculiar function to be ready to think uncomfortable thoughts, is prepared to take to heart all the drastic criticism of capitalist society and capitalist man which Marxism has to offer. For this criticism comes to a genuinely Christian mind as a mighty corroboration of its own deepest insights, as a providential renovation of its most intimate spiritual disciplines. The Christian who has the courage to accept the Marxian analysis of capitalist society may truly say: 'Who hath believed our report? and to whom hath the arm of the Lord been revealed?' For here, in the increasing bewilderments and barbarities of contemporary mechanical society, the truth of the great Pauline doctrine of 'the law of the flesh' is revealed as by a lightning flash; likewise, the truth of the great catholic doctrine of Original Sin. It can be no cause for astonishment to the Christian mind that, in an economic order of which the characteristic is that the physical energy at the disposal of society has been multiplied a thousandfold in the last hundred and fifty years, the natural man by his natural actions should be preparing to bring moral degradation and universal catastrophe upon himself. A Christianity which really believes in the necessity of dying to the old Adam and being reborn into Christ does not merely accept all the great element of truth in Marxism without any vital surrender, but must even in some sort welcome it as a confirmation of its own insight and an enhancement of its spiritual strength. For Christianity alone can accept this truth without being overwhelmed by it, without capitulating to all that is false in Marxism—the element of crude secular optimism which believes that, somehow and miraculously, out of this abandonment of political and social life to the domination of the 'natural man', a heaven on earth will emerge.

The means by which this miraculous transformation will be accomplished is 'the dictatorship of the proletariat'. It is not enough to admit that the history of post-war Europe has plainly shown that the working-class has no intention and no power to dictate, and that what happens when it is foolish enough to say that it intends to do so is that it is dictated to by a satanic Nationalism. It is imperative to realize why this happens and why it must happen. It happens and must happen because, by no conceivable operation of the 'ordinary self' of mankind, or any class of mankind, can the 'classless society' imagined by Marxist Socialism be brought into being. Such a society will be brought into being by Christian love—'that seeketh not its own'—or not at all. The 'natural man' *cannot* do it. And the 'natural man' does not change his nature by belonging to the working-class; neither does 'the natural man' of the middle-class change his nature by being received into the proletarian party. In order that the 'natural man'—the creature of appetite and selfishness—shall change his nature, he needs to be baptized into something quite different: into the death of Christ, as St. Paul knew and preached. That knowledge and that preaching, that baptism as a real experience, created the Christian Church. It and it alone can create the Christian Church anew; and the triumphant Christian Church alone, into which men are gathered from the East and the West, is the reality of that 'classless society' which the Marxist vainly dreams will be created by the 'natural' proletarian man.

So Matthew Arnold's prophecy is being realized in circumstances which he did not foresee. That fusion of Hebraism and Hellenism which he believed to be necessary if the degeneration of the new democracy was to be averted is more necessary than ever to-day. Unless it becomes the centre and source of our 'education', our education becomes merely an initiation into decay. Only the Christian mind can understand the world to-day; and that is the Christian mind which does in fact unite the selfless spiritual energy of Hebraism with the selfless intellectual honesty of Hellenism: and to-day at any rate the one is impossible without the other. To what final conclusions this new combination of Hebraism and Hellenism will lead us is a matter of relatively little moment beside the importance of understanding that this renovation of the Christian mind is essential and that it cannot be escaped by any man who is prepared to think reality to-day. That is the beginning; for thus men become instruments fit to do the will of God. That has always been the end of true education; but to-day it is the beginning of it. The very foundations of education have to be laid anew.

28

WHITMAN: POET-PROPHET OF DEMOCRACY

From Unprofessional Essays *(Cape, 1956).*

It is now nearly fifty years since my classical tutor at Oxford, H. F. Fox—whom I name, though his name will be meaningless to others, for the private satisfaction of commemorating him—pressed upon me Whitman's *Democratic Vistas.* Fox belonged to the old generation of English Liberals, who flourished in the latter decades of the nineteenth century. As a political force, they reached their apogee in the famous general election of 1906, when the Liberal party swept into power on a wave of universal reaction against the imperialist fervours of the South African war; and they were broken, permanently, by the First World War, which was undreamt of by their philosophy. But their fortunes as politicians are irrelevant. The best of the Liberals—such a one survives still in Gilbert Murray—were not politicians: they were idealists. And for one of them *Democratic Vistas* was a sort of modern Bible. I imagine that this was true of many others.

They were not mistaken in saluting Whitman as their prophet. *Democratic Vistas* is surely a permanent statement not only of the ideal of liberal democracy, but of its fundamental principles, which if it violates, it ceases to be. Democracy is a debased and ambiguous word today, when the spokesmen of totalitarian Russia make their monstrous claim that their society is a democracy, and have it granted even by some millions of Western Europeans. Therefore, I prefer to call the society which Whitman envisaged and championed, the free society. But the name is immaterial. There is no mistake possible about the kind of society of which Whitman was the prophet and champion.

That which really balances and conserves the social and political world is not so much legislation, police, treaties, and dread of punishment, as the latent eternal intuitional sense, in humanity, of fairness, manliness, decorum, etc. Indeed, this perennial regulation, control, and oversight, by self-suppliance, is *sine qua non* to democracy; and a highest, widest aim of democratic literature may well be to bring forth, cultivate, brace and strengthen this sense, in individuals and society. A strong mastership of the general inferior self by the superior self, is to be aided, secured, indirectly, but surely, by the literatus, in his works, shaping for individual or aggregate democracy, a great passionate body, in and along with which goes a great masterful spirit.

That is, at once, a proclamation of Whitman's ideal of democracy, and of the part he felt that he was called to play in its realization. It is noble and compelling. And of *Democratic Vistas* in general it may be said that, apart from its own intrinsic merits, which are very great, it is necessary to an understanding of the real purpose of *Leaves of Grass*.

Yet this was the book of which Whitman wrote to Dowden in 1872 that 'it remains quite unread, uncalled for, here in America'. Though there is the best precedent for a prophet being without honour in his own country, in the case of Whitman it needs some explanation. The one which occurs most readily to an Englishman is that the Americans of Whitman's time were too engrossed in the material mastering of a continent to have time to pause and take their spiritual bearings, whereas the little body of contemporary and influential Englishmen, who received his work with enthusiasm, had, whether consciously or not, the premonition that the epoch of their country's expansion was over, and that if Britain was to retain significance as a power for civilization, it must be as a paradigm of the free society. Whitman made his impact upon Britain at a moment when its best minds were engaged in taking spiritual stock of their country. Carlyle, Ruskin, Arnold, and Morris were the influences which had worked on the younger men who were receptive to Whitman; and Whitman seemed to corroborate and combine those influences in a radically new way. He shifted the balance from the critical to the creative, from dubiety to faith; and he added a comprehensive assertion—a poetic demonstration—of the validity of the individual which came to his English disciples as a great liberation.

What Whitman was attempting in *Leaves of Grass* cannot be better described than in the words of *Democratic Vistas*:

The literature, songs, esthetics, etc., of a country are of importance principally because they furnish the materials and suggestions of personality for the men and women of that country, and enforce them in a thousand effective ways.

Very likely, this purpose was not fully conscious in him when he began writing *Leaves of Grass*; indeed, he admitted it. But this is what he subsequently believed he had done, or tried to do. His belief was well-founded, and his claim just. This we must allow, whether or not we share his belief that a national literature is principally of importance because it offers suggestions and materials for what he elsewhere calls 'a basic model or portrait of personality for general use'. Even those who hold that literature has other purposes to serve which seem to them more important, must allow that much of the world's great literature has been valued by the people for whom it was written for the concrete ideal of personal conduct it set before them. This was the merit of Homer in the eyes of a Greek, and of Virgil in the eyes of a Roman.

Such was the sense in which Whitman claimed to be the poet-prophet of America. There was nothing narrowly national in his conception of 'these States'. If at first sight it sometimes appears to be so, only a little patience and receptiveness is needed to make us realize that his insistence on the places, the persons, and the society with which he was familiar is only an example of the working of Gœthe's poetical axiom that the universal is the particular. The universal of which 'these States' were the particular in Whitman's poetry is Democracy; and all over the world democrats, in Whitman's peculiar and profound sense of the word, that is, those who believe that a self-governing society of free and responsible individuals offers the only way of corporate progress towards the Good, have had no difficulty in regarding Whitman's America as the city of their own soul. It is for them a symbol of the ideal, of the same order as Blake's Albion and Jerusalem; and Whitman, in rhapsodizing over the rivers and prairies and people of America, is behaving as Shakespeare's poet, 'who gives to airy nothing a local habitation and a name'—except that the ideal democracy is much more than 'an airy nothing'. It is at least a compelling vision of the society towards which humanity must stumble on, if it is not to cease to be human.

At the present moment many Western Europeans, who have an emotional and intellectual loyalty to the ideal of the free society, are tempted to be a little dubious towards America's claim to be its prototype. To them the activities of Senator McCarthy loom large and ominous. They should remember that Whitman himself passed through many periods of despondence in the days of the carpet-baggers and afterwards. He too cried: 'These savage, wolfish parties alarm me—owning no law but their own will, more and more combative, less and less tolerant of the idea of ensemble and of equal brotherhood, the perfect equality of the States, the ever overarching American ideas.' Nevertheless, Whitman held to his faith that these ugly and depressing manifestations were the grim growing pains inseparable from the process of the working out of a high destiny in a mass of common humanity. Whether his faith will be justified by the event, who can say? But there is scope for tempered optimism, when we remember that, in the years immediately following Whitman's death, another idealist, of a different kidney indeed, but equally combining with his idealism a robust realism, wrote of the condition of the United States.

> Turn to Republican America. America has no Star Chamber, and no feudal barons. But it has Trusts; and it has millionaires whose factories, fenced in by live electric wires and defended by Pinkerton retainers with magazine rifles, would have made a Radical of Reginald Front de Bœuf. Would Washington or Franklin have lifted a finger in the cause of American independence if they had foreseen its reality?

So wrote Bernard Shaw at the turn of the nineteenth century. After fifty years those conditions seem to belong to a prehistoric past, as do the conditions which produced the two epoch-making strikes—of the dockers and the match-factory girls—in England. Democracy is at least free to mend its ways.

It is notable that Shaw, who no doubt imbibed much of his doctrine from Whitman, or rather found in Whitman a corroboration of his own native intuitions, agreed with him whole-heartedly in his insistence on the importance of sexual selection. The whole of *Man and Superman* might fairly be regarded as Shaw's effort to put a sharper and more paradoxical edge on one of Whitman's central doctrines: the necessity for Democracy of true and generous mating between mentally, morally and physically developed men and women. Indeed, Whitman not only anticipated Shaw's doctrine of the necessity of the Superman for viable Democracy when he inveighed against 'the appalling depletion of women in their powers of sane athletic maternity' and proclaimed that the radical weakness of the actual society in America was that 'the men believe not in the women, nor the women in the men'; but in *Children of Adam* he was the palpable forerunner of D. H. Lawrence's even more revolutionary teaching on sex. Lawrence was directly indebted to Whitman even for much of his distinctive phraseology.

This fructification in the soil of such different natures of seeds scattered from Whitman's luxuriant flowering is a simple and pertinent example of his immense seminal influence, as the poet-prophet of Democracy. That was what he justly claimed to be; and as such he is best comprehended. Or, at least, that is the best line of approach towards a complete understanding of his work: on one condition, that it is realized that Democracy can be justified and believed in only on the basis of a prior conviction of the infinite worth of the individual. Without this, Democracy is, what Plato held it to be, merely a short road to the tyranny of the baser elements in man. That can be avoided only by stubborn adherence to the sacrosanct principle of the divine right of the minority—of all minorities save one perhaps—to freedom of thought and speech. I call this right divine, because it cannot be rationally demonstrated. If it is self-evident, as I believe, it is self-evident only as a religious truth: ultimately, therefore, a matter of revelation. And since, even in the contemporary world, the truth has been categorically denied by the vast social organization of Russia, and since, in the ancient and mediaeval worlds, it was not admitted at all, it is evident that the apprehension of this religious truth is in constant need of renewal.

This was Whitman's great achievement. He vitally renewed the religious revelation on which the justification and continued existence of Democracy depends. That is to say, he experienced the revelation anew. From this derives the uniqueness of his work: the confidence with which he propounds the totality of himself—the whole experiencing nature which was Walt Whitman—as the citizen of the ideal Democracy. To the congenitally unsympathetic this has appeared as overweening arrogance, an awful example of the extravagance of romantic egotism. But no one responsive to Whitman has ever been repelled by this idiosyncrasy. It shocks only those to whom everything about Whitman is shocking. For in fact his apparent egotism is entirely justified. It follows necessarily from his vision of the ideal society: for it is implicit in the ethos of that society that the individual shall be accepted with all his imperfections—warts and all. It is a society in which the individual person is valid, because it is a society whose law is love—the same society, in fact, of which the vision came to Tchehov when he listened to music: 'where everything is forgiven and it would be strange not to forgive'. In Christian idiom, it is the Kingdom of Heaven on earth. That may seem very remote from any practical Democracy we know or can foresee, either in America or Europe: but the imaginative vitality of the ideal is absolutely necessary to the continuing existence of any Democracy at all.

That is to say, behind and beneath Whitman's promulgation of his total self as a type of the citizen of the ideal Democracy is a deeply religious humility. Unless his 'egotism' is apprehended against this background of religion it is bound to be misunderstood. Not that there is any excuse for ignoring the background. Nothing could be more explicit than, for example, *Starting from Paumanok*.

Each is not for its own sake,
I say the whole earth and all the stars in the sky are for religion's sake.

I say no man has ever yet been half devout enough,
None has ever yet ador'd or worship'd half enough,
None has begun to think how divine he himself is, and how certain the future is.

I say that the real and permanent grandeur of these States must be their
religion,
Otherwise there is no real and permanent grandeur;
(Nor character nor life worthy the name without religion,
Nor land nor man nor woman without religion.)

It may fairly be said that Whitman's great struggle as poet-prophet was to communicate his religious sense—of the divinity of the created world; of the democratic idea; of himself as part of the one and prophet of the other—without emasculating it by using the conventional language of religion. And that, in turn, is no small part of the problem for critical appreciation of him. What we are constrained to call Whitman's humility is not very like what is ordinarily understood by the word. It is the attitude of one who has been, once for all, possessed by the conviction that he is merely the vehicle and instrument of the One—'the fang'd and glittering One whose head is over all'; who, at the same time and as part of the same experience, is convinced of the uniqueness of every created person, animal and thing; who, in the words of Meister Eckhart, is as one 'who having looked upon the sun, henceforward sees the sun in all things'.

To be possessed by this conviction is, inevitably, felt as an immense privilege, for with it descends, also inevitably, a sense of one's total validity—no greater, indeed, than that of any blade of grass or lily of the field, but since it happens to a human being with the burden of consciousness and self-consciousness, bringing with it an incomparable awareness of integration, of liberation, and of ordinariness. To a man who has passed through this experience, egotism and humility are indistinguishable. The completest self-utterance is not an assertion but an annihilation of the self. The ego which, according to Pascal, is 'always hateful', is by this experience transcended or abolished.

The proof of this, in Whitman's case, is easily available. No one who has responded to the personality exposed in *Leaves of Grass* has ever felt him to be other than lovable. One may be, indeed many are, completely allergic to him; but once he has found an entry, he takes possession: and that by a quite different process from conquering our aesthetic sensibilities. Not many of Whitman's poems overcome us by the perfection of their beauty; and in face of his achievement as a whole, we remain entirely aware of the crudeness, the imperfection, the failure in transmutation, of much of it. Nevertheless, we would not have it otherwise. The roughnesses, the blemishes belong. They are necessary to the kind of communication at which he aimed, and in which he believed. He well knew what he was doing when he insisted on the interdependent wholeness of the *Leaves* he had strung together. When he said 'the words of my book nothing, the drift of it everything', or more arrestingly, but not more profoundly, that 'he who touches this book, touches a man', he was saying the same thing: that he, as a whole, had been validated.

To get to the root of this conviction, in Whitman himself and those who respond to him, we should need to inquire into the nature of the mystical experience, when it happens to a man who has worked himself free of adherence to any particular system of religion. Such an inquiry would probably not be very rewarding. It is better to accept and ponder what Whitman himself has to say of it, in the *Song of Myself*.

I believe in you my soul, the other I am must not abase itself to you,
And you must not be abased to the other.

Loafe with me on the grass, loose the stop from your throat,
Not words, not music or rhyme I want, not custom or lecture, not even the best,
Only the lull I like, the hum of your valvèd voice.

I mind how once we lay such a transparent summer morning,
How you settled your head athwart my hips and gently turn'd over upon me,
And parted the shirt from my bosom-bone, and plunged your tongue to my bare-stript heart,
And reach'd till you felt my beard, and reach'd till you held my feet.

Swiftly arose and spread around me the peace and knowledge that pass all the argument of the earth.
And I know that the hand of God is the promise of my own,
And I know that the spirit of God is the brother of my own,
And that all the men ever born are also my brothers, and the women my sisters and lovers,
And that a kelson of the creation is love,
And limitless are leaves stiff or drooping in the fields,
And brown ants in the little wells beneath them,
And mossy scabs of the worm fence, heap'd stones, elder, mullein, and poke-weed.

That seems to be a description of an actual moment of illumination, perhaps *the* moment. By its curious and impressive particularity it recalls nothing so much as some equally particular and impressive passages in Blake's prophetic books. What is peculiar to Whitman is the intensity of his physical memory of the process (which other mystics have described) by which his corporeal body was, as it were, consumed and spiritualized. He describes it, vividly and memorably, as a physical caress of his body by his soul; and this swift and sudden transcending of the distinction and opposition between body and soul is accompanied by a vision of the infinite significance of the details of the created world—what Blake called the Minute Particulars—and a simultaneous assurance that 'a kelson of the creation is love'.

One may guess that this experience is the creative kernel of the whole of the *Song of Myself*: the seed of which that great poem is an exfoliation, though of course there is no way of proving it. Anyhow, it is certain that only in the perspective established by an experience such as he describes can the apparent contradictions of the poem be naturally resolved, and seen as necessary. If the experience is not the originating germ of the poem, it is the key to it. And at no point in the amazingly rich variety of its validations does Whitman go beyond what is warranted by his mystical assurance that everything everywhere is good and divinely appointed: himself, in all his thoughts, emotions and acts, no more and no less than any other particle of the universe. The self that he 'promulges' is the self that he has discovered at the point of its unity with the All; it is beneath anything that we are accustomed to regard as personality. He has been carried back to the ground of the personal (in the metaphysical sense of the word, ground) and has found it to be of one eternal substance with everything that is, or has been, or will be. This is the firm and timeless foundation from which he vaticinates.

Quite obviously, the *Song of Myself* is just as much, if not more preponderantly, the song of Whitman's not-Self, of all the richness of the objective world. Its 'egotism' is transparent and crystalline: it is completely acknowledged, and in no way apologized for—

> I know perfectly well my own egotism,
> Know my omnivorous lines and must not write any less,
> And would fetch you, whoever you are, flush with myself.

'Flush with myself' is one of those simple and superb phrases which Whitman always had at his command. It means not merely bringing his comrade-reader to the point where he shares Whitman's perception, but bringing them both together to coalesce in a common spiritual ether. He expresses this in a splendid and homely metaphor (which may not be recognized as a metaphor) at the beginning of his *Song*.

> Houses and rooms are full of perfumes, the shelves are crowded with perfumes,
> I breathe the fragrance myself and know it and like it,
> The distillation would intoxicate me also, but I shall not let it.
>
> The atmosphere is not a perfume, it has no taste of the distillation, it is odorless,
> It is for my mouth forever, I am in love with it,
> I will go to the bank by the wood and become undisguised and naked,
> I am mad for it to be in contact with me.

That is not, what it seems, a paean to the open air; it celebrates what Blake called 'the cleansing of the doors of perception', and the entry into the new and ever-present world of things as they are. Whitman calls 'the atmosphere' what Spinoza calls the *species aeternitatis,* and more traditionally Christian mystics the all-sustaining love of God. And so Whitman ends what is in deceptive appearance an invocation of the open air with a plain declaration of his real meaning.

Have you reckon'd a thousand acres much? Have you reckon'd the earth much?
Have you practis'd so long to learn to read?
Have you felt so proud to get at the meaning of poems?

Stop this day and night with me and you shall possess the origin of all poems,
You shall possess the good of the earth and sun (there are millions of suns left),
You shall no longer take things at second or third hand, nor look through the eyes of the dead, nor feed on the spectres in books,
You shall not look through my eyes either, nor take things from me,
You shall listen to all sides and filter them from yourself.

To be intoxicated by the perfume and the distillation which he loves, but puts aside for the pure serene of 'the atmosphere', is the same as looking through the eyes of the dead. It is not enough to call the condition at which he aims for himself, and which he seeks to induce in us, freshness of vision, though no doubt where that occurs a momentary transparence has taken place. He is urging us towards not a mere 'moment of vision' but to an understanding of all that it involves: towards making the religion that underlies all such moments a permanent possession. The *Song of Myself* is crowded to overflowing not only with moments of vision but also with a rich multiplicity of statements and explorations of the background from which it arises. His focus changes incessantly. At one moment, impersonal as 'the atmosphere', his 'omnivorous lines' roam over all America; at another they pass up and down the vistas of 'the Me myself', who no less belongs to all men.

The range of this great poem is wonderful: from the picture of the negro dray-driver:

The negro holds firmly the reins of his four horses, the block swags underneath on its tied-over chain,
The negro that drives the long dray of the stone-yard, steady and tall he stands pois'd on one leg on the string-piece,
His blue shirt exposes his ample neck and breast and loosens over his hip-band,

His glance is calm and commanding, he tosses the slouch of his hat away
from his forehead,
The sun falls on his crispy hair and moustache, falls on the black of his
polish'd and perfect limbs.—

to 'the mechanic's wife with her babe at her nipple interceding for every person born'. That sudden identification of the mechanic's wife with the Blessed Virgin is of the essence of Whitman's thought.

Thus the *Song of Myself*, rightly considered, is the explication of an eternal moment. If one is required to choose, this must be pronounced Whitman's greatest poem, and certainly the one around which all the other leaves of grass—the obviously beautiful and the apparently ungainly—naturally cluster themselves. It is the heart and core of the total pattern. The only poem I know with which it can be compared is Blake's *Milton*, which is also the explication of an eternal moment. There is one salient difference between them. Blake's wonderful poem is an exploration, or re-creation of the timeless instant, whereas Whitman's equally wonderful one is a declaration of its consequences. But *Milton* is barred from the common understanding by Blake's use of his esoteric symbols, where Whitman intently addressed himself, as far as he could, to the comprehension of the common man. But, for all that, the affinities between the two poems are astonishing. How perfectly, one feels, would such a passage as this from *Milton* fall into place in the *Song of Myself*!

Thou seest the Constellations in the deep and wondrous Night:
They rise in order and continue their immortal courses
Upon the mountains and in vales with harp and heavenly song,
With flute and clarion, with cups and measures fill'd with foaming wine.
Glitt'ring the streams reflect the Vision of beatitude,
And the calm Ocean joys beneath and smooths his awful waves.
These are the Sons of Los, and these the Labourers of the Vintage.
Thou seest the gorgeous clothed Flies that dance and sport in summer
Upon the sunny brooks and meadows: every one the dance
Knows in its intricate mazes of delight artful to weave:
Each one to sound his instruments of music in the dance,
To touch each other and recede, to cross and change and return:
These are the Children of Los; thou seest the Trees on mountains,
The wind blows heavy, loud they thunder thro' the darksome sky,
Uttering prophecies and speaking instructive words to the sons
Of men: These are the Sons of Los: These the Visions of Eternity,
But we see only as it were the hem of their garments
When with our vegetable eyes we view these wondrous Visions.

Save for the repeated phrase, 'These are the sons of Los', which belongs to Blake's particular drama of the spirit, it might well be one of Whitman's canticles. And when Whitman declares that he knows that—

limitless are leaves stiff or drooping in the fields
And brown ants in the little wells beneath them.—

he is saying precisely what Blake has said before him. The leaves are 'limitless' because they are 'visions of eternity' and we see only the hem of their garments.

Thus it was right and natural that Anne Gilchrist, who devoted the first years of her widowhood to completing her husband's *Life of William Blake*, the first book in which his extraordinary genius was vindicated, should have been the first woman publicly to salute the kindred genius of Whitman. By endorsing his radical utterances on sex (essentially the same as Blake's), she gave him perhaps the most precious support he ever received—'the proudest word that ever came to me from a woman—if not the proudest word of all from any source', as he told Traubel.

Perhaps paradoxically, but rightly, Whitman believed that the immediate apprehension of an infinite significance in all existences was within the natural capacity of the common man. The truths he enunciated were self-evident to the natural vision: though he was constrained in honesty to admit that natural vision was not very common, since it required the removal of the scales of custom and prejudice—indeed of most of what was reckoned respectable.

Long enough have you dream'd contemptible dreams,
Now I wash the gum from your eyes.

Still, he insisted on the ordinariness of his own vision.

Only what proves itself to every man and woman is so,
Only what nobody denies is so.

Behind this simple asseveration is the justified assumption that, if Democracy is not a pretentious sham, a merely temporary form of social organization, produced by a favourable and quite exceptional conjunction of circumstances, and doomed to collapse under the pressure of any positive demands on its assumed morality, then there must be latent in its citizens a real fund of common and unshakable religious conviction. Every member, or at least the majority of its members, must be deeply persuaded of the infinite worth of others as well as himself. This axiomatic moral and religious truth may be overlaid, obscured and forgotten: but it must be there, or Democracy is an illusion. Whitman could not admit that it was, any more than I can. The most he could do was to admit the possibility that men might make the great refusal.

Once unquestioning obedience, once fully enslaved,
Once fully enslaved, no nation, state, city of this earth, ever afterward resumes its liberty.

But he had to make the act of faith in his fellows. The revelation that had come to consciousness in him, was latent in them. He was merely their spokesman, the interpreter of themselves to themselves.

I do not say these things for a dollar, or to fill up the time while I wait for a boat,
(It is you talking just as much as myself, I act as the tongue of you,
Tied in your mouth, in mine it begins to be loosen'd.)

And this is true, not merely of the great democratic commonplaces to which they might be expected to respond, but of the comprehensive religious realization on which alone the commonplaces can be grounded.

The moth and the fish eggs are in their place,
The bright suns I see and the dark suns I cannot see are in their place,
The palpable is in its place and the impalpable is in its place.
These are really the thoughts of all men in all ages and lands, they are not original with me,
If they are not yours as much as mine they are nothing, or next to nothing . . .

It is indeed the *philosophia perennis* which he proclaims, but with the radical variation that he proclaims it to a society which is, or claims to be, based on the belief that all its members are at least capable of it. To them he says: Have the courage of yourselves, first by discovering what your self really is. Get down to the bedrock, the point at which you know your own infinitude, stretching forward and backward in time, and upwards to eternity. From that security go your way, fulfil your own unique destiny.

I have no chair, no church, no philosophy,
I lead no man to a dinner-table, library, exchange,
But each man and each woman of you I lead upon a knoll,
My left hand hooking you around the waist,
My right hand pointing to landscapes of continents and the public road.

Not I, not anyone else can travel that road for you,
You must travel it for yourself.

It is not far, it is within reach,
Perhaps you have been on it since you were born and did not know,
Perhaps it is everywhere on water and on land.

Whitman's hope that ordinary men and women would straightway receive his utterances as the expression of their own deepest, but inarticulate, thoughts and feelings, was not realized in fact. He may have found a few such readers, but for the most part he had to depend on a few doughty defenders in his own country—Emerson supreme among them—and the enthusiastic support of a band of young English disciples. Indeeed, writing so late as 1904, Henry Bryan Binns, his English biographer, speaking of Whitman's dismissal in 1865 from his clerkship in the Indian Office in Washington, as the result of the reading of *Leaves of Grass* by his Methodist chief, says: 'Average American opinion was then undisguisedly hostile, as, of course, it still remains.' If that was really the situation in America in 1904, it was distinctly different from that in England, where by that time his book had been accepted as a classic by the Liberal intellectuals, and as a sort of Bible by the native British Socialist movement, which, though it had a fair sprinkling of intellectuals, had a solid working-class core. Perhaps the explanation of this discrepancy is that quite early in the nineteenth century the British working class had become more or less completely urbanized, and Whitman's poetry had, for that part of it which was sufficiently alert to become Socialist, a powerful nostalgic attraction as a poetry of the open country and the open air. And it is very probable that the curious, but very marked association of the early Socialist movement in England with camping and hiking, on foot or cycle, in the countryside is almost entirely due to the influence of Whitman.

But that topic, though interesting, belongs to British local history. It would appear, from what I have read, that it was as a person rather than as a poet that Whitman came closest to the common man in America: pre-eminently during his hospital experiences in Washington in the Civil War, which made so profound an impression upon him. It has been said that Whitman attributed to his war-experiences a significance for his literary development which they did not really possess. This is true, in so far as the greater part of his most characteristic work was written before the War. Nevertheless, Whitman was not mistaken about himself. The war-experience did deepen his understanding of his own poetic purposes; it intensely sharpened his sense of the appalling cost even of the partial realization of the democratic ideal; it summoned him to make his own faith stronger in that which endures beyond death. That involved no break in his development: no such catastrophic change as, for example, was enforced upon the consciousness of many Englishmen by their experiences of the First World War. Whitman's faith was as deeply grounded as any could be. There is at least one passage of the *Song of Myself* in which he deliberately compares himself with the crucified and resurrected Christ. It was a brave thing to do; but in its splendid context provokes no resistance.

> Enough! enough! enough!
> Somehow I have been stunn'd. Stand back!
> Give me a little time beyond my cuff'd head, slumbers, dreams, gaping,
> I discover myself on the verge of a usual mistake.
>
> That I could forget the mockers and insults!
> That I could forget the trickling tears and the blows of the bludgeons and hammers!
> That I could look with a separate look on my own crucifixion and bloody crowning.
>
> I remember now,
> I resume the overstaid fraction,
> The grave of rock multiplies what has been confided to it, or to any graves,
> Corpses rise, gashes heal, fastenings roll from me.
>
> I troop forth replenish'd with supreme power, one of an average unending procession,
> Inland and sea-coast we go, and pass all boundary lines,
> Our swift ordinances on their way over the whole earth,
> The blossoms we wear in our hats the growth of thousands of years.

This, again, can be paralleled in the writings of Blake, for whom the unity of all humanity is typified in 'the Divine Humanity, the One Man, even Jesus', whose sufferings must be renewed in the ascent of any single soul towards Eternity. I recall Whitman's words here only to show that there was already that in him which could endure his Civil War experiences without dismay, though receiving them with the full sensitivity of the sympathetic and compassionate imagination. He saw many Christs in the agonizing soldiers he tended.

It was wholly natural, therefore, that his participation in their heroic sacrifice should deepen his conception of the Democracy for which they died, and that he should declare:

> Only the occurrence of the Secession War, and what it show'd me as by flashes of lightning with the emotional depths it sounded and arous'd . . . only from the strong flare and provocations of that war's sights and scenes the final reasons-for-being of an autochthonic and passionate song finally came forth.

At any rate it seems to me that from this point onward, Whitman understood his purpose more clearly as that of the poet-prophet of a society to be actually realized, as it had actually been paid for in limitless human suffering. He had the satisfaction of knowing that he too had paid the price. The immense demands of the hospital-years in Washington on his vital energy were the cause of his paralysis, and of the relative poverty of his subsequent poetic output.

To compensate, there is the admirable vaticination of *Democratic Vistas.* The vision and argument of this book, more directly than any of the poetry in *Leaves of Grass,* arise from his war-experience. This, he seems to say, is the society of which that manifest heroism of the common man offers the earnest.

> The movements of the late secession war, and their results, to any sense that studies well and comprehends them, show that popular democracy, whatever its faults and dangers, practically justifies itself beyond the proudest claims and wildest hopes of its enthusiasts.

We who have lived to see much the same common men fight with no less heroism and endure no less suffering in defence of a system so remote from democracy as the Communism of Stalin's Russia or the National Socialism of Hitler's Germany, may be more dubious of the validity of this demonstration. But it seemed cogent to Whitman; and perhaps he was right. And there is no doubt at all that he was right in his vindication of the Democracy he envisioned as the only form of society which can claim the moral allegiance of the free man.

> The purpose of democracy . . . is, through many transmigrations and amid endless ridicules, arguments, and ostensible failures, to illustrate, at all hazards, this doctrine or theory that man, properly trained in highest, sanest freedom, may and must become a law, and series of laws, unto himself, surrounding and providing for, not only his own personal control, but his relations to all other individuals and to the State; and that while other theories, as in the past histories of nations, have proved wise enough, and indispensable perhaps for their conditions, *this*, as matters now stand in our civilised world is the only scheme worth working from, as warranting results like Nature's laws, reliable, when once established, to carry on of themselves.

So much, nowadays, we would all claim to see and admit; but, it is to be feared, for the most part with a kind of lip-service and formal adhesion. It was Whitman's greatness that he explored and promulgated all the tremendous assumptions and obligations involved in that comforting creed. During the eighty years that have followed the writing of *Democratic Vistas*, in spite of the fact that we have endured two wars, even more atrocious than the Civil War which served to open yet wider Whitman's wide-open eyes, and that these wars were fought, not only ostensibly but really, to maintain Democracy, we seem to have got no further in the way of understanding and conceiving and imagining Democracy, than to suppose it is achieved and realized in the establishment of adult suffrage for men and women. That is concrete, we seem to say, and comprehensible;

that is the universal yardstick, by applying which we know whether or not Democracy exists. But beyond that, everything is vague and shadowy, uncertain and insecure. Do we recognize as essential to Democracy the divine right of a minority to freedom of thought and expression and association? We hardly know. Do we declare, as essential to Democracy, that this right must be denied to a minority which seeks to undermine and overthrow and abolish even that divine right of a minority in which we vaguely believe? We hardly know. The truth is that once the obvious, elementary and mechanical condition of Democracy has been satisfied in universal suffrage, perplexity involves the urgent question: what are the further fundamental moral postulates of Democracy, even on the overtly political plane? It is as though the wind of inspiration had dropped, and the proud ship drifted becalmed. She has not even steerage way.

Granted that some of the problems with which Democracy is now confronted belong to a dimension of which Whitman had no inkling, it remains true that he alone faithfully and passionately explored the hidden moral and religious bases of Democracy from which alone an answer to all its new problems can hopefully be sought. And the main substance of his discovery is that Democracy can be secured only on the foundation of its own appropriate and necessary religion. The notion of a new religion tends, perhaps justly, to be suspect. But Whitman meant no more, but no less, than that, just as Democracy can only be understood as a growth out of former organizations of society, yet must be recognized as something entirely new, so its necessary religion will incorporate and transmute all that is valid in the religions of the societies which preceded it.

My faith is the greatest of faiths and the least of faiths,
Enclosing worship ancient and modern and all between ancient and modern.

Thus, in *Democratic Vistas*, he begins by explicitly declaring that Democracy is the development, in the further field of social organization and material opportunity, of the message of Christ that the nature of the individual soul is so transcendent that it sets all men on a common level. Democracy is the implementation of the equality of souls proclaimed by the founder of Christianity. But what is the soul? Whitman has no doubt at all that a soul distinct from the body is an illusion. Body and soul are one, not two. And whether we like it or not, it seems plain that this is the fundamental religious postulate of Democracy, however unsuspected it may be.

That, says Whitman anyhow, is what we discover when as free individuals we explore the reality of what we are. We find an ultimate and indefeasible unity of ourselves of soul and body: an individual One, which at the moment of its awareness of itself, is known to be part of the universal One. Thus that infinite worth and uniqueness of the individual, on which Democracy purports to be grounded, is a reality only when it is pursued to its religious recesses in an ultimate and immediate self-knowledge of what he calls 'the identified soul'. It is notable how close Whitman quite independently comes at this point to the language and ideas of Keats in his famous letter on 'the world as a Vale of Soul-making'. The following crucial declaration of Whitman's might be incorporated bodily into Keats's letter, without alteration and without perceptible discrepancy.

> Religion, although casually arrested, and, after a fashion preserved in the churches and creeds, does not depend at all on them, but is a part of the identified soul, which, when greatest, knows not bibles in the old way, but in new ways—the identified soul, which can really confront Religion when it extricates itself entirely from the churches, and not before.

So close is the resemblance between Whitman's and Keats's thought here that Keats supplies a better gloss than does Whitman himself on his key-phrase, 'the identified soul'. For this is exactly what Keats meant when he distinguished a Soul from an Intelligence. 'There may be intelligences or sparks of the divinity in millions—but they are not Souls till they acquire identities, till each one is personally itself.'

This religious-ethical realization, says Whitman, is the true basis of Democracy; for it is at this point, and at this point only, that the individual becomes a reality. Short of this point, he is an illusion, on which nothing solid or durable can be built. Hence the transcendent importance for enduring Democracy of the emergence of prophets of true 'personalism', as he calls it. This promulgation of 'the religious element which is, finally, at the core of Democracy' is the work of the poet-prophet, the distinctive *literatus* of Democracy. He will work, just as the poet-prophets of former ages and former modes of society, by creating a compulsive image of the concrete, unified personality which is now required, with all its particular and essentially new emotional aptitudes and ethical and religious axioms. Of such poet-prophets of Democracy Whitman claims to be a forerunner, but no more. He is, as it were, the warning and encouraging voice of the interregnum, while Democracy is still unaware of the need of imaginative patterns adequate to its own unconscious assumptions and potentialities—and dangers. The dangers he sees clearly—most apprehensively in 'the long series of tendencies, shapings, which few are strong enough to resist, and which now seem, with steam-engine speed, to be everywhere turning out the generations of humanity like uniform iron castings'.

All of which, as compared with the feudal ages, we can yet do nothing better than accept, make the best of, and even welcome, upon the whole for their oceanic practical grandeur, and their restless wholesale kneading of the masses—I say of all this tremendous and dominant play of solely materialistic bearings upon current life in the United States, with the results as already seen, accumulating, and reaching far into the future, that they must either be confronted and met by at least an equally subtle and tremendous force-infusion for purposes of spiritualization, for the pure conscience, for genuine esthetics, and for absolute and primal manliness or womanliness—or else our modern civilization, with all its improvements, is in vain, and we are on the road to a destiny, a status, equivalent in its real world, to that of the fabled damned.

The process of spiritualization which alone can save Democracy from moral disaster Whitman here defines as consisting in three things. First, the awakening of the pure conscience which is, of course, not pure in the puritan sense, because it includes a candid and delighted recognition of all the mysteries of sex—a recognition inseparable from the knowledge of our participation in and dependence upon the infinite. This knowledge is the immediate source of the pure conscience, because it binds us, with a new sense of obligation, both to the One and to our fellow-men. It is the discovery of a new and deeper meaning in the Christian summons that we shall become, by knowing ourselves to be, 'sons of God'. Second, the establishment of absolute and primal womanliness and manliness: the condition in which 'the men believe in the women and the women in the men'. By which he means the creation of a bond of true love between them, whereby they entirely trust each other: which involves, above all, for Whitman, as for Blake before him, the abolition of sexual secrecy. Man and woman recognize, revere, and delight in each other as palpable manifestations of the divine. They acknowledge their several and mutual dependence upon the infinite, each with his own sense of responsibility. Thirdly, there is genuine aesthetics—the establishment of an ideal and image of attainable beauty, moral and physical, in the common consciousness, which will attract the aspirations of men and women, and serve them as a criterion to judge themselves and others: an image and ideal corresponding to the *καλὸς κἀγαθὸς* of the Greeks, the *vir pietate gravis* of the Romans, the *honnête homme* of seventeenth-century France, or the Christian gentleman of English-speaking peoples. But these were ideals evolved in and appropriate to aristocratic societies, and almost exclusively masculine. The new ideal image must be consubstantial with the new society, in which men and women are equals and lovers, and men and men comrades; it must arise from and be prophetic of Democracy 'which alone', Whitman says magnificently, 'on anything like Nature's scale, breaks up the limitless fallows of humankind and plants the seeds of personalism'.

In this sense Whitman conceived himself as a poet-prophet co-operating with the silent workings of Democracy, and making communication to the responsive among its members of an image of the new democratic man. Yet image-making, though it was his chosen phrase, and indeed the best he could use to describe his purpose, is inadequate to what he tried to do, and did. He made a total communication of himself. His work was at once less and more than a poetic achievement. There is splendid and immortal poetry in it: perfectly formed and crystalline gems in the mass of ore. But they, without the matrix which surrounds them, would lose the greater part of their significance. And, indeed, we need them less for what they are in themselves, than as the immediate and indisputable evidence that in Whitman was a truly great poet, judged by the most conservative standards. But the matrix is more important than the gems; the total Whitman far more dynamic, far more charged with potential for humanity, than his perfected utterances. The Whitman who gropes his way from the basis of his deep and new-discovered personality, his 'identified soul', into the vast variety of his incomplete affirmations; who offers himself with all his hesitations, his contradictions, and his deep unformulable faith, to his comrades of the future, is a truly prophetic man. He is, in part, the attractive image of the citizen of the new completely human society of which the crude integument is what we call Democracy; he is, in a yet more important part, the tongue-tied soul in travail of the idea of which he is the instinctive vehicle. And this part of him, which is quite inseparable from the other, is perhaps even more durable than the image of the rounded man which he communicates. For it is inherent in this conception of Democracy, as the constant, endless breaking of the fallows of humankind for the sowing of the seed of personality, that it should never reach finality. The process is as recurrent and illimitable as the labours of the veritable husbandry of the earth. Seed-time and harvest, the quiescence of winter frost, and saving and selection of new seed, the ploughing and the fight against the weeds—

These shall go onward the same
Though dynasties pass.

So with the process of Democracy. Its faith will never be finally uttered; the final utterances will always be of faiths not its own. The image of its citizen will never be completed. Always there will be the need, to urge it onward, of that sacred and consecrated band of brothers of which Whitman dreamed.

Yet I have dreamed, merged in that hidden-tangled problem of our fate, whose long unravelling stretches mysteriously through time—

dreamed out, portrayed, hinted already—a little or a larger band—a band of brave and true, unprecedented yet—armed and equipped at every point —the members separated, it may be, by different dates and States, or south, or north, or east, or west—Pacific, Atlantic, Southern, Canadian—a year, a century here, and other centuries there—but always one, compact in soul, conscience-conserving, God-inculcating, inspired achievers, not only in literature, the greatest art, but achievers in all art—a new, undying order, dynasty, from age to age transmitted—a band, a class, at least as fit to cope with current years, our dangers, needs, as those who, for their times, so long, so well, in armour or in cowl, upheld and made illustrious, that far-back feudal, priestly world. To offset chivalry, indeed, those vanished countless knights, old altars, abbeys, priests, ages and strings of ages, a knightlier and more sacred cause today demands, and shall supply, in a New World, to larger, grander work, more than the counterpart and tally of them.

Whitman the incomplete, sustained by the inward knowledge that his own sincerely acknowledged and avowed incompleteness would make him for ever contemporary with the pioneers of responsible personality on whom the vitality, and even the continued bare existence, of the new and experimental society of Democracy will ultimately depend, is he who deserves our deepest homage. This is the man who retains, and will increase his power to stir the thoughts of men in their dumb cradles. The compulsiveness of his certainty that the person is real only in the measure of his felt and known obligation to higher powers with which he can have immediate contact; his abiding sense of the transparent miracle of personal identity—'miracle of miracles, beyond statement, most spiritual and vaguest of earth's dreams, yet hardest basic fact, and only entrance to all facts'; his refusal to push the mystery away from the field of immediate experience, by interposing the apparatus of conventional theologies; his brave and humble confidence that 'the last best dependence is to be on humanity itself, and its own normal full-grown qualities, without any superstitious support whatsoever'; his serene assurance that only this gradual, tentative, exploring attitude applied to the whole—not an arbitrary part—of a man's experience is adequately and fully religious, and that 'faith, very old, now scared away by science, must be restored, brought back, by the same power that caused her departure—restored with new sway, deeper, wider, higher than ever'—these are some of the crystallizations from the marvellous and harmonious flux of creative intuitions which Whitman has conveyed to us with all the richness of their matrix of experience. 'My opinions,' he said gently to Traubel, 'are all, always, so hazy . . . though, to be sure, when they come, they come firm.' Both statements are true; but one is often neglected. Whitman's opinions are firmer and more durable than is easily believed.

29

D. H. LAWRENCE AND T. S. ELIOT

From Love, Freedom and Society *(Cape, 1957), pages 23–38. Editor's title.*

D. H. LAWRENCE is the apocalyptic figure who marks the end of the age of Romanticism. He has a strange resemblance to Rousseau, the apocalyptic figure who marks the beginning of it. He restates Rousseau's vision of the fundamental falsity of society, but with a new accent of despair; he imagines Rousseau's natural man, or noble savage, in a new form; and he has a kindred natural magic of style. As Rousseau was the prophet of democracy to be, Lawrence is the prophet of its doom. Both were sworn enemies of the pure intellect; both were concerned to promote a renascence of the religious sense based on pure feeling; both were preoccupied with the figure of Jesus; both, in order to communicate their message, were compelled to resort to spiritual autobiography; both made a swift ascent through all the strata of society, but found no resting place; both were invariably disillusioned in their friends; and both found themselves at the last completely isolated men.

If this is the end of the age of Romanticism, and Lawrence is the last of its prophets, as I believe, there is an obvious congruity in confronting him with the chief contemporary exponent of Classicism, T. S. Eliot: quite apart from the fact that Eliot has been one of Lawrence's severest critics. With that criticism I am not concerned. It is not of Eliot's best; it does not go to the root of the opposition between them, nor does it exhibit their affiliation.

Lawrence and Eliot are roughly co-evals; both show the marks of their epoch. As Lawrence's is a romanticism of despair, so is Eliot's a classicism of despair; or if the religious reference be used, as it well may be, both Lawrence's heresy and Eliot's orthodoxy have their sources in despair. That is of course no criticism of either. Not to have despaired is to have been insensitive to the human condition. Therefore I propose, in order to establish Lawrence's significance as an apocalyptic figure of the order I have indicated, to take the shortest way I can to the heart of the matter through a comparison between two closely related works of which despair is the common theme: Lawrence's long story, *St. Mawr,* and Eliot's play, *The Cocktail Party*.

The two works correspond, and that remarkably. They deal with the 'salvation' of similar women in similar circumstances.

Lou Carrington, the 'heroine' of *St. Mawr*—St. Mawr the stallion is himself the 'hero'—is a woman who has come to an indefinable, but incessant awareness of the emptiness of her relation to her husband. Except that Rico and she *are* married, her spiritual condition is very similar to that of Celia in *The Cocktail Party* when she realizes that her relation with Edward is barren and unreal. Both women eventually find salvation; and the salvation is, at least in external circumstance, similar. Celia finds it as a Christian medical missionary on the frontiers of civilization, where she meets a painful death; Lou finds it in a dedication of herself to a solitary life in the mountains of Arizona. 'Very well, daughter,' says her mother to her, in bidding her good-bye. 'You will probably spend your life keeping to yourself.' Lou replies:

> Do you think I mind! There's something else for me, mother. There's something else even that loves me and wants me. I can't tell you what it is. It's a spirit. And it's here, on this ranch. It's here, in this landscape. It's something more real to me than men are, and it soothes me, and it holds me up. I don't know what it is, definitely. It's something wild that will hurt me sometimes and will wear me down sometimes. I know it. But it's something big, bigger than men, bigger than people, bigger than religion. It's something to do with wild America. And it's something to do with me. It's a mission, if you like. I am imbecile enough for that! —But it's my mission to keep myself for the spirit that is wild, and has waited so long here: even waited for such as me. Now I've come! Now I'm here. Now I am where I want to be: with the spirit that wants me.

We have, in Eliot's play, no words of Celia at exactly the same moment of decision. But just after she has rejected Reilly's offer 'to reconcile her to the human condition': to such a life of affectionate tolerance between husband and wife as is exhibited in the final scene between Edward and Lavinia, she says something which vibrates almost in harmony with Lou's declaration.

> I know I ought to be able to accept that
> If I might still have it. Yet it leaves me cold.
> Perhaps that's just a part of my illness,
> But I feel it would be a kind of surrender—
> No, not a surrender—more like a betrayal.
> You see, I think I really had a vision of something
> Though I don't know what it is. I don't want to forget it.

I want to live with it. I could do without everything,
Put up with anything, if I might cherish it.
In fact, I think it would really be dishonest
For me, now, to try to make a life with *any*body!
I couldn't give anyone the kind of love—
I wish I could—which belongs to that life.

Celia's vision, which she feels she must not betray, is of the ecstasy of love she had experienced with Edward, remembered

like a dream
In which one is exalted by intensity of loving
In the spirit, a vibration of delight
Without desire, for desire is fulfilled
In the delight of loving. A state one does not know
When awake. But what, or whom I loved,
Or what in me was loving, I do not know.

Lou has had no such experience. But she, no less, has had her vision to which also she must be loyal. It has come to her in the shape of the stallion, in the sudden gleam of whose entire and vivid life she sees the unreality and deathliness of the human relationships in which she is caught. Her condition after that revelation is similar to that of Celia. Indeed, Lou might have spoken Celia's words.

No. I mean that what has happened has made me aware
That I've always been alone. That one always is alone.
Not simply the ending of one relationship,
Not even simply finding that it never existed—
But a revelation about my relationship
With *everybody*. Do you know—
It no longer seems worth while to *speak* to anyone!

The visions, the absolutes, whose light reveals to Lou and Celia the deadness of their love-relations and their own isolation, are of course very different. Celia's is the remembered ecstasy of complete self-surrender to love, an experience whose reality she cannot disavow; Lou's the present vision of a mode of being made manifest to her in the quick and mysterious vitality of the horse, although that mystery is separated from her by as great a gulf as now divides Celia from her ecstasy. But the deepest difference between the conditions of the two women is that, whereas Celia is convinced that she could never 'give anyone the kind of love' she had once felt, Lou dreams, or cherishes as a possibility, that the non-human vital magic of St. Mawr might gleam undimmed in the mind and body of a man.

'Why, mother!' said Lou impatiently. 'I think one gets so tired of your men with mind, as you call it . . . Just think of St. Mawr! I've thought so much about him. We call him an animal, but we never know what it means. He seems a far greater mystery to me than a clever man. He's a horse. Why can't one say in the same way of a man: *He's a man*? There seems no mystery in being a man. But there's a terrible mystery in St. Mawr.'

In Lawrence's story we are given no hint that Lou will find the new man whom she can barely imagine. Her mother's neurotic attempt to marry Lewis the groom is to her the silliness it is. Lou has at least learned the dignity of being alone, though she will keep her lamp trimmed in case the bridegroom cometh. She is incapable of deluding herself into disaster with the notion that she will find her mate in a mindless animal man. She will await, with neither hope nor despair, the coming of the complete man. He may never come. But in the meanwhile her sex is in the keeping of something greater than she.

And neither Phoenix nor Rico nor anybody else really matters to me. They are in the world's backyard. And I am here, right deep in America, where there's a wild spirit wants me, a wild spirit more than men. And it doesn't want to save me, either. It needs me. It craves for me. And to it, my sex is sacred, deeper than I am, with a deep nature aware deep down of my sex. It saves me from cheapness, mother. And even you could never do that for me.

Both women become virginal again; but Celia's virginality is of a different kind from Lou's. She becomes virginal by vocation, knowing that she could never give to another man the kind of love she had felt in her ecstasy. Given to a person, it would—or she cannot cease to fear it would—again be based on illusion. She would be inventing her man, as she had invented Edward, and he would be inventing her. There is for her no possibility of human love between man and woman that she can at once prize and believe in: what she admits to be possible, at Reilly's suggestion, is less than what she had known. There is only one who could receive and reciprocate that love, and that is Christ.

One would like to hear Celia and Lou talking together. Lou's dream of a man in whom mind had not destroyed, or tarnished, the pristine animal spontaneity, in whom indeed the workings of the mind were infused with the pristine animal grace, might, or might not, have seemed a chimaera to Celia. Nor can I easily imagine what Lou would have thought of Celia's decision to become the bride of Christ. But I do not think they would have been totally incomprehensible to each other; I fancy they would have understood each other better than their creators would have done. That is because, in a considerable artist, creation comes from a deeper level than the conscious mind.

But, at the level of conscious doctrine, there is no reconciliation possible between Eliot's play and Lawrence's story. The possibility and the ideal of man-woman 'love' which is suggested in *St. Mawr* is not admitted in *The Cocktail Party*; and the self-sacrificial Christian resolution of *The Cocktail Party* is not within the spiritual horizon of *St. Mawr*. 'It's bigger than religion', says Lou of the spirit of wild America to which she entrusts her womanhood, and one understands her. But whether she can trust herself to it and not be destroyed is another question.

Nor do I think—to go outside the frame of this particular story—that Lawrence himself could ever have answered that question with genuine conviction. He has other Lous to tell of—in *The Princess* and *The Woman who Rode Away*, for example—and they come to a horrible end. And having regard to the whole impressive sequence of his work, culminating in *Lady Chatterley's Lover* and *The Man who Died*, we may fairly say that he returned again and again, as a compass needle to the magnetic north, to the ideal and imagination of a complete relation between a man and a woman. What, essentially, he preached, what he could never cease to imagine, was a new kind of marriage, between a regenerated man and a regenerated woman. And the new man, in the world of Lawrence's imagination, is the kind of man whom Lou conceives. There are many approximations and adumbrations of him in the characters of Lawrence's books. *St. Mawr* is, indeed, almost peculiar in that it contains no such direct presentation. There is Count Dionys in *The Ladybird*, Alexander Hepburn in *The Captain's Doll*, Henry in *The Fox,* Alan in *The Border Line*; there is Annable in *The White Peacock* at the beginning, and Mellors in *Lady Chatterley* at the end of the sequence of novels; their name, one might almost say, is legion. But by far the most convincing presentation of the new man is in those characters in which Lawrence recognizably portrayed himself: Rupert Birkin in *Women in Love,* Lilly in *Aaron's Rod,* and Somers in *Kangaroo*. With the possible exception of Mellors, the other presentations of the character strike the reader as symbols rather than individuals; or, at least, the animal element in them is much more vivid to us than the mental. Even in the case of Hepburn, who is perhaps the most successful of them, we are perplexed, as Hannele is, by a certain dumbness in him; we look in vain for some articulate assurance of the reality and validity of that 'male purpose', that 'passionate purposive activity' in man, on which Lawrence so justly insisted.

It is quite otherwise with Lawrence's objectifications of himself. Here, we feel, is a rare human reality. The vivid and impassioned dialectic of his search for a purpose, and of his relations with his wife, constitute a life and thought-exploration of the most absorbing interest. There is nothing remotely like it in English literature. The sensitive tip of an incomparable human consciousness, subtly and directly aware, through faculties which are lost or vestigial in the rest of us, of the whole environment in which it moves, is feeling its way through life on our behalf. Here, we can freely allow, mental consciousness and the deep instinctive man are in alliance, if not in harmony. That which, in other presentations, is symbolic and unsatisfying here becomes real: a matter of our own immediate experience. 'Our imagination, surpassed, is at rest.'

In that record of Lawrence's experiencing nature two main themes or quests are easily visible. They are intertwined with one another, but they are distinguishable and distinct. One is the search for a new and true relation between individuals, and above all between man and woman. The other is the search for a new and satisfying social relation of the individual to society. In both quests one can trace a crucial moment of psychic upheaval, following a catastrophic inrush of unexpected experience. These are recorded directly, the former in the sequence of poems *Look we have come through*, the latter in the 'Nightmare' chapter of *Kangaroo*.

It is well to consider the latter first, because it was the more violent in itself and more important in its consequences. In 1914, at the moment when Lawrence had become fully conscious of the uniqueness of his sensitivity and of his creative power, he suddenly had to struggle with the experience of the First World War. I can bear personal witness to the shattering effect this had upon him. Not even 'The Nightmare' fully conveys the despair and physical prostration in which he was plunged in the winter of 1914–15. I was very close to him at that time; and I too was deeply depressed: but my depression was generically different from what he suffered. Looking back to that time I see myself as a young man selfishly and personally concerned over the collapse of his hopes, beset by fears for his own security, and afraid of being engulfed in a war in which he did not believe. Lawrence's suffering was absolutely different, and of an altogether higher order. He suffered under a prophetic vision of the war as a portent of the imminent doom of modern civilization and modern man. The succeeding years since 1914 have produced little to invalidate his vision.

It was his own abnormal awareness, his sensitiveness to what had really happened in the human psyche—all that in his composition which in happier times would have put him among the highest of contemplative artists—which inexorably made him a prophet and a religious teacher. It was because he was, by endowment, a *very* great artist that he could not be one, at that point of time. His world, which was our world, was annihilated; and with that came the annihilation of himself as a social being. He was torn apart from the collective by his vision of its deathliness and doom. Nor was refuge possible for him, as it was for Eliot, in traditional Christianity. For to him Christianity was embodied in the civilization which was doomed. He was convinced that he was experiencing the end of the Christian civilization, which, under the ensign of Christian love, was engaged in mutual mass-murder. So, in his despair and isolation, he had to try to build himself up from the beginning again, to discover a reality by which, and to create a world in which, he could live. This reality and this world are not easy to describe. The whole of his works are a map of it. But some of the elements may be set down. The chief was the absolute destruction of his belief in the reality of the ideal world, which professed to be governed by love. Even his attempt to gather together a little group of friends who would trust one another, on the basis of a common faith in the necessity of passing beyond the world of the illusory idea, failed completely. The imaginative projection of this failure is to be found in *Women in Love*, where Gerald's disaster is imputed to his failure to enter into a mystical friendship or blood-brotherhood with Rupert; it occurs again in *Aaron's Rod*, and in *Kangaroo*. The more directly autobiographical record of another attempt is in 'The Nightmare'.

The essence of this new relation which he craved, was that it should rest on something deeper and firmer than 'ideal' love; and this he demanded also in the man-woman relation, and particularly in his relation with his wife, the record of which, sometimes with the barest minimum of disguise, is a main theme of his later novels. Men and women, and men and men, were to 'meet'—to use Buber's phrase—in a dark pre-mental world. How far this world was a sheer construction, how far it was a natural extrapolation of some unfamiliar dimension of subjective experience, is a difficult question. The most enthusiastic appreciations of Lawrence (such as Dr. Leavis's) leave this very important element in him severely alone. But there is no doubt that Lawrence enjoyed a kind of communion and contact with the animal and natural world which is outside the range of ordinary human experience. The convincing evidence of that is richly scattered through all his works. It is also clear enough that in his relations with his wife, he touched to his own conviction, though not to hers, unknown modes of being, which he thought he found exemplified in primitive people, and expressed in pre-Christian religions. His effort at a final imaginative synthesis of the elements of this belief of his is contained in *The Plumed Serpent*, where Ramon represents all that is still valid in the principle of love, and Don Cipriano represents the principle of the dark. These two men are the incarnations of the dual divinity of the new religion which is imagined to supersede Christianity. How far Lawrence in fact finally adhered to his belief in the reality of the 'dark gods' and the necessity of our recognizing them is hard to say. As we shall see, by the end of his work, much of the anti-human malevolence he at one period imputes to them and glorifies in them, seems to disappear; indeed, the 'dark gods' are never named in his last religious statements. And Lawrence's doctrine of marriage, as he finally presents it, is acceptable enough: it is based on a profound and religious recognition of the body, and may be described as a vital, though revolutionary, expansion of a conception of marriage which can fairly be called Christian. In fact, whatever we may think of his insistence on the 'dark gods'—to use the words as a convenient shorthand for the dubious element in his work—we must recognize that a moment comes when they vanish almost without a trace from his writings. There is a divine darkness still, but it is warm and creative and benign.

All this he put forward incessantly in novels and tales and essays and travel books and poems, which cannot be really comprehended except as a whole, for their unity lies in the fact that they are the spiritual autobiography of a man of extraordinary genius who has committed the whole of himself to the search for a new mode of human existence, a new consciousness, a new religion: who inevitably made mistakes, entered *culs de sac,* deceived himself, treated imaginations as realities, but who, with an honesty that is as remarkable as his sensitivity, recorded ruthlessly his own failures—rejected all that which, in imagination and actual experience, he had tried and found wanting, and clung to that without which he could not live. And his literary genius was put wholly to the service of this 'life-and thought-adventure', as he called it. As the exploration progressed, he made himself the protagonist of his own novels, not through any failure in his 'art', but because his 'art' could not accommodate the findings of his life-experience. His novels cease to be novels, his poems cease to be poems: because they are something more important, more charged with the immediacy of contemporary but prophetic experience, than an accepted art-form could be. Lawrence was 'beyond art', in the sense that some have claimed to be 'beyond good and evil'; or if the category of artist is to be applied to him at all, so as not to mutilate and denature the man and the message, which were one, it must be so expanded and changed as to include the whole living body of his work. His failures, his exaggerations, his perversities, his contradictions, are all vital: modes of experience in which he calls upon us to participate in order that, like him, we may discover what we are.

That is the supreme purpose of art—to reveal to man what he is.

The genius of Lawrence was appointed to a moment in history when the nature of man was undergoing a revolutionary change: when the whole fabric of his gradually grown society was in danger of becoming a steely network of impersonal and anti-human relations, the collective a sort of concentration camp furnished with the latest mechanical amenities, and religion, having lost all vital connection with man's daily life, a profound mysticism for the few, a Sunday habit for a few more, and an obsolete survival for the many.

A 'new man' was indeed looming and lurching on the horizon: the new mass-man of the totalitarian societies. Lawrence foresaw, saw, and abhorred him; but to him the mass-man of the democratic societies was not vitally different. Whether, and by how much, he was wrong in this judgment is a question on which the possibility of a specifically human future depends. Man seems to be caught in a fearful dialectic by his own technology,—a dialectic of apparent necessity, whereby the efforts of democracy against totalitarianism strengthen the hold of totalitarianism upon itself. Lawrence, prophetically, tried every issue, followed every gleam, that offered an escape from the prison, and at last he came to the conclusion that the re-creation of human marriage was the only bridge into a human future. Let marriage be made wholly alive, the mystery of the union of a man and woman conscious of each other's mystery, and the spark of vivid life might be transmitted through the imminent desolation. Here religion—and specifically all that was precious in the Christian religion—might become a reality. For those who have really followed Lawrence through his life-adventure, struggled to share his insights, been responsive to his imaginations, exposed themselves to his cauteries, been wounded by his violations, there is a compelling force in his words in the pamphlet on *Lady Chatterley's Lover*.

Marriage is the clue to human life, but there is no marriage apart from the wheeling sun and the nodding earth, from the straying of the planets and the magnificence of the fixed stars. Is not a man different, utterly different, at dawn from what he is at sunset? And does not the changing harmony and discord of their variation make the secret music of life?

And is it not so throughout life? A man is different at thirty, at forty, at fifty, at sixty, at seventy; and the woman at his side is different. But is there not some strange conjunction in their differences? Is there not some peculiar harmony, through youth, the period of childbirth, the period of florescence and young children, the period of the woman's change of life, painful yet also a renewal, the period of waning passion but mellowing delight of affection, the dim, unequal period of the approach of death, when the man and woman look at one another with the dim apprehension of separation that is not really a separation: is there not, throughout it all, some unseen, unknown interplay of balance, harmony, completion, like some soundless symphony which moves with a rhythm from phase to phase, so different, so very different in the various movements, yet one symphony, made out of the soundless singing of two strange and incompatible lives, a man's and a woman's?

This is marriage, the mystery of marriage, marriage which fulfils itself here, in this life. We may well believe that in heaven there is no marrying or giving in marriage. All this has to be fulfilled here, and if it is not fulfilled here, it will never be fulfilled. The great saints only live, even Jesus only lives to add a new fulfilment and a new beauty to the permanent sacrament of marriage.

That is clean outside the range of human possibility contained or suggested in *The Cocktail Party*; equally, it might be said, it is outside the range of *St. Mawr*. But it would not be quite true. That condition is what Lou is looking for, though she cannot define it, and probably Lawrence himself could not have done at that moment. The revelation of the stallion, the lonely vigil among the mountains: these are only clues in the search, indications of what man and woman have lost and must find.

In the picture of true marriage we have quoted, the seeming extravagance of Lou's spiritual expectations from her mountain solitude falls into place. We become aware, as we do not in the story, of its symbolism. That 'there is no marriage apart from the wheeling sun and the nodding earth, from the straying of the planets and the magnificence of the fixed stars' is a proposition of which we feel the truth, even though we are only partially capable of receiving it. That men and women must, if only in imagination and the silence of the soul, withdraw themselves from the mechanical network of this civilization and reach out for some sort of contact with the non-human world until they know themselves vehicles of the great mystery, before marriage will be revivified by their awareness of the mystery in each other—this also we feel to be true. But it is only when *St. Mawr* is interpreted in the total context of Lawrence's work that its disturbing elements of violence and exaggeration are subdued. To contend, as Dr. Leavis does in his book, *D. H. Lawrence: Novelist*, that it is, in itself, immeasurably superior to *The Cocktail Party,* because of its greater spiritual depth and its absence of snobbery, is a kind of critical perversity, or at least a *tour de force*. The spiritual superiority of *St. Mawr* over Eliot's play is potential only; and that chiefly in virtue of a latent conception of religion and marriage which Eliot deliberately rejects. I believe that the truth that is implicit and potential in Lawrence's story goes deeper, and speaks more to the real human condition than the truth that is explicit and actual in Eliot's play; but it seems to me plain that Eliot says what he has to say much more completely than Lawrence does in his story. The charge of snobbery seems to me trivial. There *is* a society such as that which Eliot presents, and in that society men and women talk as Eliot makes them talk, though seldom perhaps so absurdly or so seriously; and the conversation between Eliot's characters is as convincing in its own kind as that in Lawrence's story. As a work of art, *The Cocktail Party* has it. And so, in fairness, it should. *St. Mawr* is a mere fragment of Lawrence's work; only one, and not one of the best, of Lawrence's many tales. And, for the reason we have given, Lawrence's vision or message was necessarily impatient of art, though he was much more richly endowed with 'the more than usual organic sensibility' of the creative artist than any other of his time.

But it is only by importing into it values made explicit in Lawrence's later writing that *St. Mawr* can be made to outweigh *The Cocktail Party*. In the light of such a passage as we have quoted on marriage from *A propos Lady Chatterley's Lover* we can read into *St. Mawr* a significance which it does not itself possess.

> This is marriage, the mystery of marriage, marriage which fulfils itself here, in this life. We may well believe that in heaven there is no marrying or giving in marriage. All this has to be fulfilled here, and if it is not fulfilled here, it will never be fulfilled. The great saints only live, even Jesus only lives to add a new fulfilment and a new beauty to the permanent sacrament of marriage.

That, with all its richness of implication, of possibilities embraced and discarded, which is unfolded in his work as a whole, is the final essence of what Lawrence had positively to say. *The Cocktail Party* directly denies its truth. What Lawrence points to as the way of salvation is excluded as a possibility by Eliot. Eliot starts, like Lawrence, with people who have become aware of their own unreality. No doubt it is a different mode of awareness from that which Lawrence gives his significant characters; but, substantially, it is akin. The sudden realization in men and women that their human relations—and above all the most intimate—are illusory; that they cherish mere phantasms of each other, confront one another in masks, behave not as what they are, but as they think they ought to be, watch themselves and the others 'performing'—this is common both to Eliot and Lawrence as the necessary beginning of the soul's progress. The deep desire, the famished longing to become real, to escape from the illusory self—this, in the finding of both men—is the spiritual anguish of this age. The contradiction between our nominal religion, and our known reality is intolerable. The machine-civilization has taken our destinies out of our hands, reduced individuality to an awareness of our compelled service to a mechanism we despise, confined our freedom to that dreadful 'knowledge of necessity'—an automatic and mechanical necessity which half the civilized world deliberately worships, and the other half worships without admitting it. This is in the social macrocosm the root of the anguish. But anguish is experienced only in the individual soul, and where it is awakened, it comes in the form of a deep desire to be real, to be whole, to be spontaneous, to be free—not to be free in the foolish and fatal sense of being without limitation, but to be free in service to a purpose which commands the loyalty of our hearts and minds, our souls and bodies.

Particularly, in the individual soul, it takes the form of the longing for true marriage: for the union of a man and woman is the primal basis of human life. True marriage is the permanent relation of a man and a woman who have become real in themselves, and acknowledge and revere and delight in each other's reality. Our demand on marriage is become so great because in the world in which we live all other social relations are become so impersonal and dehumanized. Marriage is our only refuge, the only place where we can hope to be at once real and free: to be real and free is to serve. And in marriage a man and woman can hope to serve, not merely one another—a falsity which Lawrence justly denounces—but the life, the purpose, the God who is beyond them both.

Eliot is not entirely without sympathy for the hope, as his presentation of Celia shows; but he is resolute in exhibiting it as an illusion. The ecstasy of love—as it may be called—must either be transferred to the Christian God, or it must dwindle into resigned acceptance. And we must admit, there is something strangely abstract and disembodied about Eliot's conception of both the ecstasy of love and the resigned relation which is its alternative. One does not for one moment feel that Celia and Edward, or Edward and Lavinia, had been physically in love with each other. Nothing of what Lawrence means by 'sexual fulfilment' has had, we feel, any part in their lives; and although the positive sexual disgust which pervades *The Waste Land* makes no appearance in *The Cocktail Party*, we feel that it has been mitigated rather than overcome; suppressed on Christian principle rather than by new and vital conviction. Lawrence's final idea that 'sexual fulfilment' is a blessed and enduring condition, into the achievement of which all that is valid in Christian insight naturally enters, and which it is our religious duty to achieve if human life is to have its true significance and beauty, is drastically excluded from Eliot's presentation of human relations: not so much deliberately, as because Eliot is genuinely unaware of it as a possibility. *Il a pris son assiette.* And all that Lawrence intended by 'the resurrection of the flesh' is to him an uneducated heresy.

Lawrence and Eliot are indeed antithetical: they repudiate one another, I would almost say they annihilate one another. But, though I am, profoundly, with Lawrence rather than Eliot, I am not prepared to say with Dr. Leavis, that Eliot's spirituality is shallow; and I shrink absolutely from the assertion that there is a final 'human and spiritual nullity' in his plays. Eliot's spirituality belongs to a tradition of Christian spirituality which is venerable, and I am persuaded that it cost Eliot no small pains to embrace and keep hold of that tradition. But precisely because it is the traditional spirituality, it will not serve to carry us through what is to come. Too much is breaking, or has broken. The man whom the Christian tradition assumes no longer exists; and the Christian Church, either unable to discern the forces of necessity or unable to contend against them, is part of the mechanical automatism which devours us. What we need is the beginning of a new tradition of spirituality; and I believe that that beginning can be found in Lawrence.

SELECT BIBLIOGRAPHY

Fyodor Dostoevsky: A Critical Study. Secker, 1916.

Still Life (a novel). Constable, 1916.

The Critic in Judgment, or Belshazzar of Baron's Court. Hogarth Press, 1918.

The Evolution of an Intellectual. Cape, 1919.

Cinnamon and Angelica (a play). Andrew Dakers, 1920.

Aspects of Literature. Collins, 1921.

Poems, 1916–1920. Cobden Sanderson, 1921.

The Problem of Style. OUP, 1922.

Countries of the Mind. Hudson, 1922.

The Things We Are (a novel). Constable, 1922.

Pencillings. Collins, 1923.

To the Unknown God. Cape, 1924.

The Voyage (a novel). Constable, 1924.

Discoveries: Essays in Literary Criticism. Cape, 1924.

Keats and Shakespeare. OUP, 1925.

The Life of Jesus. Cape, 1926.

Things to Come. Cape, 1928.

God: an Introduction to the Science of Metabiology. Cape, 1929.

Countries of the Mind, 2nd series. OUP, 1931.

Son of Woman: the Story of D. H. Lawrence. Cape, 1931.

The Necessity of Communism. Cape, 1932.

The Life of Katherine Mansfield (with R. E. Mantz). Constable, 1933.

Reminiscences of D. H. Lawrence. Cape, 1933.

William Blake. Cape, 1933.

Between Two Worlds (an autobiography). Cape, 1935.

Shakespeare. Cape, 1936.

The Necessity of Pacifism. Cape, 1937.

The Pledge of Peace. H. Joseph, 1938.

Heaven and Earth. Cape, 1938.

The Defence of Democracy. Cape, 1939.

The Price of Leadership. S.C.M., 1939.

Europe in Travail (six broadcast talks). Sheldon Press, 1940.

The Betrayal of Christ by the Churches. Dakers, 1940.

Democracy and War. Nisbet, 1940.

Christocracy. Andrew Dakers, 1942.

Adam and Eve. Andrew Dakers, 1944.

Looking Before and After. Sheppard Press, 1948.

The Free Society. Andrew Dakers, 1948.

Katherine Mansfield and other literary portraits. Peter Nevill, 1949.

John Clare and other studies. Peter Nevill, 1950.

The Conquest of Death: a translation of Benjamin Constant's *Adolphe*, with commentary. Peter Nevill, 1951.

Community Farm. Peter Nevill, 1952.

Jonathan Swift: A Critical Biography. Cape, 1954.

Keats. Cape, 1955.

Unprofessional Essays. Cape, 1956.

Love, Freedom and Society. Cape, 1957.

Katherine Mansfield and other literary studies (preface by T. S. Eliot). Constable, 1959.

INDEX

(Major passages in bold type)

PRINTED IN GREAT BRITAIN
HAZELL WATSON AND VINEY LTD
AYLESBURY AND SLOUGH